Andrew Duncan

FAVOURITE
LONDON
WALKS

Andrew Duncan's

FAVOURITE
LONDON
WALKS

50 CLASSIC ROUTES EXPLORING
LONDON'S HERITAGE

NEW
HOLLAND

This edition first published in 2006 by
New Holland Publishers (UK) Ltd
London • Cape Town • Sydney • Auckland

Garfield House
86–88 Edgware Road
London W2 2EA
United Kingdom
www.newhollandpublishers.com

80 McKenzie Street
Cape Town 8001
South Africa

14 Aquatic Drive
Frenchs Forest, NSW 2086
Australia

218 Lake Road
Northcote
Auckland
New Zealand

ISBN 1 84537 454 1

Publishing Manager: Jo Hemmings
Senior Editor: Kate Michell
Assistant Editor: Kate Parker
Editorial Assistant: Anne Konopelski
Cartographer: William Smuts
Production: Joan Woodroffe

Edited and designed by D & N Publishing, Baydon, Wiltshire

Reproduction by Pica Digital (Pte) Ltd, Singapore
Printed and bound in Singapore by Kyodo Printing Co (Singapore) Pte Ltd

Front cover: St Paul's Cathedral and the Millennium Bridge (Geoffrey Rippingale).

CONTENTS

INTRODUCTION

Since the 1980s I've been exploring London on foot and by bike both for pleasure and profit. Sometimes I feel as if I've delved into just about every nook and cranny this great city has to offer. The results of my investigations have been published in hundreds of articles and a handful of London walking guides. The latter have, if I may be immodest for a moment, proved themselves to be reliable, accurate, interesting and well-constructed and have, as a result, sold in gratifyingly large numbers. This present book is a personal selection of my favourite walks from these earlier books and is probably the most comprehensive London walking guide on the market today.

Andrew Duncan's Favourite London Walks contains no fewer than 50 walks, many more than any of the individual source titles alone. Just over half are from *Walking London*. The other half come from *Walking Village London*, *Walking Notorious London* and *Secret London* (please visit my website at www.andrewduncan.co.uk for further details of these books). The walks cover the whole of central London and parts beyond too, not just well-known places like Richmond, Greenwich, Hampstead and Kew, but gems way off the beaten track like Walthamstow, Pinner, Carshalton and Bexley, all of which, I guarantee, are surprises in store. There are also walks along the courses of lost rivers like the Fleet and Tyburn, and theme walks, including one on Jack the Ripper and the notorious East End. Take a look at the Contents page for the full listing.

It's a truism, I know, but walking really is the only way to get to know a city – indeed anywhere – properly. It's cheap, easy, beneficial to both walker and the environment, and above all, simple. With this book, all you have to do is get yourself to your chosen start point. Once there you'll find you have everything you need conveniently to hand: detailed map, full route directions, historical and descriptive information, opening times for museums, galleries, churches and historic houses, toilet locations and suggestions for all-important refreshment stops. To choose a walk, identify a location using the map on pages 8–9 or browse through the summaries highlighting each walk's main features. The walks take, on average, about two hours and start and finish at stations, where possible the same one to make travelling easier. Places open to the public are highlighted in **bold**. Opening times are listed at the back of the book (see page 263).

If you have any comments, queries, criticisms or suggestions, please email them to me at andrew@andrewduncan.co.uk. It's always helpful to get feedback from readers. Meanwhile, I hope you get as much pleasure out of walking the walks as I have in creating and researching them.

Andrew Duncan
andrew@andrewduncan.co.uk
www.andrewduncan.co.uk

KEY TO ROUTE MAPS

Each of the walks in this book is accompanied by a detailed map on which the route of the walk is shown in blue. Places of interest along the walks, such as historic buildings, museums and churches, are clearly identified.

The following is a key to the symbols used on the maps.

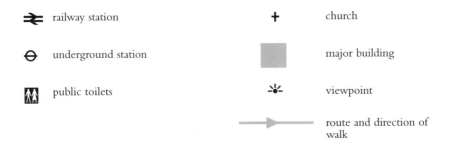

⇌	railway station	✝	church
⊖	underground station	▩	major building
⚠	public toilets	☀	viewpoint
		⟶	route and direction of walk

ACKNOWLEDGEMENTS

The author is responsible for the contents of his book, but at the end of the day any published work is more or less a team effort. This one is no exception. Over the years many people have contributed to the the evolution of the walks in this book: they are acknowledged in the various volumes from which the walks have been selected. As far as this particular book is concerned, I would like to thank a few people without whom it would not have seen the light of day in its present form: Kate Michell and David Price-Goodfellow for their editorial, design and cartographical labours; Dave Paterson for his great work behind the lens – his wonderful photographs really capture the beauty, the majesty, the idiosyncrasy, the amazing variety of London's landscape; my magazine editor Elinor Malcolm for so gracefully releasing me from my commitments to her publications so that I could concentrate on this book; and last but not least, my mother and my brother for their unstinting encouragement and support.

Map of London and Surrounds

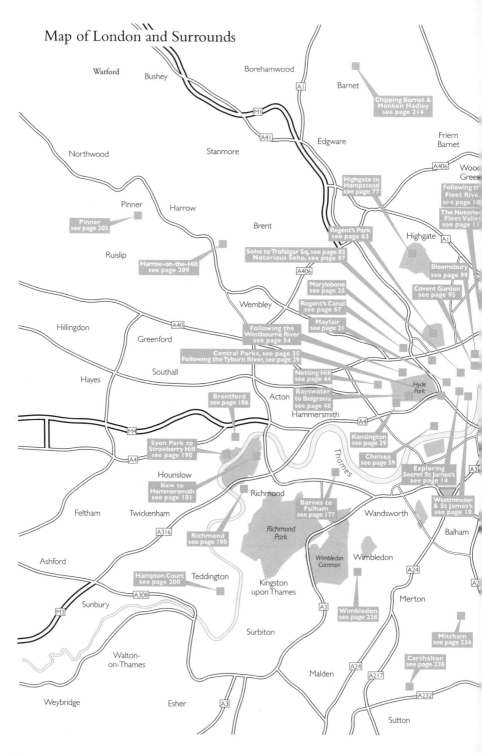

Watford

Bushey

Borehamwood

Barnet

Chipping Barnet &
Monken Hadley
see page 214

Edgware

Friern
Barnet

Northwood

Stanmore

A406

Wood
Green

Highgate to
Hampstead
see page 77

Following the
Fleet River
see page 10

The Notorious
Fleet Valley
see page 11

Pinner

Harrow

Brent

Regent's Park
see page 63

Highgate

Pinner
see page 205

Bloomsbury
see page 99

Ruislip

Harrow-on-the-Hill
see page 209

Soho to Trafalgar Sq, see page 83
Notorious Soho, see page 87

Covent Garden
see page 95

A406

Marylebone
see page 25

Wembley

Regent's Canal
see page 67

Hillingdon

Greenford

A40

Following the
Westbourne River
see page 54

Mayfair
see page 21

Central Parks, see page 35
Following the Tyburn River, see page 29

Hayes

Southall

Notting Hill
see page 44

Hyde
Park

Brentford
see page 186

Acton

Bayswater
to Belgravia
see page 48

Hammersmith

A4

Syon Park to
Strawberry Hill
see page 190

A4

Kensington
see page 39

Thames

Chelsea
see page 59

Exploring
Secret St James's
see page 14

A3

Hounslow

Kew to
Hammersmith
see page 181

Richmond

Barnes to
Fulham
see page 177

Wandsworth

Westminster
& St James's
see page 10

Feltham

Twickenham

A316

Richmond
Park

Balham

Richmond
see page 195

Wimbledon
Common

Wimbledon

Ashford

Hampton Court
see page 200

Teddington

A308

Kingston
upon Thames

A24

A2

Sunbury

M3

Merton

Wimbledon
see page 228

Mitcham
see page 234

Walton-
on-Thames

Surbiton

A3

Carshalton
see page 238

Weybridge

Esher

A3

Malden

A24

A217

A232

Sutton

Enfield

Enfield
see page 220

A10

Abridge

Loughton

M25

M11

Chigwell

Collier Row

Waltham
Forest

Hainault

A406

Redbridge

A12

Romford

Stamford Hill

Hornchurch

A10

Leyton

Stoke
Newington

Islington
see page 73

A406

Dagenham

Clerkenwell
see page 122

Stratford

Barking

Bethnal Green

The Notorious East End, see page 163

West Ham

Inns of Court
see page 103

The City around Fleet St & St Paul's, see page 127
The City between Guildhall & the Tower, see page 132
Exploring the Secret City (West of St Paul's), see page 137
Exploring the Secret City (East of St Paul's), see page 142

A13

Thames

Newham

Wapping

Wapping to Limehouse
see page 173

Thamesmead

Bermondsey to
Rotherhithe
see page 158

Woolwich

Bankside &
Southwark
see page 153

A205

Lambeth &
the South Bank
see page 148

A2

Greenwich
see page 247

East Dulwich

Lewisham

Bexleyheath

Blackheath
see page 252

A2

Dartford

Eltham

Bexley
see page 257

A205

Catford

Streatham

Dulwich
see page 244

Sidcup

A20

Crystal
Palace

A21

Swanley

Beckenham

Bromley

M20

Croydon

M25

M25

A232

Orpington

N

Purley

3,000 yards (2,740m)

Chelsfield

❖❖❖

WESTMINSTER AND ST JAMES'S

❖❖❖

Summary: A circular walk around royal Westminster and aristocratic St James's via Whitehall (a street of government offices), **St James's Park**/Square/Street/Palace, **Buckingham Palace** (the Queen's London residence), **Westminster Abbey** and School and the Houses of Parliament. Other features include Downing Street (No. 10 is the Prime Minister's official residence), **Horse Guards Parade** (including the Horse Guards and Foot Guards themselves), the gentlemen's clubs of St James's, then **Green Park** and, finally, some of the picturesque streets in the vicinity of Westminster Abbey.

Start and finish:	Westminster station (District, Circle and Jubilee Underground Lines).
Length:	3 miles (4.8km).
Time:	2 hours.
Refreshments:	Surprisingly for such a central district, refreshment stops on this walk are relatively scarce. However, there are one or two cafés and pubs close to St James's Church at the halfway stage.

Take exit 4 from Westminster Station and turn right into Bridge Street with Big Ben and the Houses of Parliament on your left. Pause for a moment at the traffic lights, as you stand at the political heart of the nation. There are statues of six prime ministers around the perimeter of Parliament Square, including, nearest to the Houses of Parliament, a bronze figure of the wartime leader Winston Churchill. On the left-hand side of the square the old parish church of Westminster (**St Margaret's**) is dwarfed by Westminster Abbey behind. Straight ahead across the square is the former Middlesex Guildhall, now law courts.

Old Whitehall Palace
Now turn right into Parliament Street leading directly into Whitehall further along. Government offices line both sides of this wide road, nearly all the way to Trafalgar Square. First on the left is the Treasury, separated from the Foreign Office by King Charles Street. In the middle of the road stands the Cenotaph, the national memorial to Britain's war dead. Leading off to the right is Richmond Terrace where Henry Stanley, the man who found Livingstone in Africa, lived before the street was claimed by the Civil Service. On the right beyond this terrace is the great grey bulk of the Ministry of Defence. The statues on the front lawn are of World War II military commanders (Montgomery, Alanbrooke and Slim) and Sir Walter Raleigh, beheaded in 1618 after an abortive expedition in search of the fabled El Dorado.

On the left-hand side of the street again, you will see the gated entrance to Downing Street. No. 10 has been the official residence of the Prime Minister since Sir Robert Walpole, the first Prime Minister, lived here in 1732. The Chancellor of the

Exchequer lives next door at No. 11. Government ministers attend cabinet meetings most Thursday mornings in Downing Street: the civil servants who service these meetings work in the Cabinet Office on the corner of Downing Street. The Privy Council, a body of specially-appointed public figures that advises the Crown on matters where it still has some political authority, has the office next to the Cabinet Office. Beyond the Privy Council is the domed entrance to the Scotland Office.

Going back onto the right-hand side of the street, beyond the Ministry of Defence is the Wales Office. Then comes the magnificent 17th-century **Banqueting House**, the only surviving building above ground of Whitehall Palace (the old palace wine cellar still exists *beneath* the Ministry of Defence). This 2,000-room royal palace occupied the whole of this area until it was destroyed by fire in 1698. On a cold morning in January 1649, King Charles I was beheaded here after stepping through a window of the Banqueting House onto a specially constructed scaffold. There is a bust of the king and a plaque above the Banqueting House entrance.

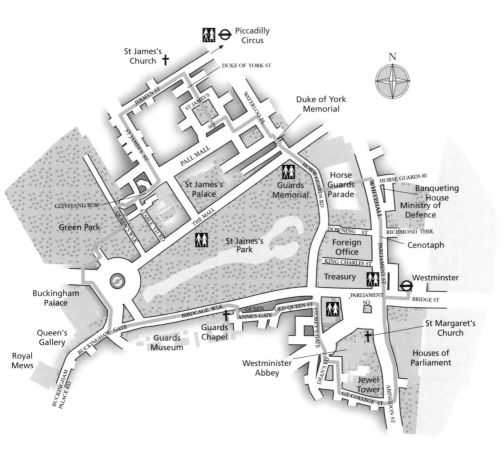

Military milieu

Cross Horse Guards Avenue beyond the Banqueting House and then cross Whitehall at the traffic lights to reach Horse Guards. The mounted guards on duty here come from the Household Cavalry, descendants of the original mounted guards for whom the Horse Guards building was constructed in the 1750s. There are notices on the inner wall of the courtyard that tell you more about the Life Guards and how the guard is mounted. What they do not tell you is that each horse and rider stands guard for one hour only at a time and not the whole day.

Go through the archway into Horse Guards Parade, the former tiltyard or jousting field of Whitehall Palace. Every year in June the square is used for the Trooping the Colour ceremony, when 2,000 red-coated foot guards together with cavalry and military bands parade their regimental flags during the Queen's birthday parade. To the left you can see the garden of 10 Downing Street. Cross Horse Guards Road at the end of the parade-ground and go into St James's Park, passing on your left the war memorial of the Household Division (the Household Cavalry and the Guards infantry combined). Turn right along the tarmac path. On the right the ivy-covered Citadel was built as a bomb-proof communications centre for the navy in World War II and is still used by the Defence Ministry today.

When you reach the Mall cross over at the traffic lights, admiring the view of Buckingham Palace to the left and Admiralty Arch to the right. Walk up the steps to the Duke of York's column. The Duke was the second son of George III and commander-in-chief of the British Army at the time of the Battle of Waterloo (1815).

Waterloo Place at the top of the steps contains many statues including, on the left, Sir John Franklin, lost while trying to find the northwest passage round Alaska, and on the right, Captain Scott, the first Englishman to reach the South Pole.

Clubs of Pall Mall

Walk down the left-hand side of Waterloo Place, past the mounting block installed for the Duke of Wellington, the British commander at Waterloo. Cross Pall Mall, which runs centrally through Waterloo Place, and turn left. Named after a game – similar to croquet – imported from France and popularized after 1660 by Charles II, Pall Mall is pre-eminently a street of gentlemen's social clubs. On the left you pass the Athenaeum, **Travellers'** and Reform Clubs, all founded in the 19th century. Take the first right turn opposite the Italian palazzo-style Reform Club into St James's Square. Turn left along the south side of the square and then right by the pavilion into the gardens (open Monday to Friday 10.00–16.30; skirt round the outside if closed). The square was developed soon after the restoration of the monarchy in 1660 and rapidly became the smartest address in London: around 1720 it was home to no fewer than six dukes and seven earls. By 1796, however, the Wedgwood china company had taken over one of the houses as a showroom and since then business has completed its conquest.

Walk straight through the gardens past the statue of King William III – to your right there is a good view of London's oldest theatre, the Haymarket, built in 1820 – and go up Duke of York Street towards **St James's Church** at the top. At the church, turn left into Jermyn Street, famous for its shirt shops and men's outfitters. Isaac Newton, discoverer of the law of gravity, lived opposite the entrance to Prince's Arcade on the right.

Continue on to St James's Street and turn left towards Henry VIII's St James's Palace at the foot of the hill. On the left, the balconied house next to the chemist's is Boodle's Club and opposite, the large house with the blue door is Brooks's Club. Both clubs have been operating for well over 200 years and have seen countless country estates lost and won at their gambling tables. Further down on the left you pass the battered shop front of Berry Brothers and Rudd, wine merchants who have been in business, originally as grocers, since the 1600s (see page 18). American readers may like to know that Pickering Place, through the archway on the left, was the base of the independent Texan Republic's legation until Texas joined the Union in 1845.

When you come to St James's Palace turn right along Cleveland Row. St James's has not been used as a royal palace since the early 1800s although foreign ambassadors are still officially accredited to the Court of St James's. Some of the Palace's contemporary functions are to provide offices for part of the Royal Household and a London base for the Prince of Wales.

Continue past the entrance to Stable Yard on the left and go through the passage to the right of the small car park into Queen's Walk. Here turn left and then almost immediately right into Green Park, opposite Milkmaid's Passage on your left. Take the left-most of the three tarmac paths and then at the crossroads turn left towards Buckingham Palace, the Queen's London home. If the flag is flying, she is in residence.

Home of the monarch

To the left beyond the palace you can see the red and white campanile of the Roman Catholic Westminster Cathedral. Go to the right of the huge wrought-iron gates and cross Constitution Hill at the traffic lights to the palace, the sovereign's main London home since 1837, when Queen Victoria took up residence. Walk along the front of the palace to Buckingham Gate. The entrances to the **Queen's Gallery** and the **Royal Mews** are further along the road on the right-hand side. Cross the road and turn left along Birdcage Walk, so called because there was a royal aviary here in the 17th century. On your left is St James's Park and on your right are the Wellington Barracks, used by the various Guards regiments detailed to protect the royal palaces. There are a total of seven regiments of Guards: five infantry (Irish, Scots, Welsh, Coldstream and Grenadier) and two cavalry (Life Guards and Blues and Royals). The two cavalry regiments wear different coloured uniforms; the uniformly red-coated foot guards are identified by different arrangements of tunic buttons. At the far end of the barracks are the modern **Guards Chapel** and the **Guards Museum**. Rising up behind is the modern Home Office building in Queen Anne's Gate.

Walk on past the chapel. When you reach the traffic lights go right into Queen Anne's Gate, architecturally one of London's finest streets. Fittingly, the National Trust, Britain's leading heritage organization, has its headquarters here (on the right as you turn left to walk down the street). Queen Anne's Gate was built in the early 18th century when Queen Anne was on the throne. There is a statue of the queen on the right where the street narrows. Nearly every house seems to have a plaque on it commemorating some worthy politician or other. Carry on to the end of the street and then turn left into Old Queen Street, also built during the 18th century. On the left you pass Cockpit Steps, site of the 17th-century royal cockfighting arena.

At the end of Old Queen Street turn right into Storey's Gate, named after Charles II's gamekeeper in St James's Park. On your left is the new Queen Elizabeth II Conference Centre. Cross the road to the forecourt of Westminster Abbey, the national church and scene of the coronation of almost every English monarch since William the Conqueror in 1066. Continue through the archway into Dean's Yard, the main abbey courtyard when Westminster was still a monastery: turning left, you will see a gateway ahead leading into the abbey's cloisters and its 900-year-old garden (free to visit when open).

Richard the Lionheart

Turn right along the east side of the quadrangle. On the left you pass the old abbey guesthouse, now the office of the cathedral chapter, and the entrance to Little Dean's Yard and Westminster School, once the abbey school and now a leading public school. Go through the archway at the end of Dean's Yard and turn left into Great College Street with the medieval abbey wall on your left. Near the end of the street, turn left along the path through Abingdon Gardens, laid out over an underground car park.

On the right is a bronze sculpture by Henry Moore, *Knife Edge Two Piece* (1962), dwarfed by the massive Victoria Tower of the Houses of Parliament. At the opposite end of the gardens on the left is the **Jewel Tower**, part of the medieval Palace of Westminster destroyed by fire in 1834 and replaced by the present Houses of Parliament. Opposite the Jewel Tower, the statue of King Richard the Lionheart brandishing his sword stands in Old Palace Yard, outside the House of Lords. Further along – spared by the fire – is the original medieval hall of the Palace of Westminster, its pitched roof, flying buttresses and plain exterior distinguishing it clearly from the ornate 19th-century Parliament building. Interestingly, the style of the new Parliament building mirrors the 15th-century east end of Westminster Abbey opposite. The statue in front of Westminster Hall is of Oliver Cromwell, leader of the Parliamentarians in their fight against King Charles I in the 1640s.

Beyond Westminster Hall, New Palace Yard is the main entrance to the House of Commons for MPs. Cross Bridge Street at the traffic lights on the corner and turn right towards Westminster station and the end of the walk.

❖❖

EXPLORING SECRET
ST JAMES'S

❖❖

Summary: After 300 years of constant building and rebuilding, St James's is honey-combed with a network of hidden passages, alleyways, courts and mews. Exploring them on foot is the best way of getting to the heart of this exclusive and fascinating little enclave. This fairly short walk starts and finishes at Piccadilly Circus and goes in an anti-clockwise direction, touching St James's Palace with its **Chapel Royal** (open for Sunday services) at its furthest point. Also featured are the local parish church,

Jermyn Street (good for clothes shopping), the **Alfred Dunhill Museum**, the Royal Over-Seas League, Pratt's and Brooks's clubs, **Spencer House** (the town house of the former Princess of Wales's family), **Green Park**, **Christie's Fine Art Auctioneers** and the London Library.

Start and finish:	Piccadilly Circus station (Bakerloo and Piccadilly Underground Lines).
Length:	1¼ miles (2km).
Time:	45 minutes.
Refreshments:	Numerous pubs and sandwich bars en route for refreshment, but Crown Passage at the halfway stage makes an ideal stopping point. Here you will find the best pub in the area – the Red Lion – and a good selection of sandwich bars and wine bars.

Walk along the south side of Piccadilly away from the underground station until you come to **St James's Church**, designed by Sir Christopher Wren. Turn left through the gates into the paved churchyard and enter the church. Continue on through the vestibule doors until you come out the far side in Jermyn Street. Here, by the entrance to the Aroma café, turn right and walk along the street, passing the entrance to Prince's Arcade. Cross Duke Street St James's (one of the lesser-known attractions of **Dunhill's** on the corner is its upstairs museum) and continue on along Jermyn Street, passing the Piccadilly Arcade.

Royal Over-Seas League

At the end of the street cross St James's Street into Bennet Street, turning left at The Blue Posts pub. This looks like a cul-de-sac, but there is a way out at the far end where some steps lead down to Park Place. Descending, you get a good idea of the steepness of the slope on which St James's is laid out. On the right at the bottom is the entrance to Over-Seas House, home of the Royal Over-Seas League, a club founded in 1910 to promote the idea of world comradeship under the aegis of the British Empire. The club occupies two fine historic houses (Vernon House and Rutland House) which you can visit on weekdays during office hours. Every September there is an open exhibition at the League for professional artists up to the age of 35. This is also open to the public.

Blue Ball Yard

Turn left in Park Place and go to the end (Brooks's Club, here since 1778, is on the left and Pratt's Club – at No. 14 – on the right). Here, turn right back onto St James's Street. Fifty yards (45m) down on the right is the arched entrance to Blue Ball Yard. It doesn't look much from the street, but when you get inside you see on the left a picturesque range of traditional mews cottages and garages. Built in 1741, they were originally coach houses, with rooms for coachmen and grooms at the top, and large cellars and wine vaults underneath. Today they make an unusual annexe to the Stafford Hotel, the entrance to whose bar and restaurant you can see at the end of the yard. Above are bedrooms. Down below, one of the ancient brick-vaulted cellars has been turned into an atmospheric subterranean dining-room. The others are used for storing the hotel's 20,000 bottles of wine.

Spencer House

Come back out onto St James's Street and turn right. At the next right, turn into St James's Place. On the left, by the red pillar box, a little courtyard gives access to the secluded Duke's Hotel, formerly chambers for wealthy bachelors. Further on and still on the left, Spencer House is the former town house of the late Princess of Wales's family. At the moment, it is on long lease to Lord Rothschild. He has spent several million pounds restoring it and opened the main rooms to the public (on Sundays). The rest of the house has been turned into offices for his various investment companies. Follow the road round to the right, go past the 80-year-old Stafford Hotel on the right and then turn left (between Nos. 22 and 23) into a gated passageway which dips and then climbs up to Queen's Walk in Green Park. Here turn left and walk down the hill, passing the garden front of Spencer House. Technically the rams' heads on the frieze are classical architectural ornaments, but I prefer to think of them as an allusion to the great flocks of sheep on the Northamptonshire uplands which made the Spencers so much money in the 15th and 16th centuries.

Bridgewater House

Beyond Spencer House is the much larger Bridgewater House with urns along its balustraded top. At the corner of its garden turn left into another gated path (don't be afraid of the sign saying it is not a public right of way and that it is liable to close without notice – it is here only for legal reasons). You come out in Cleveland Row, with the entrance to Bridgewater House on the left and Selwyn House on the right. Bridgewater House, a vast town house built in 1846 for Lord Ellesmere, heir to the vast Bridgewater estates with all their canal wealth, is today both home and office to wealthy Greek shipowner and banker Captain John Latsis. Selwyn House, named after a family that lived in an older house on this site in the 18th century, is the London office of Pilkington's glass company.

St James's Palace

Cleveland Row brings you to St James's Palace: if you look down the barred and police-guarded road to the right you can see the guards with their bearskin hats standing outside Clarence House, the home of the Prince of Wales. Go past the entrance to Little St James's Street on the left and carry on along the side of the palace. Russell Court on the left is a dead end, but as a cobbled mews of relatively traditional character – especially its little cottages right at the far end – it is worth a peep. As you enter, you can see in the stained-glass windows of a masonic hall reversed lettering reading PROVINCE OF EAST ANGLIA NORFOLK SUFFOLK CAMBRIDGE. Coming out of Russell Court and turning left, carry on down Cleveland Row with the Palace on your right. St James's Palace is the only royal palace in London which is completely closed to the public – or so most people think. There is in fact a way to see part of it, although it means coming on a Sunday and only during the winter season from October through to Easter.

The Chapel Royal

St James's Palace has two chapels. One, the Queen's Chapel, is outside the palace in Marlborough Road. The other, the Chapel Royal, is inside the palace. On most Sundays in the winter season only, services are held in the Chapel Royal which the public are free to attend. Times are published the day before in *The Times* and *Daily Telegraph* newspapers.

A feature of these services is the singing by the Chapel Royal choir. This consists of six gentlemen choristers and ten children choristers. The latter go to the City of London School, where they are called the Queen's Scholars because the Queen pays two-thirds of their fees. Dressed in their scarlet and gold state coats, they make not only a beautiful sound but a picturesque and colourful sight. Historically, they are continuing a Chapel Royal tradition of fine church music stretching back a thousand years.

Strictly speaking, the Chapel Royal is not a building but a department, an organization, a team of priests and singers charged with meeting the spiritual needs of the sovereign. In medieval times when the Court moved about a good deal, so did the

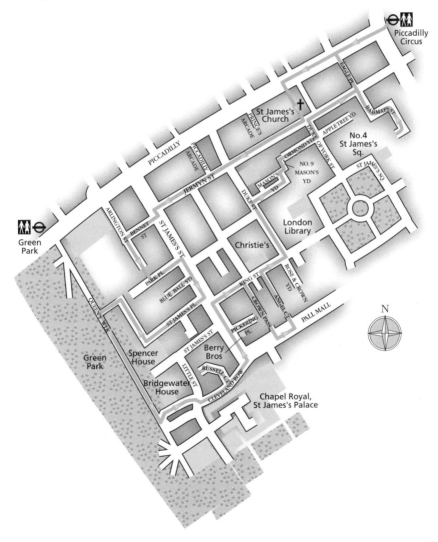

17

Chapel Royal, ferrying its vestments and service books about in panniers on two packhorses. In 1415 it went to France with Henry V and sang mass before the battle of Agincourt. As the Court gradually settled down, the Chapel Royal ceased its wanderings and settled down with it. With its royal associations, the Chapel has always been able to attract the finest musicians. Tallis, Byrd and Purcell – big names in the 16th and 17th centuries – were all Chapel Royal organists. Handel was a specially appointed composer in the 18th century. Today, musical historians describe the Chapel as nothing less than 'the cradle of English church music'.

The Holbein ceiling

The Chapel Royal organization has been at St James's Palace since 1702, but the actual chapel building forms part of the original palace put up in Henry VIII's time. It has been changed a good deal since then, particularly by the Victorians, but the richly decorated Tudor ceiling, said to have been painted by Holbein, survives. Designed in the first half of 1540 when Henry was married to Anne of Cleves, the ceiling is mainly covered in royal coats of arms and initials. These are to be expected. But there are two oddities. One is the series of vignettes incorporating the names of the Cleve family estates on the continent. A possible explanation for this is that perhaps it was the Flanders Mare's dowry that paid for the chapel. The second unusual feature is the single instance in the northwest corner of Henry's arms combined with those of Catherine Howard, his next wife after Anne. Since he divorced Anne and married Catherine in the same month, July 1540, Holbein must have been putting his finishing touches to the ceiling at that very time. So the famous story of Henry VIII and his six wives helps date one work at least in Holbein's *oeuvre*!

Outside the Palace, you can spot the location of the Chapel by looking to the right of the gatehouse: the double row of narrow windows is in the Chapel's north wall (unusually for a Christian church it is laid out on a north–south rather than an east–west axis). If you come to a Sunday service, you reach the Chapel by going through the police barrier mentioned earlier into Stable Yard; then you turn left into Ambassadors Court (ambassadors to the UK are still officially accredited to the Court of St James's); from there you pass through a surviving archway from the medieval leper house-cum-convent that preceded the Palace. This brings you into Colour Court, the Tudor section of the Palace behind the gatehouse. The Chapel is on the left.

Berry Bros & Rudd

Returning to the walk, when you reach Pall Mall cross to the far side of St James's Street on the zebra crossing and walk up the right-hand side of the street. Berry Bros at No. 3 is just the sort of old-established, up-market wine merchant you would expect to find in St James's. With its battered (but of course carefully preserved) shop front, it looks every bit the long-lived, well-established business it is. But like every commercial concern it still has to operate in a competitive market and its future, for that reason, is by no means guaranteed.

Luckily, however, it has two things to help it survive. One is 'Cutty Sark' whisky, a global seller created by the firm and a healthy generator of profits. The other is what might be called Berry Bros' very own secret weapon: its huge subterranean storage area. This enables it to supply instantly, from what looks to be just a small shop, any wine on its extensive price list – in quantity if required. No other wine merchant in central London can match this level of service, which is why no other wine merchant in central London – including those like Justerini and Brooks, which are nearly as old – has quite the same name as Berry Bros. If you go into the shop (living antique is the only term for it) and place an order (one bottle will do), an assistant will go to a raised trapdoor against the wall on the right-hand side. This is the entrance to the original shop cellar, and still the main entrance to the vastly expanded network of cellars that the moles of Berry Bros have been burrowing for the past 300 years. The latest addition came in the early 1980s when the firm acquired the cellars under Rothmans next door. These cellars are actually on two below-ground floors. Kept at a constant and fairly cool temperature by the damp London clay, these huge vaults are capable of storing 18,000 cases of wine – that's 216,000 bottles. Most of them are for sale, but some are laid down to mature. And tucked away in various nooks and crannies are the firm's choicest and oldest selections, strictly for private drinking only: Cognac from the 1830s, Lafitte from the 1860s and, of course, port. According to the cellar manager, who has personally tippled both (strictly in the line of duty), the 1863 Cockburn's is superb but the 1820 Croft's is disappointing. To get some idea of the scale of these secret vaults, stand outside the shop to the left of the entrance to Pickering Place (this, incidentally, is where the Widow Bourne established the original business – then a grocer's – in the 1690s; William Pickering was her son-in-law). Looking down St James's Street towards the Palace, the cellars come right out under the pavement and extend as far away from you as the corner of Pall Mall (the pavement on the corner is right above the tasting area). Now go into Pickering Place (it is public property), the prettiest little courtyard in St James's. Berry Bros have the houses on three of the four sides (they were built in the garden of Widow Bourne's house in the 1730s) and the cellars extend under the courtyard right to the back of the house. It should be clear now how Berry Bros can produce so much wine from what appears to be just one small shop.

Crown Passage and Angel Court

Turn right out of Pickering Place and continue on up St James's Street. A little further on you pass Lock's the hatters, here since 1764, and then Lobb's the boot- and shoe-makers, relatively new arrivals in the 1850s. Lobb's' shoes, incidentally, take up to six months to make and they have 30,000 lasts stored on ceiling-high racks in the basement, filed in alphabetical order of customer. At King Street, turn right and then when you get to Crown Passage, turn right again. Crown Passage – probably taking its name from a lost pub – is exactly what it should be, a lively little 'village' street full of useful shops and services, including an ironmonger's, for workers and residents in the surrounding streets.

Go down to the end of Crown Passage, passing the Red Lion pub on the way, and turn left along Pall Mall. After a few yards, turn left into Angel Court. Like Crown Passage, Angel Court is probably also named after a former pub, but there the resemblance ends. Where Crown Passage is full of life, Angel Court is completely dead. There is absolutely nothing at street level to interest the passing walker, and the only sound to break the otherwise dead silence is the hum of air-conditioning systems in the towering office buildings on either side. The only good thing to say about it is that no attempt has been made to create the kind of instant sham community so beloved of property developers with big ideas and no soul.

King Street

Angel Court brings you back on to King Street. Christie's world-famous auction house, founded in 1766, is directly opposite: the galleries are open every weekday for viewing and it's quite all right for you just to wander in off the street and take a look around – the sort of thing you always mean to do if you work in the area but somehow never quite get round to. From Angel Court turn right along King Street. Rose and Crown Yard on the right is a dead end and not very interesting to look at. From the yard, cross King Street and walk up the right-hand side of Duke Street St James's: Princes Place, a short dead end, is on the left. Between Nos. 12 and 13 on the right walk through the archway into Mason's Yard. This was originally built as a stableyard for St James's Square in the 1660s. The centre of the yard has always been built on, the site today being occupied by an electricity sub-station. Keep this to your left and walk to the end.

London Library

Here look right and you will see a back wall of the London Library, the famous members-only lending library conceived by historian Thomas Carlyle in 1841 and based in St James's Square since 1845. Apart from the fact that you can borrow books from it for extended periods, the beauty of the library is that readers are free to browse among the shelves in the warren of old-fashioned bookstacks lying behind the elegant St James's Square façade – provided you don't mind the occasional electric shock, that is. All the shelves and stairs in the stacks are made of metal to reduce the fire risk, and you used to get a small charge when you put your hand on a banister. Re-wiring in the late 1990s dealt with the problem, so depriving elderly members of their traditional boost as they climbed from London Topography Quarto in the basement to Periodicals and Societies on the sixth floor!

From your vantage point in Mason's Yard, you can see part of the library's new extension, completed in 1992, with some of the bookstacks clearly visible through the upper windows. Behind the windows at first-floor level lies the spacious reading-room with its main window looking onto St James's Square. In the mid-1990s, the library was extended again back to Duke Street.

Babmaes Street

Turn left round the corner of the sub-station and head for the far-right corner of the yard. Here, by the Directors Lodge Club, is a passage marked 'No. 9 Mason's Yard'. In existence probably since the building of the yard and certainly since 1720, this eventually brings you out in Ormond Yard. Here, besides a couple of clubs, is Briggs's barber shop, a favourite resort for club and business types in the surrounding streets. Go to the end of the yard. Turn left here up Duke of York Street, and then right at the top into Jermyn Street once more. Carry on along the right-hand side of the street until you get to Babmaes Street.

A long dead end with two dog-legs, Babmaes Street is really a mews penetrating as far as some of the grand houses on the northeast corner of St James's Square. The big gates on the right at the far end lead to the rear of No. 4 St James's Square, a mansion with no fewer than 77 rooms, servants' quarters, its own private courtyard garden, garaging for six cars, and to the left, at 7/9 Babmaes Street, its own little coach house last used as such in 1942. The house is now home to the Naval and Military Club. Babmaes Street's curious name is a corruption – via Babmay's – of Baptist May, the name of an adviser to the aristocratic family responsible for developing so much of the St James's area in the late 17th century.

Retrace your steps out of Babmaes Street, cross Jermyn Street and enter Eagle Place. This brings you back onto Piccadilly once more. Turn right and you arrive back at the start of the walk at Piccadilly Circus.

❖❖❖

MAYFAIR

❖❖❖

Summary: Mayfair is an exclusive shopping, residential and business district in the heart of the West End. It was developed in the 18th century, mainly by the fabulously wealthy Grosvenor family that still owns a substantial amount of property in the area. Almost every shop is a household name and nearly every house has had at least one famous occupant. This circular walk passes all of the well-known shops, such as Fortnum and Mason and Tiffany, as well as the homes of people like Beau Brummell and Clive of India. The walk includes Berkeley Square and Grosvenor Square, the Burlington Arcade and Royal Arcade, Bond Street and Savile Row, the **Royal Academy of Arts** and Royal Institution, and last but not least Shepherd Market, Mayfair's own red-light district.

Start and finish:	Piccadilly Circus station (Piccadilly and Bakerloo Underground Lines).
Length:	3 miles (4.8km).
Time:	2 hours.
Refreshments:	Shepherd Market about a third of the way along the route is undoubtedly the best place to stop because of its wide choice of venues and its friendly atmosphere. Avery Row, about two-thirds of the way, has several good sandwich bars and is similarly welcoming. Otherwise try a picnic at the halfway stage in delightful Mount Street Gardens.
Note:	The Burlington and Royal Arcades are both closed on Sundays.

Leave Piccadilly station by the 'Piccadilly (South Side)' exit and walk along Piccadilly away from the Circus. To your left you will soon see **St James's Church**, designed by Sir Christopher Wren in 1676 as the parish church for the new district of St James's being developed by the Jermyn family, earls of St Albans. The visionary artist and poet William Blake was baptized here in 1757. From Tuesday to Saturday the church forecourt is taken over by a small market selling antiques on Tuesday and clothes, jewellery, prints and souvenirs on the other days. Further along, you come to Hatchard's bookshop and then two other stores, including Fortnum and Mason, the high-class grocers. These shops all bear coats of arms, indicating that they are all official suppliers to various members of the royal family. Fortnum and Mason's connections with royalty go back to 1707 when William Fortnum became a footman in the royal household. John Hatchard founded his bookshop in Piccadilly in 1797 with less than £5 capital.

Piccadilly arcades

Opposite Hatchard's, in its own little courtyard, is Albany, a unique set of bachelors' apartments created in 1802 by architect Henry Holland out of the town house of one of George III's sons, the 'grand old Duke of York' of the nursery rhyme. The 70 apartments are owned by occupants and managed by a trust. Byron was one of the first people to live here; recent occupants include Edward Heath, Prime Minister in the 1970s, and actor Terence Stamp.

Continue along Piccadilly past the entrance to Prince's Arcade. When you get to Duke Street St James's on your left, turn right across Piccadilly and then turn left past the entrance to Burlington House, former town house of the Earls of Burlington and home of the Royal Academy of Arts, founded 1768, since 1868. Five learned societies occupy purpose-built premises around the perimeter of the courtyard. The statue in the middle is of Sir Joshua Reynolds, the first president of the Academy.

Beyond the Academy turn right into Burlington Arcade (1819), second oldest of London's five 19th-century shopping arcades (the oldest is the Royal Opera Arcade: see the Soho to Trafalgar Square walk, page 87). Turn left out of the arcade into Burlington Gardens. At the end of the road on the left, a plaque records that the corner building was once Atkinson's, a famous perfumier. The carillon is a peal of

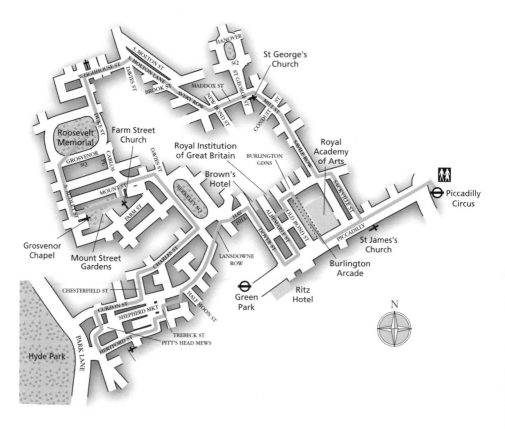

handbells housed in the black wooden steeple high above. Opposite on the other side of Old Bond Street are two famous jewellers: Tiffany and Cartier. This part of London is the most expensive shopping area in the capital as well as the centre of the fine art trade.

Turn left into Old Bond Street and then, a little further on, cross the road into the Royal Arcade. A product of the Victorian age, it lacks the Regency elegance of the Burlington Arcade. Standing at the exit of the arcade in Albemarle Street, to your right is the Royal Institution where Michael Faraday carried out his experiments with electricity (**Faraday Museum**). Opposite is Brown's Hotel, founded in 1837 by ex-manservant James Brown. Now turn left. No. 50 Albemarle Street, the second from the end on the right-hand side, has been connected with the John Murray publishing business since 1812, when Lord Byron and Jane Austen were clients of the firm. The first John Murray introduced Byron to Sir Walter Scott here and the two men, though very different in temperament, became fast friends. From the end of Albemarle Street there is a good view of the Tudor gatehouse of St James's Palace.

Turn right into Piccadilly and right again opposite the Ritz Hotel into Dover Street. No. 40 on the left is the Arts Club, founded in 1863; Dickens was an early member. Further on, the town house at No. 37 was built in 1772 for the Bishop of Ely (hence the bishop's mitre in the middle roundel above the first-floor windows) and has one of the finest classical façades of any house in Mayfair.

The May fairs

From Dover Street turn left into Hay Hill, cross the street at the bottom and go through Lansdowne Row (following the course of the Tyburn river) into Curzon Street. After Half Moon Street turn left through the arch at No. 47 into Shepherd Market, a picturesque enclave of narrow streets and old houses with many pavement cafés and restaurants. Edward Shepherd started a twice-weekly cattle market here on the banks of the Tyburn River in 1688. The two-week May fair, from which Mayfair takes its name, began a few years later but was banned in the 18th century after objections from local residents. By then the market had become a haunt of prostitutes and if you look closely at the doorbells you will see that 'French models' are still plying their time-honoured trade in the area today.

At the Grapes pub turn right and walk as far as Trebeck Street. To the right you can see Crewe House, formerly the town house of Lord Crewe and now the Saudi Arabian embassy. Turn left on Trebeck Street. On the left at first-floor level a blue plaque commemorates the May Fair. At the end of Trebeck Street turn right and left into Hertford Street. On the left at No. 10 lived General Burgoyne, the British general who lost the battle of Saratoga during the American War of Independence. The general was followed by Richard Brinsley Sheridan, the author of two evergreen comedies of the stage, *The Rivals* and *The School for Scandal*. Further along on the left at No. 20 lived Sir George Cayley, Yorkshire squire and little-known pioneer of aviation. In 1804 he built and flew the world's first flying machine.

Hertford Street ends in a small roundabout with Park Lane on the opposite side and Hyde Park beyond. Turn right here across the forecourt of the Hilton Hotel, right again into Pitt's Head Mews and then immediately left up the steps into Curzon Place. Turn right into Curzon Street. Benjamin Disraeli lived and died at

No. 19 on the right. No. 30, also on the right-hand side, houses Crockford's, the famous gambling club founded in St James's Street in 1828.

Mayfair squares

At the Curzon cinema turn left into Chesterfield Street, a virtually intact Georgian street, except for the reconstructed No. 6 on the right, former home of the novelist Somerset Maugham. Two centuries ago the narrow white house next door was the home of Beau Brummell, the famous dandy and style-king of the Regency period. So great was Brummell's influence that he is reputed to have once made the Prince Regent cry by telling him he did not like the cut of his coat. Unfortunately Brummell's finances were not as sure as his taste and he died abroad, a fugitive from his creditors.

Turn right into handsome Charles Street, leading down to Berkeley Square. This is the most attractive of Mayfair's three squares, with its 200-year-old plane trees and a fine terrace of Georgian houses along the left-hand (west) side. Walk up this terrace passing No. 45, once the home of Lord Clive, the clerk-turned-soldier whose brilliant generalship established Britain as the dominant power in India in the 18th century.

At the top of the square turn left into Mount Street. As you do so, you pass from the old Berkeley Estate into the Grosvenor Estate. Walk down to Carlos Place and turn left again into Mount Street Gardens, the former burial ground of St Mary's Hanover Square, seen later on the walk. On the left, the Church of the Immaculate Conception is the headquarters of the English Jesuits. It's popularly known as '**Farm Street**' because the main entrance is on the other side in Farm Street. Walk straight through the gardens and out by the gates on the opposite side. The church on the left is the **Grosvenor Chapel**, built in 1730 to serve the developing Grosvenor Estate. Turn right into South Audley Street, passing the famous gunmakers Purdey's on the other side of the road.

At the top of South Audley Street is Grosvenor Square, the centrepiece of the Grosvenor Estate and the third largest square in London (the largest is Ladbroke Square in Notting Hill: see the Notting Hill walk, page 46). Only one of the original Georgian houses has survived, so that the modern square is somewhat featureless and impersonal. The whole of its western side is taken up by the mono-lithic American Embassy. Cut across the square diagonally to the right. In the centre there is a statue of the American president, Franklin D. Roosevelt, and a memorial to the American and British pilots of the RAF's World War II Eagle Squadrons. In the top right corner go across the road to the left into Duke Street and then turn right into Weighhouse Street, by the Ukrainian Catholic Cathedral. Built in 1892, this was originally the King's Weigh House Chapel, and replaced the original Weigh House Chapel that occupied rooms above the medieval king's weigh house in Eastcheap in the City. Weighhouse Street will bring you to Davies Street and the former toilet-ware factory of J. Bolding, now converted into Gray's Antique Market.

Stylish shopping

Turn right into South Molton Lane, take the immediate left turn into South Molton Passage and then turn right again into pedestrianized South Molton Street. The coat of arms on the front of some of the shops indicates that you are now on land owned (since the 1620s) by the Corporation of London. At the end of South Molton Street cross Brook Street to Colefax and Fowler, leaders in country house interior design.

Plate 1: Westminster and St James's
The Westminster and St James's walk passes right by this statue of
Richard the Lionheart in Old Palace Yard, next to the House of Lords (see page 14).

Plate 2: Mayfair
*The Mayfair walk finishes with one of London's best-known
landmarks, the statue of Eros in Piccadilly Circus (see page 25).*

Plate 3: Exploring Secret St James's
Piccadilly Arcade, which connects Piccadilly with Jermyn Street, is one of several elegant covered shopping streets in the West End (see page 22).

Plate 4: Marylebone
Almost anywhere in London, look up and you will see fine architectural details like this relief on a house in Harley Street (see page 28).

Plate 5: Following the Tyburn River
The Tyburn river walk passes between the main front of Buckingham
Palace and the memorial to Queen Victoria (see page 34).

Plate 6: Central Parks
Autumn colours in Hyde Park, one of the four royal parks
traversed by the Central Parks walk (see page 38).

Plate 7: Kensington
Spring flowers make a fine show in Holland Park. Until World War II, these gardens were the private grounds of Holland House (see page 42).

Plate 8: Notting Hill
*Bargains are still to be found at the Saturday antiques market in
Notting Hill's Portobello Road (see page 46).*

Plate 9: Bayswater to Belgravia
The lavishly decorated memorial to Prince Albert, patron of the arts and
husband of Queen Victoria (see page 49).

Their shop was once the home of the Regency architect Sir Jeffry Wyatville, whose main achievement was turning Windsor Castle into the palace we know today.

Descend narrow Avery Row by the side of Colefax and Fowler. At the end of the Row, which is built over the Tyburn River, turn left and go across New Bond Street into Maddox Street – looking out for Sotheby's to the right on the opposite side of New Bond Street. **St George's Church** looms up at the end of Maddox Street. This has been one of London's most fashionable churches ever since it was built as part of the Hanover Square development in the 1720s. Hanover Square, the third of Mayfair's three squares, is to the left at the top of St George Street. The figure at the entrance to the square is of William Pitt, Prime Minister in 1783 at the tender age of 24.

Tailors and painters

Continue along Maddox Street across St George Street and turn to the right around the back of the church into Mill Street. Cross Conduit Street into Savile Row, a street famous for its men's tailors. On the left you pass a monumental building aptly named Fortress House, the headquarters of English Heritage – the organization that manages all the publicly-owned historic buildings and monuments in the country. Further on, some of the 18th-century houses retain their original exterior fixtures. No. 17 with its flagpole, first-floor balcony supported by cast-iron pillars, entrance lanterns, torch snuffers and studded front door, is a fine example. Nineteenth-century architect George Basevi lived here.

At the end of Savile Row you look straight into the rear entrance of Albany flanked by two small lodges. To the left is the tailor Gieves and Hawkes, uniform makers and another royal supplier. Turn left beside Gieves and Hawkes into Vigo Street. On the right Allen Lane's founding of Penguin Books in his apartment in Albany in 1935 is commemorated by a grey stone plaque. Turn right now into Sackville Street. There is a good view here of the former galleries of the Royal Institute of Painters in Water Colours on Piccadilly. The name of the institute is written on the façade above the busts of eight famous water-colour artists of the 18th and 19th centuries (Sandby, Cozens, Girtin, Turner, Cox, De Wint, Barret and Hunt). Founded in 1831, the institute still exists, but it now shares a building with other art societies in Carlton House Terrace.

When you reach Piccadilly, turn left and walk towards Piccadilly Circus and the statue of Eros, a somewhat inappropriate tribute to the 19th-century philanthropist Lord Shaftesbury (of Shaftesbury Avenue fame). The walk ends at Piccadilly station beneath the statue.

❖❖

MARYLEBONE

❖❖

Summary: Marylebone is just north of Oxford Street in the West End. It was one of the closest villages to central London until two landowners in the area began to lay out the regular grid of impressive streets and squares for which the area is chiefly known today. Many fine houses from that time (the 18th and early 19th centuries) still remain, although most have been converted into offices. Features of the walk include the old High Street and parish church (grave of the hymn-writer Charles Wesley), four squares (including Manchester Square where the **Wallace Collection** is based), Harley Street, **Madame Tussaud's Waxworks**, Oxford Street, and the award-winning shopping precinct, St Christopher's Place.

Start:	Edgware Road station (Circle, District and Hammersmith & City Underground Lines – the Bakerloo Line stops at a separate Edgware Road station close by).
Finish:	Baker Street station (Jubilee, Bakerloo, Metropolitan, Hammersmith & City and Circle Underground Lines).
Length:	2½ miles (4km).
Time:	1½ hours.
Refreshments:	Various pubs en route plus a wide selection of places in the second half of the walk near Oxford Street and in Marylebone High Street. James Street, just next door to St Christopher's Place, has several pavement restaurants for alfresco eating.

Take the main Chapel Street exit out of Edgware Road station, walking left to the end of the road. Go over Old Marylebone Road and continue into Homer Street, which is named after local landowner Edward Homer not the Greek poet. Turn left along Crawford Street to Wyndham Place. Wyndham Place and St Mary's Church on the left were both part of the development of Bryanston Square on the right and were designed to close the vista north from the country end of Oxford Street, a point now occupied by Marble Arch. Since the development was planned in the 1820s the trees in Bryanston Square have grown to maturity and rather spoilt the effect.

Turn right into Wyndham Place (note the decorative coal-hole covers, some of them dated) and go down the right-hand side of Bryanston Square, built on Henry Portman's estate and named after the family seat in Dorset. At the bottom turn left into George Street along the south side of the square, passing on the way the 1862 memorial to William Pitt Byrne, proprietor of the *Morning Post* newspaper (Byrne died at his house in nearby Montagu Street in April 1861). The house in front of you on the corner of Bryanston Square has a plaque to Mustapha Reschid Pasha (1800–1858), the Ottoman Empire's ambassador to Britain in 1836–37 (not 1839 as stated on the plaque).

Blue stockings

When you reach Montagu Square (1811) turn right into Montagu Street and then left into Upper Berkeley Street. The hotel on the left stands on the site of Montagu House, a large mansion destroyed by bombs in World War II. In the 18th century it was the home of Mrs Montagu, one of the cleverest women of her day and hostess of a leading intellectual salon. One regular was a man who wore blue instead of the more normal black stockings, a foible which led observers to label Mrs Montagu and her guests 'bluestockings', hence the colloquial name for an intellectual woman.

Walk on into Portman Square, the nucleus of the Portman Estate, completed in 1784. Little remains of its original architecture except for two houses on the corner.

These are Nos. 20 and 21. No. 20, Home House, was designed in the 1770s by Robert Adam for the Countess of Home and is now a private club.

Continue along the north side of the square, across Baker Street, along Fitzhardinge Street, and into Manchester Square. Completed in 1788, this was the second square to be built on the Portman Estate and is the most attractive in Marylebone. Walk to the left along the north side of the square. This is wholly taken up by Hertford House, home of the Wallace art collection. The collection was assembled by several Marquises of Hertford, the best-known being the third Marquis. Artistically his main interests were Sèvres porcelain and Dutch painting. Personally he was so unpleasant that the novelist Thackeray used him as a model for the loathsome Lord Steyne in *Vanity Fair*. Sir Richard Wallace, whose wife donated the Wallace Collection to the nation, was the natural son and heir of the fourth Marquis of Hertford.

Slum to shopping mall

Leave Manchester Square opposite Fitzhardinge Street going along Hinde Street. Cross Thayer Street and then turn right into Marylebone Lane, a vestige of the old lane from the West End to Marylebone village. Take the path that branches right at the Button Queen shop (Jason Court) and cross Wigmore Street into St Christopher's Place. This narrow street was a slum for many years, despite the efforts of reformers and local authorities to make improvements. Now, by transforming the street into a fashionable shopping enclave, it seems the property developers have succeeded where social do-gooders failed. At the southern end St Christopher's Place becomes Gees Court and narrows into an archway leading on to Oxford Street.

Turning left into Oxford Street, London's main shopping street, walk past the entrance to Stratford Place to your left (note the old porter's lodge on the eastern corner). Stratford House at the northern end was built in 1775 for Edward Stratford, second Earl of Aldborough. It is now the Oriental Club. Continue along

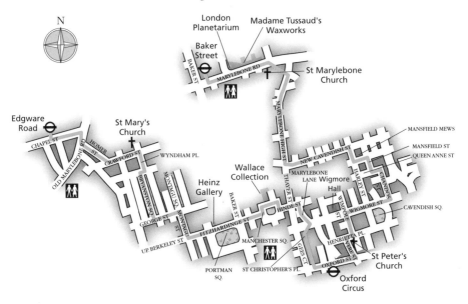

Oxford Street, crossing Marylebone Lane twice, and turn left into Vere Street. Turn right at **St Peter's Church** (1724 – see board to left of entrance) into Henrietta Place and then left into Wimpole Street. No. 1 on the right is the Royal Society of Medicine. Take the first turning on the right into Wigmore Street. To the left you can see the entrance to the Wigmore Hall, a well-known venue for classical music concerts.

Walk across Harley Street into Cavendish Square, built on land owned by Edward Harley, second Earl of Oxford. Named after the earl's wife, Lady Henrietta Cavendish Holles, Cavendish Square was both the centrepiece of the Portland Estate (which is still owned by descendants of the original owners) and the first stage of the transformation of the rural village of Marylebone into a part of urban London. On the left, beyond the surgeon Sir Jonathan Hutchinson's house, are two survivors from the original Georgian square, much of which has been rebuilt since World War II. The Convent of the Sisters of the Holy Child Jesus used to be based in one of the houses and it was they who in the 1950s commissioned the Jacob Epstein sculpture of the Madonna and Child fixed to the arch over Dean's Mews.

Take the first left turn into Chandos Street. On the left at No. 11 are the original premises of the Medical Society of London, founded in 1773 largely through the efforts of the Quaker physician John Lettsom, a seemingly tireless man who for 19 years never took a holiday and wrote all his letters, lectures and even books while driving around in his carriage visiting patients. Opposite the Medical Society is the back of the Langham, in Victorian times the grandest hotel in London.

Carry on to the end of Chandos Street. The austere, silver-grey house facing you is Chandos House, designed by Robert Adam in 1770 for the Duke of Chandos, whose family owned land here bordering the Portland Estate. This is actually a side view, as the main front originally faced east across substantial private grounds. Amongst many original features note torch snuffers on either side of the portico and rings to stand torches in.

At Chandos House turn left into Queen Anne Street and first right into Mansfield Street. On the right is a blue plaque to Sir Robert Mayer, the German-born businessman and music patron who founded the famous children's concerts of the pre-war era. He was also co-founder of the London Philharmonic Orchestra in 1932. Now turn first left into Mansfield Mews and then right into Harley Street, where top medical specialists have their consulting rooms. Almost every door has a collection of brass nameplates. Queen's College to the left is a private girls' school founded in 1848 and the first institution to provide girls with academic qualifications and access to higher education. Straight ahead as you walk up Harley Street is Regent's Park. At the first set of traffic lights turn left into New Cavendish Street. No. 48 on the left is the estate office of the Portland Estate, now called the Howard de Walden Estate, because the Howard de Walden family acquired it by a fortunate marriage with the Portlands in 1879.

St Mary-by-the-Bourne

When you get to the end of the road, turn right into Marylebone High Street. This was the main street of the village of Marylebone and still retains a little of its provincial if not rural character. Unlike most of the streets in this part of London, Marylebone High Street is not straight. This is because the High Street and Marylebone Lane developed alongside the winding Tyburn River, long before the property developers arrived with their surveying instruments and grid plans. As well as its form, Marylebone owes its name to the Tyburn. Tyburn was originally spelt Tybourne and St Marylebone Parish Church was originally St Mary-by-the-Bourne.

The manor house of Marylebone was near the north end of the street, on the right-hand side roughly where Beaumont Street is now. In adjacent fields from 1650 to 1778 were the Marylebone Pleasure Gardens. In 1668, Samuel Pepys described the gardens as 'a pretty place'; a century later Thomas Arne, composer of *Rule Britannia*, was resident conductor of the gardens' orchestra. Opposite the manor house stood the old parish church. Only the graveyard remains, now used as a public garden. Near the pavement is the grave of Charles Wesley, Methodist hymn-writer and brother of John Wesley, the founder of Methodism. A little further on beyond the local school, turn left across the open space towards the new parish church, built in 1817 as part of the Regent's Park development scheme. A notice in the garden has more of its history.

When you reach Marylebone Road in front of the church, turn left and cross the road at the traffic lights. Continue walking to the left and you will come to Madame Tussaud's Waxworks on your right. Marie Tussaud transported her wax figures from France to England in 1802 and exhibited them around the country until 1835 when she settled in nearby Baker Street. Some 30 years after her death in 1850 – by which time her show was already an institution – the figures were installed in this building. The Planetarium with its astrological displays was opened next door in 1958. Beyond the Planetarium is Baker Street station where the walk ends.

❖❖

FOLLOWING THE
TYBURN RIVER

❖❖

Summary: This walk follows the course of the lower reaches of the Tyburn, a river that once flowed above ground through Marylebone, Mayfair and Green Park into the Thames near Vauxhall Bridge. The river has long since been covered over, but many fascinating clues to its existence can be found on the surface in street names, street layout and the general lie of the land. The river rises on Haverstock Hill near Hampstead and then flows through **Regent's Park**. It may supply the lake in Regent's Park, although there is some dispute about this. The walk picks the river up as it enters the West End near Baker Street. Attractions passed on the walk (apart from the places mentioned above) include **Buckingham Palace** and the Queen's Gallery.

Start:	Baker Street station (Jubilee, Metropolitan, Bakerloo, Hammersmith & City and Circle Underground Lines).
Finish:	Pimlico or Vauxhall Bridge station (both Victoria Underground Line).

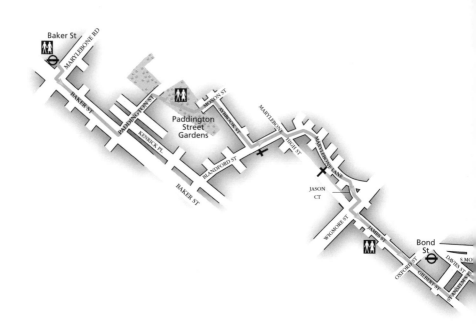

Length:	3½ miles (5.5km).
Time:	2½ hours.
Refreshments:	There are plenty of pubs, restaurants, wine bars and sandwich bars along the whole length of this walk, except for the last ½ mile (1km). Shepherd Market in Mayfair, one of London's most attractive little enclaves, is perhaps the best refreshment stop: it's about halfway and it has a good selection of all types of eating and drinking places.
Note:	If possible, plan to finish the walk at low or lowish tide on the Thames, otherwise it may not be possible to see the Tyburn's outfall. To find out when low tide is, either consult the current edition of *Whitaker's Almanack* in your local library or ring the Port of London harbourmaster on 020 7265 2656.

Come out of Baker Street Underground station on the south side of Marylebone Road and walk down the left-hand side of Baker Street, heading in the same direction as the traffic. At the second left, Paddington Street, turn left. The river actually continues south for a little way almost as far as Blandford Street before it also turns left, but because of the unhelpful street layout we have to make our turn here. If you look down Kenrick Place on the right you can see the low point where the river runs across just before Blandford Street.

30

Carry on along Paddington Street until you reach Paddington Street Gardens. Turn right into the gardens and make your way diagonally across to the far left-hand corner. Go through the gates out of the park into Moxon Street and turn right into Aybrook Street (the river was sometimes known as the Aye Brook as well as the Tyburn). At the bottom of the street, where we pick up the river again, turn left into Blandford Street.

Marylebone

When you get to Marylebone High Street, cross over to the Angel in the Fields pub and continue on along Marylebone Lane. The High Street was the centre of the old village of Marylebone, its name derived, via St Mary-le-bourne, from Tybourne (Tyburn). The lane was the road connecting the village with London. At this point the lane stuck to the riverside, hence its distinctly winding course. Elsewhere in this part of London the streets are laid out on a more or less regular grid.

Stay with Marylebone Lane until you come to a fork with a shop called The Button Queen at its dividing point. Here the lane goes off to the left away from the

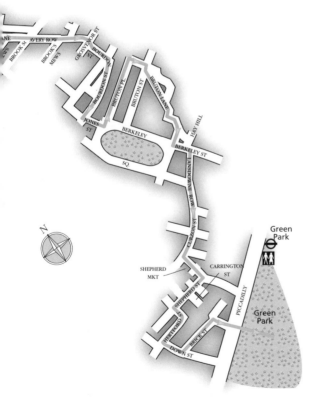

river; we go right into pedestrian-only Jason Court. At the main road (Wigmore Street) turn right and then, crossing over at the lights, turn left into James Street, a popular place to eat out in summer. Walk on down this street to its junction with Oxford

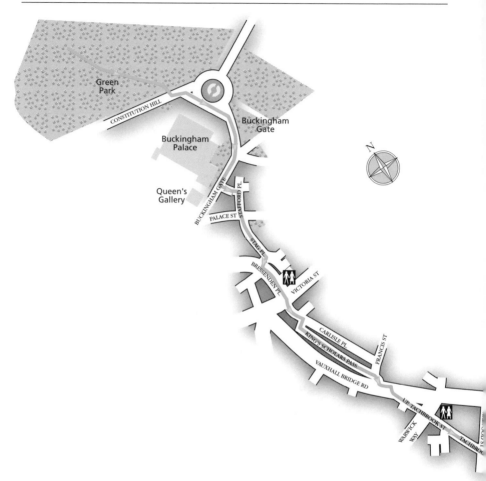

Street. Here, look left and right and you will see that you are definitely in the river valley. In 1941 the river was seen flowing through the bottom of a bomb crater here.

Mayfair

Carry on now into Gilbert Street and so into the exclusive residential district of Mayfair. Somewhere here the river bends east again, but the street levels have been so much altered that it is impossible to pinpoint the exact course. However, the steep drop into St Anselm's Place is at least a clue. Turn left here, right at the end into Davies Street and then immediately left into Davies Mews. At the end of the mews, turn right into South Molton Lane, cross Brook Street (note the watery name) and enter narrow Avery Row, built in the 1720s over the newly culverted Tyburn by bricklayer Henry Avery. The low point in the middle is the real ground level and the west side of the valley can be seen stretching up Brook's Mews to your right. Behind and in front of you, Brook Street and Grosvenor Street respectively have been raised up on artificial embankments. It's these embankments, or causeways, that create the constant ups and downs as we walk along what should be a flat river bed.

Now climb up to Grosvenor Street, cross, and go through the opening into Bourdon Street. Again, there is a marked descent to the valley bottom. As buildings now block our path, we have a short detour. Turn right up the hill (keeping left when the road forks) and then left near the top into pedestrian-only Jones Street. This brings you out into Berkeley Square. From the corner on the left, you can see the bottom of the valley at the far end of the square and the bank on the far side rising up to Piccadilly. We shall come to this point shortly, but first we return to where we left the river in Bourdon Street. Turn left into Bruton Place and go down to the bottom, past the Guinea pub. Here, follow the road round to the right, cross Bruton Street and then continue along Bruton Lane, keeping the Coach and Horses pub on the left. When Bruton Lane bends to the right, look up and left to see the 19th-century stone plaque on the wall, marking the boundary between the Berkeley estate and the City's (Conduit Mead) estate. Before these streets were built, the Tyburn river was the boundary between the two properties.

Near the end of Bruton Lane, a gated private road follows the river course. Bear right here and turn left into Berkeley Street. Hay Hill and the rising ground up to Piccadilly bar the river's southerly progress towards the Thames and force a more westerly course. To follow it, cross Berkeley Street into pedestrian-only Lansdowne Row. This little street of shops was created by paving over the river when it formed a boundary between the grounds of two former aristocratic town houses: Devonshire and Lansdowne Houses.

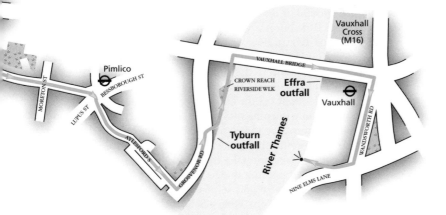

Shepherd Market

From Lansdowne Row, continue on into Curzon Street. Just beyond the Third Church of Christ Scientist on the right, turn left through the opening at No. 47 leading into Shepherd Market. Go down to the bottom by the King's Arms and turn right. The original market from which this little enclave of narrow streets, pubs and

33

restaurants takes its name must have grown up on the banks of the river, for after flowing west to avoid Hay Hill the Tyburn continues its southerly course here, possibly through Carrington Street (second on your left), Yarmouth Place and the bottom of Brick Street. Carrington Street (significantly) is a dead end, so we must detour round it to get to Yarmouth Place and Brick Street.

Carry on a little way and turn left into Hertford Street. Follow the road round to the right and take the first left into Down Street. Ahead on the right is the former entrance to Down Street Underground station, closed in 1932. Turn left again into Brick Street. Yarmouth Place is at the bottom of the hill on the left. Follow Brick Street, which used to be called Engine Street ('engine' referring to a mill or other machine powered by the river), round to the right and you come out on Piccadilly. That you are back on the actual course of the river is confirmed by the way the ground rises to both your left and your right.

Green Park

Cross Piccadilly and go through the gate into Green Park. You can now see the gently sloping valley, shorn of buildings, curving gently to the right and then, near the bottom, nudged by Constitution Hill protruding from the right, equally gently to the left. Here, in very ancient times, the open Tyburn disappeared into the marshy ground of the Thames flood plain. Later it was used to fill the lake in **St James's Park** (a function fulfilled today by artesian wells). Now, safely contained in its brick-lined tunnel, it continues on its way beneath Buckingham Palace to its meeting point with the Thames, about 1¼ miles (2km) away.

To the Thames

It has to be admitted that the walk from here to the Thames, which takes about 50 minutes and is along flat ground, is not quite as interesting or varied as the stretch from Marylebone to Green Park, but it is well worth doing nonetheless. The reward at the end is to see where the Tyburn flows out into the Thames.

To begin, cross Constitution Hill at the lights, pass in front of Buckingham Palace, and keep following the railings round to the right. After passing through Buckingham Gate, cross the main road (also called Buckingham Gate) and turn right. Turn left at No. 4 Buckingham Gate (opposite the entrance to the **Queen's Gallery**) and walk through the pedestrian-only opening into Stafford Place. Turn right here, cross Palace Street and continue on into Stag Place. At the far end, go through the colourful sculpture and then straight on into Bressenden Place. At the lights, cross straight over Victoria Street to Carlisle Place and take the first right into King's Scholars' Passage. (If the gates are closed, carry on along Carlisle Place and turn right on Francis Street.) The passage is a rather smelly service road between the backs of tall buildings. Its curious name comes from King's Scholars' Pond, into which the Tyburn flowed somewhere near here when the area was still open countryside. The King's Scholars themselves were schoolboys at nearby Westminster School. When the Tyburn was covered over, this section was christened the King's Scholars' Pond Sewer.

At the end of the passage, cross busy Vauxhall Bridge Road diagonally into Upper Tachbrook Street. You could be forgiven for thinking that Tachbrook is in some way a reference to the Tyburn. In fact it is a place in Warwickshire which in the 18th century was owned by a man who also owned land here. (The man, incidentally, was royal gardener Henry Wise.)

Carry on along Tachbrook Street, crossing Warwick Way, Charlwood Street and Moreton Street on the way. At the end, the river carries straight on across the main road (Lupus/Bessborough Street) but we have to deviate slightly and bear right along Aylesford Street. At the end of the street, cross Grosvenor Road and turn left back towards the river's course, passing the derelict Thames-side Chester Wharf.

The Tyburn outflow

When you reach Tyburn House and Rio Cottage, you are back with the river once more. This, moreover, is the precise point where it finally flows into the Thames. Beneath the houses is a semicircular opening in the river wall about 10 feet (3m) high and 15 feet (4.5m) across. Set back about 20 feet (6m) inside it is a heavy iron sluice gate, installed, as the plaque on Rio Cottage says, in 1832. To see the river's outflow channel, go round the corner into Crown Reach Riverside Walk and look over the parapet.

You used to be able to get a close-up view of the brick-lined tunnel and sluice gate by climbing down the ladder on to the mud flats, but the ladder is blocked now. The alternative is to go to the public garden on the opposite bank. To reach it, walk along the riverside to Vauxhall Bridge. Cross the bridge, turn right into Wandsworth Road and right again into Nine Elms Lane and keep going until you come to the garden. As an added incentive to make this extra effort at the end of a long walk, provided you cross the bridge on the right-hand (upstream) side you will also see – at the point where the bridge meets the bank – the sluice gate of the Effra, one of the main 'lost rivers' of the south side of the Thames. There is a similar gate on the other side of the bridge (under the headquarters of MI6, Britain's Secret Service) which is labelled 'Effra', but this is actually only a storm sewer. Locations of both Pimlico and Vauxhall Underground stations, at either of which the walk can end, are shown on the map.

❖❖

CENTRAL PARKS

❖❖

Summary: A walk from Westminster to Kensington through a green swathe of four royal parks: **St James's Park**; **Green Park**; **Hyde Park**; and **Kensington Gardens**. Places of interest include the **Houses of Parliament**, the Treasury and Foreign Office, the **Cabinet War Rooms**, **Buckingham Palace**, St James's Palace, Clarence House, Apsley House (the **Wellington Museum**) at Hyde Park Corner, the Serpentine, the Peter Pan statue and Speke memorial in Kensington Gardens, and **Kensington Palace**.

Start:	Westminster station (District, Circle and Jubilee Underground Lines).
Finish:	High Street Kensington station (District and Circle Underground Lines).
Length:	3¾ miles (6km).

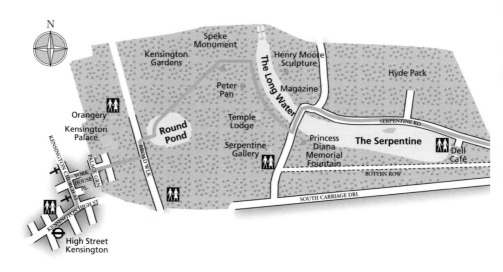

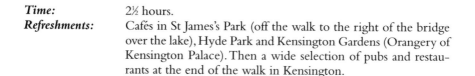

Time:	2½ hours.
Refreshments:	Cafés in St James's Park (off the walk to the right of the bridge over the lake), Hyde Park and Kensington Gardens (Orangery of Kensington Palace). Then a wide selection of pubs and restaurants at the end of the walk in Kensington.

From Westminster Station take exit 4 (Big Ben and the Houses of Parliament will be opposite) and turn right. Cross the road at the traffic lights and turn right into Parliament Street. Take the first left turn under the arch into King Charles Street (the Treasury is on the left and the Foreign Office is on the right) and go down the steps at the end of the street, passing the statue of Lord Clive, founder of the British Empire in India in the 18th century. To your left is the entrance to the subterranean Cabinet War Rooms used by Churchill and his government during World War II.

Wine-bibbing elephant
Cross Horse Guards Road and enter St James's Park, the oldest, most intimate and garden-like of the royal parks in London. In 1660, Charles II opened the park to the public, converting it into a popular resort where people strolled and talked, played games and fed the ducks. James I, grandfather to Charles II, once kept a zoo in the park: this included an elephant that drank a gallon of wine every day, and three

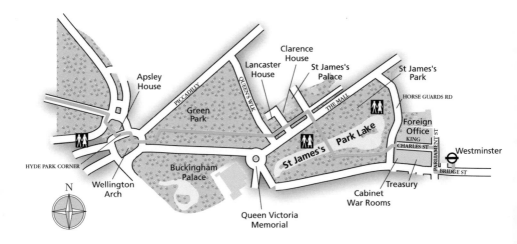

pelicans given to James I (or was it his grandson Charles II? – authorities differ) by the Russian ambassador. There are still pelicans in the park, along with over 30 other species of birds, including ducks, geese, gulls and swans.

Follow the lakeside path, with the lake on your right, until you come to a bridge. As you cross over the bridge you will see to your left the gilded memorial to Queen Victoria and the public front of Buckingham Palace, and to your right the domes and pinnacles of Horse Guards, the Old Admiralty and other government offices in Whitehall. The copper-green pitched roofs belong to the Ministry of Defence.

Once over the bridge (café to the right), carry on to the gates at the top of the bank. Cross the Mall at the traffic lights and turn left. Behind the wall on your right is the garden front of St James's Palace, originally built in the 1500s by Henry VIII. The large house next to the palace with the stuccoed façade is Clarence House, built for the royal Duke of Clarence by John Nash in 1828 and now the London home of the Prince of Wales. Beyond Clarence House is Lancaster House, a government conference centre where the Lancaster House Agreement on Zimbabwe was negotiated in 1979. Until the early part of the last century this was the palatial town house of the Dukes of Sutherland.

Military heroes
Just beyond Lancaster House turn right into Queen's Walk and then go through the opening to your left into Green Park. Continue along this wide path, crossing the

park's Broad Walk, a grassy avenue with double lines of trees on either side. This links Piccadilly at the top with Buckingham Palace at the bottom. Green Park is the plainest of the central parks, with no lake or fountains and very few flowers. The trees are mainly limes, planes and hawthorns.

When you get to the crossroads with the lamp in the middle, continue straight on (by taking the third path from the left) and when this path meets the path along the perimeter of the park, bear left towards the park's apex at Hyde Park Corner. Here, turn right out of the park, using the Green Park subway to reach the central reservation on the far side of the road. Hyde Park Corner is dominated by the Duke of Wellington, the English military hero who defeated Napoleon at Waterloo in 1815. Facing you is Apsley House, the Duke's former London home, now the Wellington Museum. Opposite the house is a mounted statue of the Duke wearing a tricorn hat. To your left there is a huge triumphal arch called the Wellington (or Constitution) Arch (housing London's second smallest police station). The other sculptures on the green here commemorate the World War I dead from the Machine Gun Corps (the nude figure of David, to your right) and the Royal Regiment of Artillery (the huge stone howitzer on the far side).

Along the Serpentine

Walk towards Apsley House and leave Hyde Park Corner by the Park Lane subway, following the signs to Hyde Park and the Wellington Museum. Turn right at the top of the steps. Go around the front of Apsley House and then turn right through the gates, crossing South Carriage Drive into Hyde Park. To the right is yet another tribute to Wellington (and also his men) – a statue of the legendary hero Achilles, cast from captured cannon. Wellington was often referred to by grateful contemporaries as the 'Achilles of England'.

There are two main paths to the left leading through Hyde Park. The one on the left with a sanded track for riding is Rotten Row, the name thought to be a corruption of *Route du Roi*, the royal road built by King William III in the 1690s, leading from Westminster to his new palace at Kensington. The walk, however, takes you along Serpentine Road, the path on the right.

Walk along the road past the cavalry memorial and bandstand. Soon you come to the Dell Café and the Serpentine lake, created in 1730 by damming the River Westbourne. Activities on the lake include swimming from the end of May to mid September and boating, and sometimes skating in winter. In 1826 a businessman won a bet of 100 guineas by driving his van and four horses over the frozen lake. To the left you can see the tower of Knightsbridge Barracks. Over to the right the large boulder was placed here by Norwegian seamen in 1978 as a token of gratitude for hospitality and support received during World War II. Further away to the right, behind the hedge and thick screen of trees, there are four acres (1.6 ha) of greenhouses, where all the bedding plants for the royal parks are grown.

Just before the bridge, take the right fork, along the left-hand side of the car park, onto the road dividing Hyde Park from Kensington Gardens. Turn left opposite the Magazine (a gunpowder and ammunition store built in 1805 and now used by park maintenance staff) and cross the bridge. Halfway across there is a fine view of the Houses of Parliament. On the far side of the bridge, turn right off the road through Temple Gate into Kensington Gardens. (If you want to see the Princess Diana memorial fountain, it's off to the left.)

Sculptures and statues

On your left now is the **Serpentine Gallery**, built in the 1930s as a tea house and now an Arts Council-sponsored gallery for modern art exhibitions. Take the path on the right leading down to the lake, here called the Long Water. To the left above the bank you can see the Temple, built in the 18th century for Queen Caroline, the wife of George II. Queen Caroline also ordered the digging of the Serpentine, and of the Round Pond which you come to shortly. On the opposite bank of the Long Water is Henry Moore's sculpture, *The Arch*. Further along, the path enters a small piece of riverside woodland and garden with an extraordinary statue of Peter Pan in the centre. J. M. Barrie was living near Kensington Gardens when he wrote the Peter Pan story, and he reputedly had the statue erected overnight so that when children came for their daily walk they would think the fairies had brought it.

Immediately beyond the woodland turn left across the grass towards the obelisk memorial to John Speke (in summer, only the base is visible through the trees). Speke was the first explorer to trace the source of the Nile to Lake Victoria in 1864. Looking left from the obelisk, the east front of Kensington Palace and the graceful spire of Kensington parish church (**St Mary Abbots**) can be seen at the end of the broad avenue to the left. Walk up the avenue (or use the tarmac path in the trees to the right if you prefer) until you come to the Round Pond.

Walk to the right of the pond, aiming for the white statue of Queen Victoria (by her daughter Princess Louise) in front of the palace. (The Orangery café is to the right.) Turn left along the Broad Walk and then take the first right turn along the south front of the palace, passing the immaculate gardens, often with rabbits playing on the lawn. The statue in the middle of the gravel walk leading up to the palace is of a wigged and hatted King William III who, in the 1690s, commissioned Wren to convert Nottingham House into Kensington Palace because he hated stuffy old Whitehall Palace down by the Thames in Westminster. Queen Victoria was born at Kensington Palace and lived there until she inherited the throne in 1837 at the age of 18. Diana, Princess of Wales, lived here until her death in Paris in 1997.

Walk straight ahead through the gates out of the park onto Palace Green. Cross the road and walk along the opposite footpath (York House Place) which brings you to Kensington Church Street. Turn left down to the junction with Kensington High Street (St Mary Abbots church is on your right). Go across Kensington High Street and turn right towards High Street Kensington station where the walk ends.

❖❖❖

KENSINGTON

❖❖❖

Summary: Kensington is an historic village suburb in West London, close to **Kensington Palace** and Kensington Gardens. It is spread out on the south-facing slope of Campden Hill and bisected by its fashionable High Street. While Kensington Palace was in use gentry and nobility dominated the area, but when the court moved out, artists and writers settled here. This circular walk starts and finishes in

Kensington High Street and includes the parish church, Kensington's two historic squares (one now 300 years old), Holland House and Park, the Melbury Road artists' colony centred on the **Leighton House Museum and Art Gallery**, and many attractive streets and houses in a rich variety of architectural styles.

Start and finish:	High Street Kensington station (Circle and District Underground Lines).
Length:	2¾ miles (4.4km).
Time:	2 hours.
Refreshments:	High-street restaurants in Kensington High Street and pubs en route. Look out for the Scarsdale pub in Edwardes Square, about halfway through the walk, the café in Holland Park after about two-thirds of the walk, and the Elephant and Castle pub near the end.

Come out of Kensington High Street Station, turn right on to the High Street and walk along towards the traffic lights. Take the first turning on the right into Derry Street. No. 99, towards the end on the right, is the entrance to the famous roof gardens built over the Derry and Toms department store in the 1930s. Derry Street leads on into the northwest corner of Kensington Square – one of the oldest and prettiest squares in London. By the mid 1600s wealthy people were moving to the then country village of Kensington in search of a healthier lifestyle. This square was developed in the 1680s to meet the growing demand. When Kensington Palace was built years later the square and surrounding houses were naturally taken over by courtiers, and Kensington itself became known as the Old Court Suburb.

Continue walking along the right-hand (western) side of the square. Many well-known people have lived here over the years. No. 33 on the right, for example, was once the home of the actress Mrs Patrick Campbell, who dominated the London stage in the 1880s and 1890s. Turn left at the bottom of the square. The utilitarian philosopher John Stuart Mill moved to No. 18 in 1837 along with his mother and unmarried brothers and sisters. The family had been living in a large house in Vicarage Square, Kensington, but after the death of Mill's father in 1836 decided to trade down. Mill remained in Kensington Square until his marriage in 1851, when he moved to Blackheath Park.

Kensington New Town

Nos. 11 and 12 are the only original 17th-century houses in the square to have survived (note the names of former occupants painted on the carved porch of No. 11). Beyond these houses take the first right into Ansdell Street. At the end of the street turn left into St Alban's Grove, passing on the left Prue Leith's School of Food and Wine. Cross Stanford Road and Victoria Road and continue into Victoria Grove, turning right into Launceston Place. These streets form a self-contained development known as Kensington New Town, which was built over market gardens in the 1840s by John Inderwick, a wealthy tobacconist and pipe-maker. He owned a clay mine in the Crimea and introduced meerschaum pipes into England. You will still find an Inderwick's tobacconist's in Carnaby Street in the West End of London. The small but elegant houses on his development have always been popular and demand will no doubt remain high so long as the New Town continues to be an official conservation area.

Before Launceston Place reaches Cornwall Gardens turn right through an archway into Kynance Mews, still paved with cobblestones from the days of horse and carriage. Opposite No. 24 turn right up some steps into Victoria Road, and then turn left by Christ Church into Eldon Road, named after a large house called Eldon Lodge that once stood near here. Opposite the church, No. 52 was the studio home of royal art tutor Edward Corbould in the 19th century. Corbould's studio is on the left side of the house: the large north-facing roof light can be glimpsed through the street window. At the end of Eldon Road take a left turn into Stanford Road and go through the passageway at the end of the cul-de-sac into Cornwall Gardens.

Fashionable flats
The character of the area changes here as the pretty, countrified houses of Kensington New Town give way to the heavy stuccoed terraces and sombre apartment blocks of High Victorian South Kensington. These were built mainly in the later 19th century when living in flats became fashionable among London's ever-expanding middle classes. From the property developer's point of view they also meant that more people could be accommodated on a given amount of land, thus generating more profit.

Turn right when you come to Cornwall Gardens and then turn left. On the left the novelist Ivy Compton-Burnett lived in the corner house from 1934 until her death in 1969. Ahead to the left is a house (No. 52) with a plaque in memory of Joaquim Nabuco, Brazilian ambassador to Britain at the turn of the century (he was here only until 1902, not 1905 as the plaque says). Nabuco, although a conservative, had been mainly responsible for the abolition of slavery in Brazil in 1888. Some years before that he had spent time as a newspaper correspondent in Britain.

Before you reach Nabuco's house, turn right down the slope of Lexham Walk, cross Cornwall Gardens Walk and enter Lexham Gardens. Keep to the right round Lexham Gardens. Take the first right turn and then turn right again into Marloes Road. Opposite the entrance to Kensington Green, a housing development covering the site of St Mary Abbots Hospital and the former Kensington workhouse, turn left into Stratford Road and follow the road as it winds left and right. When you get to the junction with Abingdon Road turn right and then first left into Scarsdale Villas. At the end, cross Earl's Court Road into Pembroke Square walking to the right of Rassell's nursery. Turn right out of Pembroke Square into Edwardes Square (Scarsdale pub on the right) and turn left, walking along the south side of the square past the Temple (the gardener's lodge).

French connection
Edwardes Square is the second of Kensington's historic squares, although it is a century younger than Kensington Square. It was built on land belonging to William Edwardes, second Lord Kensington, between 1811 and 1819 when the Napoleonic Wars were raging. The developer was French by birth and had kept his French name – Louis Léon Changeur. As building progressed, Changeur's ancestry helped to generate the rumour that he was a Napoleonic agent and that the square was being built, not for the harmless representatives of the professional middle classes, but for the officers of Napoleon's army. The feared French invasion failed to materialize so Changeur's loyalty to his adopted country – and the absurd rumour regarding it – was never put to the test.

Continue along the south side of the square and then turn right along the west side. When you reach the main road (Kensington High Street) turn right and walk

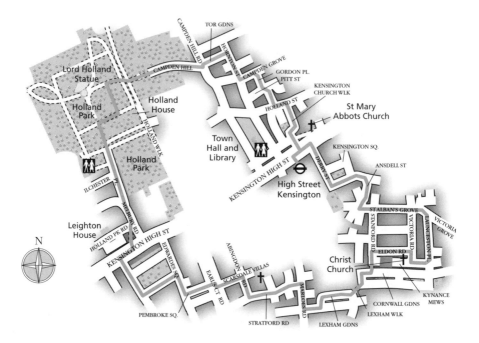

along Earl's Terrace (the earliest part of Edwardes Square) and cross the road at the first set of traffic lights. Continue along the High Street in the same direction, turning left when you reach Melbury Road.

Once part of the Holland House estate, this area was developed in the 19th century and quickly became an artists' colony. Its most famous resident was the painter, Lord Leighton, whose large house with the rear conservatory can be seen through the trees as you cross Holland Park Road on the left. It is now the Leighton House Museum and Art Gallery.

Continue on Melbury Road as far as the junction with Ilchester Place. The house on the corner here was the home of the Victorian and Edwardian painter Sir Luke Fildes, whose most famous painting, *The Doctor* (1881), hangs in the Tate Gallery. The Tower House next door to Fildes's house was once the home of the Gothic Revival architect and designer, William Burges. He designed the house and its medieval interiors himself, intending it to be 'a model residence of the 15th century'. In 1969 the actor Richard Harris bought it and completed the interior according to Burges's original designs.

The Holland Estate
Leave Melbury Road here and walk up Ilchester Place into Holland Park. This was once the park and grounds of Holland House, the large Jacobean manor house of Kensington, the remains of which can be seen ahead. In the 18th century the house was bought by Henry Fox, the first Lord Holland and the father of the great Whig (liberal) politician, Charles James Fox. While in the possession of the third Lord

Holland (1773–1840), the house was a meeting place for Whig politicians, writers and intellectuals; the names of Byron, Macaulay, Sir Walter Scott, Melbourne, Disraeli and Dickens were all recorded in Lady Holland's still-surviving dinner books. In World War II the house was virtually destroyed by bombs. The one remaining wing is now a youth hostel, the Garden Ballroom a restaurant and the Orangery an exhibition centre.

When you reach the buildings, look left through the archway where there is a superb set of murals depicting a garden party at Holland House in the 1870s. Go straight on through the colonnade (café to right) and branch right through the walled garden to the terrace on the north side of the house. Here turn right towards the house, left across the North Lawn and then walk along Rose Walk to the statue of the third Lord Holland, a good likeness by G. F. Watts and Joseph Boehm, done in 1872. Turn sharp right here, follow the path round to the right and then turn left out of the park by crossing Holland Walk (connecting Notting Hill with Kensington) into a passageway with high walls on either side. This leads through Holland Park Comprehensive School into Campden Hill.

The school was built in the 1950s following the demolition of Argyll and Moray Lodges, two of a chain of seven country lodges built along the ridge of Campden Hill between Holland House and Campden House. Beyond the school, the gate lodge of Moray Lodge and the coach house of Holly Lodge (where the historian Lord Macaulay died in 1859) still survive, dwarfed by buildings of King's College, London, on the right.

At the end of Campden Hill, cross Campden Hill Road into Tor Gardens. The second house on the right on the far side of Campden Hill Road bears a plaque in memory of Ford Madox Ford, grandson of the Pre-Raphaelite painter, Ford Madox Brown. Ford wrote over 80 books and edited some notable literary periodicals, yet only three people attended his funeral at Deauville in France in 1939. Belated recognition, however, now seems to be coming his way. The apartment block at the eastern end of Tor Gardens is Campden House Court. It stands on the site of another of Kensington's Jacobean mansions, Campden House. The house was named after its builder, Viscount Campden, whose country home was in the Gloucestershire market town of Chipping Campden.

At the end of Tor Gardens turn right into Hornton Street. At the bottom of the hill you can see the red brick and glass of Kensington's new town hall. Take the second turning on the left into Campden Grove and the first right turn into Gordon Place, crossing Pitt Street halfway down. When Kensington was a country village Gordon Place was an avenue running from Campden House at the top of the hill, down to the High Street at the bottom. Now Gordon Place ends in a pedestrian-only cul-de-sac of small houses with luxuriant front gardens.

At the Elephant and Castle pub turn left and walk along Holland Street, a pretty street with several antique shops and 18th-century houses. Originally it was a coach road along the south side of Campden Hill, connecting Holland House with Kensington Palace ahead. Just beyond No. 21 on the right, turn right into Kensington Church Walk. This leads past a group of shops to a small courtyard with half a dozen secluded houses. Go into the churchyard gardens at the west end of **St Mary Abbots**, the parish church of Kensington, built in 1872. An earlier church had been built on this site in the 1100s by the Abbot of Abingdon. The land was granted to the abbey by the lord of the manor, hence the 'abbot' part of the name. Ahead is the local church school, with 18th-century figures of a boy and girl decorating its rear wall: they originally adorned the front of the first school building which stood on Kensington High Street. Follow the path round to the right and then left past the churchyard garden until you reach Kensington High Street. The walk ends back at High Street Kensington station on the other side of the road.

❖❖❖

NOTTING HILL

❖❖❖

Summary: Located north of Kensington in West London, Notting Hill is the scene of the Notting Hill Carnival and the world-famous Portobello Road antiques market. The walk starts at the northern end of the district, runs the whole length of the Golborne Road and Portobello Road markets, and then explores steep Notting Hill itself, the site of London's finest Victorian housing development. The final part of the walk climbs leafy Holland Park and crosses Campden Hill Square to the top of Campden Hill before returning to Notting Hill Gate.

Start:	Westbourne Park station (Hammersmith & City Underground Line; trains from Paddington).
Finish:	Notting Hill Gate station (District, Circle and Central Underground Lines).
Length:	3½ miles (5.6km).
Time:	2½ hours.
Refreshments:	Pubs and a few cafés throughout the route, especially in the early stages and at the end of the walk on Notting Hill Gate, where you will also find the usual high street fast-food restaurants. Look out for the Lisboa café on Golborne Road, the Café Grove (first-floor terrace) on Portobello Road about a third of the way into the walk, and the Windsor Castle (excellent beer garden) on Campden Hill near the finish (all mentioned in the text).
Note:	Best walked early on a Saturday when the Portobello Road antiques market is open but not too busy.

Come out of Westbourne Park station and turn left into the Great Western Road. Go under the Westway overhead motorway and take the first turning on the left into Elkstone Road just beyond the Big Table furniture co-operative. Follow this road for some distance, between commercial buildings on the left and Meanwhile Gardens on the right; then railway tracks on the left (the main line to the West Country) and the 30-storey Trellick Tower on the right. Turn left, crossing over the bridge into Golborne Road. The Saturday market here trades in old clothes and every conceivable kind of junk, and is really an extension of the main Portobello Road market which begins further along the route.

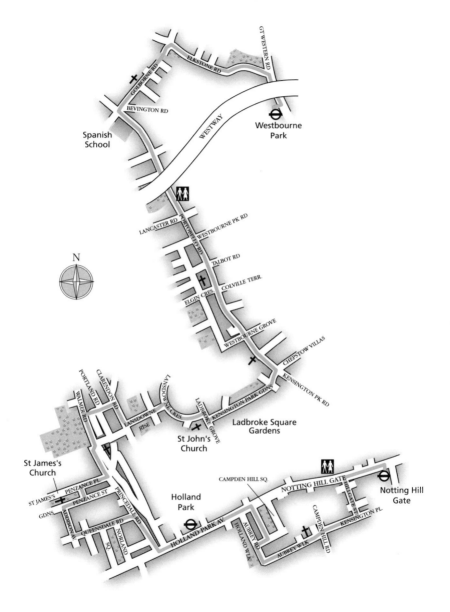

Portobello Road market

Walk along Golborne Road (past the Lisboa on the left) and, just beyond the entrance to Bevington Road, turn left into Portobello Road – the less affluent end of both the market and the Notting Hill district. This part of Notting Hill was not developed until the 1860s and the market started (unofficially) around the same time. Portobello Road was originally a farm track leading from the village of Kensington Gravel Pits (the original name of Notting Hill Gate) to Portobello Farm, which stood about where you are now. The farm was named in the 18th century in honour of the 1739 naval battle when the British defeated the Spanish off Puerto Bello in the Gulf of Mexico.

Continue along Portobello Road past the bilingual Spanish school (built as a Franciscan convent in 1862) on your right. Cross Oxford Gardens and walk down to Portobello Green under the Westway, opened in 1970. At this point the quality of the merchandise in the market begins to improve. There are also some bric-à-brac stalls, a foretaste of the antiques to come. From the Westway here to the junction with Colville Terrace and Elgin Crescent, Portobello Road is an ordinary shopping centre and thriving food market, though it has an unusual collection of shops – mostly fairly smart street fashion plus the occasional art gallery and a tattoo studio at No. 201. Café Grove is on your right at the junction with Lancaster Road.

At the end of August each year, over a million revellers pack into Portobello Road and nearby streets to enjoy the Notting Hill Carnival. This started as a school pageant in 1966 and then developed, not always happily, into today's massive Caribbean jamboree with decorated floats, steel bands and masqueraders in extravagant costumes. Many people from former British colonies in the West Indies settled in this area during the 1950s.

The proper antiques market starts at the Colville Terrace/Elgin Crescent junction and continues all the way up the hill across Westbourne Grove to Chepstow Villas. In several places it has bled into adjoining streets, in particular Westbourne Grove. Antiques, the main attraction of today's Portobello Road market, were not a feature until 1948 when dealers moved here after the closure of the Caledonian Antique Market in Islington. Virtually anything can be bought here and prices are not outrageous.

Victorian housing boom

At the end of the market turn right into Chepstow Villas. On the left, No. 39 has a plaque to Louis Kossuth, the Hungarian nationalist who sought refuge in England following the failure of Hungary's 1848–49 revolution against her Austrian masters. The house must have been very newly built then because work on the street did not start until the late 1840s. At the junction go straight across into Kensington Park Gardens. On the left, No. 7 has a plaque to Sir William Crookes, the scientist who, among other things, discovered the metal thallium in 1861. Halfway along on both sides of the street there are gates leading into large communal gardens (access for residents only). Notting Hill has 13 of these large communal gardens, and Ladbroke Square Gardens (on the left) is the largest in London. They were included in the original Victorian landscaping scheme in order to entice prospective purchasers out of the West End.

At the end of Kensington Park Gardens, cross Ladbroke Grove and walk to the right of St John's Church (1845) into Lansdowne Crescent. In pious Victorian England a church was as important a part of the infrastructure of a new and untried residential area as drains and street lighting, and many churches – like St John's – were built before the houses. St John's predecessor on this marvellous hilltop site was a racecourse grandstand.

Having built a few houses that had not proved the financial success he had hoped, the landlord of the area, James Weller Ladbroke, let some land to a local man who had the idea of laying out a racecourse round Notting Hill, using the hill itself as a natural grandstand. The racecourse opened in 1837, but was forced to close four years later when jockeys refused to ride on it, claiming the heavy going made it too dangerous.

Follow Lansdowne Crescent round to the right. Then turn left into Lansdowne Rise which plunges down the western slope of Notting Hill. At the bottom, turn right into Clarendon Road and then take the first left into Portland Road. Keep going straight ahead to Walmer Road at the bottom, passing on the way Hippodrome Mews, named after the racecourse. Turn left on Walmer Road.

A few yards further along on the left an old pottery kiln stands by the roadside. As its plaque indicates, it is a relic of the potteries and brickfields that covered this low-lying clay-land before it was developed. Pig-keepers also lived here, their animals helping to make the Potteries and the Piggeries one of the most notorious slums in the whole of Victorian England. Avondale Park behind you, which opened in 1892, was then a vast pit of stinking slurry known as the Ocean. Somehow all this squalor existed until the 1870s side by side with the middle-class suburb on the slopes of the hill above.

Walk on to the end of Walmer Road. Ahead on the left Pottery Lane connected the Potteries district to the main road (then the Uxbridge Road, now Holland Park Avenue). Keep right and continue into Princedale Road, turning first right into Penzance Place. At St James's Gardens, turn left, then right to St James's Church. The plaque on the church railings mentions that while most of the square was built in the four years after 1847, it wasn't finished until 1862 because of shortage of funds, a good indication of how costly and risky these huge middle-class Victorian developments were. This also meant that the church was not given the spire that its architect, Lewis Vulliamy, had designed.

Leafy Campden Hill

At the church turn left into Addison Avenue, the most stylish street in this development, then left again into Queensdale Road, which leads into Norland Square. Norland House, which once stood here, was a small country house with a 50-acre (20-ha) estate owned by the royal clockmaker, Benjamin Vulliamy, father of the architect Lewis Vulliamy.

When you reach the Prince of Wales pub turn right into Princedale Road (where *Oz* magazine was based at the time of the police raid following its notorious 'Schoolkids' issue) and then left into Holland Park Avenue (Lidgate's, the leading organic butchers, is on the left). At Holland Park station go over the crossing and continue up Holland Park Avenue past the statue of St Volodymyr that was erected by London's Ukrainian community in 1988. Cross the entrances to Holland Walk (leads to Kensington High Street) and Aubrey Road and turn right into steep Campden Hill Square, begun in 1826. Turner painted sunsets from the garden in the middle, and John McDouall Stuart, his health broken by hardships suffered in the first official crossing of the Australian continent, died at No. 9 in 1866.

Views from the hill

At the top of the square turn right and then left into Aubrey Road. On the right, Aubrey House, with its 2-acre (0.8-ha) walled garden, is the last of several country houses that once existed on Campden Hill. Lady Mary Coke, eccentric authoress of entertaining diaries, lived here from 1767 to 1788. One entry relates how her cow – Miss Pelham –

escaped from the grounds one day 'and went very near as far as London before I heard of her. I believe she thinks my place too retired, for she was found among a great herd of cattle.' Aubrey House is still privately owned and in the mid 1990s was sold for £20m.

At the house turn left along Aubrey Walk, which will take you to Campden Hill Road. Cross the road (Windsor Castle pub to the right) into Kensington Place. Far ahead you can see the BT Tower rising above the West End, exactly three miles (4.8km) from where you are standing. Halfway down Kensington Place at the Fox Primary School turn left into Hillgate Street. This leads through Hillgate Village, a grid of narrow streets and small but elegant mid-19th-century houses, to Notting Hill Gate. Notting Hill Gate was originally a hamlet in the parish of Kensington called Kensington Gravel Pits. The area was famed for its gravel quarries, hence the name. When the turnpike road system was developed in the 18th century, a toll gate was built across the main road running through the village. As Kensington Gravel Pits expanded into the 19th-century suburb of Notting Hill, the main road just here was renamed Notting Hill Gate.

Turn right and walk along to Notting Hill Gate Station, built roughly where the old toll gate used to stand. The gate was removed in the 1860s (along with other surviving gates in London) when road maintenance passed into local authority control. Then, Notting Hill Gate was a twisting shopping street with a bottleneck at the gate/station point. A century later demolition of protruding buildings on both north and south sides transformed it into the wide, straight boulevard it is today. The walk ends at the station.

❖❖❖

BAYSWATER TO BELGRAVIA

❖❖❖

Summary: A fairly long walk through **Kensington Gardens**, the museums area of South Kensington and the exclusive residential districts of Knightsbridge and Belgravia. Places of interest include **Kensington Palace**, the Albert Memorial, the Albert Hall, the **Victoria and Albert** and other museums, the **Brompton Oratory**, Harrods and Belgrave Square. The walk finishes at Knightsbridge station but directions are given for continuing on to Speaker's Corner in Hyde Park.

Start:	Queensway station (Central Underground Line).
Finish:	Knightsbridge station (Piccadilly Underground Line). Speaker's Corner is near Marble Arch station (Central Underground Line).
Length:	4 miles (6.4km).
Time:	2½ hours.
Refreshments:	Plenty of places in Queensway at the start, but then not many until you reach Knightsbridge about halfway along. There are some nice pubs in the Belgravia mews near the end, particularly The Grenadier in Wilton Row and the two pubs in Kinnerton Street.

Note: Do this walk on a Sunday if you want to see the Bayswater Road art market and Speaker's Corner in action.

Leave Queensway station and turn right. Cross the main road (Bayswater Road) at the traffic lights and turn right. On Sunday mornings artists and art dealers display their wares along the pavement, hanging their paintings on the park railings. At the next set of traffic lights turn left through the gates into the Broad Walk of Kensington Gardens. Far to the right you can see the mansions (most of which are embassies) in Kensington Palace Gardens. The first building you come to on your right is the Orangery of Kensington Palace. Opposite the Round Pond the palace itself comes into view beyond the sunken gardens (see the Central Parks walk, page 35, for more information about the palace). Beyond the palace and the second of the two covered seats on the left, take the second turning on the left and then immediately fork right, keeping to the right of the bandstand. Walk straight across the next path you come to, following the sign to the Flower Walk. Go straight across the next path as well and then sharp left through the gates along the Flower Walk.

Patrons of the arts

At the first crossroads turn right towards the Albert Memorial. This commemorates Queen Victoria's husband, Prince Albert, who died in 1861. The Prince is shown seated beneath an inlaid and enamelled Gothic canopy, holding a catalogue of the Great Exhibition of 1851. Around the base of the memorial is a white marble frieze depicting in life-size 169 painters, architects, poets, musicians and sculptors, a tribute to the Prince's patronage of the arts. Walk down the steps in front of the memorial and cross the road (Kensington Gore) to the Albert Hall, which opened in 1870 as another tribute to the Prince and as a major venue for a wide variety of concerts and performances, including the annual Promenade concerts of classical music.

Go left round the Hall and then left again at the back down the steps. Cross Prince Consort Road to the Royal College of Music and turn left, passing the Royal School of Mines, now part of Imperial College of Science, Technology and Medicine, itself a college of London University.

When you reach Exhibition Road, cross at the traffic lights and turn right down the hill. On your left is the Goethe Institute, a German cultural and information centre. On the right, after the entrance to Imperial College, there is a whole series of museums, beginning with the **Science Museum**. Round the corner to the right on Cromwell Road, is the **Natural History Museum**. Meanwhile on your left you pass the Henry Cole Wing of the Victoria and Albert Museum, Britain's national museum of art and design, and then the main block of the museum.

This part of South Kensington, stretching from the Albert Hall down to the V&A (Victoria and Albert) is generally called the museums area and is a direct product of the 1851 Great Exhibition that Prince Albert helped to organize. Thousands of objects from all over the world were sent to the Exhibition, which was held in an enormous glass hall in Hyde Park and visited by six million people in six months. The profits generated by the Exhibition were used to buy land and build museums, colleges, schools, and a hall of arts and sciences (the Albert Hall) to further the educational aims of the Exhibition and also to extend, in the words of the organizers, 'the influence of science and art upon productive industry'.

At the traffic lights turn left into Cromwell Gardens (leading into Thurloe Place), passing along the main front of the V&A. On the right now is the Ismaili Centre, dedicated to the religion and culture of Islam. Beyond the V&A on the left you pass first a statue of a wizened Cardinal Newman, the 19th-century Church of England clergyman whose conversion in 1845 to Catholicism, fully recognized in Britain only 16 years before, caused a national uproar. Next on the left you pass Oratory House and then Brompton Oratory, which was the main centre of Roman Catholic worship in London before Westminster Cathedral was built in 1903.

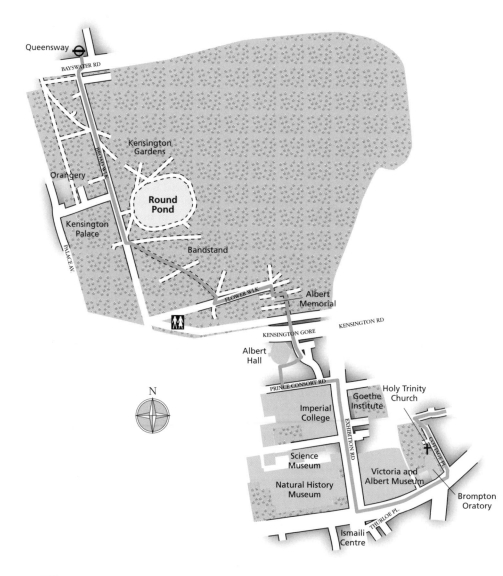

The Ennismore heritage

Beyond Brompton Oratory (just before Cottage Place) turn left between some white posts and walk along a path leading to Holy Trinity Church. The red-tiled building on the right is the former Brompton Road Underground station, opened on the Piccadilly Line in 1906 and closed in 1934. The walled-off platforms still survive deep below ground level. Follow the path around the east end of the church, past the old churchyard (now a secluded and peaceful garden) into a cobbled mews of brightly painted houses called Ennismore Gardens Mews. All the Ennismore street names in this area refer to the Earls of Listowel, also Viscounts Ennismore, who owned all the land here when it was developed in the 19th century.

Turn right along the mews and continue straight on under the arch into Ennismore Street. Walk past the Ennismore Arms, then the Clock House set back from the road in its own little courtyard, and then on the right, the entrance to Rutland Mews South. Keep going into Rutland Mews East. Near the end turn right through the gate in the boundary wall of the Rutland Estate and then left into Rutland Street. You are now in Knightsbridge. At Montpelier Walk turn left, then right into Montpelier Place and take the first left turn into Sterling Street. This brings you into Montpelier Square, with the tower of the Knightsbridge Barracks of the Household Cavalry rising up behind. This square was built in the 1830s at a time when the French resort of Montpelier was particularly popular with English tourists.

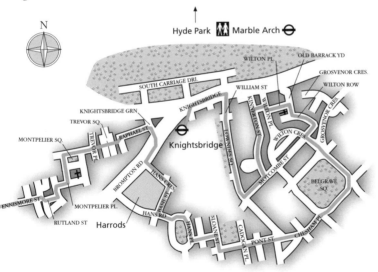

Cavalry Officers

Walk up the left side of the square and then turn right along the top. When you get to Trevor Place, turn left and then right by the pillar box along a path leading into Trevor Square. When the square was built most of the houses were apparently occupied by the mistresses of the cavalry officers. 'Trevor' was Sir John Trevor, a high-ranking 17th-century lawyer who had a small country house nearby.

Walk through the passage on the other side of the square into Raphael Street. Continue under the arch past the mural sculpture and turn right on to Knightsbridge Green. Once part of the old village of Knightsbridge, the green is now just a triangle of tarmac with a tree in the centre. Knightsbridge was so called because of the bridge that used to carry the road from London to Kensington over the River Westbourne. The river is still running but is piped underground for most of its course.

Harrods' secret

On the main road (Brompton Road) turn right towards Harrods. Cross over at the first set of traffic lights and walk along Hans Crescent between Harrods and the entrance to Knightsbridge station. Harrods now covers a whole block and is one of the largest stores in London. Its origins lie in a Knightsbridge grocer's shop that a City tea merchant called Henry Harrod bought in 1849. In 1861 his son Charles bought the shop from his father and developed it into today's world-famous emporium. His secret was impeccable service. When the store was completely destroyed by fire just before Christmas in 1883, the firm still made all its deliveries in time for Christmas Day.

Turn right round the back of the store along Basil Street. Then turn left at the end, down Hans Road. Keep to the left round Hans Place, taking the second left along Hans Street into Sloane Street. This street connects Sloane Square with Knightsbridge. The names 'Hans' and 'Sloane' came from Sir Hans Sloane, an 18th-century physician, landowner (he was lord of the manor of Chelsea) and President of the Royal Society, whose collections formed the nucleus of the British Museum.

An aristocratic quarter

Turn right on Sloane Street and then left at the traffic lights along Pont Street, with the gardens of Cadogan Place on either side. The third house on the right along the terrace bears a blue plaque to Mrs Jordan, a famous 18th-century comedy actress, known for her wit both on and off stage. When her royal lover, the Duke of Clarence, later King William IV, proposed reducing her allowance she sent him a saucy reply in the form of the bottom part of a play advert which read: 'No money returned after the rising of the curtain'!

Pont Street leads into Chesham Place and also into Belgravia, an aristocratic quarter centred on Belgrave and Eaton Squares, developed between the 1820s and 1850s on land belonging to the Dukes of Westminster. The same family still owns much of Belgravia, and Mayfair too. Eaton Hall in Cheshire is the duke's country house, and Belgrave is a small village on the Eaton estate. The family name is Grosvenor.

Maze of mews

Follow Chesham Place round into Belgrave Square and continue along the south side of the square. Although Belgravia as a whole is still largely residential, most of the houses in Belgrave Square are either embassies or the headquarters of various organizations. This side of the square is occupied by, among others, the Spiritualist Association and the German Information Centre. At the end of the south side, turn to the left and walk along the east side of the square.

At the top right corner of the square walk over the zebra crossing to the statue of the 1st Marquess of Westminster, who developed the Belgravia estate. Plaques on the statue's plinth tell the story of the Grosvenor family and their London – and in particular their Belgravia – property. Now continue straight on into gracious Wilton Row (an Earl of Wilton was father-in-law to one of the Westminsters). Follow this round to the left to the tucked-away Grenadier pub. Just before the pub, turn right through a gate into cobbled old Barrack Yard, relic of an 18th-century foot guards' barracks. At the end of this pretty Georgian street, go through the arch, turn left, immediately left again through the double gates and then right into Wilton Place, with St Paul's Church on your left.

At the end of Wilton Place cross the road (also called Wilton Place) into Kinnerton Street, turning left at the T-junction. Kinnerton Street is an attractive little backwater with two good pubs, a shop selling old newspapers, and attractive little courtyards leading off to the right. The cow-keepers, grocers, saddlers and other tradesmen who serviced the big houses in the area lived here and the then-uncovered River West-bourne flowed at the ends of the little courts.

Fireproof warehouse

Follow Kinnerton Street to the end and turn right into Motcomb Street. The Halkin Arcade, paved with enormous stone flags, leads off left and right. On the right also is the entrance front to the Pantechnicon (the name is carved high up on the façade). Built in 1830 as a fireproof complex of warehouses, stables and coach houses, it was, ironically, almost totally destroyed by fire in 1874. Part of the Wallace Collection of paintings that was stored there at the time also went up in the flames.

At the end of Motcomb Street turn right into Lowndes Square, built in the 1840s. Carry on into William Street and walk up to Knightsbridge. The walk ends at Knightsbridge station, 100 yards to the left. If you want to continue on into Hyde Park (perhaps to hear the speakers at Speaker's Corner if it is a Sunday), carry straight on over Knightsbridge and South Carriage Drive into the park, through the Dell and up the bank to the Serpentine Road. Ahead there should be five tarmac paths fanning out across the northern part of the park. The middle and widest path leads directly to Speaker's Corner and Marble Arch, and to Marble Arch station.

FOLLOWING THE WESTBOURNE RIVER

❖❖

Summary: The Westbourne is another 'lost' river like the Tyburn (see page 29). Following it, as this walk does, reveals equally fascinating surface clues as to what is going on underground. The Westbourne (meaning West Stream) begins as several streamlets flowing down the hill to the west of Hampstead. The streamlets flow together to form the main river in the region of Kilburn High Road station. From here the river flows south to Westbourne Green and then down Gloucester Place Mews and Upbrook Mews towards Hyde Park. The walk picks it up at Brook Mews North near Paddington Station and follows it as it flows through Hyde Park (passing the Serpentine), Knightsbridge, Belgravia and Sloane Square before debouching into the Thames near **Royal Hospital Chelsea.**

Start:	Paddington station (District, Circle, Hammersmith & City and Bakerloo Underground Lines).
Finish:	Sloane Square Underground station (District and Circle Lines).
Length:	3 miles (5km).
Time:	2½ hours.
Refreshments:	Around the halfway stage you have a choice of either the Dell café/restaurant in Hyde Park next to the Serpentine or, just a little bit further on, one of the cosy pubs in picturesque Kinnerton Street. Otherwise, Paddington Underground station near the beginning of the walk and Sloane Square Underground station towards the end are both surrounded by all kinds of eating places, cheap and expensive.
Note:	If possible, plan to finish the walk at low or lowish tide on the Thames, otherwise it may not be possible to see the Westbourne's outfall. To find out when low tide is, either consult the current edition of *Whitaker's Almanack* in your local library or ring the Port of London harbourmaster on 020 7265 2656.

Come out of Paddington Underground station opposite the Hilton London Paddington Hotel and turn left. Cross Spring Street and carry on down the hill, passing the entrance to Conduit Mews on the left. Spring Street and Conduit Mews (and nearby Conduit Place, which you don't see) commemorate a local spring that was used to supply the City of London with water from 1471 until 1812. This was the main spring in the area, and its name, Bayard's Watering, became, in a slightly altered fashion, that of this whole district: Bayswater.

Brooks and mews

Cross Westbourne Terrace and go past the entrance (on the left) to Smallbrook Mews, probably taking its name from a little tributary of the Westbourne. Cross Gloucester Terrace. When you get to the next mews entrances – Upbrook Mews on the right and Brook Mews North on the left – you are on the actual course of the Westbourne, which flows from right to left. Turn left into Brook Mews North and walk down to the far end. If the gate on the left is open, go through it, turn right and make your way to the far right-hand corner of the garden. Here turn left into Elms Mews. If the gate is closed, follow the road round to the right, turn left into Craven Terrace, and then, when Craven Terrace bends right, branch left down some steps (i.e. down the river bank) into Elms Mews. Elms Mews brings you out on to the Bayswater Road at a definite low point. When this was still open country there was a bridge here, with a coaching inn called the Swan next to it. The bridge has gone, but look to your right and you will see that the Swan, opened in 1775, is still very much in existence.

Hyde Park

Turn left on Bayswater Road, cross at the lights to the other side and go through Marlborough Gate into **Hyde Park**. Ahead of you now is a long stretch of water: first, four fountains and then the Long Water, the latter created in the 1730s by the simple expedient of damming up the Westbourne. In the foreground is the ornate fountain pump house, and, just in front of that, the Westbourne's original outfall into the Long Water with the tops of its three brick-lined arches poking up through the grass. Today the Westbourne flows not into the Long Water (which is filled by rainwater run-off from the surrounding slopes) but into the Ranelagh Sewer, a Victorian conduit constructed beneath the lake's left bank.

Go to the left of the pump house and walk along beside the fountains and then the lake. As you do so, you are contouring round the end of a spur of high ground running down from the Northern Heights beyond Hampstead. After a while you come to a fork. Keep right here to stay close to the water and walk underneath the bridge. On the other side (where the lake is known as the Serpentine) you can see to the right the tower of Knightsbridge cavalry barracks. Later another tower comes into view in the far distance: the Victoria Tower of the Palace of Westminster.

The Dell

Carry on to the end of the lake and the dam. Just beyond the Dell café turn right down the slope into the Dell. On the way you pass, on the right, an inscription commemorating another ancient water supply, this time not for the City but for Westminster. This one was started before the Norman Conquest (1066) and was not cut off until 1861, so it lasted for 800 years – not a bad record. The Dell is a pretty little water garden formed beneath the Serpentine's dam. The overflow from the lake here is not the Westbourne, but it does flow into the buried Westbourne (i.e. the Ranelagh Sewer) if the Serpentine is full. If the Serpentine is not getting enough run-off from its catchment area, the overflow is recycled back into the lake.

Carry straight on from the Dell, crossing first a tarmac cycle track, then the Rotten Row riding track and then South Carriage Drive. Beneath this road is a huge brick-lined cavern where the Westbourne is joined by the overflow from the

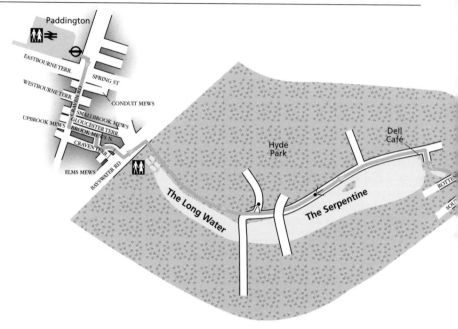

Serpentine and by a little tributary called the Tyburn Brook (not to be confused with the Tyburn) which runs down from the Marble Arch area.

Knightsbridge

Having crossed South Carriage Drive, go through Albert Gate to come into Knightsbridge. As the second part of the name suggests, there was indeed once a bridge here carrying the main road – since ancient times an important highway to the west – over the Westbourne. Where 'knight' comes from, however, is not as obvious as it seems; it is probably a corruption of a quite different word such as Neyt, the name of the adjoining manor.

From this point – the junction of Albert Gate and Knightsbridge – the Westbourne continues its southerly course across the Thames flood plain. Being so flat, the plain reveals few signs of the river's course, but there are one or two clues, for example in the layout of certain streets, which help to keep us on the right track. To find the first of these clues, we have to make a short detour to the east of the river.

The east bank

Cross Knightsbridge at the lights and turn left. Take the first right into Wilton Place and then go right again into Kinnerton Street and turn left. Off to the right there are lots of little dead-end mews running off the street at right angles. Altogether there are eight of these little enclaves, all belonging to the Duke of Westminster's Grosvenor Estate (notice the estate signs and the wheatsheaf plaque fixed to the fronts of some of the houses – the wheatsheaf is the main feature of the Grosvenor coat of arms). Today they provide bijou residences for the wealthy, but originally they were yards and workshops used by the tradesmen serving the grand houses on the Duke's newly-built Belgravia estate. The river ran along the far end of them (no doubt making a convenient lavatory and rubbish tip), which is why they are all blocked off.

At the end of Kinnerton Street, turn right into Motcomb Street. The impressive façade of the Pantechnicon (a supposedly fire-proof warehouse burnt down in 1874) stands on the right just about directly over the river's course. Carry on to the end of the street. The river crosses from left to right in the vicinity of Zafferano's restaurant at No. 15 to your right. Now turn left into Lowndes Street. When you get to the traffic lights in Chesham Place, turn right into Pont Street, so named

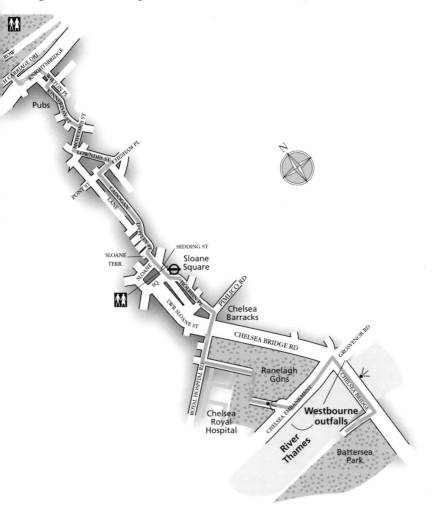

because of another bridge over the Westbourne here. The French word was probably chosen in order to make the new development (dating from the 1830s) sound more chic and attractive.

Pont Street to Sloane Square

The bridge, marked on maps up to the 1820s at least, seems to have been where Cadogan Lane now is, so turn left into the lane when you come to it and walk on right down to the end where it becomes D'Oyley Street. Follow D'Oyley Street round into Sloane Terrace and take the first left into Sedding Street. A zebra crossing at the end brings you into Sloane Square.

Sloane Square Underground station ahead provides a good opportunity to get a new fix on the exact course of the Westbourne, for the river is carried over the tracks in a huge iron pipe clearly visible from the platforms. You can try persuading the staff to let you down free to have a quick look, but they will probably make you buy a ticket first. From the station, the river carries on down Holbein Place, first left out of the station. At the end of Holbein Place it splits up into several different channels to form a kind of delta. The main one carries straight on under Chelsea Barracks and cuts across Chelsea Bridge Road and the grounds of Chelsea Hospital before flowing out into the Thames through an arched tunnel in the embankment wall.

The Chelsea Hospital channel

The barracks are inaccessible for obvious reasons so we cannot follow this route directly, but we can go through the grounds of Royal Hospital Chelsea (the home for old soldiers, founded in 1682) and pick up the river again just before its confluence with the Thames. From Holbein Place, turn right into Pimlico Road. Cross Chelsea Bridge Road at the lights and walk along Royal Hospital Road to the Hospital entrance on the left. Turn in here and walk down the road and through the big gates leading to the tree-lined avenue. The river cuts across Ranelagh Gardens – from which the Ranelagh Sewer gets its name – on the left, crosses the avenue and meets the Thames almost directly ahead. Go down the little slope in the avenue and turn right by the tennis courts. Then go left down the central path leading past the 1849 Chilianwallah memorial towards the gutted but still majestic Battersea Power Station on the far side of the river. (Chilianwallah, incidentally, was the British Army's costliest battle in the conquest of India, see page 61.)

Go through the gates at the far end and cross Chelsea Embankment using the traffic island on the left. Where the pavement meets the wall you will see the date 1858 carved into one of the granite blocks. What this refers to is not known (it can't be the building of the embankment because that was 15 years later) but it serves as a useful pointer to the mouth of the Westbourne, for if you look over the wall you will see it directly below. For the intrepid who want to get a closer look, there are some stairs about 100 yards to the right. Otherwise you can get a good view from Battersea Park opposite.

Other channels

When you come back from the park, cross the bridge on the downstream (i.e. power station) side. From here you will see two more tunnel entrances and the entrance to a large dock in between the road bridge and the railway bridge. These are the ends of the delta channels mentioned earlier.

The dock is all that remains of an extensive canal and reservoir system begun by the Chelsea Waterworks Company in 1725 to supply drinking water to Mayfair. A century later it was extended by the Grosvenor family, hence its present name, the

Grosvenor Canal. Until the mid-1990s Westminster City Council used it for barging away rubbish to tips in the Thames estuary. Now it is being regenerated with houses, shops and offices surrounding a marina. For a closer view of the dock, stand on Grosvenor Road where it crosses the dock entrance and look over the railings.

To return to Sloane Square Underground station and the end of the walk, follow Chelsea Bridge Road and its continuation, Lower Sloane Street, straight up to Sloane Square.

❖❖❖

CHELSEA

❖❖❖

Summary: Chelsea is a village suburb on the Thames close to central London. Modern Chelsea is neatly bisected by the King's Road but historic Chelsea, including the 17th-century **Royal Hospital**, **Chelsea Physic Garden**, **Chelsea Old Church**, Henry VIII's manor house, Sir Thomas More's house and the Chelsea Porcelain Works, lay between the King's Road and the Thames. This circular walk includes these historic features, plus St Luke's church, the Chelsea Farmer's Market, and the former homes of some of the writers and artists who lived in this once-bohemian district: George Eliot, James McNeill Whistler, Thomas Carlyle, Tobias Smollett and Hilaire Belloc, to name a few.

Start and finish: Sloane Square station (District and Circle Underground Lines).
Length: 3¾ miles (6km).
Time: 3 hours.
Refreshments: All manner of places to eat and drink on the King's Road, and a few pubs along the route including one at the halfway point where Milman's Street meets the King's Road. Also, various restaurants in Chelsea Farmer's Market about three-quarters of the way through the walk.
Note: Chelsea Hospital grounds are open daily 10am to 4pm but closed during the Chelsea Flower Show held at the end of May.

On leaving Sloane Square station you will find yourself in Sloane Square, named after Sir Hans Sloane, lord of the manor of Chelsea in the 18th century and one of the key figures in its history. To your right is the Royal Court Theatre where many new writers have had their plays first performed, including John Osborne with *Look Back in Anger* in 1956. Go over the zebra crossings and walk along the left-hand side of the square into the King's Road, the high street of modern Chelsea. During the 1960s the King's Road became the playground of 'swinging London' and since then has been the most fashionable shopping area outside the West End.

The Chelsea Pensioners
Continue along the King's Road, passing on the left the Duke of York's barracks, now the headquarters of Britain's Territorial Army. Cross Tenham Terrace and Walpole Street

and take the next turning on the left into Royal Avenue. Far ahead you can see the entrance to the Royal Hospital, the home for old soldiers founded by Charles II in 1682 and designed by Sir Christopher Wren. The Hospital residents are known as Chelsea Pensioners and are recognized by their old-fashioned blue or red uniforms. At the end of Royal Avenue turn left into Leonard's Terrace and then right along Franklin's Row. To your right is Burton's Court, a sports ground used by soldiers from local barracks. Cross the main road (Royal Hospital Road) to enter the Royal Hospital grounds.

At the second gate, turn right into Light Horse Court and go straight ahead through the arch leading into the colonnade. Halfway along there is a doorway on the right leading into the Hospital's dining hall and chapel. On leaving the hall, continue straight ahead into the middle of the central court (Figure Court), which is flanked by wings left and right. About 400 pensioners live here in small curtained cubicles ranged along the middle of great open dormitories known as Long Wards.

The bronze statue in the centre of the court by Grinling Gibbons depicts Charles II in the dress of a Roman emperor. Above the colonnade in the central range of the building a Latin inscription announces that the Hospital is for the support and relief of maimed and superannuated soldiers, and that it was founded by Charles II, enlarged

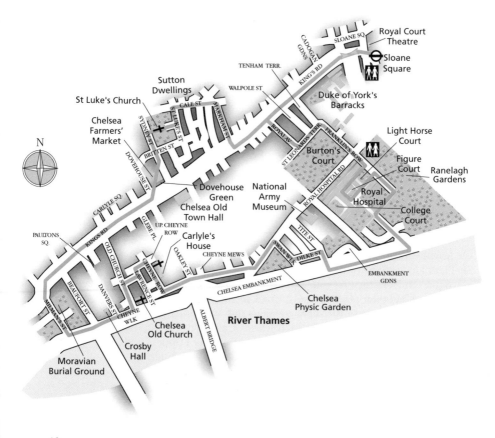

by James II and completed by William III in 1692. In the opposite direction there is a good view across the Hospital grounds to the former Battersea Power Station on the south side of the River Thames.

In front of the flagpole turn left along the terrace and pass through another arch into Light Horse Court. Turn right out of the Court and go through the gate ahead. Another gate immediately on your left leads into Ranelagh Gardens, the site of the most famous of all the pleasure gardens opened in London during the 1700s. The centrepiece of Ranelagh Gardens was a huge rotunda where visitors promenaded or drank tea and wine accompanied by an orchestra playing from a bandstand. Mozart once performed here. There is a picture of the Rotunda, which was demolished in 1805, in the little summer house in the centre of the gardens.

Walk on past the entrance to Ranelagh Gardens and turn right in front of the Hospital into the public park area. (The Chelsea Flower Show is held here in May each year. At this time you will have to retrace your steps to the Hospital entrance, turn left into Royal Hospital Road and walk past the **National Army Museum** to pick up the route at Swan Walk.) Turn left down the central walk past the 1849 Chilianwallah memorial commemorating the hardest action ever fought during the subjugation of India. Nearly a quarter of the 12,000 British troops involved were killed or wounded. Go straight on out of the park and turn right onto Chelsea Embankment.

Pagodas and power stations
Looking out over the river now you can see, from left to right, the old power station, Chelsea Bridge leading to Wandsworth and Battersea, and Battersea Park, with its Buddhist Peace Pagoda, which was built in 1985 by Nipponzan Myohoji Buddhists, on the riverside. Continue to the right along the embankment, past Embankment Gardens, and then turn right into Tite Street. Oscar Wilde and the painters James McNeill Whistler, John Singer Sargent and Augustus John all lived or worked here around the turn of the century. Almost immediately turn left into Dilke Street. On the left, No. 7 with the lantern above the front door, is the London Sketch Club, an artists' club founded in 1898 by *Punch* cartoonist Phil May.

At the end of Dilke Street turn right into Swan Walk. This one-sided street runs along the east side of Chelsea Physic Garden, which you can glimpse through the gate on the left. This botanical garden was started over 300 years ago by the City Apothecaries' Company and is still active in botanical research. Some of the first cotton seed planted in America was exported from here in 1732.

Carry on to the end of Swan Walk (where there is a plaque on the left about the Physic Garden) and turn left into Royal Hospital Road. At the end of the road turn right just before the strip of garden into Cheyne Walk, a long terrace running right along the Chelsea waterfront. Before the embankment was built in 1874 the river came right up to the side of Swan Walk. Over the centuries many famous people have lived here – No. 4 was the last home of the novelist George Eliot; Lloyd George (World War I Prime Minister) lived at No. 10; Vaughan Williams (composer) once lived on the site of Nos. 12–14; and Rosetti (painter), Swinburne (poet), and George Meredith (writer) were all former residents of No. 16 (plus Rosetti's pet wombat!).

Cheyne Walk converges with Chelsea Embankment just before Albert Bridge. A narrow lane leads off to the right, underneath No. 24 Cheyne Walk. A plaque on the right-hand wall of the lane explains that Chelsea Manor House, built by King Henry

VIII in 1536, once stood here. It was later the home of Sir Hans Sloane. After Sloane's death in 1753 the old house was demolished, although part of the garden (along with mulberry trees said to have been planted by Queen Elizabeth I) still survives beyond the wall at the end of the mews.

Go past the mews, cross Oakley Street and take the first turning on the right into Cheyne Row. You are now in the centre of the old riverside village of Chelsea. On the right, No. 10 has a plaque to Margaret Damer Dawson, founder of the women's police force of which she was first chief officer (she died in 1920 aged 45). Further along on the right, No. 24 was home for nearly half a century to the humbly born historian and social critic Thomas Carlyle, one of the most influential intellectual figures of the 19th century. **Carlyle's House** is now a National Trust museum. At the end of Cheyne Row turn left into Upper Cheyne Row and then left again into Lawrence Street.

On the right a plaque mentions the famous Chelsea Porcelain Works, which produced porcelain here for almost 40 years until the factory was moved to Derby in 1784. Nearby was a large house where the novelist Tobias Smollett lived for 12 years, keeping open house to all his friends despite his own chronic shortage of money. Further along on the left, two old houses, Duke's House and Monmouth House, share a common porch, probably a relic of a large residence known as Monmouth House that stood at the northern end of Lawrence Street. In the 17th century the mansion is said to have belonged to Charles II's illegitimate son, the Duke of Monmouth, who was beheaded in 1685 after leading an unsuccessful rebellion against his uncle, James II.

Chelsea residents

At this point turn right into Justice Walk and then left into Old Church Street. This was Chelsea's main street until 1830 when the King's Road became a public thoroughfare (until then it had been a private road used only by the royal family en route to various country retreats). Chelsea Old Church (rebuilt after being bombed in World War II) is at the southern end of the street. Henry VIII married Jane Seymour here in 1536 and Sir Hans Sloane was buried here in 1753 – his grave is marked by an urn beneath a stone canopy at the east end of the churchyard. The modern statue in front of the church facing the river is of Sir Thomas More, a Chelsea resident and Lord Chancellor under Henry VIII, who was beheaded in 1535 for refusing to accept the king's religious reforms. Parts of More's 16th-century chapel and many other fascinating old monuments survive in the church.

At the church turn right along Cheyne Walk and go past Roper's Garden, created out of a bombsite on land once given by Sir Thomas More to his son-in-law Will Roper. Cross Danvers Street. On your right is Crosby Hall, part of a medieval wool-merchant's house that was brought here from the City in the early 20th century when it was threatened with demolition. The present site of the hall was once Sir Thomas More's garden, an appropriate location for it since Crosby Hall was More's London home before he built his country house at Chelsea.

Cross Beaufort Street (the actual site of More's house – demolished in 1740) and continue along Cheyne Walk. Ahead you can see the tower and other modern residential developments covering the former wharves and railway sidings at Lots Road. On the right, No. 93 Cheyne Walk has a plaque to the novelist Mrs Gaskell, best known for her book *Cranford* (1853). No. 98 was built in 1674 for Lord Lindsey, Charles II's Lord Chamberlain. In 1752 the house was occupied by Count Zinzendorf and other members of the Moravian Protestant Church who came to England to escape persecution in their native Germany. In 1774 it was split up into seven separate houses. Whistler was a later resident and it was here that he painted the famous picture of his mother. Further along, on the corner of Milman's Street, No. 104 has two plaques, one to the writer Hilaire Belloc and the other to the Chelsea-born artist Walter Greaves who died in 1930 leaving numerous pictures of his birthplace.

Turn right into Milman's Street. Just beyond the pub on the right at the northern end of the street a large pair of gates marks the entrance to the Moravian burial ground, once part of the grounds of Lindsey House. Inside is a tiny chapel and minister's house, an exhibition room and an artist's studio. Go past the gate and onto the King's Road again. Cross over and turn right. Walk past Paultons Square (1830s) and Old Church Street on the right and on the left Carlyle Square, built as Oakley Square around 1830 and later renamed in honour of Thomas Carlyle. On the right beyond the entrance to Glebe Place are the oldest houses on the King's Road, built in 1720. There are plaques here to the actress Ellen Terry and to film director Carol Reed of *The Third Man* fame, but not to Lady Sybil Colefax, a famous society hostess who lived at No. 211 in the 1930s.

When you get to Dovehouse Green, an old burial ground on the far side of Dovehouse Street, cut diagonally across to the far left corner and go through Chelsea Farmers Market (or along the path by the fence if the market is closed) into Sydney Street. Facing up the street to the right is Chelsea's old town hall. The old borough is now part of the Royal Borough of Kensington and Chelsea and is governed from Kensington.

Cross Sydney Street and turn left, crossing over Britten Street. Then turn right into the gardens beside **St Luke's Church**. This fine 2,500-seat church, opened in 1824 to accommodate Chelsea's expanding population, was one of the first Gothic revival buildings of the 19th century. The open space all round sets it off magnificently. Charles Dickens was married here in 1836.

Cut across the gardens to the east end of the church and turn right out of the gates. Go under the arch into St Luke's Street and then turn left towards the council homes in Sutton Dwellings. Turn right onto Cale Street and follow the road to the little green surrounded by shops and restaurants. When you reach Markham Street turn right and then, at the end of the street, turn left back onto the King's Road. When you get to Cadogan Gardens just before Peter Jones, notice on No. 31 across the road to your right the plaque to the composer and folk-song collector Percy Grainger (famous for his *English Country Gardens* melody) who came to London from Australia in 1901. The walk ends back at Sloane Square station straight ahead.

❖❖

REGENT'S PARK

❖❖

Summary: **Regent's Park** and its smaller sister Primrose Hill lie immediately north of Marylebone and the West End. The walk begins in Regent's Park Road, climbs up to the viewpoint at the summit of Primrose Hill (206 feet/62.8m above sea-level) and then descends to the 400-acre (162-ha) Regent's Park directly below. Within

Regent's Park the walk passes **London Zoo**, the London Central Mosque, the boating lake and Queen Mary's Gardens, Open-Air Theatre and café. The last section of the walk is a close-up view of some of the palatial cream-stuccoed terraces that surround the park. The whole scheme was devised around 1820 by the architect John Nash as part of the grandest town-planning scheme ever executed in central London before or since.

Start:	Chalk Farm station (Northern Underground Line).
Finish:	Regent's Park station (Bakerloo Underground Line).
Length:	3½ miles (5.6km).
Time:	1½ hours.
Refreshments:	The restaurant in the centre of Regent's Park at about the halfway stage is a good place to stop to re-fuel.

Turn right out of Chalk Farm station and cross the road (Adelaide Road) into Bridge Approach. Cross the pedestrians-only bridge over the railway lines and go straight on into Regent's Park Road, the local shopping street. On the left beyond the shops, No. 122 has a plaque in memory of Friedrich Engels. A friend and collaborator of Karl Marx, Engels moved here when he was 50 years old and stayed until he was 74, the year before he died.

A bird's-eye view

When you get to Primrose Hill Road on the right, go through the gate into Primrose Hill Park and turn immediately right up the hill. The panorama from the summit includes London Zoo, Regent's Park and the West End straight ahead, and the tower blocks of the City on the left. A metal panel at the summit identifies the position of these and other major landmarks in the view.

Retrace your steps a short distance down the hill and take the first path on the right. When it forks, keep to the right and continue, crossing over all other paths until you come to the southeast corner of the park, opposite London Zoo. Cross the main road here (Prince Albert Road) and turn left. When you reach the church (St Mark's Regent's Park) turn right onto the bridge across the Regent's Canal, signposted to London Zoo.

Go across the bridge and the Outer Circle road into the Broad Walk of Regent's Park and continue past the zoo on your right. Regent's Park and the surrounding palatial terraces were all part of a huge development stretching from this point down to St James's Park by Buckingham Palace. The scheme's sponsor was the Prince Regent, later George IV, who owned much of the land (the park and terraces are still Crown property). Its designer was the Prince's favourite architect, John Nash, one of the handful of architects who did most to shape the development of London over the centuries.

The essence of Nash's scheme was a park dotted with large detached villas and surrounded by great terraces designed to look like individual mansions but, in fact, incorporating 20 or more separate houses. To the left you can see the beginning of one of these terraces – Gloucester Gate, built in 1827. There were also plans to build similar terraces to your right but the land was assigned instead to the newly-founded Zoological Society for its Zoological Gardens, first opened to the public in 1828.

Plate 10: Following the Westbourne River
Hyde Park's Serpentine lake was originally created by
damming the Westbourne river (see page 55).

Plate 11: Chelsea
The Buddhist Peace Pagoda in Battersea Park, across the river from Chelsea Embankment,
just over halfway round the Chelsea walk (see page 61).

You are warned that the elephants may take loose articles such as handbags and cameras

Plate 12: Regent's Park
Elephants are just some of the exotic animals to be found at
London Zoo, a feature of the Regent's Park walk (see page 64).

Plate 13: Regent's Canal
The Regent's Canal at colourful Little Venice, the start
point of the Regent's Canal walk (see page 68).

Plate 14: Islington
The King's Head pub in Islington, like several other pubs
in the capital, boasts its very own theatre (see page 75).

Plate 15: Highgate to Hampstead
*Kenwood House, a Georgian mansion on Hampstead Heath and
the mid-point of the Highgate to Hampstead walk (see page 80).*

Plate 16: Soho to Trafalgar Square
Fountains play in Trafalgar Square, where the Soho to Trafalgar Square
walk ends after its journey south from Fitzrovia (see page 87).

Plate 17: Notorious Soho
Modern London's Chinatown is centred on Gerrard Street where,
in the 1920s, Kate Meyrick ran her notorious 43 Club (see page 90).

Some distance ahead you can see a large drinking fountain. Just before the fountain, turn right through the shrubbery and follow the path across the middle of the park. Ahead you should be able to see the burnished copper dome of the London Central Mosque. To the left, behind the trees, is St John's Lodge, one of the eight large houses built in the park. Originally Nash planned 56 such mansions – which would of course have ruled out the creation of a public park – but the Crown Estate decided not to build the remaining 48 because it was satisfied with the revenue from the existing villas and terraces. Most of the modern park area was open to public use by 1841.

West-side terraces
When you reach the west side of the park, cross over the two bridges and turn left between the children's boating pond and the main boating lake, fed by the Tyburn River. Through the trees to the right you can see the first of the west-side terraces – Hanover Terrace (1822) – with a relief in the pediment picked out in blue and white. Sussex Place (also 1822) is next with its curving ends and pepperpots. On the other side of the boating lake there is a private house called The Holme, another of the eight original villas built in the park. The third terrace is Clarence Terrace, built in 1823 and the smallest of them all. Each terrace in the scheme takes its name from titles held by various members of the royal family during the reign of George IV.

Just before Cornwall Terrace (1821), turn left across the bridge. Turn left again and then follow the path round to the right, going past the bandstand on your left. This was the scene of the IRA bomb attack in 1982 in which seven Royal Greenjackets bandsmen were killed. The building on your right houses various organizations, including the British American College and the European Business School.

When you come to the Inner Circle road (unlike the Outer Circle this is perfectly round) cross over into Queen Mary's Gardens in the middle. Go past the restaurant and then turn left and right around the railings surrounding the sunken garden. To the left across the lawn is the entrance to the Open-Air Theatre. Continue through the gardens towards the wrought-iron gates and go through the gates, across the Inner Circle road again, then into Chester Road.

Halfway along this road, turn left into the Broad Walk again and then take the first path on the right, heading towards the Nash terraces on the east side of the park. Nash did not have time to design all the terraces, but he did personally approve each plan. Continue along the path and go through the gate out of the park. Cross the road (Outer Circle), go into Cumberland Place opposite and turn right into Chester Terrace (1825), its name blazoned across the entrance arch. This terrace is cream-coloured and clean with sharp lines and little ornamentation apart from some fluted pilasters and carved capitals. Near the far end there is a plaque on the former home of Charles Cockerell, architect of the Chilianwallah obelisk (see the Chelsea walk, page 59) and the unfinished National Monument on Edinburgh's Calton Hill. In case you are wondering what the signs with 'CEPC' on them mean, the letters stand for Crown Estate Paving Commissioners, the body responsible for the upkeep of the Regent's Park estate.

Regency entertainment
At the end of Chester Terrace turn right into Chester Gate and then left back onto the Outer Circle road with the park on your right. Cambridge Terrace (1825) is the

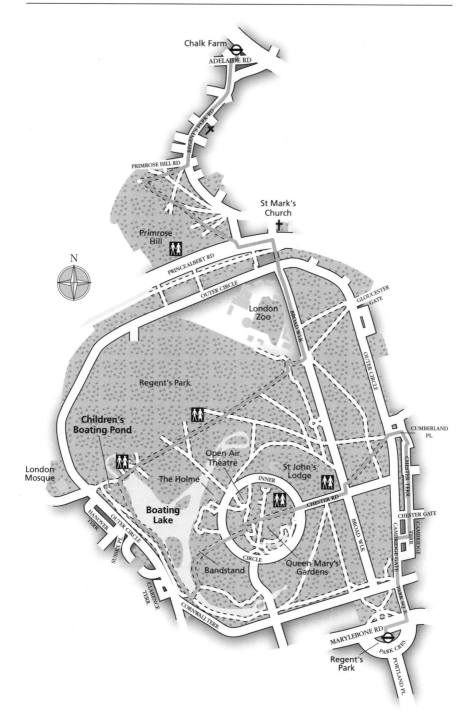

next terrace on your left; then comes Cambridge Gate. Cambridge Gate was built in 1880 and replaced an unusual feature of the Regency scheme of Nash and George IV – the Colosseum. This was a large domed building with a massive portico, similar to the Pantheon in Rome. Inside was a vast panorama of London painted from drawings made from the top of St Paul's Cathedral. Forty thousand square feet (12,192 sq.m) in extent, it took years to prepare and cost a huge amount, but it failed to draw the crowds. New attractions were added later, but the Colosseum never made any money and was eventually demolished in 1875. Beyond Cambridge Gate is the modern headquarters of the Royal College of Physicians.

Continue straight ahead into Park Square East. The central section of this terrace was occupied by another kind of entertainment not unlike the Colosseum but more fun. This was the Diorama, its name still visible after 150 years at the top of the façade. The 19th-century precursor of the cinema, the Diorama was invented by Frenchman Jacques Daguerre, better known for his later invention of the daguerreotype, the first effective form of photography. In a Diorama the spectators sat in a revolving auditorium while various special effects were used to animate scenes painted on a cotton screen – in this case the interior of Canterbury Cathedral and an alpine valley scene from Switzerland. Like the Colosseum, the Diorama was not a great success and closed down, 25 years after opening, in 1848. The three-storey glass-roofed auditorium still exists in the centre of the building, which is now the headquarters of the Prince of Wales's Princes Trust, an organization set up to help young people start their own businesses.

Across Marylebone Road, at the bottom of Park Square East, the Nash scheme continues around Park Crescent into Portland Place, and then down to the Mall bordering St James's Park. The walk, however, ends at Regent's Park station, which is to the right on Marylebone Road.

❖❖❖

REGENT'S CANAL

❖❖❖

Summary: The Regent's Canal runs from Little Venice in West London to the Thames at Limehouse in East London. This long but quite straightforward walk follows the canal along the first and most interesting section, between Little Venice and Islington. The walk passes through Regent's Park and Camden Lock Market en route and ends near Camden Passage antiques market. The canal environment is changing rapidly as the old warehouses and factories are converted or demolished to make way for waterside homes and offices. It is still possible, however, to capture something of the atmosphere of the canal as a major commercial highway, and the towpath walk will always provide an uncommon view of London.

Start:	Warwick Avenue station (Bakerloo Underground Line).
Finish:	Angel station (Northern Underground Line).
Length:	4¾ miles (7.6km).

Time: 2½ hours.

Refreshments: The Warwick Castle pub in Warwick Place and the floating café in Little Venice at the start of the walk. A variety of shops, pubs, stalls, etc. in and around Camden Lock Market at the halfway stage and at Islington at the end of the walk.

Notes: Camden Lock Market is open on Saturdays and Sundays. Camden Passage Market in Islington is open on Wednesdays and Saturdays. The canalside walk opens at 7.30am on weekdays and 9.00am on Sundays and public holidays and closes at dusk in winter.

Take the 'Clifton Villas' exit from Warwick Avenue station and walk up the right hand side of Warwick Avenue with the church behind you. Turn right into Warwick Place, left into Blomfield Road and then walk on to the bridge ahead. This area is known as Little Venice. The story of Little Venice starts with the Grand Union Canal, which enters the Thames at Brentford in West London (see page 187). This was built at the end of the 18th century to link the Thames with the new industrial areas in and around Birmingham. Later, an extension to Paddington was built to bring the canal closer to London's expanding West End. This is the canal entering the basin under the bridge. It continues in the far right corner to its original terminating basin at Paddington. Then in 1812 work began on another extension to take the canal from Paddington round North London to London's new docks downstream of the City. This new extension was called the Regent's Canal. The basin here at Little Venice was built as the junction between Regent's Canal and the Paddington branch of the Grand Union.

Horse-drawn barges

Return to Blomfield Road. Follow the road to the right along the side of the basin, keeping to the pavement since the towpath walk is blocked off ahead. Cross Warwick Avenue at the traffic lights and carry on alongside the houseboats, whose residents have exclusive use of this part of the towpath. At the end of this tree-lined stretch the canal funnels into the Maida Hill tunnel (272 yards/250m long) and the towpath disappears. In the days of horse-drawn barges the horses were released from the towropes and led over the top of the tunnel while the bargemen 'legged' the barges through the tunnel by lying on their backs and 'walking' along the tunnel roof.

When you come to Edgware Road cross over at the lights and walk up the right-hand side of Aberdeen Place. Go through the passage at the end of the road, on the far side of the electricity sub-station. At the end of the passage, descend the steps to the canal where it emerges from the tunnel. The walk now follows the towpath until the tunnel near the end of the walk at Islington.

Beyond the next bridge (Lisson Grove) the canal broadens. On the right bank here, there was once a wharf where boats loaded and unloaded at the freight yards of the Marylebone railway. The canal then runs under the bridge that carries trains into Marylebone Station. The next bridge carries the Metropolitan Underground Line and a further bridge carries Park Road, which borders the western side of Regent's Park. Lord's cricket ground is just a short distance to the left of the canal at this point.

The canal now swings to the left and enters a cutting as it follows the northern perimeter of Regent's Park. The canal was originally intended to pass through the park, but the route was changed when it was realized that commercial traffic would lower the tone of the exclusive residential development. To the left above the terraced gardens is Grove House, built in 1823 for George Bellas Greenhough, a natural scientist and the first president of the Geological Society. To the right through the trees the dome and minaret of the London Central Mosque are just visible. Then come six new villas built in various historic styles.

Blow-up Bridge
The first bridge in Regent's Park carries the Tyburn River, one of London's many hidden rivers (see page 29), over the canal. The Tyburn eventually flows into the Thames near Vauxhall Bridge. The next bridge, Macclesfield Bridge, is popularly known as Blow-up Bridge after a barge, laden with gunpowder, exploded directly underneath it in October 1874. When the bridge was rebuilt, the iron columns were turned round, which explains why the deep grooves caused by the constant rubbing of taut towropes are on the landward rather than the water side. Similar grooves can be seen in many other places along the canal.

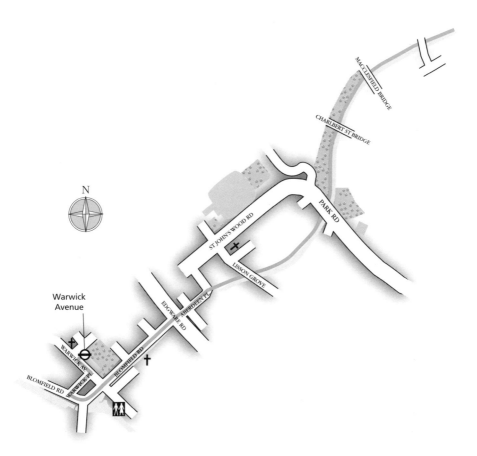

After the next bridge the canal enters London Zoo: to the left is the aviary and to the right are the animal pens (the building in the centre with the raised roof is for the giraffes). Beyond the zoo lies the Cumberland Basin, the truncated arm of the canal that once served a large market near Euston Station. Early in the 20th century the market

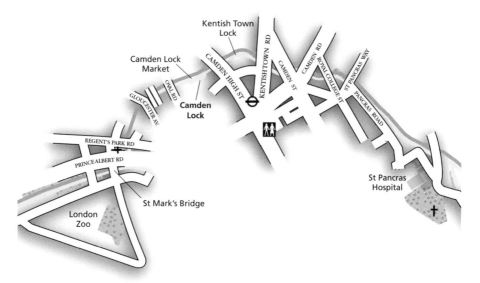

was closed and after World War II this branch of the canal was filled in with rubble from London's bombsites. (The site of the market is preserved in the street named Cumberland Market – just east of Regent's Park – and the market basin is now covered in allotments.) The canal now turns sharply to the left, another consequence of the decision to change the original route. The next short section demonstrates the charm of the canal when houses and gardens come down to the water's edge. Halfway along this section on the towpath side the bank is cut away and an underwater ramp descends to the bed of the canal. A plaque on the wall explains how this, and similar ramps elsewhere on the canal, were used to rescue barge horses when the noise made by new-fangled steam engines heading in and out of Euston caused them to bolt and fall in the water.

Beyond the next bridges, the modern bridge built in the style of a medieval castle is known as Pirate Castle. On the right-hand side is a youth club called the Pirate Club and on the left-hand side is a pumping station for the electricity network. Electricity cables have been laid under the towpath to bring power to central London from generating stations on the Thames estuary, and pumping stations like this one circulate water round the cables to keep them cool.

An old wharf market

Beyond Pirate Castle and the bridge carrying trains into Euston Station, the towpath climbs over the entrance to a subterranean basin in a former Gilbey's Gin warehouse. The towpath then crosses the canal over an iron bridge, deeply grooved by towropes. Just before the bridge, a doorway in the wall leads into Camden Lock Market, an old wharf converted into an arts and crafts centre and weekend antiques market.

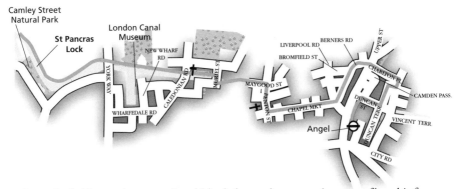

Cross the bridge and go past the old lock-keeper's cottage (now a café and information centre) on the right. This lock is the first of 12 that lower the canal down to the level of the Thames at Limehouse. At that point it is about 90 feet (27m) lower than it is now. Go through the gate onto Camden High Street, turn left over the road bridge and then left again down the slope. This will bring you back down to the towpath. Turn left under the road bridge and continue along past Hawley Lock and, on the opposite side of the canal, a former brewery converted into television studios in the 1980s. Beyond the next lock (Kentish Town) and bridge (Kentish Town Road) there are new flats and a supermarket on the right-hand bank.

Stations and freight yards

The canal now flows under three more bridges in quick succession. The first bridge is Camden Street; the second Camden Road; and the third Royal College Street. By looking up at the last bridge you can see that the original narrow brick bridge has been made much wider to carry more traffic. As the canal approaches the next bridge (St Pancras Way) it turns south towards King's Cross and St Pancras railway stations.

After quite a while you come to Camley Street bridge and a bridge carrying railway lines from the Midlands into St Pancras Station. The station concourse is raised about 20 feet (6m) above ground level in order to be level with the railway tracks after they have crossed the canal at this point. The basin beyond on the right, now used as a mooring by the St Pancras Cruising Club, once had sidings overhead from which cinders from steam locomotives were tipped into barges waiting underneath. Walking on a little further, you come to St Pancras Lock and then to the Camley Street Natural Park, opened on a former coal depot site in 1985 by Camden Council and the London Wildlife Trust. Behind the park is a clutch of 19th-century gas holders and beyond them, the spire of St Pancras Station.

Two tunnels

Now the canal makes a sharp turn to the left, round the stables of one of the old railway companies, and steers its course towards Islington. Here the canal becomes narrower but then, at the petrol station to the right, it becomes even wider than its normal width. Two tunnels run beneath the canal here, bored in 1852 to carry the Great Northern Railway (GNR) into King's Cross. If you climb the bank on the left you will be able to see both King's Cross and St Pancras Stations (the latter's roof single-span only). The Midland Railway also used King's Cross until its own station,

71

St Pancras, was opened in 1868. On the left the 19th-century freight yards and warehouses built by the GNR still await redevelopment.

Queen Boudicca

Beyond Maiden Lane Bridge (carrying York Way), Battlebridge Basin opens up on the right. Battlebridge was the old name for King's Cross and is popularly believed to have been the site of Queen Boudicca's defeat of the Romans in AD61. The name is, in fact, a corruption of Broad Ford Bridge. The ford was a crossing on the River Fleet, which flowed by King's Cross Station to the west. On the east side of the basin, which was constructed in the 1820s, is a 19th-century warehouse once used for storing ice harvested from Scandinavian lakes. Mechanical refrigeration put an end to the ice trade in the 1920s. The warehouse is now home to the **London Canal Museum**.

Beyond the bridge carrying the Caledonian Road, the canal enters the 960-yard (878-m) Islington Tunnel under Pentonville Hill. Walk up the sloping path to the left. At the top of the path go right and left through a gate to the right of an old wall along a path that winds through the Half Moon Crescent Housing Co-operative. This path leads into Maygood Street. At the far end turn right into Barnsbury Road leading into Penton Street. Opposite is the Penny Farthing pub, formerly the White Conduit House (see name above second storey). Here was founded in 1752 the White Conduit Cricket Club. A Yorkshireman called Thomas Lord was the club's groundsman. Lord later opened his own cricket ground, which became the home of the Marylebone Cricket Club (MCC) and the headquarters of the whole game.

Emigrant's friend

Look out for the Salmon and Compasses pub on the left, then go over the zebra crossing into Chapel Street Market, a Tuesday to Sunday general market. At the end turn left into Liverpool Road and then, beyond the lights, right into Bromfield Street. At the end turn left into Parkfield Street and right into Berners Road. This brings you down past the Business Design Centre (the former Royal Agricultural Hall) to Upper Street, the centre of Islington. Go straight over the zebra crossing into Charlton Place, cutting across Camden Passage and the antiques market. On the right-hand side, No. 32 Charlton Place has a plaque to Caroline Chisholm, called the 'emigrant's friend' because of the voluntary help she gave to emigrants to Australia in the 19th century. She lived in the colony for many years, giving practical help to settlers and leading parties of them into the unexplored interior. At the bottom of Charlton Place turn right into Duncan Terrace, a street of handsome Georgian terraced houses separated from Colebrooke Row by a narrow strip of railed garden. The garden marks the course of the New River, described in more detail in the Islington walk (see page 73). On reaching Duncan Street, look across to the corner of Vincent Terrace; at this point the canal emerges from the Islington Tunnel and is joined once more by the towpath. From here the walk can be extended to the end of the canal at Limehouse Basin on the Thames (about the same distance as the first section of the walk: the canal's overall length is 8½ miles (13.5km). If you walk to Limehouse, public transport details for your homeward journey can be found under the Wapping to Limehouse walk (see page 173).

Now turn right into Duncan Street. At the main road turn left. Angel station, where the walk ends, is ahead on the left.

ISLINGTON

Summary: Islington lies to the north of the City, with Clerkenwell in between. This walk starts at the historic Angel road junction and then makes its way north and uphill through the antiques market to the Canonbury Estate and Highbury Fields at the top of the hill. The middle section of the walk follows the course of the now filled-in New River, London's main water supply from 1613 until the 1980s. The 16th-century Canonbury Tower is the centrepiece of the Canonbury Estate. Other features of the walk include Charles Lamb's house and Walter Sickert's art school.

Start:	Angel station (Northern Underground Line).
Finish:	Holloway Road station (Piccadilly Underground Line).
Alternative finishes:	Highbury and Islington station (Victoria Underground Line, Silverlink Metro and trains from Moorgate). Drayton Park station (trains from Moorgate).
Length:	3 miles (4.8km).
Time:	2½ hours.
Refreshments:	Plenty of pubs and takeaway cafés/restaurants at the start of the walk in Islington and at the end (lower quality) in Holloway Road. Otherwise a few pubs en route and a few cafés around Highbury and Islington station.
Note:	This walk is best done when the Camden Passage Market is open: Wednesday, Saturday and Sunday (antiques), Thursday (books).

Come out of Angel station onto Islington High Street. To the left the Angel road junction is the meeting place of five major roads. Historically, the Angel was the starting point of the Great North Road, the main road from London to York. Entering central London, the road split at the Angel: one road went to the City, another to Smithfield Market. The domed building on the right-hand side of the junction stands on the site of the Angel coaching inn, which gave its name to the junction. The inn was the first staging post on the road to the north.

Turn right along Islington High Street. Before the property developers took over, Islington was a great dairying centre, supplying the capital with much of its fresh milk. To Londoners it was also 'merry Islington', an area vying with Clerkenwell to the south as a playground for city-dwellers in search of fresh air, exercise and entertainment. Cricket grounds, bowling greens, tea gardens and spas could all be found in Islington in the 18th century. Over 100 feet (30m) above sea level, the village was a welcome refuge from the fogs and smogs of the city.

Antique activities

Keep to the right of the High Street and follow it when it veers to the right away from the main road, which becomes Upper Street. The High Street, together with Camden Passage ahead, is the nucleus of the antiques market. The market began in

73

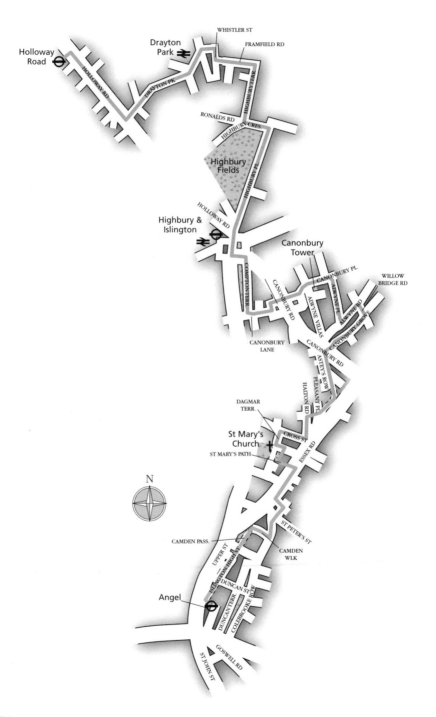

the early 1960s when antique collecting first became a popular activity. On the left, just before the passage widens in front of the Camden Head pub, No. 45 Camden Passage has a bust and plaque dedicated to an eccentric scholar and bookseller called Alexander Cruden. *The Biblical Concordance* he produced in 1761 – a system of finding a particular text in the Bible by means of a key word – is still a standard work of reference.

When you reach the Camden Head pub, turn right into the Colinsdale Estate, go left down either a ramp or steps, and then turn right through the car park and turn left. This side of the street is called Duncan Terrace after Admiral Duncan, fleet commander at the Battle of Camperdown in 1797 when the Dutch lost nine ships and the British none. The other side of the street (built around 1768, some decades before Duncan Terrace) is called Colebrooke Row after the Colebrooke family who were lords of the manor in the middle of the 18th century. The New River ran between these terraces, first as an open channel and then, from 1861, in underground pipes. The river's course today is marked by the strip gardens on your left.

At the end of Duncan Terrace on the left (just before Bridel Mews), there is a small, white, tree-hidden house with a plaque to Charles Lamb, East India Company official, critic and essayist, best known today for his *Essays of Elia*. The year these essays were published (1823) Lamb moved here to be near to his sister, who had been committed to the Islington madhouse after fatally stabbing their mother in a fit of insanity. Lamb was her legal guardian and occasionally brought her to his home whenever she was considered well enough to leave the asylum.

Cross St Peter's Street and follow Colebrooke Row round to the left onto Essex Road. Here turn right and walk along to the King's Head pub on the left. Go over the zebra crossing and walk up St Mary's Path by the side of the pub. Just before Church Cottage, turn right into the gardens behind St Mary's, the parish church of Islington.

Walk straight through the gardens into Dagmar Terrace, go through the archway and turn right into Cross Street, built around 1780. At Halton Road turn left and then first right into Halton Cross Street. Turn left into Astey's Row just before the Thatched House pub. Now you pick up the course of the New River once again.

The tale of the New River

The New River was a man-made channel, 10 feet (3m) wide and 4 feet (1m) deep, which conveyed fresh spring water from villages near Ware in Hertfordshire to the City. Completed in 1613 it was the main source of drinking water for north London and the City until superseded around 1990 by the London Tunnel Ring Main. Originally, the New River fed reservoirs at New River Head (see the Clerkenwell walk, page 122) but after World War II it was shut off just north of Islington at Stoke Newington (where it still brings water to reservoirs). Long before then sections of the river running through newly developed Islington were piped in and covered up. This section by Astey's Row was enclosed in 1893. When the flow was disconnected the pipes were dug up and the ground made into gardens, as in Colebrooke Row. The man behind this early example of commercial enterprise and civil engineering skill was City banker and MP Hugh Myddelton (there is a statue of him on Islington Green). At first capital proved hard to raise and King James I had to take a 50 per cent share in the New River Company to get the project going. But over the long term shareholders made fortunes. In 1893 one of the original 72 shares was sold for nearly £95,000. The operations of the New River Company were transferred to the Metropolitan Water Board in 1904.

When you get to Canonbury Road walk over the zebra crossing by the Myddleton (*sic*) Arms and go into Canonbury Grove, built in 1823. Here the strip gardens by the New River resume, but they are better landscaped and far better kept than the section by Astey's Row. Turn into the gardens and walk along the meandering path by the side of the river (actually duck ponds made to look like the river). There's an information panel about the New River on the right and, shortly after, an 18th-century hut used by a watchman whose job was to prevent bathing and fishing. The length of the river by the hut, still lined with (restored) wooden revetments, is the only part of the original watercourse to survive in Islington.

Monks and merchants

At the end of Canonbury Grove the gardens continue in Douglas Road, but the walk turns left over Willow Bridge (Canonbury Grove used to be called Willow Cottages and Willow Terrace) and left into Alwyne Road. Turn right into Alwyne Place, its entrance flanked by white and pink cottages. All the houses here were built in the 1840s and 1850s on Canonbury Field. At the top of Alwyne Place, turn left into Canonbury Place and walk along to an old house on the left called Canonbury Tower, on the corner with Alwyne Villas. Alwyne was one of the names of the second Marquess of Northampton.

Now leased to a theatre company, the Canonbury Tower once stood on its own on the top of a hill and for centuries was an important local landmark. In the Middle Ages the estate was owned by the Augustinian canons of St Bartholomew's Priory in Clerkenwell, after whom Canonbury is named. William Bolton, last prior of St Bartholomew's, built the Tower in the early 1500s as a manor house. After the Priory was dissolved in 1539 the estate was bought by Sir John Spencer, a rich but mean City cloth merchant who was Lord Mayor in 1594. Spencer's daughter and heiress Elizabeth eloped from the Tower with Lord Compton after being lowered from an upper-storey window in a bread basket. Lord Compton's descendants, the Marquesses of Northampton, still own the Tower, even though they have not lived here since the 1600s. Around 1770 a stockbroker called John Dawes was tenant of the Tower. He demolished some of the monastic buildings and built Canonbury House round the corner, as well as Nos. 1–5 in Canonbury Place on the far side of Canonbury House (the date 1780 is visible at the top of their drainpipes).

Continue along Canonbury Place and enter Canonbury Square: Evelyn Waugh lived here in 1928, as did George Orwell in 1945. Walk along the right-hand side of the square and follow it round to the left. Turn right into Canonbury Lane and then take the second turning on the right into Compton Terrace. Canonbury Square and Compton Terrace were built soon after 1800 by Henry Leroux. Go down the steps at the end of the terrace, go over the zebra crossing to the left and then turn right. Highbury and Islington station is round the corner to the left in Holloway Road.

All ranks and degrees

Cross Holloway Road into Highbury Place and walk along the broad walk parallel with the row of Georgian terraced houses on the right (built in 1774–79). No. 1 is where the British Impressionist painter Walter Sickert ran his painting and engraving school in the 1920s and 1930s. John Nichols, historian of literary life in the 18th century, lived at No. 14 from 1803 until his death in 1820. No. 15 was the home of Joseph Chamberlain, father of 1930s' prime minister Neville Chamberlain. After the Great

Fire of 1666 the diarist John Evelyn saw in Highbury Fields (the park on the left) a crowd of as many as '200,000 people of all ranks and degrees dispersed and lying along by their heapes of what they could save from the fire, deploring their losses, and though ready to perish for hunger and destitution, yet not asking one penny for relief'.

When you get to Highbury Crescent bisecting Highbury Fields turn left and then right along hilltop Highbury Terrace, built in 1789. From the top of Framfield Road at the end of Highbury Terrace you can see right across the 'hollow way' of Holloway to the wooded heights of Hampstead Heath beyond.

From this point there are two ways to finish the walk. You can continue to Drayton Park station (5 minutes' walk) or Holloway Road station (15 minutes' walk). Alternatively you can retrace your steps to Highbury and Islington station. To get to Drayton Park station and Holloway Road station go down Framfield Road and through the passage at the end. Then turn right and left in Whistler Street and left onto Drayton Park. Drayton Park station is opposite. Follow the road round as it bends left and right as far as the junction with Holloway Road. Then turn right and walk towards the bridge. Holloway Road station is just before the bridge on the left.

❖❖

HIGHGATE TO HAMPSTEAD

❖❖

Summary: This is a long, hilly walk across London's Northern Heights. There are fine views from many places, especially from Parliament Hill (319 feet/97m) on Hampstead Heath. The walk starts in Highgate, crosses Hampstead Heath via the grounds of 18th-century **Kenwood House**, and finishes in Hampstead, one-time spa resort and favoured retreat for generations of artists and writers. The homes of poets Coleridge and Keats and artists Constable and Romney, amongst others, are passed on the walk. Other features include **Highgate Cemetery**, where Karl Marx is buried, and the National Trust's **Fenton House**.

Start:	Archway station (Northern Underground Line).
Finish:	Hampstead station (Northern Underground Line).
Length:	6 miles (9.6km).
Time:	4½ hours.
Refreshments:	Kenwood is the ideal place to stop because it is exactly at the halfway point. In Highgate, try the terrace café in Waterlow Park or the Prince of Wales and Flask pubs in Highgate village. In Hampstead, the Wells Tavern, Holly Bush pub on Holly Hill and the café in Burgh House are all recommended. All places are mentioned in the text.
Note:	Give yourself a day for this walk, breaking for lunch at Kenwood.

77

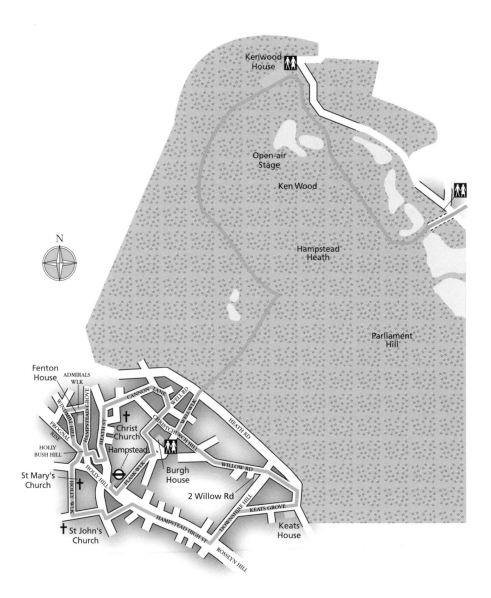

Leave Archway station by the 'Highgate Hill' exit, turn left and walk up Highgate Hill as far as the Whittington Stone pub. In front is the Whittington Stone where legend has it Dick Whittington heard Bow Bells calling him back to become Lord Mayor of London. Turn left into Magdala Avenue and, at the end, turn left then right

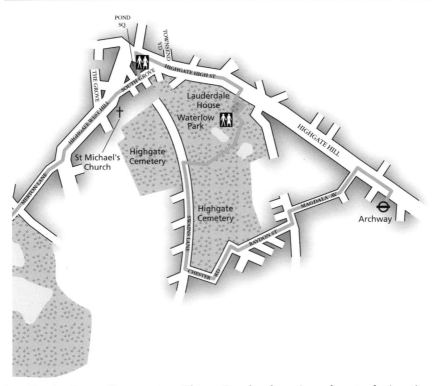

into Raydon Street. Carry on into Chester Road and continue along to the junction with Swain's Lane. The horror film-Gothic enclave on the left is called Holly Village, and was built in 1865 by the philanthropist and local landowner Baroness Burdett-Coutts for her estate workers.

Shrine of communism

Turn right up the hill until you come to the twin entrances to Highgate Cemetery, opened in 1839 and now covering 37 acres (15 ha) on both sides of the road. The western cemetery to the left is the earliest and most interesting from the point of view of its landscape and graves, but the right hosts the cemetery's most famous incumbent, Karl Marx.

Just beyond the cemetery turn right into Waterlow Park. Take the left-hand fork and then bear right through the line of trees. Cross the bridge over the terrace of pools linking the upper and lower lakes and then fork left (*not* sharp left along the lakeside). At the top of the bank turn left so that the brick wall is on your right, go to the end and then ascend onto the terrace of Lauderdale House. This 17th-century mansion was once the home of the Earl of Lauderdale and the summer retreat of Charles II's mistress, Nell Gwynn. It is now a centre for exhibitions, concerts and various other events. There is a café at the front with tables outside, and views to the west over the park.

Go round to the back of the house and through the gate onto Highgate Hill. Cross the road and turn left up the Bank, a short terrace of handsome old houses standing

79

well above street level. Turning round, there is a fine view down the hill and away over the City to the south. Continuing up the hill into the High Street of old Highgate village, archways lead off each side into yards, those on the right, particularly Townsend Yard, providing more panoramic views but this time to the east over Hornsey.

Useful and scientific knowledge

At the top of the High Street is the Gatehouse pub. The Bishop of London once owned a park up here and the pub stands on the site of one of the three gates that led into the park. The church on the right is the chapel of Highgate School, founded in 1565, which lies directly behind it. Cross the High Street here (the Prince of Wales pub is to the left) and go down a narrow passage just before No. 67 into Pond Square, once Highgate's village green. Turn left and cross the square to South Grove. No. 10a opposite is home to the Highgate Society, which organizes events for the local community. Next door, the Highgate Literary and Scientific Institution is a members-only club with a private library, reading room and meeting hall, founded in 1839 to promote 'useful and scientific knowledge'.

Turn right along South Grove and walk along to the junction with Highgate West Hill. Behind and to the right is the Flask pub, named after the flasks of Hampstead mineral water that could be bought here in the heyday of the Hampstead wells during the 18th century. Across West Hill is The Grove, Highgate's finest street. The nearest houses are the most attractive and also the oldest (they date from the 1680s). No. 3 was the home for 11 years of the poet Samuel Taylor Coleridge, author of *The Rime of the Ancient Mariner* (1798) and the opium-inspired *Kubla Khan* (1816), and much later of the writer J.B. Priestley. To the left of these houses there is a double gatehouse leading into the forecourt of Witanhurst, an enormous Edwardian mansion built by a soap magnate, billed as London's largest private house. On your left, the Old Hall and the parish church of **St Michael's** occupy a marvellous site where a great mansion called Arundel House once stood. The lawyer and philosopher Francis Bacon caught a fatal chill and died here in 1626 after making an early experiment in refrigeration by stuffing a chicken with snow.

Kenwood House

Continue on down the hill. Round the corner turn right into Merton Lane. At the bottom of the lane continue straight into the park ahead. This is Hampstead Heath, 800 hilly acres (324 ha) of mown grass, scrub and rough woodland, crisscrossed by muddy tracks and gravel and tarmac paths. Walk between the two ponds, bear right and, after 100 yards or so, take the right-hand fork. As you climb the hill on the far side of the stream you can see the main front of Witanhurst next to the church. Now you enter the woods and grounds of Kenwood House. The house itself, iced with brilliantly-painted stucco like an enormous cake, soon comes into view through the trees. A private house until as late as 1927, Kenwood is now a public museum with fine 18th-century Adam interiors and a notable collection of pictures bequeathed by its last owner, the Earl of Iveagh, head of the Guinness brewing family. There is a café at the house.

Follow the broad tarmac path along the terrace in front of the house, with the lawn sloping away to the lake on your left. At the end of the terrace, turn right through the gate back into Hampstead Heath and follow the path as it swings to the left. After quite a distance you will come to a gate in some railings. Go through the gate and bear left. Continue straight on for some way until you emerge from the trees and reach a gravel path crossing at right angles. There should be a clear view of Highgate to the left. The walk turns right here towards Hampstead, but if you have the energy you could make a 15-minute diversion to Parliament Hill for one of the best panoramic views of London. To get there, go straight on through the trees for some way. The viewpoint is easily identified by the benches standing out on the skyline.

Hampstead's health farm

To continue to Hampstead, stand on the gravel path with Highgate to your left, turn right down the hill, and then go up the other side to the main road (Heath Road). This is the western edge of Hampstead. Cross the road into Well Walk. Halfway along on the right a drinking fountain marks the site of the chalybeate spring that gave Well Walk its name and made Hampstead a popular spa resort in the early 1700s. After about a century the craze for drinking the waters died out and Hampstead was left to the artists, writers and intellectuals who had already begun to settle there in search of peace, solitude and fresh air. On the left, No. 40 Well Walk was the family home of the painter John Constable from 1827 until his death 10 years later.

At the Wells Tavern turn left down Christchurch Hill. Continue into Willow Road. On the right, No. 2 is the former home of architect Ernö Goldfinger. Designed and built by him in 1939 as part of a terrace of three, it is one of the most important examples of modernist architecture in Britain. There is a long-distance view of another of Goldfinger's best-known buildings later in the walk. Cross Downshire Hill and go round the corner of South End Road into Keats Grove on the right. John Keats, the Romantic poet, lived in the white house on the left and wrote some of his best work here, including his famous *Ode to a Nightingale*.

Continue along Keats Grove into Downshire Hill, which some say is Hampstead's grandest street. At the top of the street turn right into Rosslyn Hill, leading into Hampstead High Street. Beyond the King William IV pub on the left take the second turning on the left off the High Street under an archway into Perrins Court. At the end turn right and then left into Church Row, certainly Hampstead's most historic street. It was built in the early 1700s, just as the spa was becoming popular and not long after William of Orange became king, hence the Dutch style of the houses – tall and narrow with an abundance of glass, very similar to houses in the older parts of Amsterdam.

Authors and artists

As the street widens, it frames Hampstead's parish church of **St John's** (1745) at the end. John Constable the painter is buried in the churchyard (tomb location signposted). Keep to the right here and then turn right up Holly Walk, with the 1811 churchyard extension on your right. Further along on the right is St Mary's Catholic Church with a statue of the Virgin Mary in the blue niche above the door. Opened in 1816 for the use of French emigrés, it was tucked away in this remote spot because Catholics did not enjoy full freedom of worship at this time. At the top of Holly Walk turn right by a house where Robert Louis Stevenson, author of *Treasure Island*, once stayed, into Mount Vernon and follow the lane down to the left to the green on Holly Bush Hill. Go straight across into Windmill Hill (*not* down the slope of Frognal Rise to the left) and follow the road as it winds round to Lower Terrace. On the opposite side of the green, the terraced cottage with the blue door (No. 2) was another of John Constable's homes in Hampstead. He lived here in the 1820s making endless studies of the clouds and atmospheric effects of the big Hampstead skies.

Naval victories

Just before the green, turn right into Admiral's Walk. Round the corner is Grove Lodge, where John Galsworthy wrote most of *The Forsyte Saga* (1922). Next to Grove Lodge is Admiral's House. This house was never actually lived in by an admiral, but it does have a 'quarter-deck' from which – in the 18th century – an enthusiastic naval tenant used to fire cannons to celebrate naval victories. The prolific 19th-century architect Sir George Gilbert Scott later lived here.

Admiral's Walk joins Hampstead Grove, running left and right. Up to the left the Whitestone Pond and the former Jack Straw's Castle pub crown the highest point in London – 440 feet (134m) above sea level. The walk, however, turns to the right and passes on the left the house of George du Maurier, author of *Trilby* (1894), and on the right the National Trust's Fenton House, built by a City merchant in 1693, as it descends the hill to Holly Hill green once more. On the left, just beyond the painter George Romney's house, turn left into Holly Mount, a quiet hill-top backwater with a good pub, the Holly Bush, and more good views of the City and West London from the viewpoint at the end of the street. Conspicuous away to the right is Ernö Goldfinger's Trellick Tower, a once detested but now highly desirable apartment block in North Kensington.

West Country tales

From the viewpoint, descend the steps leading to Heath Street and turn left, going over the road on the zebra crossing. Continue up the hill and turn right by the Friends' Meeting House at the junction with Hampstead Square. Continue on into Cannon Place. Sir Flinders Petrie, the first scientific excavator of ancient Egypt, lived at No. 5 on the left. At the end of the street on the right, Cannon Hall was the home of the actor-manager Sir Gerald du Maurier, son of George, mentioned previously, and father of Daphne du Maurier, author of *Rebecca* and other famous West Country tales, who grew up here. Long before, Cannon Hall was a magistrate's house with its own gaol built into the garden wall. You pass the entrance to it after turning right beyond the hall into Cannon Lane, leading down to Well Road.

Turn right into Well Road, cross Christchurch Hill and turn left into New End Square. Further down on the left, **Burgh House** plays a central part in both Hampstead's history and its contemporary life. Built in 1703, it was the home of Dr William Gibbons, the first man to draw attention to the medicinal qualities of Hampstead's spa water and the early spa's official physician. Today it is Hampstead's community centre and local-history museum.

Past Burgh House, turn right into Flask Walk, named after the old Flask Tavern where spa water was bottled for sale in London. Funnily enough, the street is shaped rather like a bottle, wide at the bottom and narrow at the neck where it joins Hampstead High Street. Turn right out of Flask Walk onto Hampstead High Street. The walk ends at Hampstead station round the corner to the right.

SOHO TO TRAFALGAR SQUARE

Summary: Soho's image as London's red light district is fading but sex is still a major enterprise in the area. The other industries are films, music, eating and drinking – all of which reflect the cosmopolitan mix of people (mainly French Huguenots) who have lived in Soho since the first houses were built in the 1670s. The main features of the walk in Soho are its two squares (Soho and Golden), Berwick Street Market, Broadwick Street (a landmark in medical history), the birthplace of the poet William Blake and the Sixties' hangover, Carnaby Street. During the walk, you will also see **Pollock's Toy Museum**, Chinatown, John Nash's Haymarket Theatre and Royal Opera Arcade, the **National Gallery** and Nelson's Column, the last two in Trafalgar Square.

Start:	Goodge Street station (Northern Underground Line).
Finish:	Charing Cross station (Northern, Bakerloo and Jubilee Underground Lines).
Length:	2½ miles (4km).
Time:	1½–2 hours.
Refreshments:	Plenty of places en route, particularly at the halfway stage around Soho and Chinatown. These are par excellence places for eating and drinking, so take your pick. There are several pavement restaurants in Charlotte Street just before you enter Soho proper.
Note:	The Royal Opera Arcade is closed on Sundays, in which case carry on past the entrance, turn left into Regent Street and then turn left at the bottom of the street into Pall Mall.

Turn left out of Goodge Street station and then left again opposite Heal's furniture shop into Tottenham Street. The five-storey mural on the right, commissioned by the local council and painted in 1980, depicts characters and scenes from the local Fitzrovia community, named after Fitzroy Square to the right, near Euston Road. Rising up behind the mural is the BT telecommunications tower.

Take the first turning on the left into Whitfield Street. On the right now are Pollock's Theatrical Print Warehouse and, next to it in a crazy old house on the corner of Scala Street, Pollock's Toy Museum. Benjamin Pollock, who died in 1937, was one of the last producers of toy theatre scenery. The museum was added in the 1950s as an attraction to the shop and is worth seeing both for its contents and for its original 1760s' interior.

Walk along Whitfield Street past Cyberia, Britain's first internet café, and cross Goodge Street. Turn right by the garden into Colville Place and then left into Charlotte Street, which is lined with restaurants and wine bars, much like Soho. Just

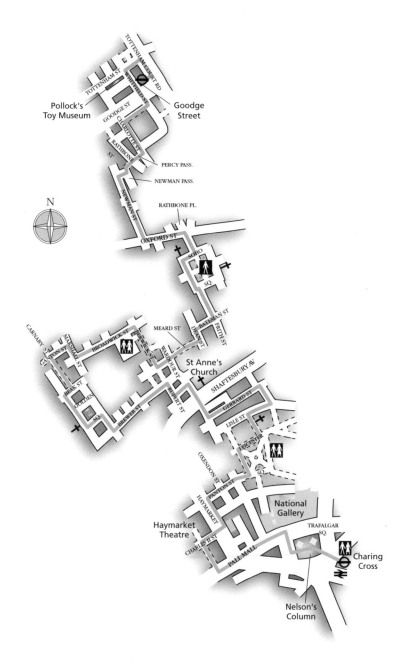

beyond Windmill Street on the left, turn right into Percy Passage, cross Rathbone Street and enter Newman Passage next to the Newman Arms pub.

The sights of Soho

At the end of Newman Passage turn left into Newman Street, centre of the textile and fashion industries, and walk down to the junction with Oxford Street. Turn left here. Thomas Edison opened his first Kinetoscope Parlour, forerunner of the cinema, on the left in 1894 (see the plaque on No. 76). When you get to Rathbone Place on the left (notice the street sign dated 1718) turn right into Soho Street and then right again into Soho Square. This is one of two squares in Soho and was built in the 1680s in open fields on the northern boundary of London. The area was once a royal hunting ground (there's a 17th-century statue of Charles II in the centre of the square), and 'Soho' was an old hunting cry. The first residents of the square were aristocrats like the Earl of Carlisle. Soon, however, Huguenot refugees from France invaded the area, the first of a series of foreign influxes that have made Soho the colourful and cosmopolitan quarter it is today.

The French Protestant Church on your right has been the centre of Huguenot life since the first refugees arrived in London in the 1550s, although the congregation did not physically come to the square until 1893. Walk around the square, crossing Carlisle Street. On the right in the corner ahead there is a stone in the wall marking the site of a house where a group of early botanists once lived, and where the Linnean Society (a botanical society founded in 1788 and still active today) met from 1821 to 1857. Twentieth Century Fox now has offices on this site.

Continue around the square and turn right into Frith Street, the first of the two streets leading out of the south side of the square. The other is Greek Street, named after the Greek Christians who settled in Soho in the 17th century. On the left is Hazlitt's Hotel, the house where writer William Hazlitt died in 1830.

When you get to Bateman Street, at the end of Frith Street, look to the left at Portland House, the white house facing you. Wedgwood, makers of the famous blue china, had their London showroom here from 1774 until 1795, when they moved to more up-market premises in St James's Square. Now turn right into Bateman Street, left into Dean Street and then right again into Meard Street, built in the 1720s though its original street sign is dated 1732.

Votes for kisses

Go across Wardour Street, the centre of the film and music business, into Peter Street. The Intrepid Fox pub on the corner bears a large relief of a scene from the fiercely contested Westminster election of 1784, with the charismatic Charles James Fox (son of a lord and champion of the people) as the candidate, and honest Sam House, the pub's landlord, as his enthusiastic supporter. Fox only won the election after enlisting the help of the beautiful Duchess of Devonshire and other great ladies who gave kisses to all the tradesmen in return for votes. Turn first right out of Peter Street into Berwick Street.

Berwick Street Market (Monday to Saturday) is reputed to have the best-quality fruit and vegetables of any street market in London. Turn left at the end of the market into Broadwick Street. Formerly called Broad Street, this was the centre of an outbreak of cholera in 1854 which killed over 10,000 people, including the occupants of 37 out of the 49 houses in this street. Many more people would have died had not the local medical officer, Dr John Snow, realized that all victims of the disease had been drinking from the same street pump. When the pump handle was removed the death rate promptly fell. Snow's discovery – that cholera is water-borne – is one of the most important in medical history. A replica of the pump stands at the junction with Poland Street and a reddish kerbstone outside the John Snow pub ahead marks the pump's actual site.

Blake's birthplace

Opposite the pub, No. 54 has a plaque to Charles Bridgman, gardener to the first two King Georges and inventor of the ha-ha, a type of sunken fence. Continue along Broadwick Street and at Marshall Street turn right. A large sign on the right marks the place of birth in 1757 of the poet and visionary artist, William Blake. Turn first left into Ganton Street and go past the entrance to cobbled Newburgh Street. Then turn left into Carnaby Street, still home to the boutiques that made it the centre of Swinging London in the 1960s. At the entrance to Broadwick Street on the left a huge modern mural depicts people and events from Soho's colourful past.

From Carnaby Street, turn right into Beak Street and first left into Upper John Street. This leads into Golden Square, its name a corruption of 'gelding'; geldings were once grazed in fields on this site. Walk along the right-hand side of the square, which was popular with embassies in the 18th century. The Portuguese embassy was at Nos. 23 and 24 on the right during the 1740s and the embassy chapel (accessed from Warwick Street) is still a Roman Catholic church. Badly damaged in the anti-Catholic Gordon Riots of 1780 and subsequently rebuilt, this is the only Catholic embassy chapel in London to survive from the period before Catholic emancipation in 1829.

Follow the square around to the left (the statue in the middle is of George II) and turn right into Lower James Street. Turn left into Brewer Street, walking until you come to Rupert Street Market. Turn right here, then take the second turn on the left into Winnett Street. Turn right into Wardour Street, passing on the left St Anne's, the parish church of Soho, only the tower of which escaped bombing in World War II. Over 10,000 corpses in the now-disused graveyard have raised it as much as 6 feet (2m) above the pavement.

Oriental history

At the bottom of Wardour Street cross Shaftesbury Avenue, leaving Soho and entering London's Chinatown. Take the second turning on the left into Chinatown's main street, Gerrard Street, with its Chinese entrance arches, street names in Chinese characters and oriental-style telephone booths.

Leave Gerrard Street, turning right into Newport Place and then right again into Lisle Street. When you reach the Chinese supermarket on the right, look up to the pediment above. 'New Lisle Street' and the 1791 date refer to the extension of existing Lisle Street in that year, made possible by the demolition of Leicester House, one of London's largest houses. As you turn left into Leicester Place, leading to Leicester Square, you are actually walking through the marble-floored hall of the house, out of the front door, and across the gravelled forecourt into what was then called Leicester Fields. During the 1700s, George, Prince of Wales, lived in Leicester House having been evicted from St James's Palace after a quarrel with his father.

Hay and straw market

Turn right into Leicester Square. For a century this has been a major centre of popular entertainment, first music halls and now clubs and cinemas. Turn left down the west side. Sir Joshua Reynolds, England's leading portrait painter in the 18th century, lived at No. 48. Leave the square from the bottom right-hand corner. Walk along Panton Street, crossing Whitcomb Street and Oxendon Street, and then turn left down Haymarket. Until 1830 Haymarket was, quite literally, the site of a hay and straw market supplying nearby stables and the Royal Mews. Towards the bottom on the left is the Haymarket Theatre, with its grand portico jutting out over the pavement. Designed by John Nash in 1820, this is the oldest theatre in London.

Opposite the theatre, turn right into Charles II Street. Halfway along cross over and go through the archway at the back of Her Majesty's Theatre into the Royal Opera Arcade. Built 1816-18 by Nash along the back of what was then the main opera house in London, this is the oldest of London's five 19th-century shopping arcades. Around the other three sides of the theatre were colonnades open to the street. A fire in 1867 seriously damaged the theatre and in 1891 it was demolished, with only Nash's arcade, which had survived the fire, being retained. By this time Covent Garden had established itself as London's new royal opera house (see the Covent Garden walk, page 95).

Turn left out of the arcade onto Pall Mall. Opposite is the Nash-designed Institute of Directors, a businessmen's association, with a fine frieze beautifully set off by its blue background. Walk along Pall Mall towards the domed National Gallery, built in 1838 on the site of the old Royal Mews. **St Martin's-in-the-Fields** Church is beyond. Cross the road at the traffic lights beside the new Sainsbury wing of the National Gallery and go into Trafalgar Square, also dating from 1838. Admiral Nelson, victor of the Battle of Trafalgar in 1805, gazes towards Big Ben and the central spire of the Houses of Parliament from the top of his 145-foot (44-m) granite column, erected in 1842. In front, isolated on a tiny traffic island, King Charles I on horseback also faces down Whitehall, but he is looking straight at the Banqueting House where, in 1649, he was beheaded. To the right, Admiralty Arch marks the beginning of the Mall leading to Buckingham Palace. Both the Arch and the Mall are part of the national memorial to Queen Victoria, who died in 1901. To your left, the Strand connects with Charing Cross Road at the point from which all road distances to and from central London are measured. On the Trafalgar Square side of the junction you can see a small round building with a lamp on top. This was once Britain's smallest police station, with its own telephone line to Scotland Yard. Nearby is a subway leading to Charing Cross station where the walk ends.

❖❖❖

NOTORIOUS SOHO

❖❖❖

Summary: This circular walk covers some of the same ground as the Soho to Trafalgar Square walk, but focuses exclusively on Soho's notorious past. Given that Soho emerged from the 1920s onwards as London's main red light district and then became in the 1940s and '50s the stage on which London's two main gangland bosses fought out their battle for underworld domination, that past is particularly rich. On the walk you will see plenty of places associated with 20th-century crime and vice (including the location of the 1952 Great Mail Van Robbery, the biggest robbery in British history until the 1963 Great Train Robbery), but also the sites of many earlier notorious events and institutions, such as the greatest homosexual scandal of the Victorian era and the flagellation brothel where the Berkeley Horse was invented.

Start and finish:	Tottenham Court Road station (Northern and Central Underground Lines).
Length:	1¾ miles (2.8km).
Time:	1½ hours
Refreshments:	There's no shortage of places in Soho, which is celebrated for its restaurants. At the halfway stage the walk passes Kettner's and the famous Coach and Horses pub in Romilly Street. Then comes Gerrard Street, the heart of Chinatown, with its many Chinese restaurants. Charlotte Street, near the end of the walk – not actually in Soho but culturally part of it – is also well known for its bars and restaurants.

Leave Tottenham Court Road station by the exit marked 'No 1 Exit, Oxford Street South Side', and turn right on Oxford Street. At the lights turn right into Charing Cross Road, passing on the right the Harmony sex shop, billed as Europe's largest licensed sex centre. Carry on for a little way and then turn right, by the Astoria, into Sutton Row. On the corner opposite the Astoria the Ann Summers shop is probably the best-known brand in the multi-million-pound sex empire created by brothers Ralph and David Gold. Besides Birmingham City Football Club, the Golds own downmarket papers like the *Daily Sport* and *Sunday Sport* and men's magazines such as *Playbirds* and *Park Lane*. The brothers got into the sex business after their mother Rose began selling 'pin-up' magazines from the shop in the front room of her East End house.

At the end of Sutton Row you come to Soho Square. At No. 21, the corner house on the right, there was, in the late 18th century, a notorious upper-class brothel known as the White House, or Hooper's Hotel, after its proprietor, Thomas Hooper. Flagellation is said to have been a speciality of the house, and the Prince of Wales, later George IV, is reputed to have been a customer. On the other side of Sutton Row, St Patrick's Catholic Church stands on the site of 18th-century Carlisle House, where Italian adventuress Theresa Cornelys hosted her lavish subscription masquerades in the 1760s. Popular with the upper classes, these were ideal for flirtations and sometimes more compromising encounters. Mrs Cornelys went bankrupt in 1772 and died a debtor in the City's Fleet prison a quarter of a century later.

Turn left by the church and then leave the square from the south side via Greek Street. When you get to the junction with Bateman Street you can see the sign for Greek Street's L'Escargot restaurant, ahead on the right. Just beyond L'Escargot is No. 47, where master of seduction Giacomo Casanova lodged in 1764. Mrs Cornelys had been a conquest of his before she came to England, and they had had a daughter, who lived with Mrs Cornelys's mother. Mrs Cornelys's son by her husband, meanwhile, lived with Casanova on the Continent. In 1763 Mrs Cornelys asked Casanova to bring her son to England, hence his visit. He stayed eight months but was in Greek Street for only a short while before his hurried departure – penniless – on 11 March. If he had stayed he would probably have been hanged for forgery.

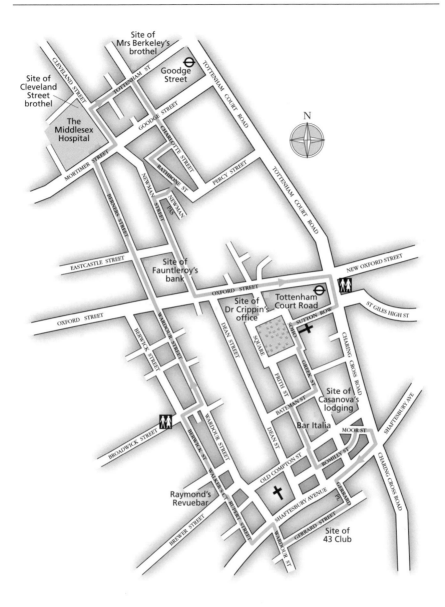

Turn right, into Bateman Street, and first left into Frith Street. Walk on down until you get to the Bar Italia on the left at 22 Frith Street (it has a large clock on the front). The so-called Battle of Frith Street started here on 11 August 1955 when gangster Jack Spot assaulted bookie Albert Dimes as a revenge attack on Billy Hill, Dimes's boss and Spot's rival for control of the London underworld. Wounded and bleeding, Dimes staggered towards Old Compton Street, taking refuge in the Continental Fruit Stores on the corner (now La Crêperie). The fight continued inside, with the proprietor's 13-stone wife belabouring the antagonists with a steel scoop. After a spell in hospital both men recovered, but the encounter is said to have contributed to Dimes's early death, aged 57, in 1972.

Looking to the right around the corner into Old Compton Street, you can see the Play 2 Win amusement arcade. On 4 September 1974, when it was called the Golden Goose, contract killer George Piggot, former henchman of notorious Notting Hill slum landlord Peter Rachman, who had died in 1962, walked in and shot dead Alfredo 'Italian Toni' Zomparelli. Zomparelli had just completed a prison sentence for killing 23-year-old David Knight at the Latin Quarter Club in Wardour Street (passed later in the walk) four years earlier. When Piggot confessed to Zomparelli's murder in 1979, Knight's elder brother Ronald, Soho club-owner and husband of the famous *Carry On* and *Eastenders* star Barbara Windsor, was tried for putting him up to it. He was acquitted in 1980. Piggot never revealed the true identity of his client, so who ordered the murder and why remain unknown.

Godfather of Soho

Cross Old Compton Street and continue along Frith Street, turning first left into Romilly Street. Cross Greek Street. Just beyond the Coach and Horses pub on the left is the original 34 Romilly Street where the so-called Godfather of Soho, Bernie Silver, and his partner, Big Frank Mifsud, ran their vice empire in the 1950s and 1960s. At that time Soho was known as 'the square mile of vice'. Silver and Mifsud's organization, the Syndicate, was by far the biggest player in the vice trade. Police reckoned, somewhat incredibly, that during its 15-year life it made £100,000 a week. Today the seedy-looking building is still part of the sex trade, as a quick glance at the names on the two doorbells indicates – Monique and Brigitte, French models.

Carry on along Romilly Street to Cambridge Circus and turn right in front of the Palace Theatre into Shaftesbury Avenue. Shaftesbury Avenue was cut through the heart of Soho in the 1880s, obliterating King Street in the process. On 10 May 1853 the Chancellor of the Exchequer, William Gladstone, got into a spot of bother here, having 'rescued' a prostitute in Long Acre and brought her back to her King Street lodgings. (The precise nature and purpose of Gladstone's nocturnal social work among London's prostitutes is still a contentious subject.) As they approached the girl's house a young man stepped out of the shadows and threatened to reveal that the Chancellor had picked up a prostitute – unless Gladstone either gave him some money or got him a job in the Inland Revenue. Gladstone refused and the case came to court. The would-be blackmailer was sentenced to a year's hard labour, but Gladstone generously arranged for his release six months early.

From Shaftesbury Avenue, turn left into Gerrard Place and then right into Gerrard Street. In the hedonistic days of the 1920s when Soho was just beginning to acquire its reputation as London's main red light district, the Loon Fung supermarket, on the left at 43 Gerrard Street, was the 43 Club, flagship of the notorious Kate Meyrick's night-club empire. When Mrs Meyrick's marriage to a Dublin doctor failed she brought her eight children to London and plunged into the burgeoning night-club business to earn a living. Although brilliantly successful and popular with the Bright Young Things, who enjoyed mixing with Soho's dangerous low life in her clubs, she frequently clashed with the police, and went to prison several times, usually for after-hours drinking but latterly for the more serious offence of bribing the local sergeant. However, she did manage to educate all her children privately and marry three daughters into the aristocracy.

Opposite the 43 Club, Chinese businessman and drug dealer 'Brilliant' Chang, real name Chan Nan, a 1920s Soho figure as notorious as Mrs Meyrick, ran the Palm Court Club, where he purveyed cocaine and heroin mainly to young women, whom he is said to have deliberately converted into addicts. Following a raid on his Limehouse hideaway, he was arrested in 1924, imprisoned for 14 months and then deported.

Carry on to the end of Gerrard Street. The Latin Quarter night-club, where David Knight was killed, was down Wardour Street to your left, on the far side at No. 13. The Knights had gone to the club to find Johnny Isaacs, who had taken part in an attack on David at a pub in Islington. Isaacs wasn't there but Zomparelli was. A fight started and Knight was stabbed to death. It later turned out that the club had been paying protection money to Knight.

Blackmailing gangs
Turn right into Wardour Street. On the right is Dansey Place. Between the world wars there was a cast-iron urinal here which was the most notorious 'cottage' (gay men's meeting place) in the West End. Called Clarkson's Cottage, after Willy Clarkson's theatrical costume shop across the road (the building with the clock on the front), it was a popular target for blackmailing gangs. Shortly after World War I a wealthy habitué is said to have been taken for £100,000. After World War II an American with fond memories bought Clarkson's Cottage and re-erected it in the grounds of his country house outside New York. It may still be there.

Sex trade
Continue to the end of Wardour Street, cross Shaftesbury Avenue and turn left. When you get to Rupert Street turn right and walk up to the junction with Brewer Street. You are now in the centre of modern Soho's licensed sex trade. Comparatively tame and small-scale compared with what it was in the 1970s when corrupt police turned a blind eye to the activities of Soho's porn barons, it consists mainly of a few sex shops, peep shows, strip clubs and video outlets. Until 2004, Walker's Court, ahead, was home to one of the oldest and certainly the most famous of Soho's strip clubs, The Raymond Revuebar, opened in April 1958 by 33-year-old Paul Raymond. In the 1960s the club made Raymond a fortune, enabling him to move into magazine publishing (titles like *Men Only* and *Club International*) and property in the 1970s; in 1990 he bought *Mayfair*, another well known men's magazine. Today Raymond owns much of Soho, including most of Brewer Street, and is said to be worth some £350m, making him one of the richest people in the country. Not bad for the son of a Liverpool lorry driver and former variety performer with a mind-reading act.

Walk through Walker's Court and cross Peter Street into Berwick Street. Somewhere here in 1751 Mrs Jane Goadby opened a brand new kind of brothel, different from anything then on offer in London. Based on the best Paris establishments, which were a cut above their rivals across the Channel, it featured beautiful and healthy girls dressed in fine clothes and presented in luxury surroundings suitable for the high-class clientele. A house surgeon was on hand to ensure that the girls remained in the peak of condition. Mrs Goadby prospered, expanding into a neighbouring house in 1754 and moving to grander premises in nearby Great Marlborough Street in 1760. After three decades as a madam she is said to have retired on the profits of her trade to a fine house in the country.

When you get to Broadwick Street, turn right and then first left into Wardour Street. The modern shop-and-office building on the left stands on the site of 153 Wardour Street, where on 10 February 1942 ex-actress Nita Ward was found dead in her flat. Her throat had been slashed and her body mutilated with a tin-opener. In succeeding days two other women were murdered in the West End, both strangled and mutilated with a razor. Two of these three women were prostitutes. That fact, plus the mutilations, led to fears that another Jack the Ripper was on the loose. For some time Soho prostitutes went in fear of their lives, until eventually police linked RAF cadet George Cummins, arrested for an attack on a woman outside a pub, with the murders. He was executed on 25 June 1942 for the murder of four women.

All Nighters Club

Carry on up Wardour Street. It was at the All Nighters Club in this street (the club is not listed in the phone books or directories of the time, so it has not been possible to establish its precise location) that two Notting Hill criminals, Lucky Gordon and Johnny Edgecombe, had a fight over Christine Keeler, an ex-girlfriend of both men, in the early hours of 28 October 1962. Gordon's badly slashed face required 17 stitches. This was the first in a series of incidents that culminated in the notorious Profumo Affair of 1963 when War Minister John Profumo resigned after it became known that he had slept with Keeler, a girl who was also the mistress of the Russian military attaché.

Mrs Bang

At the end of Wardour Street, cross Oxford Street into Berners Street. Ahead, on the right, the entrance to the Berners Hotel's Reflections restaurant stands on the site of 6 Berners Street, where the bank of Marsh, Sibbald and Co. was based from its foundation in 1782. When one of the bank's major customers went bankrupt in 1815, managing partner Henry Fauntleroy illegally sold other customers' stocks and shares in order to keep the bank afloat. Having discovered how easy fraud was, he carried on, using it to fund his secret life as a keeper of mistresses. One of these was the notorious woman-of-pleasure Mary Bertram, otherwise known as Mrs Bang. Because Fauntleroy continued to pay out dividends, his crime went undetected until 1824, by which time many small tradesmen and others had been ruined. After a sensational trial, he was hanged for forgery at Newgate on 30 November 1824 in front of a crowd estimated at 100,000.

Great Mail Van Robbery

Just beyond the Berners Hotel you come to Eastcastle Street, the scene of the robbery at 4.17am on 21 May 1952, when Soho underworld boss Billy Hill's gang hijacked a Post Office mail van carrying money from Paddington railway station to St Martin's-Le-Grand post office in the City. Meticulously planned and executed with ruthless efficiency, it netted £287,000, making Hill a wealthy man and heralding the start of what was called 'project crime'. Until another similar crime nine years later – the much more famous and lucrative Great Train Robbery – the Great Mail Van Robbery of 1952 was the biggest robbery in British criminal history.

Cross Eastcastle Street and carry on along Berners Street. The huge Sanderson building on the left covers the site of 54 Berners Street, scene of the 19th century's most notorious hoax. After he had bet his friend Samuel Beazley that he could make any quite ordinary London address the most talked about in the city, practical joker Theodore Hook decided to make an example of 54 Berners Street, the home of Mrs Tottenham, a lady who had somehow offended him. Over a period of six weeks he wrote some 4,000 letters asking all manner of tradesmen, professionals and public figures to call on Mrs Tottenham on a certain day in November 1809. On the day in question, Berners Street was packed all day long with a dense throng of horses, carts and people all trying to get to No. 54. The Governor of the Bank of England was among them, as were the Lord Mayor of London, the Chairman of the East India Company, the Archbishop of Canterbury and the royal Duke of Gloucester. Then, at 5pm, responding to ads in the papers, hundreds of unemployed servants arrived seeking positions. It took the police until late at night to clear up the confusion. The hoax duly made 54 Berners Street the talk of the capital, and Hook of course won his bet.

Going to bed with gentlemen

Continue along Berners Street. At the top, turn right into Mortimer Street, then left into Cleveland Street, and walk along to the junction with Tottenham Street. On the left, the private wing (Woolavington Wing) of the Middlesex Hospital stands on the site of 19 Cleveland Street. In 1889 when it was a male brothel, this address became the focal point of the most notorious homosexual scandal of the Victorian era. Following a theft investigation at a City post office, it was discovered that telegraph boys from the office were being paid 'for going to bed with gentlemen' at the brothel. These gentlemen apparently included Lord Arthur Somerset, son of the Duke of Beaufort and an intimate of the Prince of Wales, Lord Euston, son of the Duke of Grafton, and a Colonel Jervoise. Suspicion also hovered around the Prince of Wales's eldest son, Prince Eddy. The *North London Press* subsequently got hold of the story, claiming that the brothel proprietor had been allowed to escape and two of the boys had been given relatively mild prison sentences in order to cover up the scandal and its connection with the royal family. Lord Arthur Somerset retired into self-imposed exile on the French Riviera, where he remained until his death in 1930, but Lord Euston stayed and successfully sued for libel. The paper's editor was jailed for a year.

Too young to hang

Turn right into Tottenham Street and walk to the junction with Charlotte Street. The Margaret Pyke Centre on the left corner stands where Jay's the Jewellers was in 1947. Three armed robbers held it up on 29 April that year. Staff foiled the robbery and the gang fled on foot, their getaway car having been blocked in by a lorry. A father of six, 34-year-old Alex de Antiquis, drove his motorcycle in front of them to try to stop them, but was fatally shot in the head for his pains. The three robbers were subsequently sentenced to death, but one was too young to hang. Of the two executed, one – 23-year-old Harry Jenkins – was involved in, but not charged with, the death of Captain Ralph Binney in 1944 in another violent getaway (see page 145). On this occasion Jenkins did not fire the fatal shot, but he was hanged nonetheless, partly to discourage the increasing use of firearms in the underworld. The underworld duly got the message, and police apparently began finding discarded guns all over the place.

Opposite the Margaret Pyke Centre, 64 Charlotte Street (the Hogarth Studios) was – or at least an earlier building on the site was – once the most notorious flagellation brothel in London. Opened by Mrs Theresa Berkeley in 1828, it was a place where you could be whipped, beaten, pricked, curry-combed, scrubbed and half-strangled to your heart's content if you so desired – provided, of course, you had the wherewithal. Mrs B's particular claim to fame, and the source of her substantial and quickly acquired fortune, was the Berkeley Horse, a frame on which clients were spreadeagled to allow more efficient scourging. After her death in 1836, the Horse, bizarrely, was donated to the Society for the Promotion of the Arts, Manufacture and Commerce in the Adelphi (now called the Royal Society of Arts), one of whose members was pornographer George Cannon, a specialist in flagellant literature.

Paradise of love

Now turn right into Charlotte Street. Cross Goodge Street. Turn right into Rathbone Street and follow it round to the left. When you get to the Newman Arms pub on the right, go through the archway into Newman Passage and turn left when you come out on Newman Street. Towards the end of the 18th century, as more and more of the West End was developed, many prostitutes moved west to Marylebone, 'the new grand paradise of love', and in particular to Newman Street. A book known as *Harris's List*, published in 1793, described one Newman Street whore, a Miss H–rington, as 'a knowing one about twenty-five, with a tolerable good complexion, in company chatty, witty and agreeable'. When you entered her room she immediately took you to a sofa and showed you her 'haven of delight' – 'in return she likewise expects a view of nature's gifts from you, which if she thinks clean and properly adapted, she will unload for two pounds two'.

Walk on down to Oxford Street, cross over and turn left. The building at Nos. 55–59 Oxford Street, on the east corner of Soho Street, has intimate connections with two notorious doctors, Talbot Bridgewater and Hawley Crippen. Bridgewater housed here both his medical practice and an elaborate forgery factory staffed by several well known members of the criminal fraternity. The factory specialized in stealing things like cheques and postal orders (for example, by breaking open pillar boxes) and then forging increased values on them before cashing them in. Police discovered the factory in 1905 and Bridgewater went to prison for seven years. While he was serving his sentence, dentist Crippen worked as a partner in the Yale Tooth Specialist Company at the same address. Having fallen in love with one of the company's typists, Ethel Le Neve, he murdered his unpleasant wife and buried her under the coal cellar of their house in Hilldrop Crescent, between Holloway and Kentish Town, North London. After a dramatic chase across the Atlantic by a Scotland Yard detective, Crippen was arrested. He was executed in 1910. Ethel Le Neve later married an accountant, and died in 1967.

Continue on along Oxford Street to Tottenham Court Road station, where the walk ends.

COVENT GARDEN

Summary: North of the Strand, between the West End and the City, Covent Garden is a fashionable, vibrant and youthful quarter centred on a converted 1830s fruit and vegetable market. This circular walk includes the central market piazza (cafés, wine bars, interesting shops and street performers), Neal Street and Neal's Yard, Seven Dials, the Drury Lane Theatre and the Royal Opera House and various places associated with the Bow Street Runners and writers such as Dickens, Johnson, Boswell and Thomas de Quincey. There is also a section to the south of the Strand featuring relics of former riverside mansions (York House Watergate, Savoy Chapel), the Savoy Hotel, the Adelphi, and houses connected with Pepys, Kipling and Peter the Great of Russia.

Start and finish:	Leicester Square station (Piccadilly and Northern Underground Lines).
Length:	2 miles (3.2km).
Time:	2 hours.
Refreshments:	All kinds of places en route, but Covent Garden itself, conveniently situated halfway through the walk, will probably be the choice for most walkers, especially for visitors to London. Neal's Yard a little further on is well known for its organic and vegetarian foods.

Take the 'Charing Cross Road (South)' exit from Leicester Square station and turn left along Charing Cross Road past Wyndham's Theatre. Take the second turning on the left into Cecil Court, a pedestrian precinct lined with second-hand shops specializing in books, prints, maps, stamps and posters. When you get to St Martin's Lane, cross over and turn right. Ahead on the left, the white building with the globe on top is the Coliseum Theatre, housing the English National Opera. After passing the theatre, cross William IV Street at the traffic lights. To your right is the memorial to Edith Cavell, a British nurse executed during World War I for helping allied soldiers stranded after the German occupation of Belgium. Just before **St Martin's-in-the-Fields Church**, designed by James Gibbs in 1724, turn left, with the railings and market on your right.

Beyond the market turn right into Adelaide Street and then cross Duncannon Street and the Strand to reach the forecourt of Charing Cross Station. In the centre stands a 19th-century replica of the medieval Charing Cross, one of 12 erected by Edward I to mark the stopping places of his wife's funeral cortège as it journeyed from Lincoln to Westminster Abbey in 1290. The original cross stood in Trafalgar Square near Nelson's column, a point still officially called Charing Cross.

Riverside relics
In front of the station turn left and then right into Villiers Street, leading down the hill towards the river. Look out on the left for York Place, formerly Of Alley. In the 1600s there was a large mansion here called York House, the town house of the

95

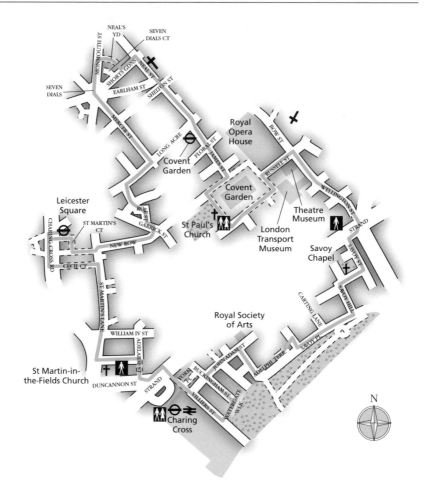

Villiers family, Dukes of Buckingham. When the second Duke sold it for redevelopment in the 1670s he insisted that every part of his name and title be used in the naming of the new streets, including the 'of ' in Duke of Buckingham. Hence Of Alley.

The arches underneath Charing Cross Station house the Players' Theatre, where the traditions of the Victorian music hall are maintained with full audience participation and dining during performances. On the left, the last house before Embankment Gardens (No. 43) is where the 24-year-old Rudyard Kipling lived on his return from India after seven years working as a journalist. It was here that he wrote his first novel, *The Light that Failed* (1890). Soon after this he married and left for America.

Turn left through the gate and go down the steps into Watergate Walk, which takes its name from the former York House gateway on the right. When the Thames was London's main highway all the big riverside houses along the Strand had their own river gates or stairs. This gateway, built in 1626, is the only one to survive. Until 1870,

Plate 18: Covent Garden

Covent Garden's old market building, now a thriving enclave of shops and restaurants,
is a good place to stop for refreshments on the Covent Garden walk (see page 98).

Plate 19: Bloomsbury
Elegant doorways with fine plaster mouldings and other details are a feature
of Bedford Square, London's finest Georgian square (see page 100).

Plate 20: Inns of Court
Lincoln's Inn Fields, one of London's oldest and largest squares and
home to the eclectic Sir John Soane Museum (see page 105).

Plate 21: Following the Fleet River
Beneath the arches of Blackfriars Bridge, where the Fleet river joins the
Thames after flowing down from the Northern Heights (see page 112).

Plate 22: The Notorious Fleet Valley

*Fleet Street, always thronged with traffic, ascends what was
once the west bank of the Fleet river (see page 116).*

Plate 23: Clerkenwell
This half-timbered gateway near Smithfield market leads to
St Bartholomew-the-Great, London's oldest church (see page 126).

Plate 24: The City around Fleet Street and St Paul's
In a little court off Fleet Street is Ye Olde Cheshire Cheese,
one of London's most historic pubs (see page 130).

Plate 25: The City between Guildhall and the Tower
Acclaimed architect Richard Rogers designed these modern offices for Lloyds of London, the City's historic insurance market (see page 133).

when the embankment was built, it stood right on the riverside. The Latin inscription along the top (*Fidei Coticula Crux* – the touchstone of faith is the cross) was the motto of the Villiers family.

Russian connections

Ascend the steps to the left into Buckingham Street. Samuel Pepys lived in this street for over 20 years, arriving in 1679 at the age of 46, when he was the senior civil servant in the Admiralty. He lived first at No. 12 (the third house on the left) and then at No. 14 (the first house on the left). He still had a house here in 1698 when Peter the Great of Russia arrived on his famous study tour of England and Holland. The tsar stayed on the right at No. 15.

At the top of the street turn right into John Adam Street. On the left, Durham House (built on the site of the original Durham House, the London house of the Bishops of Durham) has a plaque to the caricaturist Thomas Rowlandson, whose comic pictures of English life around 1800 are still widely known today. Beyond, the fine house with the flagpole and columns (No. 8) is the Royal Society of Arts (RSA), founded in 1754 as the Society for the Encouragement of Arts, Manufactures and Commerce. The Society organized the country's first art exhibition in 1760 and first photography exhibition in 1852. Its home was purpose-built in 1774 by the Adam brothers as part of their Adelphi residential development ('adelphi' is Greek for brothers). The Adelphi consisted of 24 terraced houses built high above the river over huge vaults. Most of the houses were demolished before World War II, although the dark-brick house with cream stucco work which you can see at the far end of John Adam Street is original, and the vaults (not accessible from this point) still exist. The Adelphi office block of 1938 now covers most of the site.

Life of luxury

Just before the RSA, turn right into Robert Street. Famous former residents of this street include Robert Adam and the writers Thomas Hood, John Galsworthy and J. M. Barrie. Turn left along Adelphi Terrace, looking out over Victoria Embankment Gardens. Go down the steps at the end of the terrace into Savoy Place and turn left through the colonnade underneath Shell-Mex House. Cross Carting Lane. Now you pass the rear entrance to the Savoy Hotel. Richard D'Oyly Carte started the hotel over a century ago, intending it to be the last word in luxury. The showers in the bathrooms had 12-inch (30-cm) shower heads and the huge baths could be filled in 12 seconds from 1½-inch (4-cm) water pipes. César Ritz of Ritz Hotel fame was its first manager and the legendary Auguste Escoffier its first chef. On the right, the small garden with seats, flower basin and sundial was given to London in 1989 by the hotel to mark its centenary. Beyond in the main garden there is a bust of the composer, Sir Arthur Sullivan – of the Gilbert and Sullivan duo. D'Oyly Carte, a theatrical impresario by profession, discovered Gilbert and Sullivan and had already built the Savoy Theatre for the sole purpose of staging their work before he began work on the adjacent hotel.

Take the first turning on the left into Savoy Hill, following the road round to the right to the **Savoy Chapel**, relic of the medieval Savoy Palace. The residence in the 13th century of Count Peter of Savoy, uncle of Henry III's queen, the palace was later used as a prison and hospital before being demolished in 1820 to make way for the new Waterloo Bridge. The old chapel is owned by the Queen as part of the Duchy of Lancaster Estate and is also known as the Queen's Chapel of the Savoy. As such it serves as the official Chapel of the Royal Victorian Order.

Walk past the chapel, turn left into Savoy Street and at the top of the street turn right onto the Strand. Go across the Strand at the traffic lights. Turn right and then left into Wellington Street, passing on the left the famous Lyceum Theatre founded by actor Sir Henry Irving. At the junction with Tavistock Street, the building on the right is where Charles Dickens edited his magazine *All The Year Round* for 11 years until his death in 1870. Round the corner at No. 36 Tavistock Street, Thomas de Quincey wrote *Confessions of an English Opium Eater* (1821) in a lonely little back room.

Continue walking along Wellington Street to the junction with Russell Street. To the right you can see the Theatre Royal, Drury Lane, with its long colonnade on Russell Street. Drury Lane is one of England's oldest and most famous theatres: the actress Nell Gwynn, better known as Charles II's mistress, made her debut in a previous building on this site in 1665. David Garrick, the 18th century's most distinguished actor, first appeared at this theatre in 1742. He was also manager here, as was Richard Brinsley Sheridan – author of *The School for Scandal* – after him. Ahead in Bow Street, a continuation of Wellington Street, is the Royal Opera House, originally opened as the Covent Garden Theatre in 1732. It became the Royal Opera House in 1847 when Italian composer Guiseppe Persiani took it over after the then opera house (now Her Majesty's Theatre – see the Soho to Trafalgar Square walk, page 83) refused to stage one of his works. Facing the Royal Opera House are Bow Street magistrates' court and adjacent police buildings. These are descendants of the original Bow Street court-house where, in 1749, the novelist-magistrate Henry Fielding (*Tom Jones* is his best-known work) recruited the first Bow Street Runners, forerunners of the Metropolitan Police Force.

Biographer of Dr Johnson

Turn left into Russell Street, passing on the left the **Theatre Museum** and then the Boswell Coffee House where, in 1763, Dr Johnson had his first meeting with his future biographer James Boswell. It was not actually a coffee house then, although at that time Covent Garden was famous for its coffee houses where all the great literary men of the day met and talked. Ahead is Covent Garden, originally a *convent* garden. The old market building, London's main fruit, vegetable and flower market until 1974, fills the centre of Inigo Jones's 17th-century square. Around the perimeter, starting on your left, are the **London Transport Museum**, the Jubilee Market Hall and Sports Centre, and **St Paul's Church**, known as the actors' church, the entrance to which is reached via archways in King Street and Henrietta Street. At the beginning of King Street there is a house with a plaque in memory of Admiral Edward Russell. It was his uncle, the first Duke of Bedford, who started Covent Garden Market in 1670.

Turn right in front of the coffee house and then left into James Street. Go across Floral Street and Long Acre into Neal Street. This is the main street of the regenerated warehouse area to the north of the old market, and is a curious mixture of avant-garde fashion and environmentalism. Cross Shelton Street and the entrance to Earlham Street and then turn left into Short's Gardens. On the right, the water-powered clock on the front of the Wholefood Warehouse is well worth watching if the hour is about to strike.

The sins of Seven Dials

From here turn right into the organic enclave of Neal's Yard, where you can buy bread, organic fruit and vegetables, wholefood and herbal remedies. First developed as a collection of alternative enterprises in the 1970s, Neal's Yard has spawned several well-known businesses, including Neal's Yard Remedies, which still has a shop here. Turn left through the yard and go through the gate into the little mall leading to Monmouth Street. Turn left to Seven Dials, the meeting point of seven roads. (If it is a Sunday and the gate from Neal's Yard into the little mall is shut, retrace your steps to Short's Gardens and then turn right.) The column in the centre of Seven Dials is a modern replica of the original, which was taken down in 1773 after it had become a notorious rendezvous for thieves and prostitutes. Thomas Neale, Master of the Royal Mint, started the building of the Seven Dials area in the 1690s, hence Neal Street and Neal's Yard. A plaque on the wall opposite Short's Gardens explains how to tell the time using the dial.

Take the third turning on the left into Mercer Street, go across Shelton Street again, and turn right into Long Acre. Cross over when you see Stanford's famous map shop on the opposite side and go through the arch on the right into Rose Street. Go across Floral Street and follow Rose Street round to the left and right, past the 1623 Lamb and Flag pub (where the poet Dryden was once famously beaten up) into Garrick Street. To your right, the large stone building with flagpole is the Garrick Club, founded in 1831 to promote social contact between actors and artists and the upper classes. Both club and street are named after the 18th-century actor, David Garrick.

Cross over the road to the Roundhouse pub and go round the corner into New Row. On the left, look out for the interesting scientific instrument shop on the corner of Bedfordbury. At the end of New Row cross St Martin's Lane by the Albery Theatre and go into St Martin's Court. Halfway along, turn right by the public telephone boxes and follow the court round to the left to Leicester Square station where the walk ends.

❖❖

BLOOMSBURY

❖❖

Summary: A circular walk around a once-fashionable residential district laid out between the late 17th and early 19th centuries, mainly by the Dukes of Bedford. During the early 1900s the district gave its name to the Bloomsbury Group of artists and writers, several of whom lived in the area. The main features of the walk are London University and the **British Museum**, six squares including Bloomsbury Square, Queen Square and Bedford Square (the finest surviving Georgian square in London), the **Dickens House Museum**, The Great Ormond Street Hospital for Sick Children and the **Foundling Hospital** (including the art collection). Bibliophiles will find several second-hand bookshops near the end of the walk around Museum Street.

Start and finish: Tottenham Court Road station (Central and Northern Underground Lines).

Length:	2½ miles (4km).
Time:	1½ hours.
Refreshments:	Cafés near the beginning of the walk in the Great Court of the British Museum and in Russell Square. In the last half of the walk there are plenty of places, first in Lamb's Conduit Street, then in and around Cosmo Place off Queen Square.
Note:	Pied Bull Yard is closed on Sundays but directions for a short diversion are given in the text.

Take exit 3 from Tottenham Court Road station, go straight past the Dominion Theatre and turn right into Great Russell Street by the modern YMCA building. Turn left into Adeline Place which brings you into Bedford Square, completed in 1780 as the showpiece of the Bedford Estate and today the finest complete Georgian square in London. Continue along the left-hand side of the square past

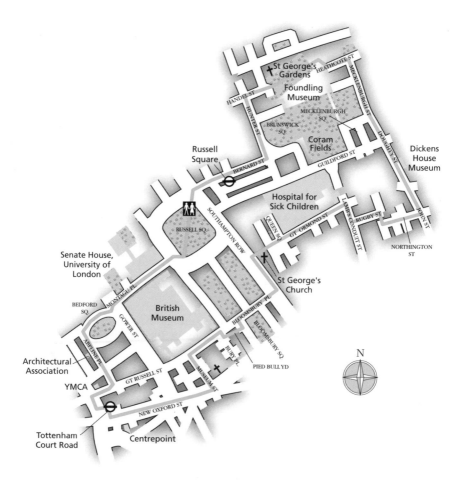

No. 35 which bears plaques relating to two 19th-century doctors: Thomas Wakley, who in 1823 founded the *Lancet*, today Britain's leading medical journal, and Thomas Hodgkin, who was one of the founders of the Aborigines' Protection Society in 1838 and did a lot of good work on behalf of persecuted Jews and the London poor. All Bedford Square's houses have been converted into offices, many of which – in keeping with the district's literary traditions – were occupied by publishers until the 1980s.

Turn right along the top of the square and go straight on across Gower Street into Montague Place. Further along on the left is Senate House (1932), the main building of London University. Opposite Senate House, on the right, is the rear entrance of the British Museum. This great museum was opened in 1759 but the building you see here (the Edward VII galleries) dates from the early 1900s.

At the end of Montague Place, cross into Russell Square gardens using the entrance to the right. Laid out in 1800 and named after the Russells, Dukes of Bedford, there is a statue of the fifth Duke (died 1805) on the right. Follow the main path diagonally across the middle of the garden, past the café, to the opposite corner. Then cross the main road into Bernard Street. Walk past Russell Square station on the right and the Brunswick Centre (a development of shops and flats built in 1972) on the left and turn left into Brunswick Square. Virginia Woolf, Leonard Woolf, Duncan Grant and John Maynard Keynes – all members of the so-called Bloomsbury Group, an association of writers, artists and intellectuals – shared a house here in the 1900s. Since then the square has been completely redeveloped.

Handel's orphan concerts

Carry on past the entrance to the Renoir cinema. If you look right down the north side of Brunswick Square you can see at the far end a statue of Captain Thomas Coram, an 18th-century sea-captain turned philanthropist. Appalled by the number of abandoned children in London, Coram established the **Foundling Hospital** in 1742. The hospital stood in large grounds behind the statue until the 1920s. Today Coram's organization, now known as the Coram Family, sponsors fostering rather than looking after orphans itself. The Foundling Museum to the left of the statue houses objects from the former hospital, including pictures donated to it by 18th-century painters such as Hogarth, Reynolds and Gainsborough.

Walk on to Hunter Street and take the first right turn into Handel Street, so named because Handel gave performances of his Messiah in the Foundling Hospital chapel to raise money for the orphans. At the end of Handel Street go into St George's Gardens. This public garden was once the burial ground of **St George's Church**, seen later in the walk. Follow the main path through the garden, bearing right towards the far end. Anna Gibson, Oliver Cromwell's grand-daughter, lies in the low tomb on the right with the pyramid-shaped top. Go through the gate at the right-hand corner of the garden, then turn left and right into Mecklenburgh Street, leading into Mecklenburgh Square. Both this square – named after George III's wife, Princess Charlotte of Mecklenburgh-Strelitz – and the original Brunswick Square were built in the 18th century on the Foundling Hospital estate, with the hospital building in the middle. Income from properties in the squares was used to support the orphanage and its pioneering work.

Dickens of Doughty Street

Walk straight on along the left-hand side of Mecklenburgh Square into Doughty Street, built around 1800. Go across Guildford Street. Clergyman and famous wit Sydney Smith (1771–1845) lived at No. 14 on the right. 'I never read a book before reviewing it; it prejudices one so' was one of his cracks. On the left at No. 48 Doughty Street is the Dickens House museum. Charles Dickens lived here from 1837 for three years and completed his first three novels here (*Pickwick Papers*, *Oliver Twist* and *Nicholas Nickleby*).

Continue up the slope into John Street and turn right into Northington Street. At the end of the street, turn right and left into Rugby Street, built around 1680 on land owned by Rugby School in Warwickshire. On the left a plaque on No. 13 records the location of the White Conduit, part of the medieval water supply of Greyfriars monastery, which was near **St Paul's** in the City.

At the end of Rugby Street turn right into Lamb's Conduit Street. After Greyfriars monastery was shut down in the mid-16th century, the conduit fell into disrepair. However, in 1577 it was rebuilt by William Lamb, a chorister in the Chapel Royal. The site of his conduit is marked by a stone plaque at the entrance to Long Yard near the far end of the street. Right at the end of the street there is still a drinking fountain. At this point you can also see the original main entrance to the old Foundling Hospital, now a children's playground known as Coram's Fields.

Halfway down Lamb's Conduit Street turn left into Great Ormond Street, completed in 1720. On the left, No. 23 has a plaque to John Howard, an 18th-century High Sheriff of Bedfordshire who spent a lifetime visiting prisons in Britain and on the continent in a pioneering attempt to improve prisoners' conditions. Apparently, the only prison Howard was unable to enter was the Bastille in Paris, though, as he said in one of his books, he 'knocked hard at the outer gate'. Howard's work is still carried on today by the Howard League for Penal Reform.

The right-hand side of Great Ormond Street is mostly taken up by the famous Hospital for Sick Children. Dr Charles West and other doctors founded it in 1852 after research had revealed that there were no hospital places for children in London, even though over 20,000 London children aged 10 or under were dying each year.

Walk along Great Ormond Street into Queen Square, built early in the 18th century during the reign of Queen Anne. Over on the left the building with the coat of arms above the door is the former Italian Hospital, opened in 1884 in a private house as a hospital for poor Italians. London's Italian community was at that time concentrated in nearby Holborn. The hospital closed in 1991.

The church of the 'climbing boys'

Cross the square and go into Cosmo Place. On one side is the Queen's Larder pub apparently named after a cellar where Queen Charlotte stored delicacies for her deranged husband, George III, while he was being treated by his doctor in Queen Square. On the other side is St George's Church, built in 1706 and once known as the sweeps' church due to a parishioner's benefaction providing Christmas dinners for 100 chimney sweeps' apprentices. Called climbing boys, these children were sent up chimneys to dislodge soot and clean flues until the practice was outlawed in 1875.

From Cosmo Place turn left onto Southampton Row and then first right into Bloomsbury Place, leading to Bloomsbury Square, originally built in the 1660s. Sir

Hans Sloane, the physician who features in the Chelsea walk (see page 59), lived at No. 4 for almost 50 years. Under the terms of his will in 1753 his enormous collections of books, manuscripts and natural history items were sold to the government for a modest sum. They subsequently formed the basic stock of the new British Museum.

Carry on along the top side of Bloomsbury Square (passing the statue of Whig politician Charles James Fox, who died in 1806) and then turn left down the far side next to No. 17, the former headquarters of the Pharmaceutical Society (note the words carved high up on the façade). Just beyond No. 15, turn right into Pied Bull Yard where you will find a café, wine bar and some interesting specialist shops. Go straight through the gate in the far right corner and turn right and then left into Great Russell Street (if the Yard is closed, carry straight on from Bloomsbury Square into Great Russell Street). The imposing main entrance of the British Museum is now on your right.

Opposite the main gates to the museum, turn left into Museum Street and at the end of the street turn right into New Oxford Street. Walk towards the Centrepoint tower block (1967) and Tottenham Court Road station, where the walk ends.

❖❖

INNS OF COURT

❖❖

Summary: This is a circular walk through the heart of legal London featuring the capital's four ancient Inns of Court where barristers (i.e. advocates) first train and then practise. These four Inns (in the order in which they are covered by the walk) are: Gray's Inn, **Lincoln's Inn**, Middle Temple and Inner Temple. Apart from the inns and their old courts and quiet gardens, features of the walk include **St Clement Danes Church**, the law courts in the Strand, Dickens's Old Curiosity Shop, Lincoln's Inn Fields, Staple Inn, Chancery Lane and the **London Silver Vaults**.

Start and finish:	Temple station (District and Circle Underground Lines). On Sundays when Temple station is closed use Blackfriars instead.
Length:	2 miles (3.2km).
Time:	1–1½ hours.
Refreshments:	Plenty of pubs, wine bars and sandwich bars between the Inns.
Note:	This walk needs to be done on a weekday because the Inns are closed at weekends.

Leave Temple station, turn left up the steps and then right into Temple Place. When the road curves to the right, turn left into Milford Lane and climb the steps into Essex Street. Middle Temple lies on the right-hand side behind the houses. Shortage of space in the Inns, including Middle Temple, has forced many barristers to seek offices (known as chambers) in nearby streets, not because the Inns are too small, but because some chambers have been let out to members of other professions, like solicitors and surveyors. Several Middle Temple barristers have their chambers in this street. Look out for

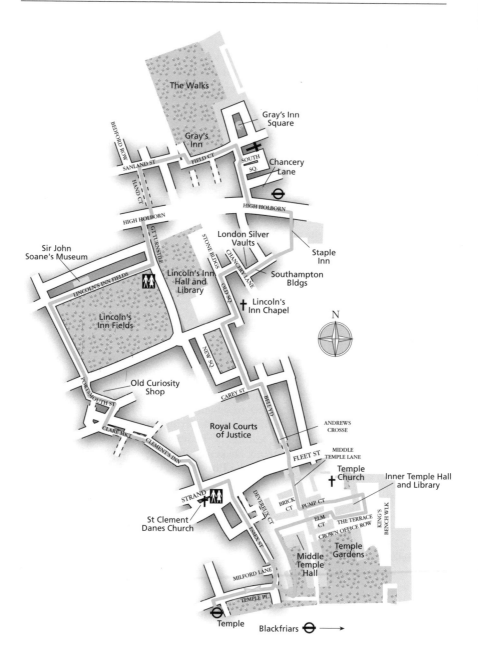

No. 11 on the left, an old house with the Middle Temple coat of arms above the door. It's easy for the tenants of these chambers to get to their Inn because there is a handy back entrance at the end of Devereux Court (opposite, by the Edgar Wallace pub).

The Young Pretender
Further along the street is Essex Hall, the main church and central office of the General Assembly of Unitarian and Free Christian Churches (Unitarianism is a liberal tendency that differs from more 'Establishment' creeds by putting reason and the individual conscience before dogma). The Hall is post-war, but the first Unitarian chapel was founded here in 1774. A stone by the door of the Temple bookshop on the left is inscribed with more details of Essex Street's 300-year history, including Bonnie Prince Charlie's five-day secret visit to London five years after the abortive Jacobite rising of 1745. The stone also records the existence of Dr Johnson's club at the Essex Head pub, now the Edgar Wallace.

You emerge from Essex Street at the east end of the Strand. St Clement Danes Church stands on an island site in the middle of the road with a figure of Dr Johnson in the paved area at its east end. The opposite side of the street here consists entirely of the **Royal Courts of Justice**. Go over the Strand at the zebra crossing to the right and turn left. There are about 60 courtrooms altogether, most of which hear only civil cases: serious criminal cases are dealt with at the Old Bailey in the City.

At the end of the wrought-iron screen that masks the administrative offices of the courts, turn right through the gate into Clement's Inn. The Inn, now an enclave of office blocks, was once one of about eight Inns of Chancery that existed side by side with the Inns of Court. Although the Inns of Chancery were able to educate budding lawyers, unlike the Inns of Court they could not qualify their students to become barristers and practise at the bar, and as a result they eventually died out. This Inn was finally demolished in 1891 after a 400-year existence.

Walk along the path between the office blocks and go up the steps into Clement's Inn Passage, leading into Clare Market. Until the beginning of this century there was a market here, but today the campus of the London School of Economics covers the area. Turn right beyond the bookshop and second left by the pub into Portsmouth Street. On the right, looking quite out of place, is the Old Curiosity Shop. Apart from being reckoned the oldest shop in London, it is also said to be the original of Dickens's eponymous novel – the one where Little Nell and her grandfather the shop-keeper are hounded by the money-lender Quilp.

Students' playground
Continue along Portsmouth Street into Lincoln's Inn Fields, the second largest square in London. Away to the right you can see the gateway into Lincoln's Inn. Walk along the left-hand side of the square. As its name suggests, it was open ground before building started in the 1600s. The only original house left is at Nos. 59-60 on this side, painted red and white and retaining the high railings and the iron cradles for torches and lanterns used before the days of street lighting. Spencer Perceval once lived here. The only British prime minister to have been assassinated, Perceval was shot in 1812 by John Bellingham, a deranged bankrupt convinced that Perceval was at the root of his problems.

The penultimate house on the left, No. 65, was the home of William Marsden, founder of both the Royal Free Hospital ('free' because it didn't charge for its services) and the Cancer Hospital, now the Royal Marsden Hospital. Next door at No. 66 are the offices of Farrer and Co, solicitors to the Queen.

Turn right along the top of the square. No. 13 in the middle is the former home of Sir John Soane, architect of the Bank of England (**Sir John Soane's Museum**).

Soane married the daughter of a wealthy builder and created a collection of historical and architectural curiosities and works of art, including many drawings and pictures. In accordance with his wishes the house was turned into a public museum after his death in 1837. It has remained virtually unchanged since and is now one of the most extraordinary time-capsule interiors in London.

Turn left at the corner opposite the 'Camdonian' sculpture, walk along Newman's Row and go through Great Turnstile (there was a turnstile here in the 1600s) into High Holborn. Go across High Holborn at the traffic lights, turn right and then left into Hand Court, an alley next to the Bung Hole wine bar. At the end turn right along Sandland Street past the entrance to Bedford Row, historically a favourite address for solicitors. Quiet and spacious, the Row has classic town architecture and a hint of the exotic in the robinia trees. Continue past the old water pump and go through the gate in the wall into Gray's Inn, the first of the four Inns of Court. This Inn is named after Reginald le Grey, Chief Justice of Chester, whose London house became the original Gray's Inn after his death in 1308.

The shame of Gray's Inn
Follow the path to the right between the buildings into Gray's Inn Place. Ahead is the Inns of Court School of Law, where trainee barristers study for their formal qualifications. Turn left into Field Court, facing the gardens that are known as The Walks (open weekday lunchtimes). Walk through the arch ahead into Gray's Inn Square and turn immediately right into South Square. The figure away to the left is Francis Bacon, one of the Inn's most famous, or infamous, old members: as Lord Chancellor in 1621 he was convicted of taking bribes, fined £40,000 and imprisoned in the Tower of London. Continue through the next two archways and you find yourself back on High Holborn.

Turn left and walk down to the traffic lights. Go across High Holborn here and turn left past the griffin on its pedestal marking the boundary of the City of London. On the right, Staple Inn, one of the old Inns of Chancery, is one of the few timber-framed buildings to have survived the Great Fire in 1666. Turn right through the archway into the shady cobbled courtyard of the Inn and go through the next archway into the small, immaculate gardens in front of the old hall. Follow the path round to the right, climb the steps and go into Southampton Buildings. On the left is the Patent Office where new inventions are registered. On the right a little further along are the London Silver Vaults, large safes once used by a safe deposit company and now converted into a subterranean arcade of silverware shops.

Cross Chancery Lane, turn right and then go left through the gates into Lincoln's Inn, the second of the Inns of Court. Stone Buildings on the right were added to the Inn around 1780. Turn left into Old Square and walk to the right of the vaulted undercroft underneath the 17th-century chapel. As you pass the corner of the building, notice on the wall the plaque recording the dropping of a bomb from a German airship in 1915. The undercroft floor is made up of the gravestones of people buried in Lincoln's Inn, one of whom was the puritan writer William Prynne, who died in 1669 and whose scurrilous writings during his lifetime caused him first to lose both his ears and then to be branded 'S L' as a seditious libeller. Such were the perils of free expression in those days. (There is a list of the gravestones and a key showing their location inside the undercroft. Prynne's is No. 44.)

Walk past the undercroft and chapel entrance towards the old hall of Lincoln's Inn and then turn right to the war memorial. Ahead you can see the other side of the gateway you saw from Lincoln's Inn Fields, to the right the Inn's new hall, library and garden (open weekday lunchtimes), and to the left, 300-year-old New Square.

Turn along the left-hand side of New Square. At the end go through the archway and turn left into Carey Street. Ahead now is the former Public Record Office, Britain's first purpose-built national archive, opened in the 1860s and closed in 1996 following the final transfer of documents to a new building in Kew in southwest London. The old PRO has now been converted into a library for King's College, part of London University. Take the first turning on the right into Bell Yard alongside the law courts. This leads into Andrews Crosse. At the end you emerge at the point where Fleet Street meets the Strand, which is also the point where the City of London meets the City of Westminster. Originally a gate called Temple Bar stood here but it was removed because it held up traffic. It now stands forgotten in the grounds of a country house north of London. The griffin marks the site. If the sovereign wishes to enter the City of London, he or she must stop here and ask permission of the Lord Mayor. The Lord Mayor in return offers his Sword of State as a sign of the City's loyalty to the sovereign. In the past, particularly at the time of the Civil War, this loyalty was not always forthcoming.

Knights Templar
The orange-brick building opposite is the main entrance to Middle Temple (1684), the third of the Inns of Court. Cross the road at the lights, turn left and through the gate into the Inn. Walk down Middle Temple Lane past Brick Court on the right and turn left through the archway with the lantern above it into Pump Court. Pass through the cloisters at the end into the open court where Lamb Buildings stood until they were destroyed by bombs in 1941. You are now in Inner Temple, the fourth and final Inn of Court. In the Middle Ages, both Inner and Middle Temple were part of the monastery of the military monks known as the Knights Templar. The Order was suppressed in 1312 and most of their premises (except for the Outer Temple which is now Essex Street) taken over by lawyers. On the left is the 12th-century Templars' church. Inner and Middle Temple separated in 1732.

Walk to the end of the courtyard (on the left is the house of the Master of the Inn), through the archway and into King's Bench Walk which stretches down the hill towards the river. Turn right here and then right again into Crown Office Row. On your left are Paper Buildings ('paper' is an old term for a house built of wood and plaster rather than stone or bricks) and Temple Gardens with their gates dating from 1730. Follow the raised terrace to the right and go through the narrow gap in the angle of the Row. This brings you into Elm Court by the side of the old buttery of the Templars on the right. A plaque on the buttery wall records the existence of vanished Fig Tree Court, first burnt in the Great Fire (1666) and then finally destroyed by bombing in World War II. Turn left here, go through the archway and cross Middle Temple Lane into Middle Temple's Fountain Court. On the left is Middle Temple Hall where Shakespeare's *Twelfth Night* was first performed – at Candlemas (2nd February) 1601. To the right are New Court and Devereux Chambers, and the other side of the gateway you saw earlier on from Essex Street.

Turn left down the steps by Middle Temple gardens (open weekday lunchtimes May–September) and follow the path out of the Inn and back into Milford Lane. From here retrace your steps the short distance to Temple station and the end of the walk.

FOLLOWING THE FLEET RIVER

Summary: The Fleet River, flowing between St Paul's Cathedral and Fleet Street, played an important part in London life for many centuries. Like the Tyburn and the Westbourne (see pages 29 and 54 respectively) it has long since been covered over, but many signs of its subterranean existence can be detected on the surface today. You see these signs on this walk, which picks the river up at King's Cross Station after its journey from its sources in the lakes on Hampstead Heath. From King's Cross the walk follows the old course of the Fleet past **Mount Pleasant Sorting Office**, the Clerk's Well, Clerkenwell Green, Smithfield Market, **St Paul's Cathedral** and Bridewell to its outflow into the Thames beneath Blackfriars Bridge.

Start:	King's Cross Station (Circle, Victoria, Northern, Piccadilly, Hammersmith & City and Metropolitan Underground Lines and mainline trains).
Finish:	Blackfriars station (District and Circle Underground Lines and mainline trains).
Length:	2 miles (3.2km).
Time:	1½ hours.
Refreshments:	There are pubs, sandwich bars and restaurants all along the route, but Clerkenwell Green is undoubtedly the best place to stop. It's got a good selection of places to eat and drink in, is exactly halfway and has a villagey atmosphere.
Note:	If possible plan to finish the walk at low or lowish tide on the Thames, otherwise it may not be possible to see the Fleet's outfall. To find out when low tide is, either consult the current edition of *Whitaker's Almanack* in your local library or ring the Port of London harbourmaster on 020 7265 2656.

On the forecourt of King's Cross Station facing away from the entrance, turn left. Cross York Way into Pentonville Road and walk along to the traffic lights. Ahead, Pentonville Road climbs the steep hill forming both the west side of the Barnsbury spur, running down from the Northern Heights, and the east side of the Fleet valley. Cross right into King's Cross Bridge, a short road covering the railway and Underground lines beneath. As you will see at various points along the course of the walk, both these lines run through a deep cutting – sometimes open, sometimes covered – as far as Farringdon station, where they divide. The railway line, continuing on through City Thameslink station and crossing the river at Blackfriars, is one of only two lines in central London to run right through the city. Significantly, both use river valleys to do so. This one, the Thameslink Line, uses the valley of the Fleet. The other, the West London Line passing the Olympia and Earl's Court exhibition centres, follows the course of Counter's Creek.

St Chad's spa

From King's Cross Bridge, take the first left into St Chad's Place and walk down the hill. Standing at the low point, you can see over the wall into King's Cross Thameslink Station in the cutting below. The building of the underground line through this district in the 1860s destroyed the last remaining part of St Chad's Gardens, a pleasure ground surrounding a once-popular medicinal well which in the 18th century attracted up to 1,000 people a week to drink its waters. Later in the walk we come to the site of another Fleet-side spa which was an even bigger draw than that.

St Chad's Place now narrows into a passage, and, bending left, brings you out on King's Cross Road. Turn right and follow the road as it bends round to the right. On the left the roads all climb up the east side of the Fleet valley and several (Weston Rise, for example) feature the tell-tale word 'Rise' in their names. Beyond the former magistrates' court and police station, the road changes direction and swings round to the left, keeping close to the river's meandering course.

Bagnigge Wells

Just beyond the garage on the right there is a terrace of houses, all with balconies at first-floor level. Here stood Bagnigge Wells, the other famous spa mentioned earlier and one of the best-attended of all the spas surrounding London during the spa-crazy 18th century. The Fleet itself flowed through the spa gardens and there were seats on the bank 'for such as chuse to smoke or drink cyder, ale etc. which are not permitted in other parts of the garden'. Today the only relic of the spa (besides the name of nearby Wells Square) is the inscribed stone set into the front wall of the first house in the terrace, thought to mark the northwestern boundary of the gardens. The stone is dated 1680, which is particularly interesting because this is about the time when Bagnigge House was used as a summer retreat by Charles II's mistress, Nell Gwynn. Nell's association with the area is commemorated in Gwynne [sic] Place on the opposite side of the road. The 'Pinder a Wakefeilde' mentioned on the plaque refers to a famous old pub called the Pindar of Wakefield on nearby Gray's Inn Road. It survived until just a few years ago when it was taken over and renamed The Water Rats. The original Pindar opened in 1517.

Mount Pleasant

Beyond the terrace turn right into Cubitt Street and then first left into Pakenham Street. The river swings right here towards Pakenham Street to avoid a knob of high ground ahead called Mount Pleasant. As you rise up towards the junction with Calthorpe Street, the knob comes into view with a huge Royal Mail sorting office on top. Go straight on into Phoenix Place and down the hill, probably an artificial one intended to graduate the incline of Calthorpe Street up the west side of the Fleet valley. When you get to the road called Mount Pleasant, the true valley bottom reappears to the right. Carry straight on here into Warner Street and go under the bridge carrying Rosebery Avenue across the valley. The river now cuts into the bank on the right, up which climb several streets with 'hill' in their names, for example Eyre Street Hill and Back Hill. The top of the hill was once a large garden attached to the Bishop of Ely's London house, hence other local horticulturally-flavoured street names such as Vine Hill and Herbal Hill. (For more about the Bishop of Ely's house and its later history, see page 139.)

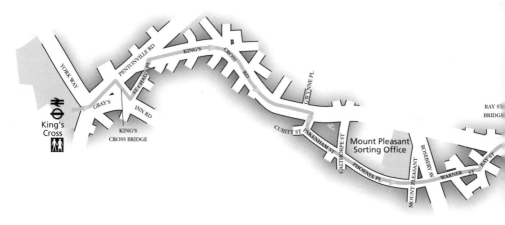

Clerkenwell

At the end of Warner Street, turn left into Ray Street, its sides framing the spire of Clerkenwell parish church ahead. Cross Farringdon Road and follow Ray Street Bridge round to the right towards the City Pride pub. Clerkenwell's name comes from the Clerks' Well, a spring of pure water on the east bank of the Fleet which in the Middle Ages was associated with the Company of Parish Clerks in the City. Having been lost for centuries, the old well was rediscovered in 1924 and is now visible through a window in No.16 Farringdon Lane (Well Court) just beyond the City Pride. The display beside the well includes an exhibition with writing big enough to read from outside and, on the left wall, an enlarged reproduction of a 16th-century map that clearly shows Clerkenwell and the broad River Fleet flowing down beside it towards the Thames.

From the well, carry on along Farringdon Lane and past the entrance to Clerkenwell Green. Cross Clerkenwell Road and continue into Turnmill Street, so named because of three water-mills worked here by the Fleet in the Middle Ages. At the end of the street, turn right by Farringdon station into Cowcross Street, cross Farringdon Road into Greville Street and turn left into Saffron Hill. This is a reminder that the Bishops of Ely grew a rich crop of saffron crocuses in their hilltop garden here, saffron being widely used in the Middle Ages to mask the taste of rancid meat. Saffron Hill slopes quite steeply down to what is probably something like real street level. At the end you have to climb up some steps to regain the artificially elevated street. The difference between the two must be all of 20 feet (6m). At the top of the steps turn left.

Ahead on the other side of the valley is Smithfield Market. When this ancient market dealt in live meat, it was the cause of many of the Fleet's problems, for the river was used to wash away the blood and entrails of butchered animals. The resulting pollution can all too easily be imagined.

Holborn Viaduct

At the crossroads, turn right into Farringdon Street and walk down to Holborn Viaduct. Climb the stairs on the right past the huge illustration of the Fleet Valley clearances of the mid 19th century. From the viaduct itself there are fine views of the valley to both north and south. To the north, Farringdon Road was constructed over the Fleet in the 1840s, erasing some of London's most infamous slums at the same time. To the south, the river had been covered over as early as the 1730s and the Fleet

Market – two rows of one-storey shops connected by a covered walkway – built on top. By the early 19th century, however, the market had become so badly dilapidated and such a nuisance that it was cleared away and replaced by Farringdon Street.

Holborn Viaduct itself was built in 1869. Connecting Holborn with Newgate Street, the new bridge put an end to the difficult and sometimes dangerous ascents and descents of the steep sides of the Fleet valley, making it much easier for horse-drawn traffic to pass to and fro between the City and the West End.

Descend from the viaduct via the south-east steps and continue along the left side of Farringdon Street. The names of several streets on the left provide more clues to the presence of the 'lost' river. Turnagain Lane was a cul-de-sac ending at the river-side: when you reached it you had to 'turn again' and go back the way you came. When Londoners cooked their food and heated their homes with open fires, much of their coal came by sea from the Newcastle area. Newcastle Close, therefore, may allude to the coal brought up the Fleet by barge, though this is not certain. Old Fleet Lane is obvious. Old Seacoal Lane is definitely a reference to coal traffic on the Fleet. The river was navigable as far as Old Seacoal Lane until 1765, when New Bridge Street, the next and final section of the walk, was built over it.

New Bridge Street and Bridewell

New Bridge Street begins at Ludgate Circus, the meeting point of two ancient thoroughfares: Fleet Street and Ludgate Hill. Here the river slices its way through the 50-foot (15-m) -high terrace forming the north bank of the Thames. As you make your way down the street, you can see how the ground continues to rise steeply on either side until quite near the Thames.

For 300 years the wide mouth of the Fleet (fleet is Anglo-Saxon for tidal inlet) was dominated by a royal palace-turned-prison called Bridewell (another watery name). Although the main part of the Tudor building was pulled down in the 1860s, a reminder of it exists in the name of Bridewell Place on the right. Also, a little further on, the prison's 1805 gatehouse, complete with black spiked gate, still stands. A little further on still is a street with the resonant name of 'Watergate'. This marks the position of the prison's river entrance. It is some distance from the modern Thames ahead, showing how much land has been reclaimed over the past couple of centuries or so, particularly at this point.

The Fleet outflow

Near the entrance to Watergate you will see an entrance to the Blackfriars subway. Go down here for the final stage of the walk: the search for the point at which the Fleet finally flows out into the Thames after its 4½-mile (7-km) journey from Hampstead Heath. At the foot of the stairs go left and then right, making for exit 5 from the subway. When you come out into the open air again, don't go up the steps onto the bridge, but turn right down to Paul's Walk. At the foot of the steps, lean out over the water and crane your head to the left: if it's low tide you should be rewarded with your Holy Grail, a clear, if oblique, view of the arched entrance to the Fleet tunnel. There is a better view of the entrance from the high-level platform of Blackfriars railway (as opposed to underground) station to your left. This runs out over the river, allowing you to look back and down at the river gate. However, you may need a ticket in order to get onto the platform in the first place.

The walk ends at Blackfriars station, accessible through the subway.

THE NOTORIOUS
FLEET VALLEY

Summary: Until it was covered over, the Fleet River was little more than an open sewer. Because of this, its valley, separating Holborn and Fleet Street from Smithfield and **St Paul's**, was for centuries one of the most pestilential and notorious parts of London – the haunt of the poor, the criminal and the outcast. Here on the banks of the Fleet, could be found pre-18th century London's main red-light district, its most notorious criminals' sanctuary, one of its three worst rookeries (a rookery was a slum criminal quarter), two of its five main places of execution and no fewer than seven of its prisons – including the famous Fleet debtors' prison, Newgate, the main prison for London and the county of Middlesex, and the Clerkenwell House of Detention. This gruesome walk visits all these places, plus – incidentally – the Inner Temple (an inn of court), St James's (the parish church of Clerkenwell) and Smithfield market.

Start and finish:	Blackfriars station (Circle and District Underground Lines).
Length:	3 miles (5km).
Time:	2½ hours.
Refreshments:	Plenty of places in Fleet Street, near the start of the walk, and around Farringdon station, about two-thirds of the way round; but Exmouth Market at the halfway stage (many new restaurants, bars and cafés) and Clerkenwell Green soon after (attractive square with seats and shade) are the natural places to stop.
Note:	If you do this walk at the weekend, you must miss a short section near the beginning which goes through the Inner Temple. Follow the dotted line on the map to pick up the walk again a little later on in Fleet Street.

From Blackfriars station, subway exit 8 brings you out on the west side of New Bridge Street, facing north up the valley of the Fleet. It was on scaffolding under Blackfriars Bridge behind you that Italian banker Roberto Calvi was found hanging on 18 June 1982, his wallet stuffed with cash and his pockets with bricks. No one has yet been convicted of his murder, but the theory is that he was killed by the Sicilian Mafia because he lost money borrowed from them to cover debts of the failed Banco Ambrosiano, of which he was chairman. The Mafia subsequently recovered its money, but Calvi was made to pay for his financial ineptitude nonetheless.

Continue along New Bridge Street, walking away from the bridge and crossing the entrance to Tudor Street. No. 14 New Bridge Street, on the left, is the former entrance to Bridewell, a former royal palace converted into a prison in the 16th century. Bridewell was the earliest of the so-called Houses of Correction, prisons where strumpets, vagrants and other petty offenders were whipped and put to work

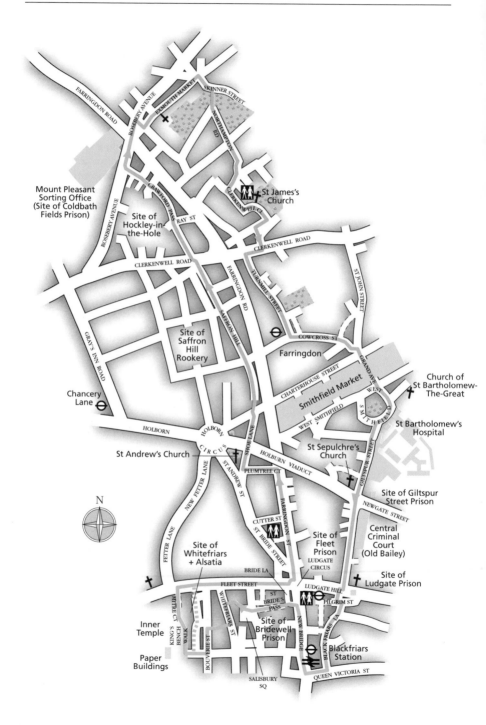

in an attempt to cure them of their disorderly ways. By the early 1700s the public whippings of semi-naked prostitutes in a black-draped room at Bridewell had become such a popular sight for men about town that a special balustraded gallery had to be built to accommodate them. The whippings were stopped later in the century, and after three centuries the prison closed in 1855.

Cross Bridewell Place, the northern limit of the prison, and turn next left into Bride Lane. When this bends round to the right, go straight on into St Bride's Passage and up the steps. The height gained represents the west bank of the Fleet River. Go straight on through the covered walkway into Salisbury Square, cross diagonally right to the covered entrance to Hanging Sword Alley, and follow the alley round to the left. This area was well known for its fencing schools during the 17th century, when men commonly wore swords. In the 18th century Hanging Sword Alley was home to a notorious criminals' drinking den called Blood Bowl House. Artist William Hogarth used it as one of the locations in his pictorial story of the Idle Apprentice, a young lad who ends his days on the gallows.

At the end of the alley, turn left into Whitefriars Street, formerly called Water Lane. Until the 1870s there was an old inn on the right where, a century earlier (on Wednesday 12 January 1763 to be precise), the 22-year-old James Boswell, later the biographer of Dr Johnson, successfully bedded actress Louisa Lewis after a month-long siege. It was the first sex Boswell had had since arriving in London two months previously, and he was mighty proud of his 'god-like' performance, climaxing no fewer than five times. Louisa was apparently satisfied after two. 'I surely may be styled a Man of Pleasure,' the would-be rake confided proudly to his diary after his night of lust.

Alsatia

When you draw abreast of the Harrow pub on the left, turn right into Ashentree Court. You are now entering what were once the precincts of the Carmelite or Whitefriars Monastery. At the end of Ashentree Court, in the basement of the modern office block on the right, you can see the little medieval vault that is the only surviving part of the monastery. After its closure in the mid-16th century the monastery was mostly built over, but its medieval right of sanctuary remained. Strictly speaking the sanctuary was for debtors only, but thieves, murderers, prostitutes and others took advantage of it to create a lawless and violent no-go area where officers of the law feared to tread. Called Alsatia – after Alsace, the disputed borderland between Germany and France where fighting was more or less constant – it was the most notorious of several similar sanctuaries in 17th-century London.

From the medieval vault continue on through Magpie Alley to Bouverie Street, turn left and then at Tudor Street turn right. Ahead you can now see a gateway leading into the Inner Temple, one of the four inns of court where barristers have their chambers. When Alsatia was in full swing, gates in the Temple wall connecting the two enclaves led to frequent battles between the lawyers and their troublesome neighbours. In July 1691 the lawyers walled this particular gate up, but the Alsatians objected and knocked it down. A fierce fight ensued in which two people were killed and several wounded. 'Captain' Francis White, the Alsatians' ringleader, was convicted of murder and hanged in nearby Fleet Street in 1693. Four years later an Act of Parliament was passed which eventually led to the final suppression of the sanctuaries.

At the end of Tudor Street carry on through the gate into the Temple. (If it is a weekend and the gate is closed, pick up the walk again by turning right into Temple Lane and making your way via Lombard Lane – one of the main streets of Alsatia – and Pleydell Court into Fleet Street.) Straight ahead is Paper Buildings where Thomas Bambridge lived in the 18th century. One of the most sadistic and corrupt keepers of London's old prisons, Bambridge was dismissed from his job as warden of the Fleet after a Parliamentary investigation in 1729 found him guilty of 'the highest crimes and misdemeanours'. Perhaps haunted by his past, Bambridge committed suicide in his chambers at 9 Paper Buildings by cutting his throat on 11 July 1741.

Robbery and Murder

Turn right now into King's Bench Walk. Bearing left towards the top you pass the Temple library and an archway leading into another part of the Temple called – before it was bombed during World War II – Tanfield Court. A young barrister living here in February 1733 found certain strange items in his rooms which it turned out his cleaner, 22-year-old Sarah Malcolm, had stolen from another of her employers, one Mrs Duncomb. During the robbery, the elderly Mrs Duncomb and two of her female servants had been murdered. Sarah admitted the robbery but denied the murders, but went to the gallows anyway. Huge crowds turned out to see her hanged in Fleet Street, just outside Temple Gate. So closely were the spectators packed together that a local woman was able to cross the road by walking on their shoulders.

Continue to the top of King's Bench Walk, and then go through the arch in Mitre Court Buildings into Old Mitre Court, passing, on the right, Serjeant's Inn, another lawyers' enclave. Just before you go through a further arch, leading into Fleet Street, turn right and then left into a little alley in the corner called Hare Place. This is all that remains of a once much longer passage called Ram Alley, which stretched back from Fleet Street to King's Bench Walk. Ram Alley was probably the most notorious thoroughfare in all Alsatia. Overhanging houses nearly met at the top, making it dark and noisome. The footway was little more than a sewer, and every house that was not a cookshop for a neighbouring inn was a brothel or an unlicensed drinking den.

Sadistic employer

As you emerge from Hare Place onto Fleet Street you are close to where Sarah Malcolm and 'Captain' White were hanged. You are also close to the site of another particularly notorious 18th-century murder. This took place in Fleur-de-Lis Court, which ran off the north side of Fleet Street until 1984, when Fetter Lane, to your left, was widened. In 1767 servant girl Mary Clifford died here of injuries received from her sadistic employer, midwife Elizabeth Brownrigg. Mrs Brownrigg was hanged at Tyburn in September that year. Her death mask is in Scotland Yard's crime museum.

Turn right down Fleet Street (picking up the weekend detour at covered Pleydell Court). When you get to Bouverie Street you are outside the main gate of Whitefriars. Another street execution took place here in 1612, when the two assassins of Whitefriars fencing master John Turner were hanged, one 6 feet (2m) higher than the other because he was of higher social rank! They had been hired for the job by Scottish peer Lord Sanquhar, who had lost an eye in a fencing match with Turner five years previously and somewhat belatedly sought his revenge. Sanquhar also went to the gallows for the crime, but outside Westminster Hall, which you pass on the Westminster and St James's walk.

At the lights just ahead, cross Fleet Street and continue on down the hill. When you get to the flamboyant Art Deco office building with the clock on the front, note the gateway at the far end marked 'IN', just before No. 133. This marks the approximate site of the house where Mary Frith lived and where she died on 26 July 1659, aged 78. By rights she should have been hanged long before because ever since her youth in Shakespeare's London she had been a notorious thief, pickpocket, highwayman and fence, usually dressing in men's clothes and much given to roistering and drinking. When she was about 30, Middleton and Dekker immortalized her in their play *The Roaring Girl* (1611) under the name by which she is best known today – Moll Cutpurse. Moll was buried in the churchyard of St Bride's across the road.

Pornographic novel

Carry on down Fleet Street to Ludgate Circus and turn left into Farringdon Street. Over on the right (effectively across the Fleet), the office building at 14 Farringdon Street, between Old Seacole Lane and Old Fleet Lane, stands on the site of the Fleet prison. Apart from the **Tower**, Newgate and the Fleet were the oldest prisons in London, having been founded in the 1100s. Originally the Fleet was moated, which cannot have done much for the health of its inmates. Later a 40-foot (12-m) wall ensured security. Until it evolved into a debtors' prison, it received prisoners from various courts, including the Court of Common Pleas, which administered it, and the infamous Court of Star Chamber, which, until its abolition in the 17th century, had the power to lock people up without trial. In the 1740s John Cleland was in the Fleet when he wrote what must be the most famous pornographic novel in the English language – *Fanny Hill* (1750).

The Liberty of the Fleet (or Rules) extended left and right of the prison and also up the hill behind it to Old Bailey. Here in the 17th and 18th centuries so-called Fleet parsons – drunken, indebted and otherwise 'fallen' clergymen – married people in taverns without banns or licences, for, of course, the appropriate fee. Fleet marriages were legal but led to so many abuses – bigamy, for example, and the forced marriages of heiresses to fortune-hunting scoundrels – that they were abolished by the Marriage Act of 1754. Thereafter people who wished to marry secretly or in haste had to cross the border into Scotland – hence the fame of Gretna Green.

Pepys and prostitutes

The north side of Fleet prison was bounded by Fleet Lane, the same as today's Old Fleet Lane. In the 17th century this was a notorious haunt of prostitutes, many of whom no doubt earned good money from frustrated debtors in the adjacent gaol. Prostitutes were regularly admitted to London's old prisons, and on one occasion in Shakespeare's time the managers of Bridewell were even found to be running it as a brothel. In July 1664 a particularly attractive Fleet Lane whore caught the attention of diarist and naval administrator Samuel Pepys. He became so obsessed with her that he came back on several occasions just to get a glimpse of her. But though sorely tempted he never actually went to bed with her.

Now continue along Farringdon Street, following the course of the Fleet River. The height of the bridge ahead, built in the 19th century to carry a new road from Holborn to the City, gives you some idea of the depth of the river valley here. Just before the bridge, turn left into Plumtree Court and then right into Shoe Lane, and continue under the bridge. Beyond the bridge, this part of Shoe Lane used to be called Field Lane. Leading as it did to the notorious thieves' rookery of Saffron Hill, the lane had an evil reputation. In the early 18th century it was the address of London's biggest male brothel, Mother Clap's molly house ('molly' was slang for homosexual). In those days sodomy was a capital offence: after a raid in February 1726, three patrons were hanged at Tyburn. By Dickens's time the place had become a 'celebrated receptacle for stolen goods'; people said you could have your handkerchief stolen at one end of the street and buy it back at the other!

When you get to Charterhouse Street you are standing at the beginning of Chick Lane, another notorious street, which ran down to the Fleet on your right and then up the hill on the far side to the sheep pens in West Smithfield, roughly where the green-domed Smithfield Market is now. An ancient house down by the river was supposed to have been a regular rendezvous of 18th-century gang leader Jonathan Wild and highwayman Jack Sheppard. It was full of hidden doors and secret hiding places, and there was a plank bridge at the back so that inmates could escape across the Fleet. The house was pulled down in 1840, some 15 years before the whole area was cleared for the Clerkenwell improvements of the mid-1850s.

Wretched place

From Shoe Lane, cross Charterhouse Street diagonally right and go down the steps into Saffron Hill. Walk along for some distance, crossing Greville Street. By the mid-19th century this area had degenerated into one of the three worst slum rookeries in Victorian London – St Giles near Covent Garden and Bermondsey in East London being the others. Even the local vicar from nearby St Andrew's Holborn dared not visit without a police escort. Dickens lived under a mile away while writing *Oliver Twist* (1837–39) and located Fagin's lair in it. 'A dirtier or more wretched place he had never seen' is Oliver's reaction when he first sets eyes on Saffron Hill. It was narrow, smelly and muddy, full of empty shops, busy pubs, screaming children and drunken, brawling people. Some of these would have been Italians, for it was at about this time that immigrants from the Mediterranean – some of them beggar-masters with troops of professional boy beggars – were beginning to turn the Holborn/Clerkenwell area into London's Italian quarter.

Just beyond St Cross Street is Saffron Street, on the right. Near here in 1865 an incident in a pub led to a fight between locals and Italian immigrants and very nearly to a tragic miscarriage of justice. One local was killed in the fight and Serafino Pelizzioni was sentenced to death for his murder. But at the last moment it was found that he had been wrongly accused in place of his cousin, who was subsequently imprisoned for manslaughter.

Continue to the end of Saffron Hill, cross Clerkenwell Road and go down Herbal Hill to Ray Street, originally known – because of its low-lying position – as Hockley-in-the-Hole. Around 1700, when Hockley-in-the-Hole was on the northern edge of London, the violent sports such as bull- and bear-baiting and swordsmen's prize fights which had traditionally been one of the attractions of Southwark's

Bankside district (where **Shakespeare's Globe** and **Tate Modern** are now) were transferred here for the entertainment of a new and less socially exalted audience – bloodthirsty Smithfield butchers mostly, who bred vicious dogs for dog fights and animal baiting. The Coach and Horses pub to your left is said to stand on the site of the ring where these sanguinary shows were held.

Cross Ray Street into Crawford Passage. At the end, cross Bakers Row, go past the trees into the remains of Coldbath Square and continue on to Rosebery Avenue. Across the road, Mount Pleasant sorting office stands on the site of Coldbath Fields Prison, built on a public dungheap in 1794. This aptly named institution soon became notorious for its punishing regime of solitary confinement and arduous treadwheeling. The latter was so hard that the Royal Artillery stopped sending its offenders here because they returned unfit for service! London's criminals were so shocked by the harsh conditions they encountered at Coldbath Fields that they nicknamed the gaol the Bastille, usually shortened to Steel. The Steel closed in 1877.

Fenian explosion

Turn right past the fire station and cross Farringdon Road into Exmouth Market. At the end, turn right into Rosoman Street and, when the road bends left, carry straight on, joining up with Northampton Road. Carry on along here as far as Corporation Row. Behind the wall, Kingsway College stands on the site of an old prison known as the Clerkenwell House of Detention, dating from the early 17th century. In 1724 notorious highwayman Jack Sheppard escaped from the prison by scaling the 22-foot (6.7-m) wall with his fat mistress Edgeworth Bess on his back. In 1867 Irish Fenians, forerunners of the IRA, blew a hole in the prison's north wall in a bid to free two colleagues. The attempt failed, but the explosion wrecked many of the houses that then stood in Corporation Row; six people, including two children, were killed instantly, nine died later and about 40 were injured or disabled for life. The prison closed in 1877.

From the entrance to Corporation Row, go slightly right into Clerkenwell Close and follow this road round to the left, past the entrance to St James's Church, which has a memorial to the Fenians' victims. Clerkenwell Close brings you to Clerkenwell Green. In Tudor times and earlier, the Green was occasionally used as a place of execution. In 1538, for example, 20,000 Londoners saw three men, including one of the city's hangmen, hanged for robbery at Smithfield's St Bartholomew's Fair.

Wild oats

Turn right now, and then left in front of the old Middlesex Sessions (or court) House. At Clerkenwell Road, go right and then first left into Turnmill Street, an ancient thoroughfare that ran along the east side of the Fleet River. Turnmill Street was already known for its whores in the 15th century. By the time of Shakespeare (who has Justice Shallow in *Henry IV Part II* boasting about sowing his wild oats in Turnmill Street) it had become London's main red-light district north of the river. Court records reveal at least five brothels in the street between 1613 and 1616.

At the end, turn left into Cowcross Street. Follow this round to Charterhouse Street and cross over into Grand Avenue, which takes you through Smithfield Meat Market into West Smithfield. Keep left round the square. In the corner you come to the west entrance of **St Bartholomew's Church**. The victims of Smithfield burnings had to face this entrance, so the executions must have taken place very near here. Ahead of you, on the wall of St Bartholomew's Hospital (Museum of), is a memorial to Sir William Wallace, the Scottish patriot hung, drawn and quartered at Smithfield on 23 August 1305. Not all executions here were official. In 1754 two thief-takers called Egan and Salmon, pilloried at Smithfield for luring young men into crime and then betraying them to gain the rewards, were actually stoned to death by a crowd outraged that the two principals should have escaped the death sentence when several of their victims had gone to the gallows.

Turn left out of West Smithfield into Giltspur Street. Cock Lane, on the right, was one of the few places in the Middle Ages where prostitutes were legally allowed to ply their trade. In 1762 the notorious Cock Lane Ghost hoax was perpetrated at a house about halfway down on the left-hand side. Well known people including the Duke of York and Dr Johnson came to investigate, but it turned out that the noises supposedly made by the ghost – said to be the spirit of a young woman poisoned with arsenic – were in fact the product of a young girl scratching and knocking on a board concealed beneath her stays. Note the inscription on the right-hand corner of the entrance to the street, with its references to resurrection men. Although it is questionable that the Fortune of War pub that once stood here was in fact the main port of call for bodysnatchers north of the river (if indeed there ever was such a place), two notorious snatchers called Bishop and Williams of whom more in a moment, certainly used it as a rendezvous.

At the end of Giltspur Street is **St Sepulchre's Church**. Murderess Sarah Malcolm, whom you encountered at the start of this walk, was briefly interred here after her execution. Later her skeleton was exhumed and sent to the Botanical Garden at Cambridge, whence, the Garden says, it has since disappeared. Opposite St Sepulchre's, the Merrill Lynch building stands on the site of the Giltspur Street prison, opened in 1791 and closed in 1855. One of the two prisons belonging to the sheriffs of London, this was the third and last incarnation of a medieval prison which originally stood in Bread Street. The sheriffs' other prison was the Wood Street Compter (pronounced counter), remains of which can be seen on the Exploring the Secret City (East of St Paul's) walk (page 142).

Executioner's kitchen

Cross Newgate Street into Old Bailey. On the left-hand corner the **Central Criminal Court**, better known as the Old Bailey, stands on the site of Newgate Prison, closed in 1902. In this broad open space thousands gathered to watch public executions outside Newgate from 1783 until 1868. The better-off folk rented rooms in houses and pubs opposite, like the Magpie and Stump, which survives in modern form. The hoi-polloi thronged the street, risking death in the crush. The gallows were erected outside the debtors' door, which was approximately where the disused gated entrance to the Central Criminal Court is now. The gaol was to the left of where you are standing (the original gaol was in the gatehouse straddling Newgate) and the sessions (or court) house was to the right. In between was the infamous Press Yard, off which was the Press Room where murderers and others who refused to plead were 'pressed' with increasingly heavy weights until they either agreed to plead or, in a few cases, died. On the prison side was the executioner's kitchen, where the heads and limbs of dismembered traitors would be boiled in bay salt and cumin seed to preserve them when they were impaled on spikes fixed to the top of London's various gates, especially the one at the south end of London Bridge. It was not unknown for the executioner and inmates to chuck the heads about like a football. In 1820 the last beheadings in England took place outside Newgate when, for a fee of 20 guineas, a masked resurrection man armed with an amputating knife cut off the heads of five men who had just been hanged for their part in a plot to assassinate members of the Cabinet.

Just beyond the Old Bailey sessions house – where the modern court extension is now – stood Surgeons' Hall, the headquarters of what later became the Royal College of Surgeons. Here, from 1752 onwards, were brought the corpses of executed murderers, either for public dissection on the premises or for clearance for dissection at one of the teaching hospitals. Like street execution, dissection was regarded as an especial humiliation. Lord Ferrers, hanged at Tyburn for murdering his steward, not surprisingly felt the insult particularly acutely; his body was delivered to Surgeons' Hall in his own coach on 5 May 1760. It was in the late 18th century, when the supply of bodies from Surgeons' Hall proved inadequate to meet the increasing demands of the expanding surgical profession, that bodysnatchers, also known as resurrection men, began digging up corpses from graveyards and selling them to the hospitals. The bodysnatchers, John Bishop and Thomas Williams, mentioned earlier, went one step further and actually resorted to murder to obtain bodies to sell. The Burke and Hare of London, they were caught in 1831 and hanged outside Newgate in front of a crowd estimated at 30,000.

Criminal Mastermind

Carry on down Old Bailey. On the right No. 30 (the middle one of a parade of modern shops) stands approximately on the site of Jonathan Wild's 'Office for the Recovery of Lost and Stolen Property', deliberately positioned close to Newgate and the Old Bailey. In the early 18th century Wild earned himself the title of Thief-Taker General for his success at recovering stolen goods and securing the conviction and execution of criminals, for both of which he was rewarded under the official thief-taking system. In reality he was the biggest gangster of them all, achieving his success by controlling the very criminals who carried out the crimes that he purported to solve. In 1725 this criminal mastermind – perhaps the greatest London has ever known – himself went to the gallows for his part in handling stolen lace worth just £10. His skeleton survives in the Royal College of Surgeons in Lincoln's Inn Fields.

At the end of Old Bailey you come to Ludgate Hill. Just to your left stood Ludgate itself, used from early times, like Newgate, as a gaol. Ludgate was a debtors' gaol for relatively high-status freemen of the City of London, and as such was more comfortable than other London prisons. But inmates were still mulcted for every last penny and, if a harsh keeper was in charge, badly treated as well. The gate was removed in 1760, but the prison lived on as the Ludgate wing of various other prisons, latterly Whitecross Street, closed in 1870.

Cross straight over Ludgate Hill into Pageantmaster Court. Turn left into Pilgrim Street and right into Ludgate Broadway, and carry on into Black Friars Lane. Follow this all the way down the hill until you come to Blackfriars station, where the walk ends.

CLERKENWELL

Summary: Close to the **St Paul's Cathedral** end of the City, Clerkenwell is particularly rich in historical features, including the remains of three medieval monasteries (St Bartholomew's, Charterhouse and the Priory of St John of Jerusalem), London's oldest church (**St Bartholomew-the-Great**), London's oldest hospital (St Bartholomew's), a centuries-old market (Smithfield), a medieval well (the Clerks' Well), an old prison (Clerkenwell House of Detention), a village green (now tarmac rather than grass), an historic theatre (Sadler's Wells) and two Georgian squares (Claremont and Myddelton). As if this were not enough, it also has connections with historic events like the Peasants' Revolt, the Reformation and the Spa Fields Riots.

Start:	Angel station (Northern Underground Line).
Finish:	Barbican station (Circle, Metropolitan and Hammersmith & City Underground Lines).
Length:	2 miles (3.2km).
Time:	1½ hours.
Refreshments:	Pubs, sandwich bars and restaurants en route in Exmouth Market (a third of the way along the route), Clerkenwell Green (two-thirds of the way and the nicest place to stop) and Smithfield (near the end of the walk).
Note:	By doing this walk in the morning you could combine it with an afternoon visit to the **Museum of London**, which is just a short distance from the end of the walk.

Turn left out of Angel station and walk down to the traffic lights. Turn right into Pentonville Road, cross over at the lights and take the first turning on the left into Claremont Square. The embankment in the centre of the square hides the upper of the two reservoirs constructed to collect water from the New River (see the Islington walk, page 73). This one dates from 1709. Walk straight down Mylne Street into the west side of Myddelton Square. Both squares were developed in the 1820s by the New River Company.

Spas and wells

At the bottom of the square cross River Street and go into Myddelton Passage. Follow this road round to the left and then turn right into Arlington Way. On your left is the back of Sadler's Wells Theatre. On your right is New River Head, the original termination of the New River, an artificial watercourse that, from 1613, brought water to London from springs 20 miles (32km) away in Hertfordshire. Looking right, through the fountain gardens, you can see remains of the old water-works, including the base of the windmill that from the early 18th century was used to pump water up to the reservoir in Claremont Square. From there, gravity-fed pipes carried it to customers. In the 1680s natural springs around the reservoirs were

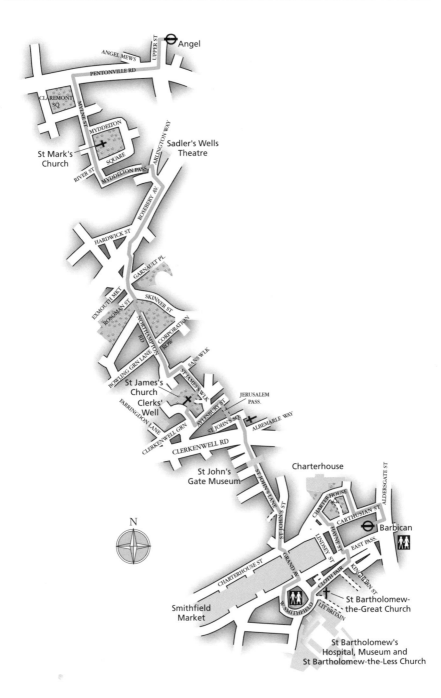

Angel

ANGEL MEWS
PENTONVILLE RD
UPPER ST

CLAREMONT SQ
MYLNE ST

MYDDELTON
SQUARE
ARLINGTON WAY
RIVER ST
MYDDELTON PASS

St Mark's
Church

Sadler's Wells
Theatre

ROSEBERY AV

HARDWICK ST

GARNAULT PL

EXMOUTH MKT
ROSOMAN ST
SKINNER ST
NORTHAMPTON RD
BOWLING GRN LANE
CORPORATION ROW

SANS WLK

ST JAMES'S WLK

St James's
Church

Clerks'
Well

FARRINGDON LANE
CLERKENWELL GRN
AYLESBURY ST
ST JOHN'S SQ

JERUSALEM
PASS.

ALBEMARLE WAY

CLERKENWELL RD

St John's
Gate Museum

Charterhouse

N

ST JOHN'S LANE
ST JOHN ST
CHARTERHOUSE
CARTHUSIAN ST
ALDERSGATE ST

Barbican

EAST PASS.

CHARTERHOUSE ST
GRAND AV
LINDSEY ST
HAYNE ST
KING FORN ST

CLOTH FAIR

Smithfield
Market

W SMITHFIELD
LIT BRITAIN

St Bartholomew-
the-Great Church

St Bartholomew's
Hospital, Museum and
St Bartholomew-the-Less Church

found to have medicinal properties and at least a dozen were developed into commercial spas.

From Arlington Way turn right onto Rosebery Avenue, transferring to the other side of the road when you get to the zebra crossing. The statue in the gardens on this side of the road is part of the Finsbury war memorial. Continue along Rosebery Avenue and take the next turning on the left into Garnault Place. Then go over the zebra crossings towards Exmouth Market and turn left into Rosoman Street. Walk straight on between the gardens when the road bends to the left. The open space here is known as Spa Fields, and it was here that the patrons of the spas danced, played games and strolled through shady walks. In 1816 the Spa Fields Riots took place here when a parliamentary reform meeting got out of hand and an attempt was made to seize the Tower of London.

Bowling green
Keep going straight on down Northampton Road towards Clerkenwell church, past the sunken playground on the left. Beyond the playground, slum clearance and rebuilding – following World War II bombing raids – have done away with the old streets and replaced them with one huge and unattractive housing estate. Cross the junction of Corporation Row (left) and Bowling Green Lane (right). There was once a bowling green here – one of Clerkenwell's many attractions for the City dwellers to the south. Once again, walk straight ahead when the road bends to the right. On the left now is the former Hugh Myddelton School, now flats and offices. Before the school a prison called the Clerkenwell House of Detention was here. Some of the subterranean cells were converted into a museum a few years ago, but this has now closed. To the right you can see evidence of recent rebuilding in Clerkenwell. Many of the new developments consist of workshops and industrial units for craftspeople and small-scale manufacturers, the aim being to support Clerkenwell's craft tradition, historically centred on clock- and watch-making.

Fenian explosion
Turn left into Sans Walk, right into St James's Walk and halfway along right again into the graveyard garden of St James's, the parish church of Clerkenwell. Go round to the left of the church to the main entrance. Inside there are memorials to the Protestant martyrs of the Reformation and to the victims of the 1867 explosion at the aforementioned House of Detention when members of the Fenian Conspiracy (forerunner of the IRA) blew a hole in the wall in an attempt to release two of their compatriots.

Turn left through the gate out of the churchyard into triangular Clerkenwell Green, historically an open space between St John's Priory (of which more later) and St Mary's Nunnery to the north. At the base of the triangle stands the old Middlesex Sessions House, built as a courthouse in 1782, used until 1920 and now occupied by freemasons. To the right of the Sessions House round the corner in Farringdon Lane is Well Court, an office block built over the Clerks' Well after which Clerkenwell is named. The well in turn is thought to have been named after London's parish clerks who gathered here annually in the Middle Ages to perform mystery plays. The well was rediscovered in 1924 and has been preserved in a small room in the office block, which is visible from the street outside.

Nearby on the right at No. 37a, in a former charity school dating from 1737, is the Marx Memorial Library. After the Spa Fields Riots Clerkenwell became a popular meeting place for radical movements and earned itself a reputation as 'the headquarters of republicanism and revolution'. Various radical organizations made use of the old charity school building and Lenin even edited one of his revolutionary papers here. The library and research centre, specializing in the labour movement, was founded in 1933.

Knights of St John

Leave Clerkenwell Green by turning left into Aylesbury Street and then right into Jerusalem Passage, the northern entrance to the medieval Priory of St John of Jerusalem. On the corner there is a plaque to Thomas Britton (1644–1714), a charcoal dealer and music scholar who held weekly concerts in the room above his warehouse where musicians of the stature of Handel regularly played. Jerusalem Passage leads into St John's Square, the main courtyard of the priory. The Knights of St John, along with the Knights Templar, were military monks charged with protecting pilgrims in the Holy Land. In 1539 the English section of the order was abolished by Henry VIII. In 1831 it was refounded as a Protestant organization and set up its headquarters in the new priory on the left of the square. In 1873 it acquired St John's Gate ahead, the 1504 southern entrance to the old priory and now a Hospitaller museum. The new order launched the St John Ambulance Brigade here in 1877.

Now cross Clerkenwell Road – driven through the square in 1878 – and go straight through the gate. Continue along St John's Lane to the junction with St John's Street. The road bellies out here because Hick's Hall, the predecessor of the Middlesex Sessions House on Clerkenwell Green, was built in the middle of the road in 1612. After that time the cattle, sheep and pigs destined for Smithfield market just passed by on either side.

Place of execution

Turn right along St John's Street into the Grand Avenue of Smithfield Market. At the end of the avenue turn right and walk in an anti-clockwise direction around the central gardens, a relic of old Smithfield, originally called Smoothfield. This open space has a long history going back to the early Middle Ages. Just outside the City wall, it was used for jousts, tournaments, fairs and meetings. St Bartholomew's Fair was held here from 1123 to 1855. During the Peasants' Revolt of 1381 the rebels were confronted by young King Richard II here and their leader, Wat Tyler, was stabbed by Lord Mayor William Walworth. Smithfield was also a place of execution; criminals were hanged while traitors, heretics and others were roasted, boiled or burnt. Over 200 Protestants were burned alive here during the six years of Queen Mary's reign in the 1550s. Smithfield was used for a regular Friday horse market as early as 1200. In 1638 a live cattle market was started. As houses surrounded the field, the market became such a nuisance that it was closed and then in 1855 moved to Islington. The dead meat market, still flourishing today, opened in 1868.

Walk around the gardens until you come to St Bartholomew's Hospital. Founded in 1123 as part of St Bartholomew's Augustinian priory, also founded in that year, this is the oldest hospital in London. In 1381 Wat Tyler was brought into the hospital after being stabbed by the Lord Mayor, but soldiers dragged him back outside and decapitated him on the spot. Behind the hospital's main gate, rebuilt in 1702 with a statue of Henry VIII in the niche above the arch, you can see the tower and roof of the hospital chapel. After Henry VIII closed the medieval priory in 1538, he allowed the hospital not only to survive but to become a new parish in its own right. The old hospital chapel became the new parish church of **St Bartholomew-the-Less** while the old priory church became the parish church of St Bartholomew-the-Great.

London's oldest church

Continue around the square to the archway beneath the black and white half-timbered building straight ahead. At second-floor level there is a statue of St Bartholomew holding the knife with which he was supposedly flayed alive while on a missionary journey to Armenia. The gateway leads to the parish church of St Bartholomew-the-Great, London's oldest church and, apart from the St Bart's hospital chapel, the only surviving part of the original Augustinian priory.

Turn left and then first right into Cloth Fair (on Sundays you can enter the church precincts and cut diagonally left across the churchyard to a gate in the railings). Cloth Fair is part of a maze of narrow streets and passageways surrounding the church. In the 15th and 16th centuries cloth was the main source of England's wealth and St Bartholomew's Fair (held over three days around St Bartholomew's Day – 24 August) was the country's biggest cloth trade fair. Merchants came from all parts of Europe to buy the famous English broadcloth. Walk along the side of the church. When you get to Kinghorn Street on the right, turn left to Ye Olde Red Cow pub. Go through the archway, across the road into Hayne Street, and then across Charterhouse Street into Charterhouse Square. Turn right past the arched entrance to Charterhouse.

Richest commoner

Charterhouse was a Carthusian monastery founded in 1370. After its closure in 1537 and the execution of 20 monks, including the prior, the building was put to a variety of uses, including storing the royal hunting tents. In 1611 Thomas Sutton, the 'richest commoner in England', bought Charterhouse and converted it into a school and an almshouse. The school became one of England's best-known public schools and still exists at Godalming in Surrey, where it moved about a hundred years ago. The almshouses are still in the Charterhouse – **Charterhouse Sutton's Hospital**.

Walk along the top of the square, passing the Charterhouse chapel behind the railings. In the corner on the left, Rutland Place leads to St Bartholomew's Hospital Medical School, built over the Great Cloister and other parts of Charterhouse destroyed in World War II bombing raids. Turn right here and then left out of the gates into Carthusian Street and walk towards the Barbican. At the main road (Aldersgate Street) turn right to Barbican station. The walk ends here, but signs point the short distance to the Museum of London for those who have the energy and desire to find out more about London's past.

THE CITY AROUND FLEET STREET AND ST PAUL'S

Summary: Until quite recently the western part of the City was the traditional centre of London's printing, publishing and newspaper industries. This circular walk includes many places associated with the area's literary past, such as St Paul's Churchyard and Fleet Street, the printers' church of **St Bride's**, Stationers' Hall and **Dr Johnson's House**. The walk's other main features include the Old Bailey courthouse together with Newgate and Bridewell prisons, the **College of Arms**, the site of Blackfriars Monastery, **St Paul's Cathedral** and other Wren churches, and Playhouse Yard, site of Shakespeare's Blackfriars Playhouse.

Start and finish:	St Paul's station (Central Underground Line).
Length:	2 miles (3.2km).
Time:	1½ hours.
Refreshments:	Various places en route, but there are two pubs worth visiting, both mentioned in the text: Ye Olde Cheshire Cheese in Vine Office Court off Fleet Street (just over halfway round the walk) and the Blackfriar near Blackfriars Bridge (about two-thirds of the way round the walk).

Take the 'St Paul's' exit from St Paul's station, turn left and make a U-turn back towards the cathedral. St Paul's is the major work of London's great architect, Sir Christopher Wren. The foundation stone was laid in 1675 when Wren was 43 years old and the last stone was put in place by his son 35 years later. Although Wren visited the site weekly, daily supervision was provided throughout the whole period by just one master-builder, Thomas Strong, of a well-known family of Cotswold masons. The original Norman cathedral, destroyed in the Great Fire, was even larger than Wren's new building and must have dwarfed the medieval city.

London book trade

Turn right along the churchyard railings towards the deanery and chapter house. A plaque on the wall on the right commemorates John Newbery, the first children's book publisher. *Little Goody Two Shoes* is probably his best-known production. In the middle of the 18th century, St Paul's Churchyard was the centre of the London book trade, as it had been for hundreds of years, even before printing arrived in England in 1476. 'Churchyard' was really a loose term for the precincts of the cathedral which over the years had become crowded with shops and houses.

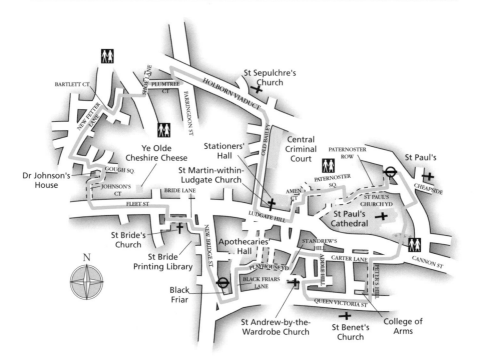

Paternosters

Go past the deanery and turn right between the chapter house and Paternoster Lodge into Paternoster Square. Built on a World War II bomb site, the square is named after nearby Paternoster Row, an ancient street where strings of prayer beads (known as paternosters) were made before the 16th-century Protestant Reformation. Turn left into Bishop's Lane and walk towards the gateway into Amen Court on the far side of Ave Maria Lane. Go to the left of the gateway and under the modern office building into the forecourt of Stationers' Hall, the livery hall of the Stationers' and Newspaper Makers' Company. In the 16th and 17th centuries the Company effectively controlled the printing and publishing trades, and until as late as 1911 all new books had to be registered at Stationers' Hall. On the front of the hall there is a plaque to Wynkyn de Worde, 'Father of Fleet Street'. We will catch up with this oddly-named person later in the walk.

Go straight past the hall and the gateway into the courtyard; along the alley called Stationer's Hall Court; and right into Ludgate Hill. On your right is the inconspicuous entrance to Wren's church of **St Martin-within-Ludgate**, situated just inside the Lud Gate of the old city. Beyond the church, turn right into Old Bailey which runs just inside the line of the old city wall. At the end of the street the **Central Criminal Court**, popularly known as the Old Bailey, is on the right (the public entrance is in covered Warwick Passage). Built in 1902, the court partially replaced the infamous Newgate Prison where in May 1868 the last public hanging in Britain took place. The victim was Michael Barrett, one of a group of Irish terrorists who had killed six innocent people in a bomb outrage the previous year (see the Clerkenwell walk, page 122). Over the road from the Old Bailey is **St Sepulchre's Church**. Originally dedicated to the martyred King Edmund, it acquired its unusual name in the Middle Ages when crusading knights heading off to the Holy Land to fight for the Holy Sepulchre in Jerusalem took to starting their journeys here. St Sepulchre's is the largest city church after St Paul's Cathedral: its contents include the old executioner's bell from Newgate Prison.

Stinking sewer

From Old Bailey turn left into Holborn Viaduct. Built in 1869, Holborn Viaduct spans Farringdon Street some way below. Beneath Farringdon Street flows the Fleet River which rises on Hampstead Heath and joins the Thames nearby. For hundreds of years the Fleet was a stinking open sewer and dump for butchers' offal, even after Wren made this section into a decent canal, flanked by 30-foot (9-m) wide wharves. It was eventually piped in and covered over in 1766. The Fleet still flows into the Thames under Blackfriars Bridge (see page 112).

After crossing the viaduct, turn left down the stairs and take two right turns into Plumtree Court. Turn left into Shoe Lane, cross the road ahead and climb the steps on the other side, going through the modern office block. At the top of the steps keep to the right, ascend another short flight of steps and then turn left and right into Bartlett Court. This brings you to New Fetter Lane where you turn left. On the right at the junction with Fetter Lane stands a statue of John Wilkes, 'champion of English freedom'. In the 1760s, Wilkes fought the Government when it tried to close his newspaper and imprison him for sedition. The Government also tried to stop him taking his seat in Parliament after his election as an MP, but violent 'Wilkes and Liberty' riots forced it to concede. The common people loved Wilkes, especially in the City where he was elected Lord Mayor in 1774. The building on the right just beyond the Wilkes statue is the former Public Record Office. It is now the library of King's College, which is part of London University. Opposite is a modern plaque commemorating the Moravian chapel and congregation, established here in the mid-18th century. The Moravians were Protestant refugees from Germany: their old burial ground still survives in Chelsea (see page 63).

Great dictionary

When you come to West Harding Street, turn left and follow the signs to Dr Johnson's House in Gough Square (that is, branch right into Pemberton Row and then right again under the arch). Johnson moved to Gough Square in 1746 and immediately set to work on the great dictionary that was to make his name – though not his fortune – when it was published nine years later. In 1759 he moved to lodgings in the Temple. This house, which he rented for £30 a year, was opened as a Johnson museum in 1914. Over at the far end of the square is a statue of Johnson's beloved cat, Hodge.

Go past the front of the house into Johnson's Court (named after a different Johnson) and follow it to Fleet Street. Turn left here towards St Paul's Cathedral, high on Ludgate Hill on the far side of the Fleet valley. The second court on the left, Bolt Court, is where Johnson died in 1784. The fourth court, Wine Office Court, was the site of an office where licences to sell wine were issued. No doubt the clerks in the office were regulars at Ye Olde Cheshire Cheese pub here. Most evenings they would have seen Johnson (he once said, 'a tavern chair is the throne of human felicity'), and many other famous literary men.

Further along Fleet Street you come to the former offices of two famous newspapers: the *Daily Telegraph* (Peterborough Court, Nos. 133–141) and *Daily Express* (building with the black glass front). Fleet Street has been synonymous with newspapers since the first daily newspaper, the *Daily Courant*, was produced here in 1702. Now all the big national newspapers and news agencies have moved elsewhere. The last to go was the famous Reuters news agency, which departed in June 2005. The exodus was prompted by a revolution in printing technology and began amid acrimonious disputes in 1986 when the *Sun* and the *News of the World* moved to Wapping.

The Father of Fleet Street

Go across Fleet Street to Wren's St Bride's Church, known as the printers' church. Now we catch up with the Alsatian printer Wynkyn de Worde for it was here, opposite the entrance to Shoe Lane, that in about 1500 he got himself a small house and workshop, and set up the first printing press in Fleet Street. He had previously been working in Westminster, first as assistant to William Caxton (the man who brought printing to England in 1476) and then as proprietor of the business after Caxton's death. It was the increasing competition in the printing world that forced him to move closer to the main book market in St Paul's Churchyard.

Turn left alongside St Bride's. Go down the steps and turn right into Bride Lane and follow the lane past the entrance to **St Bride's Institute and Printing Library**. In the library exhibition room there is an old wooden hand press, of the sort widely used from the 1400s until around 1800. When you get to New Bridge Street cross over and turn right towards Blackfriars Bridge.

The building on the right with the flagpole on the front (No. 14) is the 1802 gatehouse of the old Bridewell House of Correction. Formerly a medieval riverside palace beside the Thames, the prison was opened around 1555 and closed 300 years later when the women-only Holloway Prison was built in north London. To start with, vagrants and unruly orphaned apprentices were its main clientele. Later, large numbers of prostitutes were sent here. For many years a popular amusement for male Londoners was a visit to Bridewell to see the twice-weekly whipping of prostitutes stripped to the waist in the black-draped 'correction' room.

Memorials to the Black Friars

When you get to The Blackfriar pub – decorated in art nouveau style and the only one like it in London – turn left round the corner under the figure of the stout Black Friar and go under the railway bridge. Then turn left into Black Friars Lane. These names all come from the Black Friars (i.e. Dominican) monastery that stood here from 1278 until its dissolution in 1538. Most of the buildings were then demolished but some parts survived until the Great Fire.

Ahead, the building on the right-hand corner is **Apothecaries' Hall**, built in 1688 as the livery hall of the Apothecaries' Company, one of the City livery companies. Just before the hall, turn right into Playhouse Yard, site of the former refectory of the monastery. In Shakespeare's time the refectory was converted into the Blackfriars Playhouse, an indoor theatre (unusual for the time) with three galleries and 600 seats. Shakespeare was a partner in the theatre, and it was used in the winter by his company, the King's Men. In summer the company used their other premises, the famous open-air Globe Theatre on Bankside (see the Bankside and Southwark walk, page 153). Both theatres were closed by the Puritans in the 1640s.

Continue straight on past Church Entry into Ireland Yard. A haberdasher called William Ireland kept a shop here in the ground floor of the old monastery gatehouse. In 1613 Shakespeare bought the shop and then left it to his daughter Susannah when he died three years later. On the left, the little courtyard is part of the churchyard of St Ann Blackfriars, which was burnt in the Great Fire. Part of a wall from the monastery still stands just inside the churchyard gate.

The Dragon, the King and the Wardrobe

At the end of this alley, turn left along St Andrew's Hill and then right into Carter Lane. On the right, opposite the youth hostel, an archway leads into Wardrobe Place where the king's Master of the Wardrobe had his office and storeroom from 1359 until the Great Fire. This official was responsible for looking after all the king's ceremonial robes and spare cloth. In 1604 Shakespeare was issued with 4½ yards (4m) of scarlet cloth from the Wardrobe so that he could make himself a new suit for James I's state entry into London.

Take the next turning on the right into Addle Hill. Near the bottom of the lane go right into Wardrobe Terrace which takes you round the back of **St Andrew-by-the-Wardrobe**, Wren's last City church, finished in 1695. On the main road (Queen Victoria Street), turn left. On the right beyond Baynard House are Wren's Benet's Church and the City of London School. On this side of the road is the College of Arms – the office (and, for some, also the home) of the royal heralds who arrange all the great state occasions like coronations and state openings of Parliament. They also devise new coats of arms (for a fee) and undertake genealogical work. Heralds have picturesque names like Garter King of Arms, Bluemantle and Rouge Dragon, and this college was built for them after the Great Fire on a site – handy for the Wardrobe – that they had occupied since 1555.

Paul's Cross

On the other side of the college, turn left up Peter's Hill towards St Paul's and then, just before the main road at the top, right into Carter Lane. At the end of the lane, cross Cannon Street and walk to the left of the garden through the gate into St Paul's Churchyard. Follow the path round the end of the cathedral, passing St Paul's Choir School on the right. This is a remnant of St Paul's School that was here from 1512 until 1884 when it moved out to Hammersmith. On the far side of the cathedral is Paul's Cross, a column marking the site of an open-air pulpit that was used until 1643 for making public announcements and reading royal proclamations. The historian Carlyle called the cross '*The Times* newspaper of the Middle Ages'. Turn right here out of the churchyard and follow the road (Change Alley) to the left to St Paul's station where the walk ends.

THE CITY BETWEEN GUILDHALL AND THE TOWER

Summary: The eastern half of the City is both the oldest part and the financial centre of modern London. This circular walk sticks mainly to the City's many narrow lanes and alleys, but still manages to cover all the main institutions such as Lloyd's, the Royal Exchange, the Stock Exchange, the **Bank of England**, the **Guildhall**, **Mansion House** and Custom House, as well as taking in other features such as the site of Dick Whittington's house, the Great Fire **Monument**, the **Tower of London**, Bow Bells, Leadenhall Market, the old Billingsgate Market, many City churches and livery halls as well as several traditional City pubs and eating houses.

Start and finish:	Tower Hill station (District and Circle Underground Lines). Fenchurch Street railway station and the Docklands Light Rail's Tower Gateway station are both nearby.
Length:	2½ miles (4km).
Time:	1¾ hours.
Refreshments:	No shortage of pubs, restaurants, wine bars and sandwich bars en route plus several old-fashioned City watering holes spread out along the course of the walk and all mentioned in the text (the Jamaica Wine House, the George and Vulture – ties compulsory – the Old Dr Butler's Head, Williamson's Tavern, the Olde Wine Shades).

Leave Tower Hill Station by the 'Fenchurch Street' exit and walk round the top of Trinity Square between, on the left, Trinity Square Gardens, where prisoners from the Tower of London were executed, usually by decapitation, and on the right, Trinity House, headquarters of the 16th-century Trinity House Corporation, which is responsible for the lighthouses on the coasts of England and Wales.

Beyond Trinity House turn right into Savage Gardens, left into Pepys Street and then right into Seething Lane. In the 17th century Samuel Pepys lived and worked in the Navy Office here, and worshipped regularly in **St Olave's Church** during the period covered by his diary. He was also buried in the church after his death in 1703. St Olave's is in the City's Tower Ward and a noticeboard to the right of the churchyard gate lists the ward's alderman and common councillors. The City is divided into 26 wards, each of which elects a number of common councillors and an alderman who together form the City Corporation, presided over by the Lord Mayor.

The legend of Lloyd's

At the end of Seething Lane turn left and then right into New London Street. Go up the steps, walk straight across the forecourt of Fenchurch Street station (to the left you can see the remains of All Hallows Staining) and then go across Fenchurch Street into Billiter Street to the left. Take the first turning on the left into Fenchurch Avenue. Ahead is the new high-tech headquarters of Lloyd's, the world-famous insurance market originally started in Edward Lloyd's coffee house in Tower Street in the 1680s.

Turn left and right by Lloyd's into Leadenhall Market, established here in the 1300s and rebuilt in 1881. Turn left at the central crossroads, take the second turning on the right into Bull's Head Passage by Kent's the fruiterers, cross Gracechurch Street and go into Bell Inn Yard ahead on the left. Bell Inn was a casualty of the Great Fire of 1666.

Turn right into St Michael's Alley at the end of the yard and go into the former churchyard of **St Michael Cornhill** with Christopher Wren's church on the far side. Turn left here and go as far as the first crossroads in this maze of narrow passages. On the right is the Jamaica Wine House, built on the site of London's first coffee house, the Sign of the Pasqua Rosee's Head, which opened in 1652. In the 1670s it became the Jamaica Coffee House, an unofficial post office for letters to the West Indies and a general rendezvous for merchants and sea captains involved in the Jamaica trade. On the left, the George and Vulture, a traditional City pub and chop house (ties compulsory), has been serving bankers, brokers, merchants and clerks for the best part of 300 years.

Walk on past the jeweller's shop into Castle Court. Turn right into Ball Court at the sign pointing to Simpson's Tavern (opened 1757). On Cornhill, turn left and cross the road at the traffic lights. Go left again and then right into the open space of Royal Exchange Buildings. The Royal Exchange on the left was founded in 1570 by Sir Thomas Gresham as a meeting place for merchants. This is the third building on the site and it was last used for its original purpose in 1939.

Home of the Old Lady

At the end of Royal Exchange Buildings is a statue of George Peabody, the American-born founder of the 19th-century Peabody housing trust. Peabody Buildings are still a common sight in London, and the City recognized his work on behalf of the poor by making him a freeman. Standing by the statue, you can see to the right the former Stock Exchange, made redundant by the introduction of electronic trading, and the International Financial Centre – at 600 feet (183m) the tallest building in central London.

Turn left now and cross Threadneedle Street into Bartholomew Lane. As you do so look left to the porticoed façade of the 18th-century Mansion House, official residence of the City's Lord Mayor during his (or her) one-year term of office. On the left now is the back of the Bank of England, its 18th-century walls windowless for extra security. Familiarly known as the Old Lady of Threadneedle Street and founded in 1694 to raise money for war, the bank now issues banknotes, stores the national gold reserves and supervises financial activities in the City.

At the end of Bartholomew Lane, turn left into Lothbury and then right into Tokenhouse Yard. In the 1600s tokens were minted and issued here whenever coin

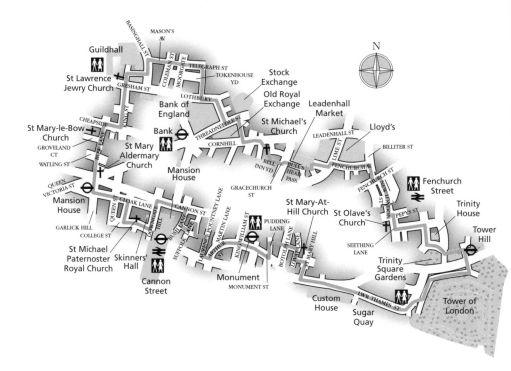

of the realm was in short supply. Most of the buildings at the end of the yard are occupied by Cazenove's, the most fashionable of the old stock-broking firms in the City and one of the few to remain independent following deregulation of the City's financial markets in 1987.

Shock treatment

Go straight through the passage under Cazenove's and turn left into Telegraph Street. Cross Moorgate – a road that led north towards one of the old City gates – into Great Bell Alley. Then cross Coleman Street into Mason's Avenue. The Old Dr Butler's Head here was one of several pubs founded around 1616 to sell a successful brand of medicinal ale concocted by Dr William Butler, the king's physician. Dr Butler's speciality was shock treatment: he once cured a patient by having him thrown out of a window into the Thames!

Mason's Avenue leads to Basinghall Street where Hugh Myddelton had his office (see the Islington walk, page 73). Turn left here and then first right into Guildhall Buildings, passing on the left the Mayor's and City of London Court (the Lord Mayor is also the City's chief magistrate) into Guildhall Yard, where the City Corporation does its work. On the right-hand side is the 15th-century Guildhall, much repaired after the Great Fire and the Blitz, and the new Guildhall Art Gallery, which incorporates remains of London's 2,000-year-old Roman amphitheatre. Opposite stands **St Lawrence Jewry Church**, so named because in medieval times it stood in the Jewish quarter of the City. It now serves as the official church of the Corporation of London.

Turn left by the church and cross Gresham Street into King Street. Turn right into Cheapside and then left into Bow Lane by Wren's **St Mary-le-Bow Church**. Traditionally, anyone born within the sound of Bow bells was said to be a true Cockney, or pure Londoner. That was in the days when the City was densely populated. Today only a few thousand actually live here: most people simply commute to work.

Continue along Bow Lane. To the right in Groveland Court is Williamson's Tavern, started in 1739 by Robert Williamson in what had previously been the Lord Mayor's house. The gates at the end were presented to the then Lord Mayor by William III and Queen Mary after a visit to the City. Go across Watling Street, the Roman road from Dover in Kent to Shropshire on the Welsh border. Wren is said to have built what is now Ye Olde Watling pub and to have worked here while **St Paul's Cathedral** (visible to the right) was being built. Walk past St Aldermary Church and cross Queen Victoria Street into Garlick Hill by Mansion House station, where the ground begins to drop steeply away towards the river. Garlic was once sold in this district; more recently it was the centre of the fur and skin trade. Take the first turning on the left into Great St Thomas Apostle Street; at the end you pass the site of St Thomas the Apostle church and some handsome merchants' houses. Go across Queen Street into Cloak Lane. The view right is of Southwark Bridge and the *Financial Times* building on the south side of the Thames.

Pantomime hero

From Cloak Lane take the first turning on the right down College Hill. Here on the left lived Richard Whittington, the most famous of all London's citizens. The youngest son of a Gloucestershire landowner, Whittington made his fortune as a mercer (dealer in textiles) and was Lord Mayor four times between 1397 and 1419. Although he married, he died childless so he left most of his enormous wealth to various charities. His generosity made him a popular hero and he is still celebrated in children's stories and Christmas pantomimes.

At the bottom of College Hill is the church of **St Michael Paternoster Royal**: Whittington was buried in its Great Fire predecessor in 1423. Turn left along winding College Street past the livery hall of the Innholders' Company. Then turn left again into Dowgate Hill past three more livery halls: first, the Dyers' Company; second, the Skinners' Company (a fine Georgian stuccoed building of 1778 – the actual **Skinners' Hall** is in a courtyard to the rear); and third, the Tallow Chandlers' Company (only the gate is visible – again the hall is in a rear courtyard). The oldest City livery companies (modern creations have taken the total to over 100) are the descendants of the trade guilds that controlled all business life in the medieval City. Today they are mainly charitable and social bodies. All livery men are freemen and all vote in the Lord Mayor's election.

At the top of the hill turn right past Cannon Street station and then right again into Bush Lane. Then take the first turning on the left into Gophir Lane and turn left again into cobbled Suffolk Lane. Follow this round to the right and turn right into Laurence Pountney Hill. On the right now are two merchants' houses, built in 1703 and the finest houses of their date in the City. In the little square turn left along the sunken path between the two churchyard gardens. Here stood Laurence Pountney Church and Corpus Christi College, both destroyed in the Great Fire. They were founded by Sir John de Pulteney, a Drapers' Company man and Lord Mayor in the 1330s. His house, which was later inhabited by the Black Prince, eldest son of Edward III, stood on the site of the two merchants' houses.

Continue straight across Laurence Pountney Lane and through the small car park to Martin Lane. On the left corner is the Olde Wine Shades, started just before the Great Fire and one of only a couple of City taverns to have survived the conflagration. Turn right here and then immediately left into Arthur Street. Then cross King William Street (subway to left) to the Monument, built by Wren in 1677 as the City's memorial to the Great Fire of 1666 (see the panel on the base for more history). The panorama from the top is well worth the climb up the spiral staircase inside.

The City ablaze

Go past the Monument along Monument Street and take the first turning on the left into Pudding Lane. The Great Fire started here during the night of 2 September 1666 in the ovens of the king's baker – aptly named Faryner ('farine' is French for flour). Take the first turning on the right into St George's Lane and go straight across Botolph Lane and through Botolph Alley to **St Mary-at-Hill Church** in Lovat Lane. This church was gutted in 1986 by a fire, a more than usually sad event because it was the only Wren City church to have retained its original interior more or less as the architect designed it. Go through the passage to the right of the church to **St Mary-at-Hill** (the church entrance is through a door-way up the hill to the left) and then turn right and left into cobbled St Dunstan's Lane. With the exception of its tower, now used as a chapel, Wren's church of St Dunstan-in-the-East at the end of the lane was largely destroyed during World War II. It has since been converted into a public garden.

Turn right here and cross over the main road (Lower Thames Street) to the Custom House, where customs duties on all goods imported into London have been collected since at least the 1200s. To the right is the former Billingsgate fish market, which was used from the early Middle Ages until the market moved to a new docklands' site in 1982. Turn left along Lower Thames Street, and walk straight on when the road bends left up the hill. On the right is Sugar Quay where the great sugar firm of Tate and Lyle has its offices. Turn right on to the quayside to see the 1,200 foot- (366 metre-) long river frontage of the Custom House. Then turn left along the quayside walk. You come out of Three Quays Walk by Tower Pier and the entrance to the 900-year-old Tower of London, built just outside the City boundary by William the Conqueror to overawe potentially troublesome citizens. Go through the gates by the ticket office and along the moat-side walk. Turn left into the subway under the road and climb the steps to Tower Hill Station, where the walk ends.

Plate 26: Exploring the Secret City (West of St Paul's)
The golden figure of Justice presides over the City's Central
Criminal Court, better known as the Old Bailey (see page 139).

Plate 27: Exploring the Secret City (East of St Paul's)
The Bank of England, founded in 1694, is the geographical
and financial heart of the City (see page 147).

Plate 28: Lambeth and the South Bank
Love it or loathe it, the late 20th-century architecture of the South Bank arts complex has a certain stark beauty (see page 152).

Plate 29: Bankside and Southwark
Shakespeare's Globe theatre has been rebuilt close to its original
Bankside site opposite the City in Southwark (see page 155).

Plate 30: Bermondsey to Rotherhithe
A spectacular view across the Thames to Canary Wharf
from Rotherhithe Street (see page 162).

Plate 31: The Notorious East End
The Blind Beggar pub in the East End where gangster
Ronnie Kray shot George Cornell in 1966 (see page 168).

Plate 32: Wapping to Limehouse
*The former St Katharine's Dock next to Tower Bridge
is now a thriving yacht marina (see page 173).*

Plate 33: Barnes to Fulham
*Rowing starts early on the Thames at Putney, a great boating
centre and the start point of the University Boat Race (see page 179).*

Plate 34: Kew to Hammersmith
*Chiswick House, the beautiful 18th-century villa at the
mid-point of the Kew to Hammersmith walk (see page 183).*

EXPLORING THE
SECRET CITY
(WEST OF ST PAUL'S)

Summary: This circular walk covers roughly the same part of the City as the walk around Fleet Street and St Paul's, but – like its counterpart in the eastern part of the City – is designed specifically to explore the area's extraordinary network of passages, courts and other obscure little thoroughfares. All these various ways are relics of the City's largely medieval street layout, itself one of the most wonderful features of London. Other things worthy of note on this walk are Postman's Park and the heroes' memorial, **Dr Johnson's House**, a medieval crypt and hall, a private road that is part of Cambridgeshire, the Newgate execution bell, the **Central Criminal Court** (Old Bailey), London's hardest-to-find pub and the **St Bride Printing Library**.

Start and finish:	St Paul's station (Central Underground Line).
Length:	2 miles (3km).
Time:	1½ hours.
Refreshments:	Pubs all along the route and nests of sandwich bars on Fleet Street (halfway) and in the Carter Lane area near the end, but a special place to look out for is Ely Place, a third of the way along. Here you will find the ancient Olde Mitre pub and at St Etheldreda's Church, a café serving lunch and afternoon tea 12 noon–2.30pm and 3pm–4.30pm Monday to Friday.
Note:	See note (a) to the Exploring the Secret City (East of St Paul's) walk on page 142.

Take the main exit from St Paul's station and turn left at the top of the stairs, heading north along St Martin's le Grand towards the tree on the left at the far end. Nomura House to your left was built about a century ago following the demolition of three earlier buildings, as the blue plaques indicate. At the tree turn left into Postman's Park and walk towards the building in the middle with the tiled roof. This is an extraordinary monument, a memorial to 53 men, women and children who gave their lives to save others from disaster: fires, drowning, out-of-control trains and other everyday catastrophes. It was the inspiration of Victorian artist G. F. Watts. He had been struck by the story of Alice Ayres, a 26-year-old live-in maid who had rescued her employer's three children from a fire and then lost her own life while attempting to jump to safety from an upstairs window. Watts felt that such people deserved some permanent memorial so, after due negotiations, he began this wall of plaques. His wife added a few after his death but the idea never really caught on so even now there are still some blanks to be filled up.

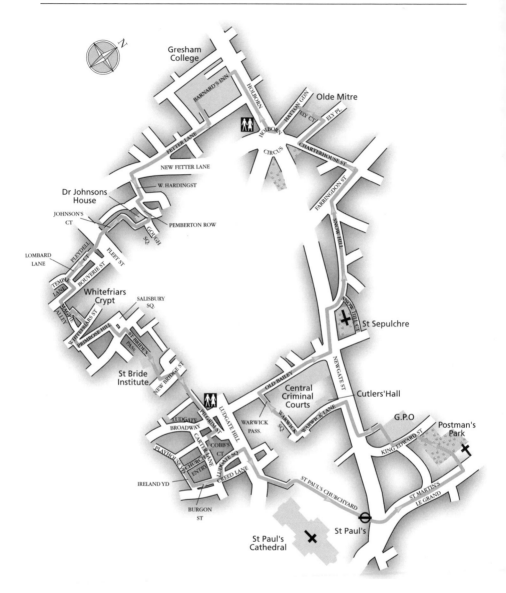

Cutlers' Hall

Go straight on past the memorial and out of the park, cross the road and turn left beside the Merrill Lynch building. At the far end is an archway with a plaque on it. Turn right into the gated path to the left of the archway and follow it round to the left between the remains of Christ Church Greyfriars (bombed in the Blitz) and its former churchyard. On Newgate Street turn right and then left into Warwick Lane. On the right now, the red-brick building with the terracotta frieze showing craftsmen forging metal is the livery Hall of the Cutlers' Company, No. 18 in the order of company precedence and chartered since 1416. Cutlers, of course, make knives and forks and other eating implements.

Beyond the Hall turn first right into Warwick Square, site of the London home of the Earls of Warwick in the 15th century. In the far corner go left into Warwick Passage. This takes you under the **Central Criminal Court** and out onto Old Bailey. Turn right towards the lights and cross over Newgate Street to the corner of **St Sepulchre's** churchyard. Here you can see the first drinking fountain installed by the Metropolitan Drinking Fountain and Cattle Trough Association in 1859. To the right is the Merrill Lynch building, beneath which is preserved in a special chamber a section of London's Roman wall complete with later Saxon bastion.

For whom the bell tolls

Turn away from the yard along the side of the churchyard to the junction with Snow Hill. Snow Hill Court behind the church, reached by a gate outside the west door, is worth a quick look. Formerly the parish hall, it now serves as the Snow Hill Medical Centre. In the church itself is a poignant relic of Newgate Prison, precursor of the Central Criminal Courts. At midnight on the eve of an execution the bellman of St Sepulchre's used to rouse the prisoners in the condemned cell with a handbell and exhort them to make their peace with God while they still had the chance. The practice died out over two centuries ago but somehow the old bell has survived. It is now in a glass case mounted on a pillar in front of the pulpit. There is a similar bell in the Whitechapel Bell Foundry in the East End. Could one be an imposter?

Make your way down Snow Hill, passing first the police station on the site of the old Saracen's Head Inn (where Wackford Squeers meets Nicholas Nickleby in Dickens' novel of that name) and then a rather run-down part of Smithfield market. At the bottom of the hill turn right into Farringdon Street and then at the lights left into Charterhouse Street. Walk up the hill on the right-hand side and at the top turn right into Ely Place. This is a private road belonging to the Crown, hence the gates and the gatekeeper. Another curiosity is that, though within the bounds of the City, the road is technically part of the county of Cambridgeshire. This strange anomaly arises from the fact that for centuries Ely Place was the town house of the Bishops of Ely (Ely being in Cambridgeshire). Attached to the episcopal palace was an ancient church dedicated to St Etheldreda. When the bishops moved to the more fashionable West End in 1772, Ely Place was built over with the elegant terraces you see today, but the church, halfway down on the left, was preserved. Today it is used for Roman Catholic worship and has a convent attached next door. The crypt chapel beneath the main church is the oldest centre of Roman Catholic worship in London.

Hidden pub

Before you get to St Etheldreda's turn left opposite No. 33 into narrow Ely Court. This leads to what must be the most out-of-the-way pub in London, the Olde Mitre (mitres being the hats that bishops wear). Bishop Goodrich started it in 1546 for the use of his London servants and it has been here ever since. It has small dark rooms and old wooden furniture and the stump of an ancient cherry tree around which Queen Elizabeth I is said – no doubt apocryphally – to have danced.

Carry on to the end of Ely Court, cross Hatton Garden (famous for diamonds) and turn left. At Holborn cross to the far side of the road and turn right. After a while you will come to a doorway with the words 'Barnard's Inn' over it. Turn in here. At the end of the tiled passage you come to the only surviving buildings of the original Inn, namely a small 18th-century house on the left, and, to the right, a beautiful little 15th-century hall which has miraculously survived 500 years of bombs and rebuilding. Barnard's Inn was one of the Inns of Chancery. These were colleges associated with solicitors and attorneys and similar to the Inns of Court which were for barristers or advocates. Having lost their educational function, the Chancery Inns finally died out in the 19th century. Barnard's Inn was bought by the Mercers' Company for their school, which moved here from Whittington College in 1892 and stayed until 1959. Then in 1991 the Inn became the base of another old-established City educational institution, **Gresham College**.

Free lectures

Gresham College is unique in London and probably in the country. As established by public-spirited City merchant Sir Thomas Gresham in 1597 it is essentially a public lecture foundation. The College appoints eminent scholars to professorships in seven ancient disciplines – astronomy, divinity, geometry, law, music, physic and rhetoric – and since 1985 one modern one (commerce) and pays them to deliver free lectures to the public. Originally the aim was to convey the new learning of the Renaissance to the mass of illiterate people. Today, besides giving their lectures, usually in the old hall, the professors also do research and hold seminars, and prepare reports and studies on pressing contemporary issues. In short, the College has become a kind of university, but with several important differences. There is no formal teaching, the students (i.e. the public) do not have to turn up for lectures and there are certainly no exams! The funding for the whole exercise comes from income generated by Gresham's estate. He bequeathed it jointly to the City Corporation and his own livery company, the Mercers', and they now administer it through the augustly named Joint Grand Gresham Committee. Go straight on through the archway by the hall into the court-yard and then through another archway. Now bear left and exit on Fetter Lane. Turn right here and walk down to the junction with New Fetter Lane, where stands the statue of John Wilkes, an 18th-century Lord Mayor of the City and MP. The inscription calls him 'the champion of English freedom' because he stood up to a brow-beating government that first tried to muzzle his satirical newspaper, the *North Briton*, and then to deprive him of his seat in Parliament. He succeeded in the first but not in the second and this of course made him a martyr and popular hero in the process.

Dr Johnson's House

Cross New Fetter Lane here and turn right past the plaque on the left commemo-rating the Moravians, a Protestant sect from Germany who sought refuge in England in the 18th century. (Their original burial ground still exists behind a high wall at World's End in Chelsea.) On the right you pass the eastern boundary of the Bacon Estate, and the former Public Record Office, before turning left into West Harding Street and its continuation (bearing right) Pemberton Row. Follow the signs to Dr Johnson's House in Gough Square. Here the Doctor compiled his great dictionary, published in 1755. The adjoining curator's house is said to be the smallest house in the City: one can easily believe it. Carrying on past the house into Johnson's Court you eventually come out on Fleet Street (St Paul's to the left). Cross straight over into Pleydell Court and continue down Lombard Lane towards the river.

Medieval crypt

At the bottom turn left into Temple Lane, right into Bouverie Street and then left into Magpie Alley. This brings you to the back of 65 Fleet Street, the offices of Fresh-fields, one of the top law firms in the City. It looks normal enough, but if you peep over the railings into the glass-walled basement you will see a most extraordinary thing: a complete little medieval building encased within the modern structure above and around it. This is the modern way of preserving and displaying archaeological remains – of which there are many in the City – and it seems to work very well. The crypt, for that is what it is, is the only surviving building from the medieval monastery of **Whitefriars**. For centuries it lay hidden beneath a house in Britton Court, serving as a coal cellar. When Britton Court was swept away it was unearthed and incorporated in this new building, still in its original position. It has now stood here for something like 700 years. If you would like to take a closer look, there are steps down on the left. Continue on into Ashentree Court. Turn right on Whitefriars Street and then left into Primrose Hill and follow it round to the left up past the back of the Harrow pub. At the end under the office block, climb the steps up to Salisbury Square and turn right. In the middle stands a memorial to yet another freedom-loving Lord Mayor and MP, this one being Robert Waithman, a self-made man and a powerful advocate of parliamentary reform and other radical causes in the early 19th century. He just lived to see the passing of the Reform Act in 1832.

Printing library

Go past the obelisk into St Bride's Passage, a sort of raised courtyard with **St Bride's Church** on the left and the St Bride Foundation Institute and Printing Library ahead. Go down the steps by the library entrance and turn right at the bottom. At New Bridge Street, cross over (you may have to use the lights, left) into Pilgrim Street and go up the steps. Carry on at the top and take the first right into Ludgate Broadway followed by an immediate left into Cobb's Court. Follow this round to the right and cross Carter Lane into Church Entry. Church Entry follows the exact line of the cross-ing between the nave and chancel of the great church of the Blackfriars Monastery that at one time sprawled over this whole area. After the dissolution of the monaster-ies in the 1530s the nave was turned into the local parish church of St Ann Black-friars, the little churchyard of which survives on the right as a garden. Church Entry leads into Playhouse Yard where, in 1600, Richard Burbage, Shakespeare's friend, opened the Blackfriar's Playhouse in one of the old monastic buildings. Turn left into Ireland Yard. Haberdasher William Ireland lived here in one of the monastery gate-houses before Shakespeare bought it in 1613. Walk along past the second little church garden (the actual site of the church of St Ann Blackfriars) and take the second left into Burgon Street. At Carter Lane cross over into Creed Lane and turn immediately left into Ludgate Square. This curving street (not a square at all) brings you out on the main thoroughfare of Ludgate Hill. Here turn right. Cross over to the forecourt of **St Paul's Cathedral** and make your way round its left-hand side, staying outside the railed churchyard. St Paul's station, where the walk ends, is at the far end on the left.

EXPLORING THE SECRET CITY (EAST OF ST PAUL'S)

Summary: This circular walk covers roughly the same part of the City as the walk between **Guildhall** and the **Tower**, but it is specifically designed to explore the area's maze of lanes, alleyways and passages. It's these narrow thoroughfares – which have survived major rebuildings following the Great Fire of 1666 and the air Blitz of 1940 – that give the City its special charm. As it threads its way east from St Paul's station and then back again, the walk passes City insitutions like the **Mansion House** and the **Bank of England**, the **Monument** to the Great Fire, the halls of the Carpenters', Drapers', Grocers', Mercers' and Sadlers' livery companies, numerous City churches (including the least altered of Sir Christopher Wren's) and Britain's oldest synagogue (the **Spanish and Portuguese Synagogue**).

Start and finish:	St Paul's station (Central Underground Line).
Length:	3 miles (5km).
Time:	2½ hours.
Refreshments:	No shortage of places of all kinds throughout the walk, but two to look out for in particular are Talbot Court about a third of the way round (restaurant, pub and sandwich bar/café) and Priest's Court towards the end (sandwich bar and cheap restaurant).
Note:	(a) This walk should be done between Monday and Friday during office hours. Not only is it during the working day that the City is at its liveliest and most exciting, it is also when the greatest number of places – including some of the passages which are an integral part of the walk – are open.
	(b) This is quite a long walk for such a dense place as the City so you might prefer to do it in two goes. A natural halfway break is Fenchurch Street.

Take Exit 2 from St Paul's station and turn right towards Cheapside and Bow Church. Cross New Change and enter Cheapside. Beyond the first terrace of shops, turn right onto the forecourt with the flowerbeds and go through the central archway between the two banks. In the courtyard (this is an extension of the Bank of England) turn immediately left through another archway and go down the steps and across the road into a passage with a Japanese fast-food restaurant at the entrance. This brings you out into a garden area, formerly the churchyard of **St Mary-le-Bow**. St Mary's has a crypt restaurant which is now about 20 feet (6m) below ground level. In Roman times it was at street level.

Colony of Virginia

In the middle of the garden stands a statue of Captain John Smith, a City man and one of the founders of the colony of Virginia in 1606. A Corporation board explains in more detail why exactly the statue is here. Keep the statue to your left and carry straight on down the alley behind the church. Turn right into Bow Lane – a narrow pedestrian-only street thronged with office workers at lunchtime – and then almost immediately left through the archway into Well Court, which no doubt takes its name from a well that was once here. Follow this round to the right into the court proper and turn left. Cross Queen Street – Guildhall to the left, Southwark Bridge to the right – into Pancras Lane. St Pancras Church was here until the Great Fire of 1666. Its churchyard is now a small, rather scruffy, garden, often used as a bicycle park. A little further on is the site of another church destroyed in the Great Fire – St Benet Sherehog. From its name (a 'shere hog' is a ram castrated after its first shearing) it is evident that this church stood in the heart of the medieval City's wool district.

At the end of Pancras Lane, cross Queen Victoria Street – Royal Exchange to the left, exposed remains of the Roman Temple of Mithras to the right – into Bucklersbury. Walk on down here (crossing the course of the Walbrook River in the process) towards the Mansion House and the church of St Stephen Walbrook. Chad Varah, founder of the Samaritans, is rector of the church. The Lord Mayor is one of the churchwardens.

Go into the alley between the two buildings and follow it round to the left past St Stephen's churchyard. When you meet the road, turn right and then at the T-junction (St Mary Woolnoth on the left) go right again into St Swithin's Lane. On the right there are two large courts leading off this narrow lane. The first – New Court – has been the home of Rothschild's merchant bank since 1804. The second was the Hall of the Founders' Company until they moved to Smithfield in 1987. It is now let as offices.

Near the bottom, just after the Bankers Books bookshop, turn right through the parking area into Salters Hall Court, home of the Salters' Company until bombed out in 1941. They had come here 300 years previously when they bought Oxford House, hence the name Oxford Court you can see on the garden wall. The garden is the old churchyard of St Swithin's London Stone, destroyed in the same blitz raid as the hall.

The London Stone

Turn left out of the court and then left again on Cannon Street. Here you will find, set into the building on the left, the 'London Stone' from which the church took its name. The plaque tells you more about it. Continue on. Having crossed St Swithin's Lane, you come to Abchurch Lane. Here turn left and then left again across the churchyard of St Mary Abchurch. It's worth having a look inside this church, built in 1676. With its large painted dome and rich dark woodwork, it is the least altered of all Sir Christopher Wren's post-Great Fire City churches.

'Shitteborwe' Lane

Go round the corner of the church into Sherborne Lane, where if windows are open you can hear dealers trading in an office somewhere up above. In other parts of the

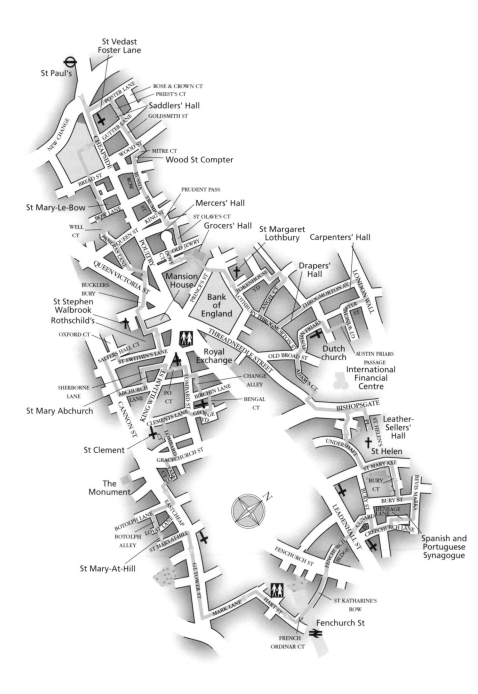

St Vedast
Foster Lane

St Paul's

ROSE & CROWN CT

PRIEST'S CT

FOSTER LANE

Saddlers' Hall

GOLDSMITH ST

NEW CHANGE

GUTTER LANE

WOOD ST

MITRE CT

CHEAPSIDE

Wood St Compter

BREAD ST

RUSSIA

PRUDENT PASS.

St Mary-Le-Bow

BOW

TRUMP

Mercers' Hall

KING ST

ST OLAVE'S CT

BOW LANE

Grocers' Hall

WELL
CT

St Margaret
Lothbury

Carpenters' Hall

QUEEN ST

PANCRAS LANE

POULTRY

OLD JEWRY

DOVE
CT

QUEEN VICTORIA ST

BUCKLERS-
BURY

Mansion
House

PRINCE'S ST

Drapers'
Hall

TOKENHOUSE
YD

St Stephen
Walbrook

Bank
of
England

LOTHBURY

ANGEL CT

THROGMORTON AV.

LONDON WALL

Rothschild's

OXFORD CT

THROGMORTON

AUSTIN FRIARS

GT WINCHESTER
ST

SALTERS HALL CT

ST SWITHIN'S LANE

THREADNEEDLE STREET

OLD BROAD ST

Royal
Exchange

Dutch
church

AUSTIN FRIARS

PASSAGE

SHERBORNE
LANE

ABCHURCH
LANE

PO.
CT

KING WILLIAM ST

LOMBARD ST

CHANGE
ALLEY

ADAM'S CT

International
Financial
Centre

St Mary Abchurch

BIRCHIN LANE

BENGAL
CT

BISHOPSGATE

CANNON ST

CLEMENTS LANE

GEORGE
YD

Leather-
Sellers'
Hall

St Clement

LOMBARD

ST HELEN'S

St Helen

GRACECHURCH ST

UNDERSHAFT

ST MARY AXE

The
Monument

BURY
CT

BEVIS MARKS

EASTCHEAP

BURY ST

LEADENHALL ST

HENEAGE
LANE

N

BOTOLPH LANE

LOVAT LANE

CUNARD LANE

CREECHURCH LANE

BOTOLPH
ALLEY

ST MARY-AT-HILL

Spanish and
Portuguese
Synagogue

FENCHURCH ST

FENCHURCH
BLDGS

St Mary-At-Hill

GT TOWER ST

MARK LANE

HART ST

ST KATHARINE'S
ROW

Fenchurch St

FRENCH
ORDINAR CT

country – Dorset for example – Sherborne is a perfectly innocuous name meaning 'clear stream'. Here, however, it has slightly less lyrical connotations. Apparently it is a corruption of Shitteborwe (presumably pronounced 'shitborough'), a medieval colloquialism for 'public lavatory'!

At the end of the lane go straight over King William Street into Post Office Court, site of the General Post Office in the 18th century. This completely covered passageway brings you onto Lombard Street, the traditional centre of the banking community, hence the old-fashioned signs hanging outside the various branches. Coutts' on the right occupies the site of Lloyd's Coffee House, the 17th-century precursor of the modern Lloyd's insurance market.

Cross Lombard Street diagonally right and enter Change Alley, short for Exchange Alley and so called because of its proximity to the Royal Exchange, whose green gates you can see at the far end. Take the first turn on the right. At the crossing, a blue plaque on the left marks the site of the Kings Arms Tavern where the first meeting of the Marine Society was held in 1756. Founded to promote careers at sea, particularly for poor boys, the Society continues its maritime work from its current headquarters in Lambeth.

Naval officer killed
Carrying straight on, Change Alley brings you to Birchin Lane. Turn left and then right here into a narrow passageway called Bengal Court. (A modern plaque at the entrance commemorates naval officer Captain Binney, killed in the 1940s while trying to stop a gang of jewel thieves, see page 94.) At the end of Bengal Court, the entrance to the ancient George and Vulture restaurant is on the left, while George Yard is on the right. Take the right turn and walk through the yard to Lombard Street. To the left you see the tower-block office of Dresdner Kleinwort Benson, another old-established merchant bank. Cross Lombard Street into Clements Lane, leading to the church of St Clement at the bottom. Walk down to the church and take a look into Church Court with its well-kept but unfortunately seatless churchyard (and the plaque at the entrance recording the residence in 1784 of the first Serbian Minister of Education) before retracing your steps a short distance back up the lane and turning right into Lombard Court. This brings you to Gracechurch Street. Cross over – the 202-foot (61-m) high Monument to the Great Fire is the major landmark to the right – into Talbot Court, one of the places mentioned at the beginning as a good place to stop for something to eat or drink. As you can see, it's got a nice pub, The Ship, and round the corner is a good sandwich bar with seats.

St Mary-at-Hill
Emerging on Eastcheap – 'cheap', as also in Cheapside and in place names like Chipping Norton, means market – turn left and then first right into Botolph Lane. Halfway down turn left into Botolph Alley. At Lovat Lane cross over and go down the alley on the right-hand side of the church. At the next lane, St Mary-at-Hill, also the name of the church, turn left up the hill. The doorway on the left marked 'Entrance to Church' leads to the tiny little churchyard as well as to the church. The church has been rebuilt in a plain dignified manner following a disastrous fire in the 1980s.

Continue on up the hill and turn right onto the main road, heading for All Hallows Church and, in the distance, the Tower of London. Cross where you can and turn left into Mark Lane and then right into Hart Street. Having passed The Ship pub and **St Olave's Church** with its Samuel Pepys and naval associations, turn left just before the bridge into French Ordinary Court. The French Ordinary was an eating-house catering for French Protestant refugees in the 17th century ('ordinaries' served simple meals at fixed prices). The cavernous court takes you under Fenchurch Street railway station and brings you out into St Katherine's Row, next to the old churchyard of St Katharine (*sic*) Coleman, demolished in 1926.

At Fenchurch Street (the halfway point of the walk) – St Botolph Aldgate to the right – cross over and go into Fenchurch Buildings. At Leadenhall Street, cross diagonally left into Cunard Place and then turn right into Bury Street and left into Creechurch Lane. As you turn left, a plaque on the right-hand corner marks a seminal spot: the site of London's first synagogue, built after the re-admission of Jews to England during the Commonwealth Interregnum. They had been kicked out 350 years before following vicious persecution.

Turning left off Creechurch Lane into Heneage Lane and following the latter round to the right you come to the back of the second synagogue built after the re-admission (the Spanish and Portuguese Synagogue). This one has fortunately managed to survive and is now the oldest such structure in Britain. At the end of Heneage Lane, turn left on to Bevis Marks. A little way along you can see the front of the synagogue through the gates, the date of its construction (1701) clearly visible above the door. Immediately after the synagogue, turn left into Bury Street and then right into tiled Bury Court. On St Mary Axe, turn left towards the new Lloyd's building and then right into Undershaft (the 'shaft' was a medieval maypole). Where the road divides, bear right to stay close to St Helen's Church and its pretty churchyard, unusually open for the City. Carry on past and out into Bishopsgate. Here turn right and walk up to St Helen's Place, a private gated road owned by the Leathersellers' Company who have their Hall at the far end on the left. Feel free to go into the road for a look – the gates are for cars, not people.

When you have finished, retrace your steps back down Bishopsgate. At the lights turn right into Threadneedle Street (corruption of 'three needles' – no doubt a shop sign, perhaps of a haberdasher's) and then turn right again through the gates at No. 40. Passing under an archway you come to a quiet courtyard garden with the International Financial Centre rising high above. Turn left down some steps into Adam's Court and then go straight over Old Broad Street into Austin Friars.

This narrow winding lane is the main thoroughfare of an enclave that covers the site of the main Augustinian monastery in medieval England. After the Dissolution of the Monasteries the nave of the friars' church was given to Protestant refugees from Holland for use as a Dutch church. As you can see, after 450 years the Dutch are still here, though their present house of worship is a 1950s' rebuild.

Carpenters' and Drapers' road

Go right round the end of the church and then left into Austin Friars Passage. At the road turn left and follow it round to the right to London Wall. Here turn left and then left again into gated Throgmorton Avenue. The arms on the gates belong to the Carpenters' Company, who have their Hall on the left of the entrance. They also own the first section of the avenue, hence the little coats of arms stuck on the fronts of the buildings.

Where the road widens out and the tarmac turns to granite setts, the ownership changes to the Drapers' Company. It's now their coat of arms you see on the lampstands and by the drainpipe halfway up the building on the left. Keep going straight down the avenue and you come to Drapers' Hall with its little garden. Though perhaps large by current City standards, the garden is a mere fragment of what it used to be when the drapers dried and bleached their clothes in it.

Throgmorton Avenue brings you out onto Throgmorton Street by the Stock Exchange. Turn right and then right again into Angel Court, where a comprehensive redevelopment has obliterated all traces of whatever may have been here before. There is an interesting inscription, however, that says that the land is owned by the Clothworkers' Company (their Hall is elsewhere) and that part of it was bequeathed to them by a 16th-century master, Thomas Ormiston. It is rare to find such explicit statements of land ownership in London.

Go to the left of the inscription and turn left, carrying straight on by the phone box when the road bends to the right. Where the sign says No. 1 Telegraph Street, turn left into the unnamed passage. You come out in Tokenhouse Yard, the site of an office where, in the 17th century, special business tokens were issued at times of coin shortage. Go down to the end of the yard and turn right on Lothbury. Have a look in St Margaret's Close behind the church of St Margaret Lothbury before crossing over to the Bank of England, by the statue of the bank's architect, and walking along to the corner.

Cut left through the colonnade here and cross the road to the vehicle barrier barring the entrance on the far side. You are now on Grocers' Company land. Go through the barrier into the courtyard in front of Grocers' Hall and walk along in front of the Hall, turning right at the far end into another yard. Near the end turn right into Dove Court and then right again into Old Jewry, London's medieval Jewish quarter before the great expulsion of 1291. Frederick's Place on the left is an attractive little cobbled cul-de-sac savouring of the old, pre-Blitz, City. Mercers' Hall is at the end. The blue plaque on the big house on the left relates to the time when, as a young man, Benjamin Disraeli, later novelist and Prime Minister, worked here as an articled clerk in a solicitor's office.

Forgotten prison
Just beyond Frederick's Place, named after a 17th-century Lord Mayor, turn left into St Olave's Court leading to the converted church of St Olave Jewry and its tiny churchyard garden. At the end turn left and then right into white-tiled Prudent Passage – derivation unknown – and then cross King Street into Trump Street, which becomes Russia Row. At the end of Russia Row go straight on into the entrance of Mitre Court. Besides covering the yard of an old inn called the Mitre, this also conceals the site of one of the old City prisons, the Wood Street Compter (pronounced 'counter'), demolished in 1816. In the middle, steps lead down to one of the old prison dungeons, now used as a storeroom by the adjacent Four Vintners wine merchants. The manager is happy to show people around provided he has an assistant to look after the shop. Continue on past the steps and out of the court into Goldsmith Street. Straight ahead now is Saddlers' Hall. Just to the right of the Gutter Lane street sign is the easily missed entrance to a passage with railings on the right and also a plaque relating to old Broderers' Hall. (Having lost

their Hall in the Blitz, the Broderers, or Embroiderers, sold up and moved out to a new address near Hampton Court). Go down the passage to Priest's Court, which links up with Rose and Crown Court to make a little island block where there is a cheap restaurant, ideal for lunch. Go straight on through Priest's Court and turn left on Foster Lane. On the left, the first door you come to gives access to a pretty little courtyard attached to the adjacent church of St Vedast Foster Lane. If the door is open you are welcome to go in. At the far end is the parish hall. This end is the rectory with roof-garden and first-floor gallery leading to the church. A relatively recent occupant was the late Canon Gonville Ffrench-Beytagh, the brave Dean of Johannesburg expelled from South Africa in the 1970s for helping channel funds to the African National Congress.

Now carry on to the end of Foster Lane. Here once more is Cheapside and, to the right, St Paul's station, where the walk ends.

❖❖❖

LAMBETH AND THE SOUTH BANK

❖❖❖

Summary: The first part of this walk takes you round the back of Waterloo Station through Lower Marsh (Monday to Saturday market for household items) to Archbishop's Park and the ancient palace of the Archbishops of Canterbury at Lambeth (the **Museum of Garden History** is next to the palace). The next section is along the riverside embankment to the South Bank arts complex, passing on the opposite bank the **Houses of Parliament**, Whitehall and Cleopatra's Needle. Finally, the walk crosses Waterloo Bridge (best bridge view of Westminster and the City) to Somerset House, **St Mary-le-Strand Church** and the Surrey Street **'Roman' Bath** on the north bank.

Start:	Waterloo Station (Northern, Bakerloo, Jubilee and Waterloo & City Underground Lines; mainline trains from the south and west).
Finish:	Temple station (District and Circle Underground Lines). On Sundays when Temple station is closed use Blackfriars instead.
Length:	2½ miles (4km).
Time:	1½ hours.
Refreshments:	Plenty of places in Waterloo Station and Lower Marsh, then nothing until you reach the South Bank between Westminster and Waterloo bridges. Near the end of the walk, Somerset House has a café with a raised terrace overlooking the river.

Take the 'South Bank' exit from Waterloo Underground station, cross York Road and turn left towards the bridge. Go straight over the entrance to the road on the right, which slopes upwards to the main entrance to Waterloo Station, and turn right into Mepham Street immediately before the bridge. When you reach the main road (Waterloo Road), turn right and walk past the ground-level entrance to Waterloo Station.

Home of Shakespeare

The Old Vic Theatre stands to your left on the corner of The Cut. Built in 1818 and later named after Queen Victoria, this famous old theatre enjoyed its heyday under the management of Lilian Baylis. Taking over from her social-reformer aunt, Emma Cons, in 1912, Baylis transformed the theatre from an alcohol-free music hall with religious overtones into the 'home of Shakespeare' in London and a popular opera house, all without losing its local (mostly working-class) audience. In 1982 the theatre was again revamped and relaunched by the Canadian entrepreneur Ed Mirvish.

Walk to the right into Baylis Road, and keep right into Lower Marsh and its small market. Until the 19th century, when it was drained and developed, this area was marshland much prized for duck shooting, hence the street name.

At the end of Lower Marsh cross Westminster Bridge Road and go straight on into Carlisle Lane. Continue under the railway bridge, going past the car park on the right, and turn right into Archbishop's Park. Even though it is open to the public, this park is still owned by the Archbishops of Canterbury and was once part of the grounds of Lambeth Palace, which you can see behind the trees in the opposite corner. Further round to the right you can see the top of the Victoria Tower in the Houses of Parliament rising up over the medical school of St Thomas's Hospital.

Follow the path to the end of the park and when it curves to the right (the Lambeth millennium path inset with historical plaques starts here), walk straight ahead into the alley and out into Lambeth Road. Turn right here along the side of the former Archbishop Tait's Infants' School and various precincts of Lambeth Palace. When you get to St Mary-at-Lambeth Church on the right, go into the churchyard.

The redundant church and part of the churchyard now house the Museum of Garden History operated by the Tradescant Trust. John Tradescant and his son were famous professional gardeners in the 17th century and were employed both by James I and his son Charles I. They were also great travellers and brought many new plants back to England, including lilac, evening primrose, Virginia creeper and the parent of the London plane. Their home was in Lambeth where they had a famous museum called 'Tradescant's Ark' containing 'all things strange and rare' including a 'natural dragon' and 'blood that rained in the Isle of Wight'. The Tradescants are buried in the museum part of the churchyard. Also buried here is Admiral William Bligh, better known as Captain Bligh of *Mutiny on the Bounty* fame. His harsh discipline provoked his crew into mutiny in 1789. With only 18 loyal crewmen he was set adrift in a small boat in the middle of the Pacific but still made it to land after an heroic 4,000-mile (6,400-km) journey. Bligh lived at No. 100 Lambeth Road.

Leave the churchyard and go across the forecourt of the Tudor gatehouse of Lambeth Palace. The Archbishops of Canterbury acquired the manor of Lambeth in 1197, conveniently close to the royal palace at Westminster across the river, and have had their main palace here ever since. Cross Lambeth Palace Road to Lambeth Pier and turn right along the Albert Embankment. There is a fine view of the Houses of

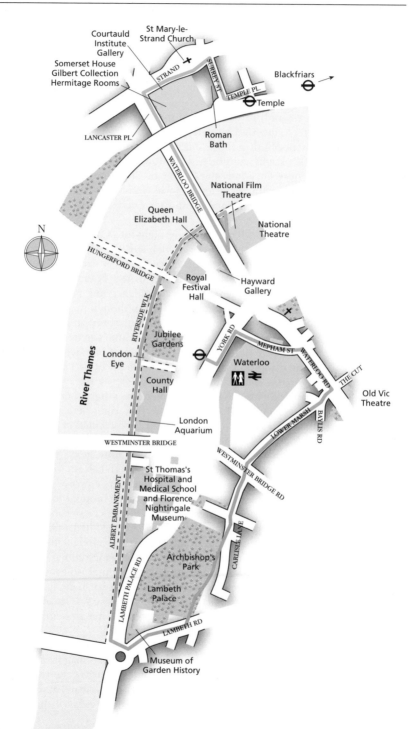

St Mary-le-
Strand Church

Courtauld
Institute
Gallery

Somerset House
Gilbert Collection
Hermitage Rooms

Blackfriars

STRAND

SURREY ST.

TEMPLE PL.

Temple

LANCASTER PL.

Roman
Bath

WATERLOO BRIDGE

National Film
Theatre

Queen
Elizabeth Hall

National
Theatre

N

HUNGERFORD BRIDGE

Royal
Festival
Hall

Hayward
Gallery

RIVERSIDE WLK

Jubilee
Gardens

YORK RD

MEPHAM ST

WATERLOO RD

London
Eye

Waterloo

THE CUT

County
Hall

Old Vic
Theatre

River Thames

London
Aquarium

LOWER MARSH

BAYLIS RD

WESTMINSTER BRIDGE

St Thomas's
Hospital and
Medical School
and Florence
Nightingale
Museum

WESTMINSTER BRIDGE RD

ALBERT EMBANKMENT

CARLISLE LANE

Archbishop's
Park

LAMBETH PALACE RD

Lambeth
Palace

LAMBETH RD

Museum of
Garden History

150

Parliament on the opposite bank, including the riverside terrace, which is invisible from the Westminster bank.

The Albert Embankment was completed in 1870, as you can see from the date on the base of the ornate lamp-posts. Subsequently the embankment wall was raised by 18 inches (45cm) in order to protect the city from rising flood-tide levels. At the same time the embankment seats were raised on plinths to preserve the view. Recently a special Thames barrier was built to protect London from floods. In view of this the extra blocks on top of the wall have been removed, but the benches have been allowed to stay on their plinths.

Riverside nightingales

When you come to the wall on the right, note the plaque to Lt-Col John By, builder of the Rideau canal in Canada. The wall belongs to St Thomas's Hospital and its medical school. The hospital was founded around 1200 at the Southwark side of London Bridge (see the Bankside and Southwark walk, page 153) and then in 1871 it moved to what was then the more peaceful location of Lambeth. The first training school for nurses, inspired by the pioneering work of Florence Nightingale, was founded at St Thomas's in 1860 and there is now a **Florence Nightingale Museum** in the hospital.

Go through the subway under Westminster Bridge. As you emerge, look back and up at the huge stone lion. A well-known riverside feature since 1837, it used to stand a little further downstream by Hungerford Bridge, over the entrance to the Lion Brewery. The Brewery was demolished in 1949 and the lion was moved to this position in 1966. It is made of Coade Stone, the most weatherproof artificial stone ever made, but the stone's formula was lost when the Coade factory, founded in the 1760s by Mrs Eleanor Coade, closed in 1840. The Coade factory stood just here where County Hall now stands. County Hall was the headquarters of the London County Council and then the Greater London Council until the latter's abolition in 1986. The building has since been converted into a hotel, conference centre, offices, shops, restaurants and the **London Aquarium**.

South Bank celebrations

Continue along the riverside walk. On the left now is the London Eye viewing wheel, put up to mark the millennium. To the right is the Shell Centre building, separated from the river by the Jubilee Gardens, laid out to mark the Queen's Silver Jubilee in 1977. Previously the site had been used for the 1951 Festival of Britain, a celebration of national achievements a century after the 1851 Great Exhibition, designed to lift the spirits of the nation after six years of post-war austerity. Near the Jubilee Oracle sculpture look out for two verses inscribed in the pavement: a humorous piece about swans and buses from comedian Spike Milligan and something rather more elegiac from 19th-century poet and designer William Morris:

> *Forget six counties overhung with smoke*
> *Forget the snorting steam and piston stroke,*
> *Forget the spreading of the hideous town;*
> *Think rather of the pack-horse on the down,*
> *And dream of London, small, and white, and clean,*
> *The clear Thames bordered by its gardens green.*

Nearby, there is an immense flagpole cut from the forests of British Columbia especially for the Festival of Britain. After the Festival the flagpole was taken down but then re-erected by the British Columbian government to mark the Queen's Silver Jubilee. On the north bank in front of the Ministry of Defence there is a gold eagle on a large pedestal; this is the Royal Air Force war memorial for World Wars I and II.

Egyptian obelisk

Continue along the embankment and under Hungerford Bridge. On the right, the Royal Festival Hall, built for the Festival of Britain, marks the start of the South Bank arts complex, which itself grew out of the Festival. Next on the right is the Queen Elizabeth Hall and the Purcell Room, with the **Hayward Gallery** behind. On the other side of the river you can see Cleopatra's Needle, an ancient Egyptian obelisk given to Britain in 1819 by Egypt's Turkish overlords and floated here in 1878 from Alexandria. The National Film Theatre is underneath Waterloo Bridge and beyond the bridge is the **National Theatre**, incorporating three separate theatres – the Olivier, the Lyttelton and the Cottesloe. The appearance of these South Bank block-houses has provoked a good deal of criticism over the years, but so far none of the schemes put forward for making them easier on the eye (including a transparent roof covering the whole complex) have met with much support.

Somerset House

Go under Waterloo Bridge, turn immediately right up the steps and then turn right again over the bridge, towards Somerset House on the north bank. Half-way between the City and Westminster, the bridge provides superb views in both directions (the main landmarks are identified on panels halfway across the bridge). At the far end turn right on to the terrace in front of Somerset House. If the terrace is closed carry on into Lancaster Place and then turn right into the Strand.

The most important 18th-century public building in London, Somerset House was built in 1775 for various government departments, primarily the Navy Office. Then for years it was the place to go for birth certificates and wills. Today it is home to the Inland Revenue and three important art collections: the **Courtauld Institute of Art**, the Gilbert Collection and the Hermitage Rooms.

Halfway along the terrace, turn left and pass through the former Seamen's Waiting Hall into the courtyard. Walking either through or round the water jets, cross the courtyard to the archway and turn right on to the Strand. On the right now is King's College, part of London University. On the left is St Mary-le-Strand Church, built in 1717, with Bush House behind, occupied by BBC Radio and its World Service.

Roman bath

Take the first turning on the right into Surrey Street, walking down towards the river. Look out for Surrey Steps, halfway along the street on the right. These steps lead to an alley called Surrey Lane where there is what is traditionally claimed to be a Roman bath – now owned by the National Trust – in a basement of a King's College building. You can view the bath from outside through a window and there is an information board that will tell you more about its possible origins (probably not Roman). At the end of Surrey Street turn left along Temple Place to Temple station where the walk ends. (If the station is closed, continue along the embankment to Blackfriars station.)

BANKSIDE AND SOUTHWARK

Summary: Bankside and Southwark lie on the south bank of the Thames opposite the City. Historically, they were always part of the City and vie with it in terms of atmosphere and historical appeal. The main features of the walk are: in Bankside, the reconstructed **Shakespeare's Globe** and the sites of three Elizabethan theatres (including the original Globe); in Southwark, the **Clink Museum**, the Bishop of Winchester's medieval palace, St Mary Overie Dock, **Southwark Cathedral**, the George Inn, the site of Chaucer's Tabard tavern and the old operating theatre-cum-herb garret of St Thomas's Hospital; and in the final section of the walk through the new London Bridge City, Hay's Galleria, **HMS** *Belfast* and **Tower Bridge**. There are splendid views of the City throughout the walk.

Start: Blackfriars station (District and Circle Underground Lines and mainline trains).

Finish: Tower Hill station (District and Circle Underground Lines). Fenchurch Street railway station and the Docklands Light Rail's Tower Gateway station are both nearby.

Length: 2½ miles (4km).

Time: 2 hours.

Refreshments: Plenty of places all along the route. Two famous historic pubs worth trying are the Anchor, situated on Bankside and the George in Borough High Street. Southwark Cathedral, also at the halfway stage, has a refectory.

Take Exit 3 from Blackfriars station and cross Blackfriars Bridge, the third bridge over the River Thames to be built in central London. This bridge was erected in 1869, though the first Blackfriars Bridge, known as William Pitt Bridge, was built a century earlier. Next to the road bridge is one Victorian railway bridge and the piers of another. Both bridges were built for the London, Chatham and Dover Railway Company, the dismantled one being the first railway bridge across the Thames.

Down to the river
Over the bridge, turn left between the bollards and go down the steps. (In the underpass left are some old views of the railway bridges and the first Blackfriars Bridge.) Turn right through the gate and follow the riverside walk. Beyond the railway bridges there is a fine view of the City. In the east the International Financial Centre is the tallest building, while the western end of the City is still dominated by **St Paul's Cathedral**. Until the Hilton Hotel was built in 1963 St Paul's was the tallest building in London. Even now, planning controls dictate that the buildings

153

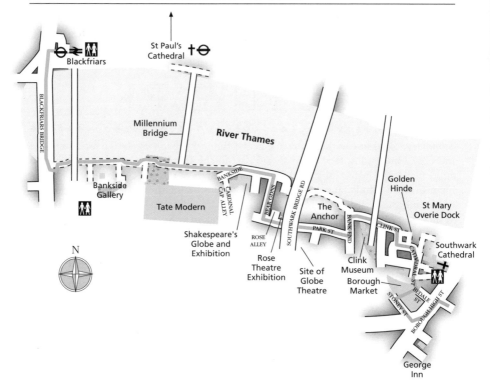

around the cathedral must be no higher than around 130 feet (40m). St Paul's itself is 365 feet (111m) high.

Go past the Founders Arms, built on the site of the foundry where all the iron-work for St Paul's was forged. On the right is the 1980 Bankside Gallery, home of the Royal Societies of Painters in Watercolours and Painter-Etchers and Engravers. Next on the riverside is the former Bankside Power Station, completed in 1947 and converted in the 1990s into the **Tate Modern** – a gallery housing the Tate Gallery's collection of international modern art. In Tudor times (16th century) there were fish ponds here supplying pike to local religious houses and the royal palaces across the river. Beyond the power station, Cardinal's Wharf retains some of its old houses. The house on the left has a plaque recording that Sir Christopher Wren lived here while St Paul's was being built, though there is no evidence to prove this. On the right, Provost's Lodging belongs to the Provost of Southwark Cathedral, a building that you come to later in the walk.

In between the houses is Cardinal Cap Alley, which once led to a tavern and brothel called the Cardinal's Hat. Until the 1600s Bankside was – as a royal proclamation of 1547 put it – a 'naughty place', full of taverns, brothels (called 'stews' from the stewhouses, which were steam baths doubling as brothels), bear- and bull-baiting pits and, in the time of Shakespeare, public theatres. These were all enormously popular forms of entertainment, but the prudish City authorities refused to tolerate them within their own jurisdiction on the north bank of the river.

Ironically, they all flourished here in Bankside, even though part of this area, known as the Liberty of the Clink, was under the control of the Bishops of Winchester, whose London palace was nearby. The other part of the area was called Paris Garden,

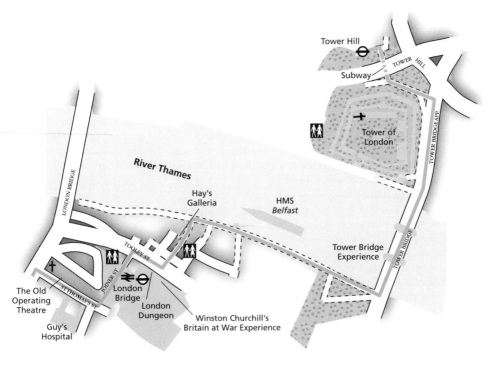

'better termed a foule den than a faire garden' as one writer referred to it in 1632. In 1556 the City authorities gained control of the area but conditions did not really change. It was the 17th-century Puritans who really put an end to Bankside's debauchery and dissipation by closing down the theatres during the Commonwealth.

Global development
Next to Cardinal's Wharf is the new International Shakespeare Globe Centre. This enormous project is the fruit of 20 years' hard lobbying by the late American actor and director, Sam Wanamaker, and features a reconstructed Globe Theatre, complete with thatched roof, in which 1,500 people can watch performances of Shakespeare's plays in a partly open-air setting, just as they were staged four centuries ago. The season is May to September.

Take the second turning on the right after the Globe Centre into cobbled Bear Gardens, the site of Bankside's bear-baiting arena. At the end on the left the print gallery marks the position more exactly. In 1613 the bear pit was replaced by the Hope Theatre after the nearby Globe Theatre had burned down (the Hope Theatre's owner, Philip Henslowe, was a business rival of Cuthbert and Richard

Burbage, who ran the Globe). Although it was the most modern of the four Bankside theatres in Shakespeare's time, the Hope only survived for three years as a playhouse. Bear-baiting – presumably more profitable – was then resumed. In 1656 the Hope was demolished and, as the plaque on the wall of the centre records, was replaced by the Davies Amphitheatre, the last bear-baiting ring built on Bankside. Bear-baiting and bull-baiting were both finally banned in 1835.

Turn left out of Bear Gardens into Park Street, formerly called Maiden Lane because it was a red-light area. The next street on the left is Rose Alley with the site of the Rose Theatre on the corner nearest to the bridge. This theatre, built in 1587, was the first theatre on Bankside and (like the Hope Theatre) was built by Henslowe. Edward Alleyn, founder of Dulwich College and the most famous actor of his day, made his name here, and Shakespeare's *Henry VI* and *Titus Andronicus* were first performed here. Peer through the windows of the modern office block now covering the site and you will see the remains of the Rose's foundations, revealed during excavations for the building in 1989 and preserved after a vigorous campaign by thespians and archaeologists. The remains are now displayed in the Rose Theatre Exhibition.

Continue along Park Street, going underneath the approach to Southwark Bridge. On the left are the offices of the *Financial Times* newspaper. Opposite is the actual site of Shakespeare's Globe (the 'wooden O' as he called it in *Henry V*) with information about the excavations carried out here in the 1990s. Any remains that were discovered at that time were preserved and then sealed beneath the ground. Shakespeare was both an actor and a shareholder in the Globe, which was built in 1599 by the Burbages using materials from their old theatre in Shoreditch. The Puritans closed the theatre in 1642 and in 1644 it was demolished to make room for houses. In the 18th century there was a brewery on the site owned by the Thrale family (see plaque on right further on). The Thrales were good friends of another literary giant, Dr Samuel Johnson, who had his own room here at their house next to the brewery. One cannot help wondering whether he ever knew that his illustrious predecessor once trod the boards here. The fourth Bankside theatre was the Swan, built in 1595 near Blackfriars Bridge.

The Liberty of the Clink

At the end of Park Street turn left into Bank End and then right at the Anchor Inn, dating from around 1775, into Clink Street with its old warehouses and derelict sites. This part of Southwark retains many features – and much of the atmosphere – of its recent commercial past. The Clink debtors' prison (the origin of the slang word 'clink' meaning prison) stood here until it was set on fire and destroyed during the Gordon Riots in 1780. On the right, in an old warehouse, there is a museum about Bankside, including the Clink and the 'Liberty' around it which was controlled by the Bishop of Winchester.

Further along on the same side of the road are the remains of Winchester Palace, the London house of the Bishops of Winchester from about 1150 to the mid-17th century. There is very little to see apart from the foundations, although the west wall with its 14th-century rose window is still standing. On the left, Pickford's Wharf has been renovated as part of the redevelopment of Southwark's ancient dock, St Mary Overie. The **Golden Hinde**, a full-sized reconstruction of the ship in which Sir Francis

Drake became the first Englishman to circumnavigate the globe, is now moored here. To the left there is another good view of the City and a key to the landmarks, and also a plaque recounting the legend of St Mary Overie.

Follow the road round to the right and then cross over Cathedral Street to get to Southwark Cathedral. The building dates from 1220 and is full of historic monuments and tombs, including that of John Gower (died 1408), the poet and friend of Chaucer. At that time the church was part of the Priory of St Mary Overie, where Gower lived for the last 20 years of his life. Also buried in the cathedral are Edmund Shakespeare, William's youngest brother, and the dramatists Fletcher and Massinger. John Harvard, founder of Harvard University, was born in Southwark and baptized here in 1607.

Walk past the entrance to the churchyard on the left. Underneath the railway bridge turn right into the covered Borough Market and then immediately fork left (notice the 'schedule of rents' behind you). Established in 1756, Borough Market is London's oldest wholesale fruit and vegetable market on its original site. On Friday afternoons and Saturdays it now hosts a fine food retail market. Having crossed the central alley of the market, turn left into Stoney Street and then cross the road to the traffic lights in front of the HSBC Bank. You are now on Borough High Street.

Borough High Street leads to London Bridge on the left. Until 1750 London Bridge was the only way across the Thames in London, so Borough High Street was the main road to the south and the English Channel. Inns for travellers entering and leaving the City lined the length of the street. One actually survives – the George, a galleried inn dating from 1677. You can see the entrance to its yard across the road to the right next to Lloyd's Bank. Further on from the George, Talbot Yard marks the site of the Tabard where Chaucer stayed before setting out on his pilgrimage to Canterbury. In the introduction to the *Canterbury Tales* he says: 'In Southwerk at the Tabard as I lay, Ready to wenden on my pilgrimage to Caunterbury …'. Further still down the High Street were two notorious debtors' prisons, the King's Bench and the Marshalsea. Charles Dickens set much of his novel *Little Dorrit* in the Marshalsea after his father had been imprisoned there in 1824. Later, imprisonment for debt was abolished and both prisons were closed.

Hospital to horror house

Now cross Borough High Street and turn left away from the George, and then right into St Thomas's Street. On the left is St Thomas's Church, once a parish church within medieval St Thomas's Hospital and also the hospital chapel. In 1865 the hospital moved to Lambeth (see the Lambeth and the South Bank walk, page 148) to make way for London Bridge Station. The church meanwhile has become the chapter house of Southwark Cathedral. The church loft, which was used both as a storehouse for medicinal herbs and as an operating theatre for the hospital, was rediscovered in 1956 and opened as a museum. Beyond the church, the row of Georgian houses was built for the use of various hospital officials. Nos. 11–19 are still occupied by local health officials.

Opposite is the 1725 entrance court of Guy's Hospital with a statue of its founder, Thomas Guy, MP and a wealthy printer and publisher, in the middle. It was here that John Keats spent a year training to be a surgeon before giving up medicine for poetry.

Turn left into Joiner Street and go through the tunnel under London Bridge Station, opened in 1837 as London's first railway terminus. Cross Tooley Street to the

London Bridge Hospital and turn right past the **London Dungeon**. Opposite **Winston Churchill's Britain at War Experience** turn left into Hay's Galleria, converted from the warehouses on the former Hay's Wharf – the biggest wharf in the Pool of London – as part of the London Bridge City redevelopment scheme (local heritage centre in lower level). Walk over the filled-in dock to the riverside terrace: the Custom House is opposite and the former Billingsgate fish market to the left of it. Turn right here to HMS *Belfast,* the largest cruiser ever built for the Royal Navy – weighing in at 11,000 tons (11,220t) – and now the only one of its old big-gun ships in existence. The ship was built in 1938, taken out of service in 1965 and opened as a museum in 1971.

Walk on past the entrance to the ship and continue along the riverside walk. On the right the centrepiece of the new London Bridge City is the Greater London Authority's headquarters, where the capital's mayor and assembly are based. To the left is a fine view of the Tower of London. When you get to Tower Bridge, climb the steps and turn left, crossing the river using the left-hand pavement. Completed in 1894, when tall ships still used the Pool of London just below London Bridge, Tower Bridge was provided with a central section that could be opened to let high-masted ships through, and an overhead walkway so that pedestrians could use the bridge even when it was closed to road traffic. The walkway is now included in the bridge museum.

Once over the bridge, continue along Tower Bridge Approach round behind the Tower to the bus stop. Here, take the subway to Tower Hill station, which is where the walk ends.

❖❖❖

BERMONDSEY TO ROTHERHITHE

❖❖❖

Summary: This walk, half of which is along the Thames, links two former villages close to central London. Bermondsey originated as a settlement around Bermondsey Abbey and developed into the centre of London's leather industry. Rotherhithe was a great maritime centre and the home port of the ship that carried the Pilgrim Fathers to America. On the walk you see Bermondsey's **St Mary Magdalen Church** and remains of Bermondsey Abbey, the **New Caledonian Antiques Market** (Friday mornings, early), the excavated remains of a 14th-century royal manor house, fine river views, and, in Rotherhithe, old warehouses, **St Mary's Church**, **Brunel's Engine House** and the famous Mayflower pub.

Start:	London Bridge Station (Northern Underground Line and mainline trains to the southeast).
Finish:	Rotherhithe station (East London Underground Line).
Length:	3½ miles (5.6km).
Time:	2¾ hours.

Refreshments: Numerous places around London Bridge Station, Tooley Street
and Bermondsey High Street. Otherwise try the Angel pub on
the riverside halfway between Bermondsey and Rotherhithe, or
the riverside Mayflower pub in Rotherhithe. Rotherhithe also
has a Chinese restaurant and a burger-kebab bar.

Turn right out of London Bridge Station onto Tooley Street. Opposite the entrance
to Hay's Galleria, turn right into Weston Street and walk underneath the station.
Turn left onto St Thomas Street and then right into Bermondsey Street, the main
street of the former village of Bermondsey. Apart from some warehouses and
factories at this top end, Bermondsey Street retains – unusually for this part of
London – much of its original character as a community high street, and also many
of its original houses, particularly the little row on the right, of which No. 78, with
its oriel window and weatherboarded attic workroom, is the highlight. Restoration
will no doubt reach these houses before long, for Bermondsey Street is now a
conservation area and much refurbishment work has already been done in the
lower half of the street.

St Mary Magdalen

Further on, the street names of Tanner Street and Morocco Street, where Bermondsey Street crossed the now lost River Neckinger, flag the site of the former leather
market. In the Middle Ages, drawn by the water supply and the availability of oak
bark for tanning, leatherworkers settled at Bermondsey and made it the centre not
only of London's, but the country's, leather industry. Skins came from the Smithfield slaughterhouses to be processed at Bermondsey before being marketed at
Leadenhall Market in the City. When Leadenhall became too small in the 19th
century, the leather market was brought to Bermondsey, so making the area the
centre of the leather trade as well as the leather industry. The market building,
now converted into offices, stands on the far side of the market area at the end of
Morocco Street. The parish church of St Mary Magdalen, built around 1680 on the
site of an earlier church which had become unsafe, is at the bottom of the street,
with the old Georgian rectory on one side and the modern rectory on the other.
All around are warehouses full of antiques, spilling over from the Friday morning
New Caledonian Antiques Market, which moved here from north London after
World War II following closure of the leather market. It is mainly a market for
dealers, but collectors come here too. You have to be here early to get the best
bargains though: like most wholesale markets, most of the day's business is done
while ordinary folk are still tucked up in bed.

Resurrection men

Carry on past the church and the disused graveyard. The building on the corner is
the old parish watch-house where the parish constables reported for duty, and where
a watch was kept on the graveyard to prevent resurrection men stealing fresh corpses
to sell to nearby hospitals for dissection. At this point you are standing on the site of
the north gate of the former Bermondsey Abbey, founded in 1082 and endowed
with the manor of Bermondsey by King William Rufus. The village of Bermondsey grew up along the lane connecting the north gate with London Bridge.

Bermondsey Square ahead represents the main quadrangle of the abbey. The abbey church lay along Abbey Road to your left. After acquiring the dissolved abbey in the 1540s, courtier Sir Thomas Pope (founder of Trinity College in Oxford) knocked the church down and used the stone to build Bermondsey House on the eastern side of the old abbey quadrangle. As you can see, nothing substantial is left of the abbey now, or indeed of Pope's house. Even Georgian Bermondsey Square has almost entirely disappeared: only a rather forlorn group of houses from the southwestern corner is left. On Friday mornings the open space in the middle of the square is filled with antiques stalls.

Cross the square diagonally to its southeastern corner and turn into Grange Walk. Grange Walk ran from the abbey's eastern gatehouse to the abbey grange or farm. Several very old houses survive on the right-hand side of the street. No. 7, one of the oldest, must have been part of the gatehouse, for the gate hinges still protrude from its pink-coloured façade. Having passed the disused 1830 girls' charity school building on the right, you come to No. 67 on the left, the most handsome house in the street, recently restored with the assistance of English Heritage.

Now you are at the eastern extremity of the Bermondsey village area. Open fields originally stretched from this point to the neighbouring village of Rotherhithe, a large part of which was also owned by Bermondsey Abbey. Today housing estates, industrial buildings and main roads are more in evidence. We now have to make our way through all these developments until we reach the docklands strip beside the Thames.

London's first railway line

Turn left into The Grange and then right into Abbey Street. Ahead Canary Wharf Tower rises above the bridge carrying the railway line to London Bridge Station. Opened in 1836 and extending as far as Greenwich, this was the first railway line in the capital. As you pass beneath the bridge, note the handsome fluted columns and fine brickwork of the original structure and the way it has been widened over the years to accommodate more tracks.

At Jamaica Road turn right and then first left into George Row. Jacob Street at the far end marks both the beginning of the riverside warehouse area and the site of Jacob's Island, a notorious Victorian slum surrounded by polluted mill streams. This is where Dickens set the death of Bill Sikes in *Oliver Twist*. Turn right into Chambers Street, where there are still many vacant warehouses and mills, and then left into Loftie Street. Here film studios and scenery makers have put some of the empty spaces to productive use. At the end of Loftie Street turn right into Bermondsey Wall East and then left through modern Fountain Green Square to reach the riverside directly opposite Wapping Pier Head, the former entrance to the London Docks. Turning right along the riverside there are fine views of the great terraces of warehouses on both sides of the river. On the left, the modern building painted white and blue is the base of the river police. On the right, in front of Canada Tower, are the warehouses and church spire of Rotherhithe, your ultimate destination.

Turner's *Téméraire*

At Cherry Garden Pier, named after a 17th-century resort visited by Samuel Pepys and the spot where Turner stood to paint his National Gallery picture of the

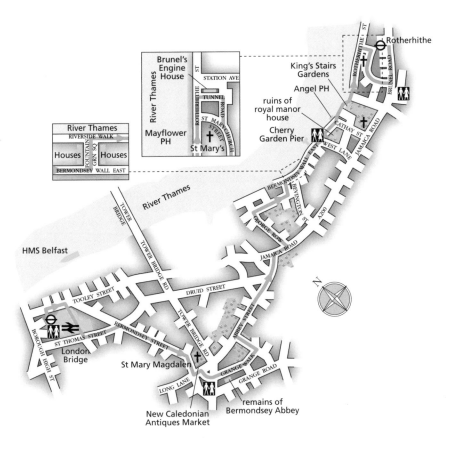

warship *Téméraire* on its way to a Rotherhithe breaker's yard, you have to leave the riverside walk and return to the road. As you pass the entrance to West Lane on your right you cross from the ancient parish of Bermondsey into Rotherhithe. The first feature you come to is an open area with the Angel pub on the riverside and, in the centre, the partially excavated remains of Edward III's 14th-century moated manor house. Three panels around the site tell the story of the house, which was probably the manor house for that part of Rotherhithe not granted to Bermondsey Abbey. Originally in the hands of the noble Clare family, the house and land seem to have passed into royal control in or shortly before Edward III's time. A successor, Henry IV, is said to have lived here in 1412 while recovering from leprosy.

Royal landing stage
Carrying on, you come to the solitary office of Braithwaite and Dean, one of the few surviving firms of Thames lightermen. For centuries, lightermen have conveyed

cargoes from ships out in the middle of the river to the warehouses on the riverside quays. Beyond Braithwaite and Dean are the King's Stairs Gardens, the King's Stairs being the landing stage for the royal manor house. In the gardens you rejoin the riverside and walk through an arcade under a modern apartment block before coming back onto the road at the start of Rotherhithe Street. Because it is very narrow at this point and hemmed in by tall warehouses, it is difficult to imagine the street ever amounting to much. But in actual fact it extends for almost 2 miles (3km) and is one of the longest streets in London. It was originally laid out over a great flood wall (possibly begun by the Romans) and up to the 18th century formed the main thoroughfare of a major ship-building centre. In the 19th century, as Britain's trading empire grew, docks, mills, wharves and warehouses replaced the old Rotherhithe shipyards.

From this narrow section of Rotherhithe Street you emerge in the centre of the old village of Rotherhithe. On the left beyond the Thames Tunnel Mills, one of the first industrial buildings in docklands to be converted into residential use, the Mayflower pub provides a clue to Rotherhithe's main claim to fame: the *Mayflower*, the ship that carried the Pilgrim Fathers over to America in 1620, was berthed here. Its master and part-owner, Captain Christopher Jones, moved to Rotherhithe from Harwich in 1611. He is buried in the churchyard, as are the three co-owners of the ship.

Continue on under the gantry. The late 18th-century warehouses left and right were formerly a granary belonging to the Grice family. Now they are home to Sands Studios, where the film *Little Dorrit* was made, and the Rotherhithe picture library. Behind the granary you come to Brunel's Engine House. This is the original pump house used during construction of the Wapping–Rotherhithe tunnel between 1824 and 1843. Inside, an exhibition tells the story of the tunnel – the first ever built under water – and the heroic struggle needed to complete it. Engineered by the Brunels, father and son, it is now used by the East London Underground Line.

Prince Lee Boo

Turn right into Tunnel Road between the Engine House and the granary and then right again into St Marychurch Street. **St Mary's Church** was built by local people in 1715 and deliberately raised up high on a plinth to protect it from flooding. Inside there are many memorials to local ships' captains and some pieces of furniture made by wood salvaged from the *Téméraire*. The pillars look like stone, but are in fact tree trunks encased in plaster. The roof, resembling an upturned boat, must have been a doddle for the local boatbuilders who fashioned it. Outside the west end of the church are two interesting memorials: a modern one to the captain of the *Mayflower* and an original commemorating two people linked together by a fascinating story. In 1783 Captain Henry Wilson's ship was wrecked and he and his crew were cast away on the Pacific island of Cooroora, east of the Philippines. They got on so well with the islanders that, when they had built themselves a new ship and were about to return to England, the king of the island asked them to take his son with them to be educated in an English school. Wilson gladly brought Prince Lee Boo to his home in Rotherhithe and sent him to the local school. Although much older than the other pupils he was a great favourite, but unfortunately had no defences against western diseases. After only six months he succumbed to smallpox.

You come out of the churchyard directly opposite the rectory and the former village school with its little figures of a boy and a girl above the door. The charity school was founded in 1612 by Robert Bell and Peter Hills, a seaman, to whom there is a brass memorial inside the church. In Prince Lee Boo's day the school house was at the east end of the church, but in 1797 it moved to this house, where the master also resided. It still survives today as a modern primary school in Beatson Walk.

Sufferance Wharf

Turn right past the school. On the left now are the village watch-house and fire-engine house, both built in 1821, and on the right Hope Sufferance Wharf. From Tudor times onwards goods could only be unloaded in the port of London at 'legal' quays. When these became congested, other quays were licensed or 'suffered' to admit goods bearing low customs duties. Hope Wharf at Rotherhithe, stretching back from the riverside to this point, was one of these sufferance wharves.

Follow the road round to the left, and at the end turn left into Brunel Road. Rotherhithe Underground station, where the walk ends, is about 100 yards (90m) ahead on the left.

❖❖❖

THE NOTORIOUS
EAST END

❖❖❖

Summary: This walk explores the East End's notorious past, which is dominated by two names: Jack the Ripper, presumed to be responsible for the Whitechapel murders of the 1880s, and the Kray twins, Ronnie and Reggie, London's most successful and notorious underworld bosses in the 1960s. The walk visits places connected with both Jack and the Krays, including all six commonly accepted Ripper murder sites (since no-one knows who the Ripper was it is impossible to say how many murders – if any – he actually committed), the home of the Krays and the Blind Beggar pub where Ronnie Kray shot fellow criminal George Cornell. Also featured on the walk are other notorious East End events, such as Henry Wainwright's murder of his mistress in 1874, the 1911 siege of Sidney Street, involving Winston Churchill and a gang of Russian anarchists, and the 1936 Battle of Cable Street, caused by British blackshirts attempting to march through the East End with its large Jewish population.

Start and finish:	Aldgate East station (District and Hammersmith & City Underground Lines).
Length:	3¾ miles (6km).
Time:	2½ hours.

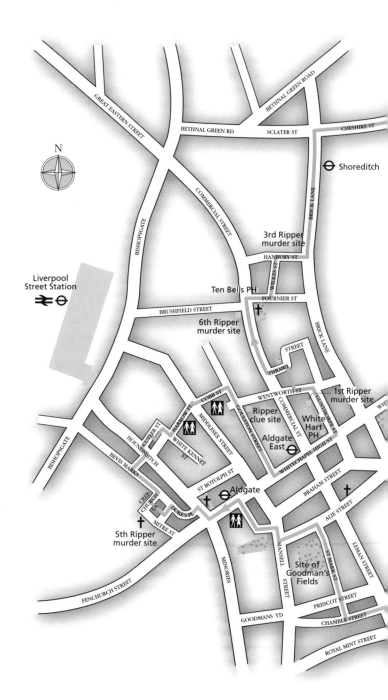

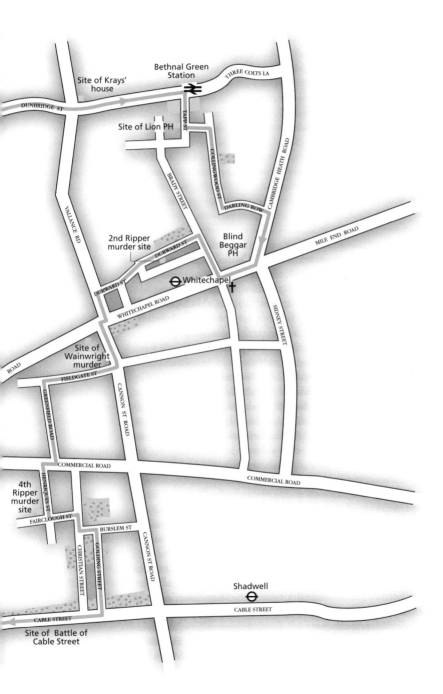

Refreshments: The Blind Beggar pub is at the halfway stage and serves
lunchtime food and so is the obvious place to stop, but it is
nothing special in itself and its interior is completely different
from what it was at the time of the Kray murder. Near the
beginning of the walk, Brick Lane is famous for its Asian
restaurants, and towards the end the Houndsditch area has many
sandwich bars and takeaways catering to City office workers.

Take the 'High Street (north side)' exit from Aldgate East station and turn left. Cross
Commercial Street at the lights and continue along Whitechapel High Street. After a
while you come to the White Hart pub, on the left. In 1890 Severin Klosowski, a
qualified junior surgeon from Poland who came to England in 1887 and worked as a
hairdresser in the East End, kept a barber shop in the basement of this pub. Later, in
1903, having changed his name to George Chapman and turned to pub-keeping in
Southwark, he was hanged for poisoning three women. After Chapman's arrest,
Inspector Abberline, head of the Whitechapel Murders investigation, thought it possible he might have been the Jack the Ripper, but Chapman's preferred method of killing
suggests otherwise and there is no actual evidence to link him with the Ripper's crimes.

Just beyond the pub, turn left through the archway into Gunthorpe Street (note
the tiled history display on the left of the arch and, further on, the painted board on
the side of the pub mentioning Klosowski-alias-Chapman). In the Ripper's day this
street was called George Yard. Still narrow and cobbled, it retains more of its original
appearance and atmosphere than any other Ripper-associated site. Near the far end,
on the left, the red-brick Sunley House stands on the site of George Yard Buildings,
the tenement block where Martha Tabram, possibly the Ripper's first victim, was
murdered in the early hours of 7 August 1888.

A 39-year-old prostitute estranged from her husband, Martha had lived with
William Turner for ten years off and on – more off than on because of her drinking.
At the time of her death the relationship was in an off phase. Martha was last seen
just before midnight on Bank Holiday Monday, 6 August 1888, when she went into
George Yard for sex with a soldier she had picked up in a local pub. Her body was
found on the first-floor landing of the George Yard Buildings tenement at 4.50 the
next morning by labourer John Reeves as he set off for work. Medical examination
showed that she had died about 2.30am as the result of a frenzied knife attack
during which she had been stabbed 39 times (but not mutilated). One of the stab
wounds appeared to have been inflicted with a bayonet-type weapon, raising the
possibility of a connection between the soldier and her death.

Wicked quarter mile

When you get to Wentworth Street, turn left and then cross right to go through the
gate into Flower and Dean Walk. Flower and Dean Walk takes its name from Flower
and Dean Street, one of several streets which in the 1880s formed a notorious
rookery or criminal quarter. This was the milieu in which the Ripper's victims lived
and in which he operated. The local clergyman described it as the 'wicked quarter
mile' because of its many prostitutes. Most of these prostitutes – including the
Ripper's victims – lodged in the rookery's numerous doss-houses, where beds could
be hired for a few pence a night.

When you reach the crossroads in the middle of this modern housing development, turn left and carry on along Thrawl Street, another of the rookery's more notorious streets. At the end turn right into Commercial Street. The first street you come to on the right is Lolesworth Close: this is the only remaining part of the original Flower and Dean Street. At least three of the Ripper's victims lodged here at one time or another. The eastern part of the old street is now covered by the Attlee Adventure Playground.

Carry on along Commercial Street, crossing the entrance to Fashion Street. When you get to the disused drinking fountain set into the churchyard railings on the right, look left along the 'Private Road' between White's Row car park on the left and the old Fruit and Wool Exchange (once part of Spitalfields Market) on the right. In the Ripper's time this road, towards the northern end of the 'wicked quarter mile', was called Dorset Street. Miller's Court, where Mary Kelly – supposed to be the Ripper's final victim – was murdered, was about one-third of the way along the street on the right-hand (north) side.

Born in Ireland, 25-year-old Mary Kelly grew up in Wales and married a miner. After his death in a pit accident, she came to London and worked in a West End brothel before moving to the East End. She was last seen alive at 2am on Friday 9 November 1888 picking up a client in Commercial Street and taking him back to her ground-floor room in Miller's Court behind No. 26 Dorset Street. She was probably killed about 4am but her naked body was not found till 10.45am when the rent collector called. With time and privacy, the killer had been able to mutilate her much more severely than any previous victim. Bits of her were found on the bedside table and under the bed. Her breasts had been cut off and her face was cut up beyond recognition. It was subsequently discovered that her heart was missing.

Mary Kelly was the Ripper's last definite victim. Some people think that after the Miller's Court orgy he either died, went mad and was committed to an asylum or possibly committed suicide. However, in the three following years there were two more murders which bore some Ripper hallmarks. But after 1891 there were no more Ripper-style murders in Whitechapel and in 1892 – the year in which Inspector Abberline retired – the Metropolitan Police finally closed their file on the case. It has been reopened many times since, but to little effect. After the Whitechapel murders, Dorset Street was renamed Duval Street before being demolished in 1929 to make way for an extension to Spitalfields Market.

Drinking haunt

Carry on past the churchyard to Fournier Street. The Ten Bells pub on the corner, here in Ripper times, was a favourite drinking haunt of Ripper victims Annie Chapman, Elizabeth Stride, Catherine Eddowes and Mary Kelly. Turn right into Fournier Street and first left into Wilkes Street. At the end of Wilkes Street, turn right into Hanbury Street. A disused brewery completely fills the north side of this street but many original houses remain on the south side. No. 29 Hanbury Street – the house where Annie Chapman, believed to be the Ripper's third victim, was killed on 8 September 1888 – was on the north side roughly opposite the present-day Nos. 28 and 30.

Forty-seven-year-old Annie Chapman abandoned her husband and three children in Windsor in the early 1880s and came to London, where she earned a precarious living selling – besides her body – matches, flowers and her own crochet work. She was last seen outside No. 29 Hanbury Street haggling with a respectably – but shabbily – dressed man at 5.30am on Saturday 8 September 1888. Half an hour later one of the many occupants of the house, Leadenhall market porter John Davis, found her body in the back yard. Her throat had been cut, her dress pushed up and her intestines ripped out and strewn across her left shoulder. A post-mortem subsequently showed that her uterus was missing. Amongst several items found near her body was a leather apron. This chimed in with a scare then current in the neighbourhood about a man wearing a leather apron going round threatening and blackmailing prostitutes. The man was successfully identified but was ruled out as a Ripper suspect after the murder-scene apron was found to belong to an innocent resident of No. 29 Hanbury Street.

Swords and knives

Carry on to Brick Lane. Turn left and walk along to the railway bridge. Just beyond it, take the second right into Cheshire Street. Cheshire Street eventually turns into Dunbridge Street. A short distance after that, Dunbridge Street joins Vallance Road at a roundabout by the railway line. The modern version of the original No. 178 Vallance Road, where the Kray twins lived with their mother while establishing themselves as East End gangsters, stands on the far side of the road to the left. Violet Kray moved here in 1939 to be near her family, the Lees. Two sisters lived either side of her, and her father and brother lived across the road above their café. The Kray twins, born in Hoxton in 1934, lived at No. 178 until they were well into their 20s, by which time they had already made their name as villains. For Ronnie in particular the house was a haven. All he needed to be happy was to be at home with his mother, his dog, his sharp suits and his collection of swords and knives.

Cross Vallance Road and carry on along Dunbridge Street, past the garages in the railway arches. When you get to the end, turn left by the Cavalier pub into Brady Street and then right into Three Colts Street. By the entrance to Bethnal Green station turn right into Tapp Street. Beyond the railway line on the right, there was, until 2003, a typical East End backstreets pub called The Lion. Ronnie Kray, a homo-sexual schizophrenic, was drinking here at about 8pm on 9 April 1966 when his spies (local boys, some of whom he slept with) brought him word that George Cornell was in the nearby Blind Beggar. Cornell was in Kray's sights because he was believed to have shot and killed Kray's cousin and ally Dickie Hart in a gun battle in a south London club the previous month. Accompanied by henchman Ian Barrie and a driver, Kray went home to get his gun and then made his way to the Blind Beggar to find Cornell. The walk passes the Blind Beggar shortly.

Beyond the pub, follow the road round to the left and then turn first right into Collingwood Street. After a while this bends left into Darling Row, which runs into Cambridge Heath Road. On Cambridge Heath Road itself, turn right and walk down to the junction with Mile End Road (left) and Whitechapel Road (right). Straight ahead, halfway along Sidney Street on the left-hand side, is a tall block of flats with rows of balconies along the front and a partly glass-walled staircase tower to the right. Called Wexford House, this block stands on a site once occupied by several houses, including No. 100, where the famous Siege of Sidney Street took place on 3 January 1911. After attempting to rob a jeweller's shop and killing three policemen in the process, two, possibly three, well-armed Russian anarchists holed up in the front room on the first floor and kept not only their 400 police pursuers but also the Fire Brigade, a military force including artillery and the Home Secretary, Winston Churchill, at bay for seven hours. After a fire started mysteriously on the top floor, the house burned down. Two charred bodies were later found inside, but neither proved to be the man regarded by many as the anarchists' mastermind, the elusive, almost legendary, Peter Piatkow, better known as Peter the Painter and rumoured to have been in the house when the siege started.

Turn right into Whitechapel Road. On the right is the Blind Beggar pub, where Ronnie Kray killed George Cornell. Since the mid-1960s, when the murder took place, the interior has been modernized – probably several times – so there is little point in looking for the holes left by the two warning shots Ian Barrie fired into the ceiling as Kray strode up to his victim. Not realizing what was happening, Cornell calmly announced, 'Well, look who's here,' before Kray shot him at point-blank range. There were several onlookers, but of course nobody saw a thing – at least not until much later when Kray was safely locked away in a police cell. This was in 1969 when the twins – each of whom had committed at least one murder – were sentenced to at least 30 years in prison. Ronnie Kray served almost 28 years before dying of a heart attack in Broadmoor asylum on 17 March 1995, aged 61. Reggie Kray served more than 30 years before being released a few weeks before his death in September 2000. A third brother, Charlie, seven years older than the twins, also died in 2000, having been convicted of drug dealing in 1997 at the age of 70 and sent to prison again (he was also gaoled after the 1969 convictions).

Continue along Whitechapel Road past the entrance to Sainsbury's, turn right into Brady Street and then go first left into Durward Street, called Buck's Row until 1892. Walk past the new block of flats on the left to the space at the end between it and the converted school building ahead. This is the spot where Polly Nichols, believed to have been the Ripper's second victim, was found lying half in the road and half on the pavement, in front of the entrance to a stableyard between the school and a row of what were then new houses.

Forty-two-year-old Mary Ann Nichols – Polly to her friends – was married with five children but had been separated from her family since 1880, the year after the birth of her last child. Like most of her fellow Ripper victims, she earned money through prostitution and spent it on drink and a bed at the doss-house. On the night of her death she had already earned and spent her doss money three times and was last seen – drunk and staggering – by a friend at 2.30am on 31 August 1888 going out to earn it for a fourth time. An hour and ten minutes later her body was found by Police Constable John Neill. Her throat had been cut twice, the second cut almost severing her head from her body. She was the first victim to be mutilated and is therefore regarded by Ripper students as the killer's first definite victim. Her skirts had been pushed up and her abdomen ripped open to expose her intestines.

Human hand
Walk along to the far end of Durward Road and turn left into Vallance Road. At the lights, look to the right across Whitechapel Road to a pair of tall brick-gabled buildings with a date-stone saying 'AWB 1901' at the top. The one on the left (No. 130) stands on the site of the warehouse where mat-and-brush-maker Henry Wainwright shot and then buried his mistress Harriet Lane on 11 September 1874. A year later,

having gone bankrupt, Wainwright had to quit the warehouse, which meant he also had to get rid of the body. Dismembering it and wrapping it up in two parcels, he got someone to help him carry the parcels into the street. While Wainwright went for a cab this person peeked inside one of the parcels and was horrified to find a human hand. Wainwright then drove with the parcels across London Bridge to Southwark, where he intended to bury the remains beneath his brother's shop in Borough High Street. However, the police were waiting for him and he was immediately arrested. Wainwright went to the gallows outside Newgate on 21 December the same year, the first man to be hanged in London for seven years.

Now cross over Whitechapel Road into New Road and take the first right into Fieldgate Street. When you get to Greenfield Street, turn left and walk down to Commercial Road. Here turn right to the lights, cross, turn left and then immediately right into Henriques Street (Berner Street in the Ripper's day). Walk on down as far as the entrance to Bernhard Baron House. The gateway almost opposite marks the approximate position of the entrance to Dutfield's Yard where Elizabeth Stride, believed to have been the Ripper's fourth victim, was found dead early on 30 September 1888.

Doss-house world

Born in Sweden in 1843, Elizabeth Gustafsdotter came to England in 1866 and married a carpenter named John Stride. After the marriage broke down in 1882, Elizabeth descended into the doss-house world of prostitution and drunkenness (for which she was convicted eight times in 1887 and 1888). Soon after midnight on Saturday 29 September she was seen several times in Berner Street with various men. At 1am the next morning her body was found at the entrance to Dutfield's Yard behind No. 40 Berner Street by Louis Diemschütz, steward of the adjacent International Working Men's Educational Club. Her throat had been cut, but that was her only injury. However, it is thought that the murderer had intended to mutilate her as usual but was scared off by the arrival of Diemschütz in his pony and trap. The theory is that the Ripper then stalked off in a westerly direction in search of another victim, for the dreadfully mutilated body of Catherine Eddowes was found in Mitre Square in the City less than an hour later. The walk passes through Mitre Square in due course.

At the end of Henriques Street, turn left into Fairclough Street, right into Christian Street, left into Burslem Street and right into Golding Street, formerly called Grove Street. Peter the Painter lodged at No. 59 Grove Street (no longer standing). When the Sidney Street anarchists were retreating from Houndsditch with their fatally wounded leader, George Gardstein, they left him to die at the Painter's house before moving on to Sidney Street for the final showdown with the authorities.

Walk under the railway line to the end of Golding Street and turn right into Cable Street. Continue along Cable Street to the lights at the junction with Dock Street/Leman Street and Royal Mint Street ahead. Here, on Sunday 4 October 1936, was fought the so-called Battle of Cable Street, a street fight between East Enders and the police prompted by British fascists' plans to march through the East End, with its large Jewish population. The fascists gathered in Royal Mint Street to begin the march; local East Enders, mobilized by communists and other left-wing groups, manned a barricade across Cable Street to stop them. The unlucky police were, as usual, caught in the middle. The battle started when the police tried to clear the route for the fascists by moving the barricade. This largely consisted of an overturned lorry full of bricks which the defenders then used as missiles against their attackers. The police failed to clear the barricade and the march was accordingly called off.

Turn right into Leman Street, go under the railway lines and turn first left into Chamber Street. Halfway along turn right into (unsigned) Magdalen Passage, which crosses the site of the 18th-century Magdalen Hospital, London's first home for repentant prostitutes. Dr William Dodd, the 18th-century's most notorious clergyman, preached the inaugural sermon at the institution's foundation in 1758 and afterwards became its official chaplain, on a salary of £100 a year. Dodd later became a successful society preacher in the West End, but got into debt funding his lavish lifestyle and unwisely forged a bond to raise money in the City. Forgery was then a capital offence and the unfortunate Dr Dodd duly went to the gallows in June 1777.

Notorious highwayman

At the end, cross Prescot Street into St Mark Street. St Mark Street cuts through what in the 18th century was open meadow known as Goodman's Fields. England's most notorious highwayman, Dick Turpin, was involved in a gun battle here in 1737 when constables tried to arrest him and his partner Robert King after they had stabled a horse stolen at Epping in a nearby inn. King was fatally wounded in the shoot-out. Turpin escaped, only to die on the gallows at York two years later.

When you get to Alie Street, turn left, cross Mansell Street, turn right and then go first left into Little Somerset Street. Follow this round to the right and into the open space with the Still and Star pub on your right and Aldgate station across the road ahead. Using the lights, cross Aldgate High Street to the station and turn left. Walk round the corner in front of the church to the subway entrance (marked 'Exit 7'). Go down into the subway and come out at Exit 6 and turn right into Duke's Place. Just beyond the primary school, turn left into St James's Passage.

This leads into Mitre Square, the place where the Ripper killed for the second time on the night he was prevented from mutilating Elizabeth Stride in Berner (now Henriques) Street. The square has been completely rebuilt since the Ripper's day, but its shape and size are the same. Over in the far left-hand corner there were some vacant cottages where the flowerbeds and benches are now. It was in the corner by these cottages, early on 30 September 1888, that the Ripper murdered Catherine Eddowes, believed to have been his fifth and penultimate victim.

Having spent the previous evening sobering up in a cell in Bishopsgate police station, Catherine – separated from her partner and three children for the last eight years – was last seen at 1.35am at one of the entrances to Mitre Square talking amicably to a man with her hand on his chest. Just ten minutes later Police Constable Watkins of the City Police found her body at the southwest corner of the square. As one ripperologist has observed, whoever the Ripper was, he was a professional: in less than 15 minutes he inveigled his victim into Mitre Square, killed her, mutilated her and made good his escape, taking her left kidney and womb with him, all virtually under the noses of four serving or former policemen.

Turn right along the near side of the square and exit via Mitre Passage. Turn right into Creechurch Lane and then left into Bevis Marks. After a while, take the first right into Goring Street. At its end, look across to the other side of Houndsditch. This is the site of the jewellers' shop (No. 119) that the Sidney Street anarchists, encountered earlier on the walk, were attempting to rob in 1910.

Cross Houndsditch diagonally to the left and go into Cutler Street. Almost immediately turn right through the covered entrance into Clothier Street. Little more than a back yard, Clothier Street roughly covers a cul-de-sac known in 1910 as Exchange Buildings. It was from a house here on 16 December 1910 that the Sidney Street anarchists were attempting to break into the rear of the jeweller's shop when they were surprised by police at 11.30pm. Opening fire, the anarchists killed three unarmed officers and seriously wounded two others before making their escape eastwards towards Sidney Street. The dead policemen were the first City officers to have been killed on duty within living memory, which says something about the state of law and order in London at that time.

Follow Clothier Street round to the left and turn right, back into Cutler Street. Then turn first left into Harrow Place. At the end you come to Middlesex Street, better known as Petticoat Lane, a market street notorious historically as a recycling centre for stolen property. Cross Middlesex Street into Cobb Street and walk on to Bell Lane. In the early 19th century – a time when the capital's crime rate was probably higher than it has ever been before or since – No. 12 Bell Lane (no longer standing) was home to 'the great Ikey Solomons', the most notorious fence in London and a major player in the Petticoat Lane property exchange. Solomon's ten-year reign ended in May 1826 when police raided his house in search of stolen watch movements. Although Solomons himself managed to escape on that occasion, his empire was effectively broken up. He was later captured and transported as a convict to Van Diemen's Land (Tasmania), where he died in 1850.

Ripper's only clue

Turn right into Bell Lane and cross Wentworth Street into Goulston Street. The flats on the left stand on the site of a 19th-century tenement block called Wentworth Model Dwellings. It was on the pavement outside one of the entrances to this block that the Ripper left his only known clue: a piece of Catherine Eddowes's apron, stained with her blood. The fact that it was dropped here suggests that the Ripper made his escape from Mitre Square in an easterly direction. When police discovered the apron remnant they also found a strange graffito chalked on the wall immediately above it: 'The Juwes are The Men that Will not be Blamed for nothing.' Although there was nothing to suggest that this had anything to do with the Ripper or the murders, the police feared it would fuel already prevalent rumours that the Ripper was a foreign Jew, so they hastily erased it before most people were up and about. It is possible, of course, that the Ripper also saw the graffito and deliberately dropped the piece of apron by it in order to make people think there was some connection between the murders and the Jewish community, even though there wasn't. If this was his plan it succeeded brilliantly, for ripperologists are still discussing it endlessly today.

Walk on down to the end of Goulston Street and turn left on Whitechapel High Street. Aldgate East Underground station, which is where the walk ends, is ahead on the left.

WAPPING TO LIMEHOUSE

Summary: This walk goes straight along the riverside through the old dockland areas of Wapping, Shadwell and Limehouse, the original Tower Hamlets immediately east of the City. These districts are all at various stages of redevelopment following the wholesale closure of London's moribund docks in the late 1960s. The walk starts at St Katharine's Dock by Tower Bridge. Wapping High Street and Pier Head follow; then Wapping Wall, Shadwell Basin and Park, Narrow Street, Limehouse Basin and Limehouse's famous parish church of **St Anne's**. Other features are three old dockland's pubs and views of the river from stairs, wharves and waterfront parks.

Start:	Tower Hill station (District and Circle Underground Lines). Fenchurch Street railway station and the Docklands Light Rail's Tower Gateway station are both nearby.
Finish:	Westferry station (Docklands Light Rail).
Length:	3¼ miles (5.2km).
Time:	2½ hours.
Refreshments:	Apart from places like the Dickens Inn in St Katharine's Dock, the only places to stop on this walk are a handful of historic riverside pubs strung out along the route, all of which are mentioned in the text.

Come out of Tower Hill station and go down the steps into the subway with a section of the old City wall on your left and the Tower of London ahead. When you get to the ruins of the old postern gate in the City wall, turn left along the side of the Tower moat, following the signs to St Katharine's Dock. Go under the next road and then branch right across the small bridge into the water garden. Turn left by the World Trade Centre into Commodity Quay, which faces one of the three basins in St Katharine's Dock. A hospital, a medieval church and over 1,000 houses were demolished to make room for St Katharine's dock, which opened in 1828. Tea, rubber, wool, marble, sugar, tallow and ivory were all unloaded at the quays and stored in the dock's multi-storey warehouses supported on their thick iron columns.

Commercial commodities

At the end of Commodity Quay, turn right along the flagged terrace in front of the new shops in the ground floor of the warehouse. Go through the archway into the entrance basin connecting with the river. Turn right here and then cross the bridge by the Madison coffee house, marking the approximate position of old St Katharine's Church.

Go to the left under the Tower Hotel and then left again over the red bridge across the entrance to the dock. The entrance's relatively small size was one reason why St

Katharine's was never a great commercial success. It survived, however, along with London's other wet docks until competition from the new container ports further downstream forced them all to close in the 1960s.

Keep to the left along the dockside and then turn right round the end of the Dickens Inn. Turn left behind the row of houses facing the basin. Go left again at the end and then right to the gate leading into Thomas More Street, bordered by dock walls. Turn right here, right again at the first junction and then left at the second junction into Wapping High Street, a long street that follows the course of the river almost as far as Limehouse. The road was built around 1570 to link the legal quays in the City – the only quays at which ships could lawfully unload their cargo – to new storage warehouses downstream at New Crane Wharf. Inevitably, people settled along the road and it was later described by John Stow, a 16th-century historian of London, as a 'filthy strait passage, with alleys of small tenements or cottages … inhabited by sailors' victuallers'. So began the maritime community of the East End.

On the left you pass new housing developments built over the London Docks. Opened in 1805, the year of Nelson's victory at Trafalgar, London Docks were about three times larger than St Katharine's Dock and, with their monopoly on the import of tobacco, rice, wine and brandy, were commercially very successful. So prosperous were they, in fact, that in 1864 they took over St Katharine's. Apart from the two entrance basins, most of the docks have now been filled in, the 20-acre (8-ha) western dock being buried beneath the new headquarters of Rupert Murdoch's News International, publishers of the *Sun* and *The Times*.

After a while you come to Wapping Pier Head, a double row of Georgian houses facing each other across railed gardens. The houses were built for officials of the dock company and the central gardens cover the original entrance to the docks. Cobblestones set in the garden on the left describe the arc of the dock entrance gates.

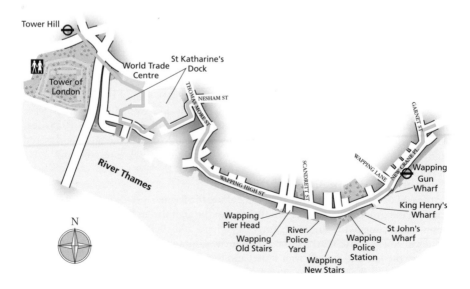

Convicts' quay

Continue through the Pier Head houses. On the right the Town of Ramsgate pub marks the entrance to a narrow alleyway leading to Wapping Old Stairs. At low tide you can go down these stairs onto the rocky riverside and get a good view of both Butler's Wharf on the Surrey bank, and of Tower Bridge. During the bloodless revolution of 1688 it is said that the bloodthirsty Judge Jeffreys was captured here as he tried to flee the country in a collier bound for Hamburg. Later, convicts were chained up in the pub's cellars before being transported to Australia. More recently the warehouses here were used for oranges and spices. An old lady I met who had lived in Wapping all her life told me how the dockers used to break open a crate of oranges each morning and throw the fruit to the children as they passed by on their way to school. On the left in Scandrett Street are Wapping's former 18th-century charity school and parish church, both of which have now been converted into homes.

Further along, the white building covered in abstract concrete shapes is the boat-yard of the river police. Set up in 1798 to deal with endemic pilfering from the thousands of merchant ships in the river (a contemporary estimate put the value of goods stolen at £½ million/year), they were the first properly organized police force in the country. They are now part of the Metropolitan Police and patrol the Thames in a fleet of 33 boats.

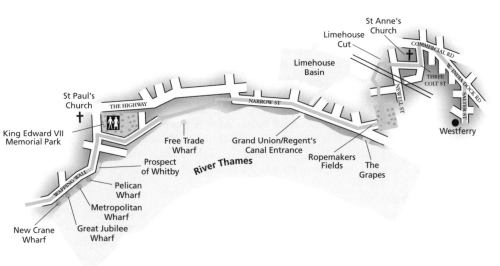

Next to the boatyard is a riverside garden from which there is a fine view of the lonely Angel pub on the south side of the river in Bermondsey. Beyond the next ware-houses are Wapping New Stairs and the station of the river police. After the Captain Kidd pub and Swan Wharf you come to King Henry's Stairs leading to a riverboat pier from which there is a good view of Rotherhithe and the former Surrey Docks. In the 16th century there was a cannon foundry here making guns for Henry VIII's navy, hence the local names of King Henry's Wharf and Gun Wharf. Later the spot became the traditional place of execution for convicted pirates. Captain Kidd – the naval officer who, having been sent on an anti-pirate mission to Madagascar, turned pirate himself – was hanged here in 1701. For maximum deterrent effect the sentence was usually carried out at low tide and three high tides were allowed to wash over the corpse before it was cut down and buried. The last hanging at Execution Dock took place in 1830.

The High Street now curves to the left beside Gun Wharf and then passes Wapping station. The Underground line runs under the river through the world's first underwater tunnel. Engineered by the Brunels, it was completed in 1843 after 20 years of tunnelling. Follow the road round to the left into New Crane Place and then turn right into Wapping Wall. The original road was laid out on top of a sea wall, constructed between St Katharine's and Shadwell after the old medieval flood defences had been washed away by heavy tides in the 1560s.

New wharf development

Now you pass New Crane Wharf and Great Jubilee Wharf, and then Metropolitan Wharf, an old pepper warehouse converted into offices and studios. Next is Pelican Wharf, and beyond that on the corner is the Prospect of Whitby pub, named after a ship from the Yorkshire port that once berthed here regularly. Like the Angel at Bermondsey, this is another pub of great antiquity, though its claim to be the oldest riverside inn in London should be taken with a substantial bucket of salt.

Follow the road round to the left past the old London Hydraulic Power Company's pumping station (now a restaurant). Between 1893 and 1977 this supplied hydraulic power for cranes and lifts not only to the wharves here in Docklands but also to theatres and office buildings as far away as Earl's Court in West London. You now cross the bridge over the entrance to Shadwell Basin. Once the eastern entrance to London Docks, this basin is now used for swimming and canoeing, and new houses have been built on the quays. To the right of the basin you can see the spire of St Paul's Shadwell Church, traditionally known as the church of the sea captains. Captain Cook, the discoverer of Australia, was a regular worshipper in the church and in 1763 James, his eldest son, was baptized here. Like his father, James also served in the navy but was drowned in 1794. American readers will be interested to know that President Jefferson's mother was baptized here early in the 18th century. To see the church, walk round the north side of the basin and climb the steps into the churchyard.

Intrepid explorers

Immediately after the bridge turn right into a path besides the sports ground leading to the King Edward VII Memorial Park. Opened in 1922, the park covers the site of the old Shadwell fish market which lay between Shadwell High Street (now The Highway) and the river. On the right adjoining the Rotherhithe Tunnel ventilation shaft is a coloured tablet commemorating the Elizabethan navigators who sailed from the Thames to find a northeast passage round Russia to China. The expedition set sail in 1563 but had not gone far before all the ships were separated in a gale. Sir Hugh Willoughby and his crew froze to death in the Arctic winter but the others returned safely, one of them via the court of Ivan the Terrible in Russia. Sir Francis Drake found a way to China 25 years later, using the southerly route round Cape Horn. The Ratcliff Cross mentioned on the tablet stood on the riverside marking the position of Ratcliff Stairs, the most important station for Thames watermen east of the Tower. The walk passes the site of the stairs shortly.

Plate 35: Brentford
Boston Manor in west London was once the
manor house of Brentford (see page 187).

Plate 36: Syon Park to Strawberry Hill
*The railway bridge spanning Richmond lock and weir on
the Syon Park to Strawberry Hill walk (see page 193).*

Plate 37: Richmond
*Evening sun bathes Richmond's restored Riverside and
original Georgian bridge over the Thames (see page 196).*

Plate 38: Hampton Court
*The immaculate gardens to the east of Hampton Court palace are
one of the highlights of the Hampton Court walk (see page 201).*

Plate 39: Pinner
Pinner's parish church of St John was built out of local flint in the
14th century and given a tower in the 15th century (see page 206).

Plate 40: Harrow-on-the-Hill
The buildings of historic Harrow School dominate the hilltop village
of Harrow-on-the-Hill in north-west London (see page 211).

Plate 41: Chipping Barnet and Monken Hadley
Chipping Barnet's Elizabethan grammar school, built in
1573 and now part of Barnet College (see page 219).

Plate 42: Enfield
*Enfield's Chase Green, public park and remnant of a former royal hunting
ground, is now decorated with a Millennium Fountain (see page 220).*

Now walk along the riverside, from which there is a good view of Canary Wharf on the Isle of Dogs. Go through the gate and continue in front of the new flats on what was Free Trade Wharf.

The riverside walk eventually brings you to Narrow Street, the old link between Shadwell and Limehouse. Just here is the site of Ratcliff Stairs. Away to your left the old house across the road behind the trees is the present base of the Royal Foundation of St Katharine, the organization displaced to make way for the eponymous dock in 1828. Continue along Narrow Street. After a while the road crosses the entrance to Limehouse Basin, itself the entrance to the Regent's Canal and thus to the whole of the national canal network. A short canal called the Limehouse Cut also runs from Limehouse Basin, linking up with the River Lee navigation to the east. The Barley Mow pub, once the dockmaster's house, is a good place to stop for refreshments.

Sailors' leisure

Further along this street you come to The Grapes, the third of the old riverside pubs on the north bank. Once there were dozens of pubs along the river – 36 in Wapping High Street alone – where originally sailors and then dockers slaked their thirst. Fork left here into Ropemakers Fields. When you get to the bar/restaurant continue on into the park and turn left. Just before the path enters the circular railed enclosure sloping up to the footbridge, go right, round the outside of the railings and onto the towpath of the Limehouse Cut. Here turn right. Just beyond the railway bridge turn right up some steps and then left along a path that brings you out on Newell Street, a rare survivor of Georgian Limehouse. The bow-fronted house on the corner of Newell Street ahead was often visited by the London novelist Charles Dickens, whose godfather, Christopher Huffam, lived here. Cross Newell Street and approach the famous parish church of Limehouse – St Anne's – built by Nicholas Hawksmoor in the early 18th century (see the sign on the right-hand gate pier for more about the church's history).

Go to the right of the church and leave the churchyard by the gate at the opposite end. Turn left into Three Colt Street and then right onto the main road (Commercial Road). Fork right into West India Dock Road (on the left, notice the old ship chandlers' and sail makers' building). Opposite the police station turn right into Salter Street. Westferry Station, where the walk ends, is straight ahead.

❖❖

BARNES TO FULHAM

❖❖

Summary: Barnes and Fulham, with Putney in between, straddle the River Thames in west London. The central section of the walk follows the river, first along the towpath and then on Putney Embankment, a great rowing centre. Otherwise, apart from its first stage in the old village of Barnes (still with its green, duckpond, pub and

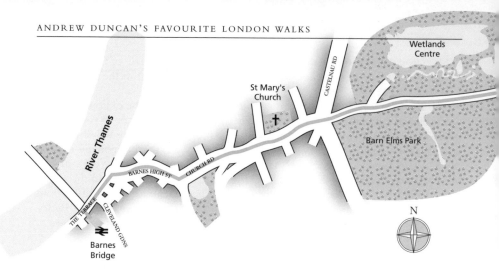

church), the walk goes mainly through parks and gardens, including the public grounds of 16th-century **Fulham Palace**, the former summer retreat of the Bishops of London. The palace's gardens are among the loveliest and least known in London. Other features of the walk include Putney and Fulham churches with their Civil War associations, and the remains of the 300-year-old Fulham Pottery.

Start:	Barnes Bridge station (mainline trains from Waterloo).
Finish:	Putney Bridge station (District Underground Line).
Length:	3½ miles (5.6km).
Time:	2 hours.
Refreshments:	Plenty of places in Barnes at the start of the walk (including the Sun Inn on the village green) and in Putney High Street by Putney Bridge, a little over halfway into the walk. Near the end there is a good café in Fulham's Bishop's Park.

Come out of Barnes Bridge station, cross the road and turn right along a breezy, open stretch of the River Thames. This is the last stage of the 4½-mile (7-km) Oxford and Cambridge University Boat Race, which ends upstream of the bridge at Mortlake. On the right, the red-brick house on the corner of Cleveland Gardens was home to *Planets* composer Gustav Holst while he was teaching music at nearby St Paul's School.

Suburban village
Follow the road round to the right into Barnes High Street. Although it is a suburb firmly entrenched in the London conurbation, Barnes still retains much of its old village character. Round the corner at the end of the High Street you will find the village green with a duckpond in the middle and a central island where swans breed. On the right of the pond, Milbourne House – the oldest house in Barnes – was home briefly to the 18th-century novelist Henry Fielding, author of *Tom Jones*. As you turn left along Church Road you pass the village pub overlooking the green and the pond. Further on along Church Road you come to Barnes' church, **St Mary's**, looking every bit the rustic country church with its lychgate, yews and well-tended graveyard.

178

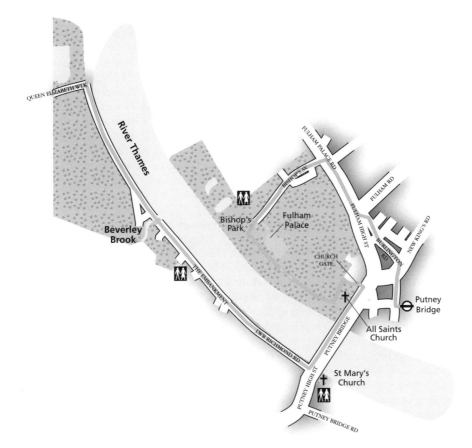

When you come to the traffic lights at the junction with Castelnau Road, go straight across into the lane that runs alongside Barn Elms Park. Barn Elms House, demolished after a fire in 1954, was the manor house of Barnes and the modern park its grounds. The only relic today is a section of the old lake. Previous residents include Queen Elizabeth I's minister and spymaster, Sir Francis Walsingham, and the 18th-century banker and Lord Mayor of London, Sir Richard Hoare, who is buried in St Mary's Church. From 1894 until 1939 the old house was an upper-class country club. On the left the **Wetlands Centre** stands on what was, until the early 1990s, a vast reservoir as big as the park itself.

When the road enters the sports centre, keep to the pavement and go through the gate into Queen Elizabeth Walk. This will bring you out onto one of the quietest and most rural stretches of the Thames towpath in London. Opposite you can see Fulham football ground, and to the right of the ground, Bishop's Park, your eventual destination. Turn right and walk along to a small dock where the Beverley Brook joins the Thames. Here the towpath turns into Putney Embankment, a great rowing centre and the start point of the Oxford and Cambridge boat race since it

179

was first held over the full Putney to Mortlake course in 1845. There are lots of boathouses here and boats are constantly being carried in and out, so watch out as you walk along.

Follow the Embankment along to Putney Bridge. Putney Church, on the other side of Putney High Street, is dwarfed by the office blocks behind. In this church in 1647, England's anti-royalist New Model Army held a two-week conference known to history as the Putney Debates. Ostensibly the debates were about whether the army should be disbanded without back-pay or indemnity for damage done during the war against the king. In practice, they ranged over a whole spectrum of political ideas embodied in the 'Agreement of the People', including the then-revolutionary concept of 'one man, one vote'. The army radicals lost the argument and Oliver Cromwell finally crushed them after a mutiny two years later.

Fulham and its palace

At this point, turn left over the bridge towards Fulham and its parish church of **All Saints** on the opposite side. When you come to the junction with New King's Road (which branches right) turn left into Church Gate. On the right at the end is a fine range of almshouses, still used by local people. These were built in 1869, having been endowed in 1680 by Hereford MP and local landowner Sir William Powell. (The original Powell almshouses were in nearby Burlington Road which you come to in a minute.) Go through the gate into the churchyard. As well as being Fulham's parish church, All Saints also has close connections with the Bishops of London because it was the closest church to their summer home, Fulham Palace, and at least 10 bishops are buried in the churchyard. Inside there are many fine monuments, including two from the Civil War. One commemorates William Rumbold, a royal official who was both Surveyor-General of the Customs and Comptroller of the Great Wardrobe. In his latter capacity, he carried off the royal standard to Charles I at Nottingham when the Civil War broke out. Rumbold died in 1667 at nearby Parson's Green. The other monument, dated 1665, commemorates 25-year-old Thomas Carlos, whose father, Colonel William Carlos, hid in the oak tree at Boscobel with the future Charles II, after the defeat of the royalists at Worcester in 1651.

Go to the right round the west end of the church, and turn right into Bishop's Park. The park was originally part of the grounds of Bishop's Palace, which you will come to shortly. Walk through the park, either along the riverside or through the centre, and when you come to the crossroads next to the open-air performance area turn right out of the park between, on the left, the café and aviary and, on the right, the entrance lodge of Fulham Palace. Immediately turn right into the grounds of the palace and walk straight through to the gateway leading into the central court-yard. It was only in 1973 that the Bishops of London gave up Fulham Palace, having used it – mainly as a summer home – for a thousand years. In its present form, the building is only about 500 years old, being essentially a Tudor mansion of the 16th century ranged round a cobbled courtyard. The garden front was added much later in 1814.

Secret garden

To gain access to the gardens and the palace museum, go back out of the courtyard gateway, turn right, go through the gate and then turn right again. The palace gardens are among the most attractive and secluded in London, particularly the walled garden, which is reached through a low Tudor archway in the old brick wall on the opposite side of the gracious lawns. Here in this old kitchen garden, which, with its dilapidated greenhouses, feels like some kind of secret garden, you could be a million miles from central London.

Retrace your steps to the original entrance to the palace grounds near the exit from the park and turn right along Bishop's Avenue, with bowling green and tennis courts on your left and the Warren allotment gardens on your right. Beyond the school, Moat Garden on the right has been created out of the remains of the huge moat system that once surrounded Fulham Palace. Archaeologists say this defensive system is at least as old as the time of the Danish occupation (9th to 11th centuries) and could even date from Roman times several hundred years before that.

On the main road (Fulham Palace Road) cross over at the lights left, and turn right. At the roundabout junction with Fulham Road, go over the zebra crossing to the left and into Burlington Road – this is where the almshouses used to be. At the end of this road there is a disused 19th-century pottery kiln, part of the old Fulham Pottery that was based here until lack of space forced it to move to Battersea in the 1980s. The move severed a 300-year-old link with the past, for the pottery had been here since 1672. Ex-lawyer John Dwight established it after learning how to produce a much sought-after type of pottery called salt-glazed stoneware, until then only obtainable in Germany. Dwight also tried to manufacture porcelain in England for the first time – without success.

At the end of Burlington Road, turn right onto New King's Road, cross the road using the traffic island, and go along the path by the bus stop, which leads to Putney Bridge station and the end of the walk.

❖❖❖

KEW TO HAMMERSMITH

❖❖❖

Summary: Kew and Hammersmith, with Chiswick in between, are all on the River Thames in west London. Apart from the first section of the walk around Kew Green and a short-cut through the landscaped grounds of 18th-century **Chiswick House** (a beautiful Palladian villa), the walk follows the river throughout, first along Strand-on-the-Green and then along Chiswick Mall and Hammersmith's Upper and Lower Malls. These are all one-sided streets, separated from the river by a path or quiet road, and lined with fine 18th-century houses interspersed with old pubs such as the City Barge or the Dove. The most famous of the riverside houses is Kelmscott House where William Morris spent the last two decades of his productive life.

Start:	Kew Gardens station (District Underground Line; Silverlink Metro mainline trains; riverboats from Westminster Pier – spring to autumn only).
Finish:	Hammersmith station (District, Metropolitan and Piccadilly Underground Lines).
Length:	4½ miles (7.2km).
Time:	2½ hours.
Refreshments:	Pubs and tea rooms in and around Kew and Kew Green (particularly the outstanding Newens' tea rooms in Kew Road near the start of the walk) and later on several historic riverside pubs: the City Barge at Strand-on-the-Green (a third of the way along the route) and the Ship and the Dove on the Upper Mall at Hammersmith (three-quarters of the way along the route). There is also a good café in the grounds of Chiswick House at the halfway point.

Standing at the main exit from Kew Gardens station, take the right fork of the road and then turn right onto Kew Gardens Road. Follow it round to Kew Road where you will see the wall of the **Royal Botanic Gardens** on the far side. Turn right past Newens' tea rooms, resisting, if you can, the temptation to sample their deservedly famous Maids of Honour tarts. When you reach the traffic lights some way ahead on this busy stretch of road, cross the road to your left, turn right briefly, and then go left again into Kew Green, walking along the south side with Kew's 18th-century church on your right.

Before the Botanic Gardens

The old village green, with its pond in one corner and cricket pitch behind the church, is overlooked by elegant Georgian houses. Most of these houses were built in the 18th century for the courtiers and officials attached to the royal court during its summer residence in Kew. What is now the Royal Botanic Gardens was once the site of the royal palaces, of which only Kew Palace, bought by George III in 1770 and now a museum, survives. George III's mother, Princess Augusta, founded the botanic gardens in 1759, and Queen Victoria handed them over to the nation in 1841. In the beginning the gardens were only 9 acres (3.6 ha), but they now cover over 300 acres (121 ha).

Continue along the south side of the green past **St Anne's Church**, burial place of two famous painters, Johann Zoffany (died 1810) and Thomas Gainsborough (died 1788). The latter's grave is the flat slab surrounded by black railings on the south side. Both had houses nearby. Further along on your left, No. 47 is now the administrative offices of the gardens. Its gates were the gardens' original entrance. Today the main entrance is through the massive black and gilt gates ahead at the western corner of the green. Follow the road round past the entrance and along the north side of the green, passing on the left the Herbarium (where dried specimens of all the world's plants are stored) and then Ferry Lane, which once led to the now-defunct Brentford Ferry. When you reach the main road again, go over the road at the zebra crossing and then turn left over Kew Bridge towards Brentford. The island on the left is Brentford Ait and the graceful tower to its right is part of the former Grand Junction Water Works, now the **Kew Bridge Steam Museum**.

Along the Strand
On the other side of the bridge turn right down the steps and follow the road round to the left along the river. When the road diverges from the river, bear right along the footpath between the river and Strand-on-the-Green. The Strand was just a small fishing community until the great Court era of Kew from the mid-18th century onwards. Zoffany lived in one of the biggest of the new houses built at that time (No. 65) and used the local fishermen as models for a painting of the Last Supper he executed for a local church.

Further along the Strand you come to the old City Barge pub, which claims to date from 1484 and was originally called the Navigator's Arms. The name was changed after a boathouse was built nearby to store the lord mayor of London's state barge. Beyond the bridge are the 17th-century Bull's Head pub and some tiny almshouses, built in 1724. The squat, modern building on the opposite side of the river is the Public Record Office, where national archives stretching back to the time of William the Conqueror are stored.

When the path comes to an end continue straight on into Grove Park Road, bearing left when Grove Park Road branches off the main thoroughfare. The Grove Park Estate was built in the grounds of Grove House, an 18th-century mansion that was still standing in 1928. At the end of the road (on the right is St Paul's Church) turn left and then left again over Grove Park Bridge. When you are halfway over the bridge, turn right down the steps and walk up to Chiswick station. Turn left into Park Road, then right into Staveley Road and left through the gates into the grounds of Chiswick House. At the toilets near the entrance turn right and walk straight on.

Chiswick House was built in the 1720s by the amateur architect Lord Burlington, essentially as a place where he could display his art collection and entertain his friends. It was one of the earliest Palladian houses in England and is, therefore, an important architectural monument. The gardens are significant too, because they were the first to break away from the formal Dutch style and experiment with a more natural approach. Both house and garden owe much to the 18th century's reverence for classical antiquity, so you will find numerous temples, columns and urns.

When you get to the bridge, go straight over and right up the bank. Pass the sunken pond with the central obelisk and then walk down the avenue of urns to the house. Go round the house to the right, between the gate pillars, and then turn immediately left along a path that leads past the café and eventually to a small lodge. Leave the park by the gate to the right of the lodge.

Artists and actors
Turn left along Burlington Lane towards Paxton Road, crossing the lane at the traffic lights. Beyond St Mary's Convent turn right into Powell's Walk. This ancient right of way takes you to Chiswick Old Burying Ground and **St Nicholas's Church**, the nucleus of the old riverside village of Chiswick. Modern Chiswick's centre of gravity has since shifted north to Chiswick High Road, leaving old Chiswick a quiet backwater, cut off from the rest of London by the Great West Road, driven through the suburban streets between old and new Chiswick in the 1950s.

Go round to the right of St Nicholas's 15th-century tower and through the south porch into the little churchyard. Several well-known people are buried at

St Nicholas's, including Lord Burlington of Chiswick House and his landscape designer William Kent. The most prominent grave in this part of the graveyard (on the right, surrounded by railings) belongs to 18th-century artist William Hogarth and his wife and mother-in-law. They all lived together in Hogarth's little country house at Chiswick, now a museum – **Hogarth's House**.

Go straight past Hogarth's tomb and out of the churchyard into Chiswick Mall (Hogarth's house is to the left: along Church Street, under the roundabout, and into Hogarth Lane). Handsome houses face south across the river. The first is the local

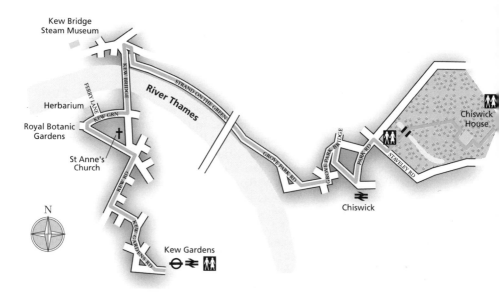

parsonage. Bedford House was the home of the acting family, the Redgraves. The finest is Walpole House, the one with the railings and gate in front, nearly opposite the far end of the island (Chiswick Eyot). Relations of Sir Robert Walpole, England's first Prime Minister, lived here in the 18th century. Later it was used as a school. William Thackeray boarded there for a while and probably used it as the model for Miss Pinkerton's Academy in *Vanity Fair*. One of the first occupants of Walpole House was Charles II's mistress, the Duchess of Cleveland, 'fairest and lewdest of the royal concubines'.

Private printing presses

At the end of Chiswick Mall the small cottages of Durham Wharf interpose between the river and the road so that the river is temporarily lost to view. The cottages are followed by the more substantial houses in Hammersmith Terrace, built in the 1750s with gardens right on the river. No. 7 bears a plaque to Sir Emery Walker (1851–1933), an expert on printing types and a partner in two local printing presses, the Kelmscott Press and the Doves Press. No. 3 was the home of calligrapher Edward Johnston (1872–1944), teacher of graphic designer and artist

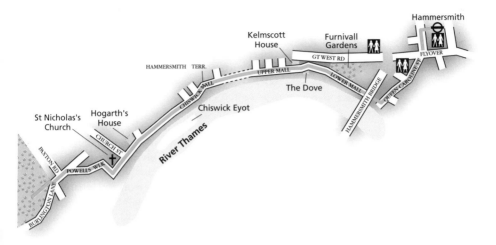

Eric Gill, and a collaborator on the Doves Press. A.P. Herbert, a colourful MP who wrote many books about the Thames before his death in 1971, lived for more than 50 years at Nos. 12–13.

At the end of the terrace the walk returns to the riverside in a public garden laid out on the site of the old West Middlesex Water Company pumping station, part of which remains as a brick arcade. Ahead, there is a fine view of Hammersmith Mall as it curves round to Hammersmith Bridge. Continue past the 18th-century Old Ship pub, through the tunnel created by the overhang of a modern apartment block, and then past Linden House, for over a century the headquarters of the London Corinthian Sailing Club, founded in 1894. Races are started from the box on the right. The long, low building on the opposite bank is St Paul's School, which was founded in the shadow of **St Paul's Cathedral** in the City in 1512, moved to Hammersmith in 1884 and to this site in 1968.

This stretch of the river (Hammersmith Reach) offers the best sailing on the tidal part of the Thames. But it is probably used as much by rowers as by sailors (and it is roughly the halfway stage of the Oxford and Cambridge boat-race course). You can see the first boathouses in Hammersmith Upper Mall soon after the road rejoins the riverside a few steps ahead. The five-bay Georgian house at the end of the Mall, with its own front garden behind walls and railings, is Kelmscott House, designer William Morris's London home from 1877 until his death in 1896. Morris named the house after his country home in Kelmscott, Oxfordshire. This was also on the Thames and more than once Morris rowed with family and friends the whole way upriver from one house to the other. An earlier occupant was Sir Francis Ronalds (1788–1873), who developed the world's first electric telegraph in the garden. He was forced to abandon it after the government, blind to its revolutionary importance, said it could not see a use for it!

Fine book-making

Thomas Cobden-Sanderson, a friend of Morris, lived next door at No. 22. Sanderson gave up being a barrister while in his 40s and started the Doves book-bindery, where he carried out a lot of work for William Morris's Kelmscott Press. Later, after Morris had died and the Kelmscott Press had folded, Cobden-Sanderson and Emery Walker from Hammersmith Terrace founded the Doves Press alongside the bindery. During the 19th century the craft of good book-making had sunk to a low ebb in Britain. These three men – Walker, Cobden-Sanderson and Morris – were largely responsible for reviving it and starting the private press movement that is still flourishing today. Cobden-Sanderson also invented the term 'arts and crafts' for the movement that Morris inspired.

The Doves Press and Bindery occupied a small house just beyond the 18th-century Dove pub on the right. It was here, in the 18th century when the Dove was a coffee house, that poet James Thomson wrote part of his famous poem *The Seasons*, and also the words of *Rule Britannia*.

Walk on into Furnivall Gardens, laid out over Hammersmith's wharf area following World War II bombing, and then along the Lower Mall past more boat-houses, pubs and houses. Continue under colourful Hammersmith Bridge, dating from 1887, to the end of the riverside walk. Turn left into Queen Caroline Street and walk to the flyover. There is a subway further on that will take you to Hammersmith station and the bus station in the traffic island on the right, where the walk ends.

❖❖

BRENTFORD

❖❖

Summary: Brentford is a former west London village on the north bank of the Thames directly opposite Kew Gardens. It grew up at the point where the Great West Road forded the River Brent, and where the River Brent flowed into the Thames. Thanks to better than average road and water communications, it was at one time an important commercial centre and the county town of Middlesex where the parliamentary elections were held. This circular walk starts at the manor house north of the old village centre and then follows the now-canalized River Brent down to its confluence with the Thames, a picturesque area of locks, marina, wharves and boatyards. There are fine views from here downstream and across to Kew. The walk returns to the start point via the centre of Brentford and The Butts, a square of lovely old houses hidden away on the north side of the High Street and one of west London's best-kept secrets.

Start and finish: Boston Manor station (Piccadilly Underground Line). Brentford station (mainline trains from Waterloo) can be used if more convenient: it is on the walk and, being closer to the village centre, cuts out the longish walk between Boston Manor station and Boston Manor House.

Length: 3½ miles (5.6km).

Time: 2¾ hours.

Refreshments: Pubs, cafés, fish and chip shop, pizza restaurant and bakery in the High Street. On the actual walk route you'll find a bar/restaurant overlooking the marina, the Brewery Tap pub in the wharf area and the White Horse pub (with a riverside garden) near The Butts. St Paul's Church serves morning coffee and cheap hot lunches.

Come out of the Underground station and turn right down Boston Manor Lane. After about 200 yards (180m) you come to the gates of **Boston Manor House**. Turn in here and make your way round to the left of the house to the garden front with its stately old cedars. Originally built in the 1620s, Boston Manor was once the manor house of Brentford village, about ¾ mile (1.2km) to the south. James Clitherow, son of Sir Christopher Clitherow of Pinner, bought the house in the 1670s and remodelled it after a fire. His descendants remained lords of the manor until 1924 when the arrival of the new Great West Road induced them to sell up and move away.

Today, the view from the garden is of the M4 flyover, but originally the house looked over parkland to the River Brent and, beyond, to Osterley Park, former home of the Child banking family. Before the area was built up Brentford was surrounded by a whole string of country mansions: **Syon House**, Osterley Park, Boston Manor House, Gunnersbury House (home of the Rothschild family) and, south of the river, Kew Palace. Remarkably, all survive today and all are open to the public.

Turn left down the broad tarmac walk, aiming for the tall office blocks. At the bottom by the toilets and the little car park, turn right and walk down the gently sloping hill towards the Brent. Here the river is actually part of the Grand Union canal, constructed from the 1790s onwards to link London with the industrializing Midlands. At Hanwell, about a mile (1.6km) north of here, the river and canal diverge. The canal heads off west towards Uxbridge and so to Braunston in Northamptonshire where it links up with other waterways, while the river makes its way northeast to its source near Barnet. Cross over the footbridge and turn left, heading in the direction of the Samsung tower and the Great West Road bridge. Beyond the bridge you go round a corner and under a railway bridge before passing through a covered dock. Now you can see, ahead left, the old village centre on the far bank of the Brent with the spire of **St Paul's Church** rising up behind. The wide loop of the Brent here was cut off by the canal partly as a short cut and partly to create a backwater basin.

St Lawrence's Church and Brentford Lock

Carrying on, St Lawrence's Church comes into view straight ahead through the trees and beyond Brentford Lock. Although it was strategically important, Brentford was not a particularly populous place in the Middle Ages and so was part of the parish of Hanwell rather than being a parish in its own right. However, Hanwell church was a fairly long walk away, so Brentford had its own church, dedicated to St Lawrence. Brentford at last became a parish in 1749. Fifteen years later, when the radical political writer Horne Tooke was parson, the bulk of the church was rebuilt in brick next to the original 15th-century stone tower. Rationalization of parishes led to the church's closure in 1961. Plans to convert it into a theatre in the 1980s fell through and now the building stands redundant beside the busy High Street.

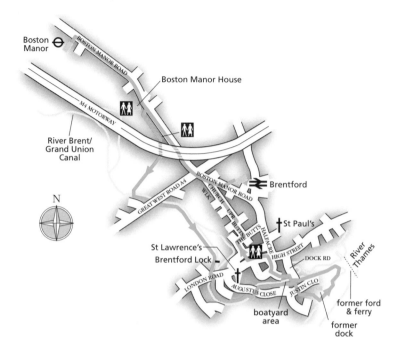

Looking back just after you pass Brentford Lock, you get a good view of The Butts, seen close up later on the walk. Built for Brentford's expanding middle class from the late 17th century onwards, The Butts was laid out on high ground to protect it from flooding. Brentford's less fortunate working class population lived in low-lying areas near the Thames, also seen close up later on the walk. Serious inundations in these low-lying areas were not infrequent in the days before the development of water management techniques.

Turn left over the bridge where the old Great West Road originally forded the Brent and then go immediately right and down the steps to continue the towpath walk (signposted). Having flowed south until now, the canalized river here turns sharply east as it nears the Thames. Over on the far side the trees denote the grounds of the Duke of Northumberland's Syon House. On this side new houses and offices are being built among the small factories and workshops that crowd what is called The Ham – a former piece of riverside common. When you reach the bridge that once carried the railway to Brentford Dock, you have to turn left onto the road to pass underneath it. A flight of shallow up-and-down steps brings you back onto the towpath and into Brentford's main waterfront and boatyard area.

Brentford began to develop as a commercial and industrial centre about the time the Clitherows arrived. Inns and shops lined the High Street, serving travellers on the Great West Road. Corn and garden produce from orchards and market gardens were traded in the market place. To the south, industry (including several breweries and distilleries) crammed into the narrow space between the High Street and the wharf-lined waterfront. Here also lived Brentford's working population. Brentford's economic significance increased with the arrival of the canal in the 1790s. Some 40 years later the town was given another boost when famous engineer Isambard Kingdom Brunel built a large dock at Brentford and connected it to his Great Western Railway by a branch line leading north to Southall. Brentford Dock, of which more in a moment, no longer exists, but, as you can see, the canal and busy waterfront remain and the land between the High Street and the waterfront is still packed with boat-building firms and many other small businesses.

Brentford Dock

Cross the footbridge and once you are on the other side do not go back down to the towpath but continue along the riverside, keeping to the tarmac (and do not go up the ramp). Good views of the basins and boatyards open up to the left. When you reach the lock, turn right on Dock Road and go under the arch by the dock management office. Carry on over the road and up the steps, now walking on red tarmac with flats to your left and a little car park on the right. You are now in what was once Brunel's dock, built on an islanded spit of land called Old England. The dock basin could accommodate boats up to 300 tons and all around were loading bays, warehouses and railway sidings. Like London docks downriver, Brentford Dock closed in the 1960s and was subsequently redeveloped as a marina with surrounding flats and houses.

Turn left at the small fountain. Go under the walkway into a garden area and then up the steps ahead onto the terrace of the marina bar and restaurant. Cross the terrace diagonally to the right, go down the bank and turn left along the gravel walk by the river. Kew Gardens is surprisingly close on the right. Ahead rises the graceful campanile of **Kew Bridge Steam Museum**, formerly the Grand Junction Waterworks Company.

Cross the entrance to the dock basin and follow the path round to the right, up the steps and back onto the red tarmac. From the viewpoint here you can see, away to the right, George III's Kew Palace, and, near to the left, the entrance to the ferry basin. The King's ferry operated between here and the opposite bank of the Thames, carrying horses and carriages as well as people, from at least the mid-17th century. Ferrying people continued until well into the 20th century, even though there was a bridge at Kew from the mid-18th century.

Soap and starch

To the left of the ferry basin there used to be a large soap factory which, as early as the 1820s, was the biggest hard soap factory in southeast England. Production at the works – which, apart from the dock, was the largest enterprise in Brentford – ceased in 1961. Turn sharp left back along the entrance to the canal, which strictly speaking starts at the lock crossed by Dock Road. Cross the lock on the black and white foot-bridge and walk back along the canal. First you cross a weir and then a pair of disused floodgates called Dr Johnson's Lock after Dr William Johnson, the proprietor of a starch mill in Catherine Wheel Yard in the 18th century. Turn right by the Brewery Tap pub and walk up Catherine Wheel Road (the Catherine Wheel was an inn). When you reach the High Street turn left and cross at the lights into the Market Place. Both the High Street and the Market Place have been dramatically altered in the 20th century to allow the main road to be widened and to provide more up-to-date shopping facilities. The market was forced to move as long ago as the 1850s when the new courthouse was built. It went first to a site near Kew Bridge and then in 1974 to Heston.

Pass to the right of the courthouse. To the left of the White Horse, the artist J. W. Turner spent four years as a boy living with his uncle, a local butcher, before going on to study at the Royal Academy. The White Horse has been here since at least 1603, though it has, of course, been rebuilt since then. Beyond the White Horse you come to an unexpectedly beautiful enclave of lovely old houses called The Butts.

The Butts

Originally common land, used since at least the 16th century for compulsory archery practice (a butt is a target, hence the name), The Butts was enclosed and sold off for building in 1664. Most of the houses around the square – built for Brentford's increasingly prosperous commercial and professional classes – date from soon after that time. Throughout the 18th century, and for much of the 19th, the elections for Middlesex's two MPs were held here. Local traders benefited enormously from what was effectively a two-week jamboree, but the reputation of the town suffered badly from the bribery, brawling, drunkenness and violence that tended to accompany elections in those days.

Make your way across to the far right-hand corner of the square. Here there is a wide avenue leading from the square to Half Acre. The houses on either side are rather later in date than those in the square. This is because on the left side at least, until well into the 19th century, this was the site of Ronald's Nursery, one of the largest in the area and a supplier to Kew when the botanical garden was being developed. St Raphael's Convent takes up most of the avenue's right-hand side.

Exit the square via Upper Butts. At the end turn right into Somerset Road and then left into the continuation of Upper Butts. Go straight on down to the end (now Church Walk) and cross the bridge over the railway line, constructed through Barnes in 1849. When you reach the road you can either turn left, cross the Great West Road and continue up Boston Manor Road to Boston Manor station, or turn right for Brentford station (entrance over the bridge) for trains to Waterloo.

❖ ❖

SYON PARK TO
STRAWBERRY HILL

❖ ❖

Summary: This is a riverside walk in west London on the opposite bank to the better-known Kew and Richmond, going upstream from Syon Park to Strawberry Hill. On the way the walk passes through the old village centres of Isleworth and Twicken-ham and includes the handful of riverside mansions that remain from the whole string that once lined this stretch of the Thames: **Syon House, Marble Hill House, Orleans**

House, York House and Horace Walpole's Gothic fantasy, **Strawberry Hill**. One of the more unexpected sights on the walk is the British Legion's poppy factory in Richmond.

Start:	Syon Lane station (trains from Waterloo).
Finish:	Strawberry Hill station (trains from Waterloo).
Length:	4½ miles (7.2 km).
Time:	2½ hours.
Refreshments:	Near the beginning of the walk, try the café-restaurant in Syon Park or the riverside London Apprentice pub in Isleworth a little further on. Places to stop in the middle of the walk are non-existent unless you cross the road bridge into Richmond. In the second half of the walk, there is another café at Marble Hill House and then plenty of places, including riverside pubs, in Twickenham.

Come out of Syon Lane station onto the road bridge, turn right and then immediately fork left. Eventually you come out onto London Road opposite a grand but disused entrance into Syon Park, complete with iron brackets ready to receive flaming torches and a stone lion above the central arch. The lion is the heraldic crest of the Percy family, Dukes of Northumberland, who have owned Syon Park since the time of Elizabeth I. Before that it was a monastery. Turn left along London Road past the Park Tavern and then cross at the traffic lights into the lane signposted Thames Path and Syon House.

Syon House tragedies

The first landmark you see is the glass dome of the Great Conservatory. The house itself does not come into view until you have passed the entrance to the restaurant and garden centre and have joined the road leading out of the park. All you actually see from this distance are the castellated façade of the north front and the matching lodges at either end of the ha-ha. To your right is the large expanse of parkland cushioning the house from surrounding suburbia. There is more parkland, including gardens landscaped by Capability Brown, behind the house and between it and the River Thames.

The early history of Syon House has its sad episodes. As a plaque on one of the barns indicates, Richard Reynolds, a senior monk at Syon Abbey, was executed in 1535 for refusing to accept Henry VIII's religious reforms. Soon after, young Katherine Howard, Henry VIII's fifth wife, was imprisoned here before she was beheaded for treason in 1542. A few years later Lady Jane Grey, married to the son of the Earl of Northumberland, was offered the crown at Syon after the death of Edward VI. Her reign lasted for only nine days and within a year she too had gone to the block.

Follow the road to the park gate and turn left along Park Street towards the riverside by Isleworth churchyard. Only the old tower remains of the original village church, most of which was destroyed by fire in 1943. Several stones are set in the corner of the churchyard wall recording various floodwater levels. The earliest is March 1774; the highest is 1928 when 14 people were drowned in central London. The island opposite is Isleworth Ait (sometimes spelt 'Eyot', meaning island). At low tide the river retreats, leaving a land bridge across to the island. The Romans are said to have crossed the Thames here in 54BC.

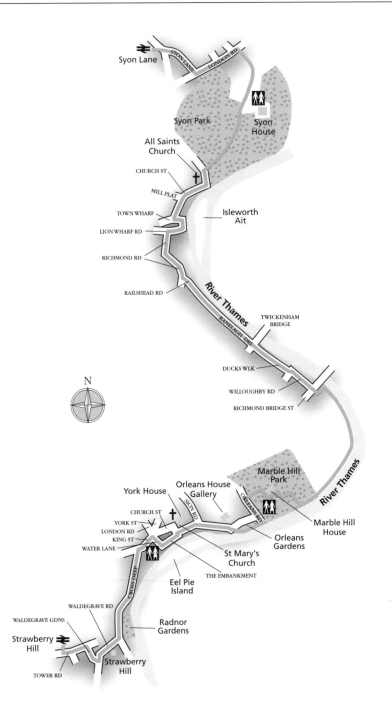

Syon Lane

SYON LANE
LONDON RD

Syon Park

Syon House

All Saints Church

CHURCH ST

MILL PLAT

Isleworth Ait

TOWN WHARF

LION WHARF RD

RICHMOND RD

RAILSHEAD RD

River Thames

RANELAGH DRI

TWICKENHAM BRIDGE

DUCKS WLK

WILLOUGHBY RD

RICHMOND BRIDGE ST

N

Marble Hill Park

Orleans House Gallery

York House

River Thames

CHURCH ST

YORK ST

LONDON RD

KING ST

WATER LANE

SION RD

ORLEANS RD

Marble Hill House

Orleans Gardens

St Mary's Church

Eel Pie Island

THE EMBANKMENT

CROSS DEEP

WALDEGRAVE RD

WALDEGRAVE GDNS

Radnor Gardens

Strawberry Hill

Strawberry Hill

TOWER RD

Continue along Church Street between the 15th-century London Apprentice pub (so-called because City apprentices used to row here on their days off) and the attractive houses by the church. Just before you reach the bridge over the Duke of Northumberland's River, a lane leads off to the right giving access to the tiny Ingram almshouses built in 1664. Called Mill Plat, the name recalls the mill that not long ago stood on the river here. Local people still remember buying bread in the village made from flour ground at the mill.

Go past the lane and straight over the bridge into the new square, in the middle of which stands the former village school, founded 1630. Keep left of the school and just beyond turn left along Town Wharf to the new Town Wharf pub on the riverside. Isleworth's non-unionized dock operated well into the 1960s, accommodating ships bringing wood and coal from as far away as Scandinavia. Some local people also remember barges carrying blocks of ice for local butchers' shops. There is still some commercial boat-building and repairing in the yards on the ait. Looking left, there is a good view of the church and pub on the riverside corner. Turn right along the terrace and then right again – *before* the gardens in front of the new houses – into unsignposted Lion Wharf Road. Turn left along the main road at the top (Richmond Road) past the Nazareth House Convent and home for the elderly, founded in 1892.

Richmond riverside

When you get to the River Crane, turn left into Railshead Road and rejoin the River Thames. On the right Gordon House, residence in the 19th-century of Lord Frederick Gordon, is now the Twickenham campus of Brunel University. On the opposite bank is the Old Deer Park at Richmond, now the Royal Mid-Surrey golf course. Far ahead you can see houses and the Star and Garter home for disabled servicemen on top of Richmond Hill. In the foreground an iron footbridge crosses over Richmond Weir and Lock. This is actually only a half-lock because the weir can be lowered when the water level is sufficiently high. The real barrier between the tidal and non-tidal Thames is upstream at Teddington, just beyond the end of this walk. As you pass the bridge the road rejoins the river on Ranelagh Drive. The next bridge is Twickenham road bridge and immediately beyond that is a small turret-like building that gives access to a large underground water main. Continue under the next bridge, the railway bridge linking Twickenham and Richmond.

Just past the railway bridge the private moorings and houses on Ducks Walk obstruct the view of the river. Ducks Walk leads straight into Willoughby Road. At the end of Willoughby Road cross the main road (Richmond Bridge Road) at the traffic lights and turn left beside (not over) Richmond Bridge to rejoin the river. The walk now follows the river all the way to Twickenham, apart from a brief deviation around Marble Hill House.

As you proceed along the riverside path you draw abreast of the British Legion poppy factory – the long white building with the flagpole – halfway up the hill on the opposite bank. The red paper poppies worn on Remembrance Day are made here. The river now begins to bend to the right, away from Richmond Hill and the Star and Garter Home (see the Richmond walk, page 195). On the far bank Petersham House stares at you across Petersham Meadows. Behind the house the red brick campanile of what used to be All Saints' Church at Petersham is also conspicuous. Beyond Glover's Island, Petersham's River Lane ends in a public slipway on the opposite bank.

On this side of the river, private gardens give way to the public park surrounding Marble Hill House. Turn right into the park when you come to the gateway in the railings and pass the huge walnut tree, reputedly over 200 years old and probably part of the original 18th-century garden design. Further along the path turn left towards Lady Suffolk's subterranean grotto. Just beyond the grotto turn right round the corner of the wood towards the house. George II's lover, the Countess of Suffolk, built it in 1729 as a refuge from Court and her husband, as she detested both.

Orleans' exile

Go right or left to the entrance front of the house and head off left past the ice house towards the coach house café. Pass by the left-hand side of the coach house and then turn left back down to the river along (unsignposted) Orleans Road. A gateway in the wall on the right leads to the Orleans House Gallery, a council-owned collection of pictures, including many local views, housed in the remains of another 18th-century riverside mansion. Louis-Philippe, King of France 1830–48, lived here as the emigré Duc d'Orléans from 1815 to 1817. Later his widow lived here, and then his son, the Duc d'Aumale. At the bottom of Orleans Road, Hammerton's Ferry, one of the last full-time Thames foot ferries, carries walkers to and from the National Trust's **Ham House** on the opposite bank.

At this point turn right into Orleans Gardens and walk along the riverside beside the horse chestnuts, carefully pruned to hang over the water rather than the park. Towards the end of the gardens the remains of Orleans House come into view. The main block, which was demolished in 1926, was on the right of the octagon. Rejoin the road (Riverside) and turn left towards Twickenham.

Beyond the pub, Sion Road on the right is an attractive 18th-century terrace with an unusual Egyptian-style decoration under the eaves, picked out in black. Notice the street sign high up on the right bearing the date 1721. Sion Road leads up to the council offices in York House, a 300-year-old mansion set in fine gardens, including a sunken garden, a water garden and a balustraded riverside terrace reached by a bridge over the road. The Yorke (sic) family originally owned the estate, hence the name, but in the 19th century the exiled French royal family used it in addition to Orleans House and seven other houses in the vicinity. Have a look around York House gardens if time and energy permit.

Continue along Riverside, under the York House gardens' bridge and on to Twickenham Embankment by **St Mary's Church**, where poet and local resident Alexander Pope was buried in 1744. Opposite is car-free Eel Pie Island, named after a famous hotel that, in the 19th century, was the island's only building. In the early 1960s the old hotel ballroom was a jazz club where several famous groups like the Rolling Stones cut their teeth. The island's former boatyard now provides workspace for a community of artists and craftspeople.

Turn right by the Eel Pie Island bridge into Water Lane. At the end of the lane paved Church Street on the right leads back down to the church (halfway along on the right is a shop selling products from the Eel Pie Island studios). Ahead, London Road will take you towards Twickenham rugby stadium, Harlequins' club ground and venue for England internationals. The walk, however, goes to the left, along King Street, before turning left at the traffic lights into Cross Deep, a road running parallel to a stretch of the Thames called Cross Deep.

Beyond Cross Deep House and St James's School turn left opposite the Pope's Grotto pub into riverside Radnor Gardens, once the site of a house belonging to the Earl of Radnor. The local council bought it in 1902 which explains why the remarkable Twickenham war memorial is here. Alexander Pope's villa, one of the best-known riverside houses in the 18th century, stood on the downstream side of the gardens with a tunnel-grotto linking it to its 5-acre (2-ha) gardens on the other side of Cross Deep road. By all accounts Pope's Villa was a remarkable place, but sadly a later owner, fed up with the number of pilgrims coming to see where the great poet lived, knocked it down.

Gothic humour

Leave the gardens by the gate at the end and cross the road into the left of the two roads that lead off on the far side (Waldegrave Road). The road passes the entrance to Strawberry Hill, probably the most famous of all the old riverside mansions in southwest London. At a time when the classical style of ancient Greece and Rome was fashionable, Horace Walpole, author of the Gothic novel *The Castle of Otranto* and son of the prime minister Sir Robert Walpole, built this mansion in a medieval Gothic style with turrets, battlements and pointed windows. Although it was intended as a joke (he actually called it his 'little plaything ... the prettiest bauble you ever saw'), it had a great influence on the next generation of architects. The house is now part of Surrey University.

Walk round the corner, turn right into Waldegrave Gardens and then turn left into Tower Road. Walk along to the level crossing and Strawberry Hill station where the walk ends.

❖❖

RICHMOND

❖❖

Summary: Richmond, Ham and Petersham are all by the River Thames in southwest London. This circular walk starts on Richmond Green where part of an old royal palace and many fine Court houses still stand. It then joins the Thames towpath before climbing Richmond Hill. The panoramic view from the top is one of the best on the river. The walk passes through **Richmond Park** before descending the western slope of the hill into Petersham (burial place of the discoverer of Vancouver Island) and Ham. Old mansions abound. The walk loops round **Ham House** and then returns to Richmond along the towpath through Petersham Meadows.

Start and finish: Richmond station (District Underground Line, Silverlink Metro and mainline trains from Waterloo; boats from Westminster Pier).
Length: 4½ miles (7.2km).
Time: 3 hours.
Refreshments: Variety of pubs, restaurants and takeaway places at the beginning and end of the walk in Richmond, plus a pub (Dysarts) at the halfway stage in Petersham. There are also cafés in Pembroke Lodge in Richmond Park (about a third of the way through the

Note:
walk – recommended for its spectacular views) and at Ham House, where the walk turns back along the river to Richmond. The walk passes the grounds of Ham Polo Club. Matches are played on Sunday afternoons, May to September.

Leave Richmond station, turn left and go over The Quadrant at the zebra crossing. The Station Hotel was home to the Crawdaddy Club in the early 1960s. The unknown Rolling Stones were gigging here in 1963 when they were discovered and hit the big time with their first single. Mick Jagger now lives in Richmond – the walk passes his house later on. Go through the arch to the right and turn left over the bridge into Little Green. Continue straight ahead into Richmond Green. In Tudor times this served as the jousting field of the royal palace that was situated in the far right corner. Much later, houses, many of which remain, were built along the left and far sides of the green for court attendants and servants. The best of these houses are at the opposite end in Old Palace Terrace and Old Palace Place and further round to the right in Maids of Honour Row. The latter was built in 1724 for the maids of honour attending on the Princess of Wales, Princess Caroline of Anspach. Newer houses occupy the other two sides.

Richmond's royal residence
Walk to the end of the green and then turn right past Old Palace Place and Maids of Honour Row. The next house, set back behind the wall, is part of the old palace. Turn left by the ancient pine tree in the corner of the garden and go through the old palace gatehouse with Henry VII's arms above the arch into Old Palace Yard. There had been a royal house at Richmond throughout the medieval period but Henry VII, who preferred this palace to all his others, was the first to make it into a major royal residence. He even changed its name from Shene to Richmond after his earldom of Richmond in Yorkshire. Elizabeth I, the last of Henry's Tudor dynasty, was the last monarch to use the palace. Most of it was demolished after Charles I's execution in 1649.

Leave the Yard via the path marked by two white bollards in the far right corner. Turn left into Old Palace Lane and walk down towards the river past the White Swan pub. At the end of the lane on the left stands Asgill House, built in 1758 for Sir Charles Asgill, banker and City lord mayor. A stone plaque on the wall records that the royal palace extended to the river here and that Edward III, Henry VII and Elizabeth I all died here (in 1377, 1509 and 1603 respectively).

Walk to the left along the Thames towpath (here called Cholmondeley Walk) past the gardens of Asgill House, with its superb copper beech (planted in 1813) and gazebo, and then the gardens of Trumpeters' House, the garden front visible at the end of a long lawn framed by trees. Trees are the glory of Richmond.

On the left, Friar's Lane, marking the site of the Franciscan friary of Shene founded by Henry VII in 1501, now joins the riverside. Next on the left is Water Lane by the White Cross Hotel (the friary's badge was a white cross). Beyond Water Lane is a terraced garden with a 1980s' development of neo-Georgian offices on top of the bank. The Victorian building on the left is the old Richmond town hall, now the central library, tourist information office and local museum.

Terrace panorama
When you get to Richmond's Georgian bridge climb the steps on the left and walk to

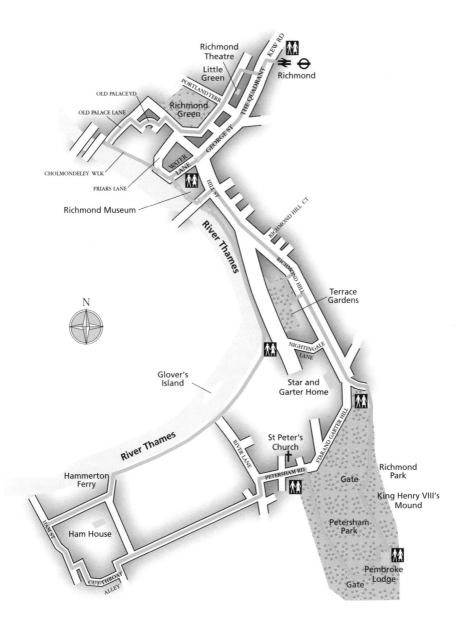

Richmond Theatre

Little Green

Richmond

KEW RD

THE QUADRANT

OLD PALACE YD

OLD PALACE LANE

Richmond Green

PORTLAND TERR

GEORGE ST

CHOLMONDELEY WLK

WATER LANE

FRIARS LANE

Richmond Museum

HILL ST

River Thames

RICHMOND HILL CT

RICHMOND HILL

Terrace Gardens

N

Glover's Island

NIGHTINGALE LANE

Star and Garter Home

River Thames

RIVER LANE

St Peter's Church

STAR AND GARTER HILL

Richmond Park

Hammerton Ferry

PETERSHAM RD

Gate

King Henry VIII's Mound

HAM ST

Ham House

Petersham Park

Pembroke Lodge

CUT-THROAT ALLEY

Gate

the roundabout. Here turn right into Hill Street and then go across the road using the zebra crossing. Continue up the hill, taking the left fork when the road divides. When you get to Richmond Hill Court (near the top of the hill on the left) cross over to the path along the top edge of the Terrace Gardens that cover the side of the hill. The second flight of steps carries you up to the top terrace with its views far away to the west over the river. 'Heavens! What a goodly prospect spreads around, of hills and dales, and woods, and lawns and spires and glittering towns and gilded streams', exclaimed poet and Richmond resident James Thomson in 1727. Explanatory panels in the middle of the top terrace pinpoint the main landmarks in the panorama. Directly ahead, the roof of Ham House is visible above the trees to the left of the river; below are Petersham Meadows and the white Petersham Lodge; to the left of the meadows are Petersham House and Petersham Church. The large brick building near left is the Petersham Hotel. Behind you is Downe House, the home of Rolling Stone Mick Jagger.

Cross Nightingale Lane. The Wick on the corner belongs to The Who's Pete Townshend. Beyond, Wick House was built for painter Sir Joshua Reynolds in 1771. It's now a hostel for nurses at the Royal Star and Garter Home on the summit of the hill that you come to shortly. Founded after World War I, the Star and Garter cares for disabled servicemen and takes its name from its predecessor on the site, the Star and Garter Hotel, opened in 1738. Like other hotels and inns on the river, the Star and Garter's heyday came in the 19th century when hordes of visitors travelled out from London on the new railway in search of fun and fresh air. The novelist Charles Dickens held an annual private dinner at the hotel to celebrate his wedding anniversary. Fire put an end to the hotel in 1870.

Cross the busy road (Star and Garter Hill) to the right of the roundabout and go through the gate into Richmond Park. Created for deer hunting in 1637 by Charles I, Richmond Park, unlike the Old Deer Park on the other side of Richmond, still has deer in it: about 600 is the normal stock level. Of course, the park is no longer used for hunting, but many people still ride through the woodland or on the rough open ground. There is also plenty of space for two golf courses, several cricket fields and over 20 football pitches, plus lakes for fishing.

The highest point of the park

Take the hard path to the right along the edge of the hill, not the rough path going *down* the hill. After a few hundred yards, go through a big gate into Pembroke Lodge Gardens and then along the terrace, past flower beds and seats on the left and the ugly memorial to poet James Thomson on the right. Continue through the John Beer Laburnum Walk. Then turn left and climb to the top of King Henry VIII's Mound, the highest point in the park. Sadly, the story that Henry VIII stood here in 1536 waiting to see a rocket fired from the Tower of London to announce that his second wife, Ann Boleyn, had been successfully beheaded, is demonstrably false. Today, you are supposed to be able to see both **St Paul's Cathedral** in the City and Windsor Castle from this point. St Paul's is plainly visible through the park's trees and across west London and the view to it is now protected by law. Windsor Castle is not so easy to make out. In fact, I do not think I have ever managed to pinpoint it.

Descend the knoll on the opposite side and continue along the hillside terrace until you come to Pembroke Lodge, a molecatcher's cottage converted for the Countess of Pembroke in 1780. Queen Victoria's Prime Minister and Foreign Secretary Lord John

Russell lived here for 30 years. Disliking society in London, he held cabinet meetings and did much of his government work here. Later his grandson, the philosopher and mathematician Bertrand Russell, spent his childhood in the Lodge before going to university. Today the Lodge is a café and restaurant with views from its terrace rivalling if not surpassing those from the Lauderdale House café in Highgate.

Go down the steps in front of the terrace and follow the fence to the left for a few yards until you come to the garden gate. Go through the gate and head off right, down the hill to the broad track you can see running left and right. Ahead is the white gateway leading into Sudbrook Park, now a golf course with a grand 18th-century club-house. The red-brick campanile belongs to Petersham's redundant All Saints' Church, now used as a recording studio.

Walk to the right along the broad track and head for the village of Petersham, aiming for the timber-framed Dysarts pub ahead. Cross Petersham Road here – the road is very busy – and turn left. Along the lane to the right is Petersham's little parish church, with the grave of George Vancouver, discoverer of Vancouver Island, in its churchyard. Described in the 18th century as the most elegant village in England, Petersham still has many fine houses today. Next on this side of the road is Petersham House, built around 1674. Beyond is Rutland Lodge, built in the 1660s, occupied by the Duchess of Rutland in the 1740s and converted into flats after a serious fire in 1967. In River Lane on the right 37-year-old George Vancouver settled in 1795 to write up his voyages for publication. He died three years later. Opposite, on the corner, is Montrose House, built for a judge around 1700; the Dowager Duchess of Montrose lived here in the 1840s.

Follow the road round the sharp left-hand bend and then, just before the Fox and Duck pub on the left, turn right. Go to the right of the gatehouse and then, when you reach the gate into the Deutsche Schüle (built in 1690 as Douglas House and bought by Germany in 1969 for use as a German school), branch left onto the long straight avenue that was once the drive to Ham House. Walk past Ham Polo Club to the end of the avenue by the garden wall of Ham House. The south front is visible through the gates on the right. To the left, Melancholy Walk leads to Ham Common. Follow the wall of Ham House to the left and then right round the corner into Cut-Throat Alley. This brings you out on Ham Street, connecting Ham Common with the river.

Whipping boy

On Ham Street, turn right and follow the wall until you come to the entrance to Ham House. Turn right again and walk along the avenue towards the north front of the house. Now owned by the National Trust and open to the public, this fine Stuart house was the home of the Earls of Dysart until 1948. The first earl was granted the house, along with other property in Ham and Petersham, by Charles I in 1637. The earl had grown up with the king and, some say, had been his whipping boy: whenever the young prince did anything wrong, it was poor Dysart that was punished for it, not the prince.

Orleans House on the opposite bank of the river is just visible through the trees to the left. At the end of the avenue take the path to the left leading to the Thames towpath. Hammerton's foot ferry operates here on a daily basis for most of the year (weekends only November–January). Turn right along the towpath towards Glover's Island and Richmond Hill. The view is nearly as good as the one from the top of the hill, especially if the sun is behind you. On the left, **Marble Hill House** gradually appears (for this and Orleans House see the Syon Park to Strawberry Hill walk, page 190).

Follow the towpath alongside Petersham Meadows, grazed by cattle from Petersham Farm. After a while the towpath bears right and then left into riverside Buccleugh Gardens, once the grounds of Buccleugh House. Nothing remains of the house except the brick shelter on the right and, just beyond, the tunnel that led from the house to more gardens on the other side of Petersham Road. Here, now a public park called Terrace Gardens, there is still a fine river-god statue which the then occupant of Buccleugh House bought from the Coade factory at Lambeth in 1781 (see the Lambeth and South Bank walk, page 148).

Continue along the riverside path under the bridge and back along the new terrace. By the White Cross Hotel turn right into Water Lane. Walk up to the main road (George Street) and follow it along to the left until you come to Richmond station, where the walk ends.

❖❖❖

HAMPTON COURT

❖❖❖

Summary: The great Tudor palace of **Hampton Court** sits on the Thames in southwest London, surrounded by beautifully kept gardens and 1,100 acres (445 ha) of rough deer park (Hampton Court Park and Bushy Park). The walk begins in the palace grounds. Next comes **Bushy Park**, with the path following the Chestnut Avenue to begin with, and then meandering through the glades in the secluded Waterhouse Woodland Garden in the centre of the park. The last leg of the walk is set in the riverside village of Hampton, the main features of which are the 18th-century Garrick's Villa and **Shakespeare Temple**. The village also has a fine church, riverside gardens, an excellent antiquarian bookshop and several pubs.

Start:	Hampton Court station (mainline trains from Waterloo; riverboats from Westminster Pier).
Finish:	Hampton station (mainline trains from Waterloo but different line from above).
Length:	3½ miles (5.6km).
Time:	2 hours.
Refreshments:	Various pubs and restaurants around the entrance and exit to the palace grounds, plus more pubs and takeaways in Hampton village. There is a restaurant within the grounds of Hampton Court, and the Waterhouse Garden in Bushy Park at the halfway point is a fine site for a picnic.
Note:	Access to the formal garden area of Hampton Court Palace is free November–February only. Charge applies at other times. A dotted line indicates the affected section of the walk.

From Hampton Court station go straight over the bridge across the River Thames towards the palace, its fantastic roofscape is a forest of bulbous, twisting Tudor chimneys with the pitched roof of Henry VIII's great hall rising up in the middle. Henry's Lord Chancellor, Cardinal Wolsey, began the palace as his own residence after buying the estate in 1514. Then, when his credit with the king began to sink, Wolsey handed the palace over to Henry in a desperate attempt to retain royal favour. It failed and in 1530 Wolsey died in disgrace. Nearly 200 years later, William III and Queen Mary commissioned Sir Christopher Wren to demolish the Tudor state and royal apartments and replace them with a completely new building grafted on to the stock of the old. George II (reigned 1727–60) was the last monarch to actually reside in the palace, though it is still owned by the sovereign.

Tudor palace
After the bridge you draw abreast of the Mitre hotel on the left. Just beyond the Mitre, the road leading off to the left passes former homes (both marked by plaques) of palace architect Sir Christopher Wren and pioneering scientist Michael Faraday (see the Mayfair walk, page 23). Turn right through the palace's main gate into the drive leading to the great gatehouse. Left of the gatehouse, a lower and wider gateway leads to the enormous kitchens, cellars and other domestic offices on the north side of the palace. The long, low building immediately on your left was once the palace stable block.

In front of the gatehouse turn left and go through the ivy-covered archway into the Tiltyard Garden. Before you get to the Tiltyard Tearooms, turn right through the gate and go straight on into the Wilderness garden area with the palace on your right. When you reach the far side you come to the entrance to the palace's immaculate formal gardens. These gardens used to be free all year round, but now you have to pay during the summer. If you don't want to pay for entrance, skip the next couple of paragraphs. If you do want to pay, or you are doing this walk during the winter when access to the gardens is free, go through the gate and turn right along the gravelled path. On the right the balconied building is the palace real tennis court where successive monarchs played the ancient game of real (or royal) tennis. The game is still played here by a local club (the court may be open, in which case you can go in and have a look). Then comes the east front of the palace itself. From the mid point three walks radiate left towards Hampton Court Park, the central one following Charles II's Long Water canal towards Kingston-upon-Thames.

At the end of the east front is the entrance to the Privy Garden, where the king and queen were able to walk in private protected from the public gaze. Turn right into the Privy Garden, laid out as it was in William and Mary's time, and walk along the palace's south front. At the far end go through the gate into the Pond Gardens area, passing the little Knot Garden and the Lower Orangery on your right and the Pond Gardens themselves on your left. The sunken pond gardens were originally ornamental ponds used for holding freshwater fish such as carp and bream, which were consumed in vast quantities at Tudor banquets. At the far end is the green house containing the Great Vine, planted in 1768 by royal gardener 'Capability' Brown. Grapes from the vine are sold in the palace shops in late August. The ground outside is kept bare of other plants so that the roots of the vine get the maximum amount of nutrients from the soil.

Turn left past this fallow area and then left again, with the pond gardens now on your left and William III's banqueting house on your right (the letters VR on the drainpipe stand for Victoria Regina, i.e. Queen Victoria). At the far end turn climb the steps, turn right and then go down the steps to the south end of the Privy Garden, bounded by

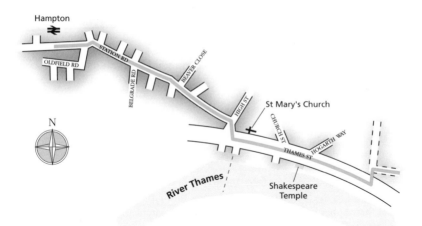

the amazing iron railings and gates (some picked out in gold) wrought by master crafts-man Jean Tijou, one of the many artists employed by Wren on the new palace.

Follow the railings round and climb the steps to the east terrace. Looking towards the palace now you can see how Wren's grand new building was simply grafted on to the older Tudor stock. At the end of the terrace, go back out of the Privy Garden and retrace your steps to the gate. After a while you come to the palace's famous maze and the Lion Gate, the northern entrance to the palace grounds.

Verdant parks
Go through the Lion Gate, cross the road dividing Hampton Court Park and Bushy Park, and then go through the gate into Bushy Park, keeping to the grass on the left-hand side of the Chestnut Avenue. This straight road runs for 1 mile (1.6km) through the park, broken only by the round pond and Diana Fountain visible a short distance ahead. Cardinal Wolsey created Bushy Park out of three older parks in 1514. Wren later added the Chestnut Avenue and Lion Gate to form an impressive approach to his new palace.

When the road divides to skirt the pond, keep to the left-hand side. On the far side of the pond keep the rows of trees bordering the avenue's left-hand side on *your* right and follow the grassy track towards the palisade surrounding the Waterhouse Woodland Garden – your next destination. Just before you reach the little bridge over the stream, veer left towards the white sign marking the entrance to the woodland garden. Go through the gate and turn left along the zigzag path, keeping the water on your right. Laid out in the 1940s in this remote location, the woodland garden remains little known, despite its obvious charms, and is often completely deserted, especially on weekdays. The river is the Longford river, an artificial watercourse 11 miles (18 kilo-metres) long, constructed in 1629 to supply gravity-fed water to Hampton Court and to all the fountains and lakes in its grounds, a function it continues to perform today.

Follow the path as it winds through the trees, passing a bridge and a gardener's house en route. Go through the gate at the end of the garden, cross the tarmac path and go through the next gate by the police box. Walk about 20 yards (18m) and then take the first turning on the left along a narrow path. Follow this path round to the right over a stream, and then to the left, walking straight along the right bank of the stream. Cross over a second bridge and turn right into a woodland glade with a worn path. Aim for the opposite right-hand corner and rejoin the path by a tree stump. Follow this path round to the left until you come to a small embanked reservoir. Turn left here so that

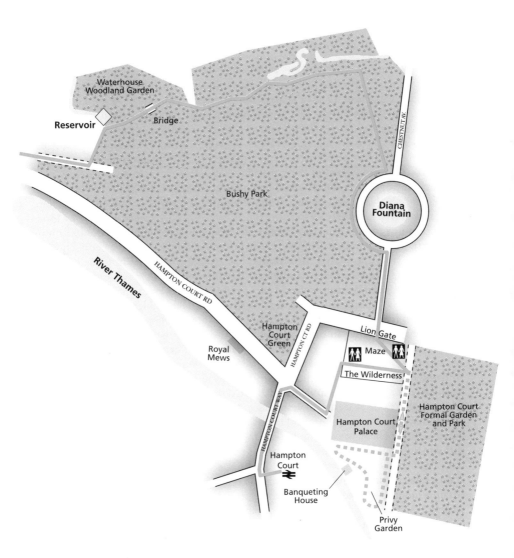

the reservoir is on your right, and follow the path past the reservoir and water house, and then alongside a stream flowing out of the reservoir and eventually into the Thames.

203

You will soon come to a gate leading out of the garden back into the deer park. Go through the gate and turn right along the lime avenue leading to the old park-keeper's lodge and the stockyard and park headquarters, site of the medieval Hampton farm. Stay on the avenue or walk on the tarmac path on your left. Near the end, follow the tarmac path as it veers to the left to a gate leading out of the park. Go through the gate and turn right onto the busy riverside Hampton Court Road leading to the village of Hampton. (Turning left here will take you back to Hampton Court.)

Hampton's heritage
After a while you come to the entrance to the stockyard on the right. Opposite is Garrick's House where David Garrick, army officer and nephew of his namesake, David Garrick, the leading actor of the 18th century, lived from 1778 until his death in 1795. Cross Hogarth Way. The large house on the right, converted into flats in the 1920s, was Garrick the actor's country house, bought in 1754 and known as Garrick's Villa. The following year he built the temple on the left to house a statue of Shakespeare which is now in the British Museum. The temple stands in its own little park and is connected to the house by a tunnel under the road.

Continue past the house and cross Church Street. Hampton Church on the right was completely rebuilt in 1831, but its ancient monuments were preserved, including one to Sibel Penn, nurse to Henry VIII's only son, Edward VI. Sibel died of smallpox in 1562 and her kindly, grey-cloaked ghost is said to haunt not only this church, but also Hampton Court where she worked and the house now standing on the site of her old home, Penn's Place, which is marked by a plaque back round the corner in Church Street.

Walk past the church and the Bell Inn. Until 1995 Betty's confectionery and tobacco shop stood on the corner at no. 18. It was run by an extraordinary woman called Betty Kenton who, under her maiden name of Ambler, had been British champion women's sculler in 1935 and 1938. There was a photograph of her in the shop to prove it. Betty's husband ran the boatyard across the road and operated one of the last remaining foot ferries on the Thames. The grumpy old ferryman, who had been doing the job for 50 years, waited inside the shop for custom. In 1995 the Kenton's lease of the ferry expired and they decided to close the shop and retire. The following year two local couples acquired the lease and they now run the ferry, which is said to be at least 500 years old.

The walk now turns right into Hampton High Street, but first take a peep down Thames Street ahead in order to see the local antiquarian bookshop. It has old sofas and armchairs and classical music playing on an ancient radiogram and its huge stock is well worth a leisurely browse.

Now turn right into the High Street and take the first turning on the left into Station Road for the last part of the walk. On the right beyond Beaver Close the road passes some pretty cottages, and then a terrace of small, plain three-storey Georgian houses, the first with a little stable and loft in the front garden. Beyond the shops and Belgrade Road on the left, new housing and a village green cover water filter beds originally built in 1855 by the Southwark and Vauxhall Water Company after central London's private water companies had been forced to move their Thames intakes upstream to the cleaner, non-tidal part of the river. The old pumping houses still stand on the riverside.

Continue to the end of the wall and cross Oldfield Road (the Railway Bell pub is opposite). Hampton station, where the walk ends, is further along on the right.

❖❖

PINNER

❖❖

Summary: No name is more redolent of Home Counties suburbia than Pinner. But this former village in northwest London, now one of the capital's most attractive suburbs, retains many of its original features and is well worth exploring. Of particular note are its beautiful High Street with timber-framed pub, medieval church, handsome old houses and places connected with such characters as 19th-century garden writer and designer John Claudius Loudon, Lord Nelson's daughter, Horatia, and illustrator Heath Robinson. This circular walk, starting and finishing at the local underground station, takes in all these features and also includes some fine views of open park and farmland towards Harrow Weald. It's worth trying to combine the walk with a separate visit to moated Headstone Manor, home of the **Harrow Museum and Heritage Centre** (Pinner was once part of the manor of Harrow). Unfortunately, Headstone is slightly too far away from Pinner itself to be included on the walk.

Start and finish:	Pinner station (Metropolitan Underground Line).
Length:	2¼ miles (4.4km).
Time:	2 hours.
Refreshments:	In High Street: the Queen's Head and Victory pubs, Pizza Express, Italian restaurant and a café/wine bar. In Bridge Street: the Oddfellows Arms pub, McDonald's, Wenzel's bakery and coffee house, a Chinese restaurant and a fish and chip shop.
Note:	**Pinner Fair** is held annually in the High Street and neighbouring Bridge Street.

Come out of the station and turn left down the hill. At the bottom turn right onto the main road and then right again into the High Street. Bridge Street is really Pinner's main shopping street and has most of the big stores you would expect to find in any modern town centre. Fittingly, High Street is reserved for more individual shops, including Corbett's bookshop and one or two antique shops. It also has a couple of ancient pubs, the Queen's Head on the left and the Victory on the right. The latter is dated 1580, but while the building itself might be that old, the pub has only been here since the late 1950s. They have been pulling pints at the Queen's Head, on the other hand, since at least the days of Charles I (1625–1649).

The High Street is without question Pinner's chief glory. Stretching uphill from the River Pinn at one end to the parish church at the other, this broad sloping thoroughfare is lined with houses, shops and pubs built over the last four centuries, providing a wonderful lesson in architectural styles and building materials. Here, and in neighbouring Bridge Street, is held Pinner's famous fair, first authorized in 1336 and a regular annual event since at least the 18th century.

At the top of the street on the left – beyond the green donated to the village in 1924 – is the long, low Church Farm, one of the oldest buildings in Pinner. The fact that this was a farmhouse as late as 1906 shows just how relatively recent a phenomenon the modern suburb of Pinner is. Opposite, the Hilltop Wine Bar was a butcher's shop from the 1600s until the 1930s. Animals were slaughtered in the building to the right with the louvred roof (now a chiropodist's surgery). Between Church Farm and the wine bar is a house with an unusually large window facing down the High Street. As the Harrow Heritage Trust plaque says, this was a Victorian temperance tavern and tea garden called Ye Cocoa Tree. Opened in 1878 by 45-year-old local resident and property lawyer William Barber, who must have been something of a temperance enthusiast, it was popular with day trippers from London (the Metropolitan Line railway arrived at Pinner in 1886) and lasted well into the 1920s, by which time much of the central area of the village had been developed.

St John's Church
Continue to the right into Church Lane. Built in flint, the only building material available in any quantity locally, **St John's Church** was dedicated in 1321, though it did not become a parish church in its own right until 1766 when Pinner broke away from Harrow. St John's great tower, which dominates Pinner High Street, is a 15th-century addition. The entrance to the church is via the lychgate and the sunken path leading to the south door. To the right, the curious monument with the stone coffin

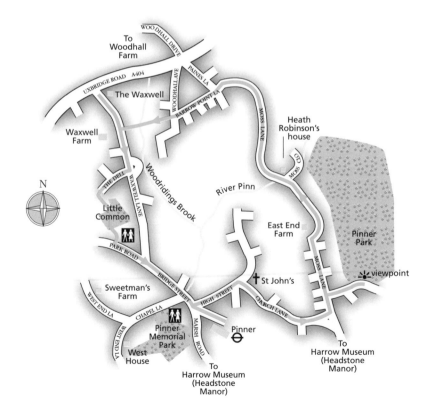

sticking out either side commemorates the parents of John Claudius Loudon, the early 19th-century garden writer and designer of cottages ornées and model farms, and is no doubt a product of his fertile, if slightly eccentric, imagination. Loudon senior was a tenant farmer in Pinner. Inside the church there is a memorial to the poet laureate Henry Pye, of whom more later when we come to East End.

Pinner House

Carry on past the church. Round the corner you come across Pinner House, the grandest house in Pinner village proper. Dating from around 1700 when an increasing number of wealthy Londoners were building country houses in outlying villages like Pinner, it has a remarkably gracious aspect and must at one time have enjoyed wonderful views southwards across the fields towards Harrow. Apart from Pinner Hill away to the north (now a golf club), it is the only one of Pinner's mansions to survive into the 21st century. Since the late 1940s it has been an old people's home. Further on around another corner you come to a cluster of comfortable-looking old houses: on the right The Grange; on the left the grey-painted Bay House (timber-framed behind a deceptive Victorian façade); and then, on the right again, the substantial Elmdene facing Nower Hill Green. Here, in the 19th century, lived the daughter of Horatio Nelson and Lady Hamilton, Horatia Nelson Ward. Horatia died when she was 81 and is buried in the village cemetery in Paines Lane. More recent occupants of the house include the comedian Ronnie Barker and the actor David Suchet, star of the TV series *Poirot*.

Nower Hill Green is sometimes known as Tooke's Green because of the Victorian drinking fountain in the centre that commemorates village benefactor William Tooke. Tooke, who lived at Pinner Hill, was as near to a squire as Pinner could have had in the 19th century. He paid for the rebuilding of the church in 1880. His clergyman grandfather – whose inheritance of a fortune in 1792 enabled him to devote himself to historical studies – was one of the first historians of Russia.

From deer park to farm

Walk past the memorial to the top of the green and turn left and then right into Wakehams Hill. At the top where the road bends right, bear left down the track. From the gate, where there is a thoughtfully provided seat, there is a splendid view north over Pinner Park towards the high ground beyond. Up in that high ground, near the River Pinn's source, are two of Pinner's three surviving farms: Pinnerwood Farm and Oxhey Lane Farm. The third is the one you can see in the middle of Pinner Park, just beyond the main road. Sometimes called Hall's Farm, it is named after the family that have tenanted it (from St Thomas's Hospital in central London) since the end of the 19th century. Before that the Halls were at nearby Headstone Manor (the manor house of Harrow and now the Harrow Museum and Heritage Centre). In medieval times Pinner Park was a 250-acre (100-ha) deer park used for hunting. Farming gradually took over in the 16th century.

East End

Retrace your steps down Wakehams Hill. Facing you across Moss Lane at the bottom is The Fives Court, a notable Arts and Crafts house designed at the beginning of the last century by Cecil Brewer for Ambrose Heal of Heal's furnishing store in

Tottenham Court Road. Turn right into Moss Lane. A fairly long section now ensues until you come to the nucleus of a former outlying settlement of Pinner called East End. You will know it when you see it, for the ancient houses are conspicuous among the newer buildings. Three houses remain out of the original half dozen or so. First, on the left behind a crazy wall, is Tudor Cottage, an old house tarted up with an assortment of architectural antiques. Beyond is East End Farm, the brick indicating a later date and greater prosperity. Here lived George III's poet laureate Henry Pye (1745–1813), whose memorial is in the church. Ridiculed even in his own day, he is only remembered now, if at all, because of fellow writer George Steevens' punning put-down of his first birthday ode to the king using the line 'When the PYE was opened' from the 'Sing a song of sixpence' nursery rhyme. At the end of the farmyard is the 15th-century East End Farm Cottage, the oldest house in Pinner, if not in the whole of the county of Middlesex. Amazing enough from the outside, inside it has a superb, roughly contemporary, wall painting. Originally the house must have been considerably grander than the farm labourer's cottage it later became. The old farmyard on the right survives virtually intact and is still in semi-agricultural use (by a firm of fruit and potato merchants).

River Pinn
Carry on along Moss Lane, around the corner and down the hill. At the bottom you cross over the River Pinn: the name Pinner is thought to mean 'settlement on the banks of the Pinn'. The path on the left leads through to Paines Lane. No. 75 on the right has a blue plaque to the illustrator William Heath Robinson, a resident of Pinner for some 13 years. He actually lived in this house for five years from 1913.

Another long section now ensues until you reach the junction of Moss Lane with Paines Lane (Moss Cottage is on the left). Paines Lane originally led north from Pinner to Woodhall Farm, where the Loudons lived. The original farmhouse, complete with neo-Gothic features such as pointed windows, probably designed by John Claudius Loudon himself (he stayed on the farm once while convalescing from rheumatic fever), still stands in Woodhall Drive. To see it, turn right here, walk to the end of the road, cross the main road into Woodhall Drive and walk up the left-hand side for about 100 yards (90m). Otherwise, cross Paines Lane diagonally to the left into Barrow Point Lane and carry on to the bottom.

Waxwell Lane
Where the lane turns sharp left, bear right through the hedge and then immediately left into the footpath, signposted Waxwell Lane, though the name has been painted over. At the low point in the middle of the path you cross over Woodridings Brook, a tributary of the Pinn. Emerging in Waxwell Lane, Waxwell Farm is immediately opposite. No longer a farm, it still has a huge garden and is another reminder of Pinner's not too distant agricultural past. The house is now used by the Holy Grail, a Roman Catholic organization.

Waxwell Lane takes its name from a medieval spring or well, which until the arrival of piped water was a major source of fresh drinking water in the area. If you turn right in Waxwell Lane you will find the well, reached by a short flight of steps but now bricked up, just by the junction with the main road, on the right-hand side. The main route of the walk turns left along Waxwell Lane and then, opposite Waxwell Close, an elegant crescent of 'artisan' housing dating from the 1920s, right into the Dell. The great hollow of the Dell, now filled with modern houses, was man-made over the centuries by locals digging for lime and flint. Both were used for building, but lime, of course, was also in demand as a farmland dressing. Elsewhere in Pinner, people mined underground for these valuable materials. Some of the mines, which still exist but are not open to the public, are over 100 feet (30m) below ground level.

Pinner Common

As you approach the Dell, keep on the left-hand side and walk along the pavement as the ground drops away to the right. Just beyond White Cottage, turn left through the gate into Little Common, relic of a once much larger piece of common land (another area, called Pinner Green, survives to the north). Follow the path out of the park and turn left on Park Road. Ahead you can see the spire of Harrow church breaking out of the trees on top of Harrow Hill. Carry on down the hill to the Oddfellows Arms pub at the junction with Waxwell Lane. Here there is an old milestone giving the distance to London. Around the corner in Waxwell Lane there are two charming old timber-framed cottages, Orchard Cottage and Bee Cottage, which are well worth a look.

Carry on down Bridge Street. At the bottom you pass the entrance to Chapel Lane, leading to West End (balancing East End on the other side of the village) and West House whose grounds are now a public park. You then cross (although you are not really aware of it) the bridge over the Pinn, from which, of course, Bridge Street takes its name. The Pinn flows to the right here in a southwesterly direction and eventually joins the Colne (and thence the Thames) a few miles south of Uxbridge. Pinner station, and the end of the walk, is 100 yards (90m) or so ahead, this side of the railway line.

❖❖

HARROW-ON-
THE-HILL

❖❖

Summary: Harrow-on-the-Hill is an attractive hilltop village in northwest London dominated by **Harrow School**, a famous public school second only to Eton in terms of social exclusivity, and alma mater of such illustrious figures as Byron, Sheridan, Trollope, Palmerston and Churchill. School and village mingle together so you see much of the school on the walk, including classrooms, boarding houses, tuck shop and the original school building housing the **Harrow Old Speech Room Gallery** and its collection of school treasures. Besides fine views, other features of this circular walk, which starts and finishes at the station at the foot of the hill, are the extraordinary **Cat Museum**, Harrow's ancient parish church with its great spire visible for miles around, Byron's boarding house and the famous spot in the church-yard where the young poet used to spend hours gazing out over the surrounding countryside. It's worth trying to combine the walk with a separate visit to moated Headstone Manor, once the manor house of Harrow and now the **Harrow Museum and Heritage Centre**. Unfortunately, the museum is too far away to be included on the walk.

Start and finish: Harrow-on-the-Hill station (Metropolitan Underground Line; mainline trains from Marylebone Station).
Length: 1¾ miles (2.8km).
Time: 1½ hours.
Refreshments: High Street: French restaurant, Drift In tearooms (much used by boys from the school), Chinese restaurant, hotel/bar, tapas bar, bar-brasserie. West Street: Tea at Three tea rooms, Castle pub. Station Road Shopping Centre (by the station): range of fast-food outlets.

Take the south exit from Harrow station, walk straight down to the end of the road and turn left with the rising ground of the park to your right. After a while turn right into Grove Hill and begin the climb up to the top of the hill. Just before the

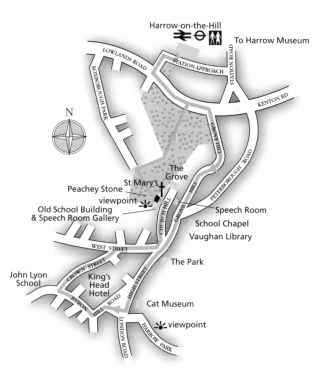

junction with Davidson Lane you pass between two large houses: Elmfield and The Copse. These are the first of the Harrow School boarding houses in the village. There are 11 in all. Another three are below you to your left on Peterborough Road. The remaining six are strung out along the High Street on top of the hill. Around the corner ahead you come to the main complex of school buildings, with more boarding houses on the left and the first classrooms on the right.

King Charles's Well
Just beyond the path on the right ascending to Church Hill there is a metal plaque high on the Art School wall recounting how Charles I stopped here in 1646 to water his horse and take a last look at London before going on to surrender himself to the Scottish Army. King Charles's Well, as the place came to be called, was just one of three places on Harrow Hill where villagers could obtain water until the Harrow Waterworks Company started piping in supplies in 1855. The difficulty of obtaining water on this hilltop site was an important factor in limiting the expansion of the village before the mid-19th century.

Speech Room
Opposite the massive Speech Room (assembly hall) built to commemorate Harrow School's tercentenary in the 1870s, there is a plaque in the wall at the junction of Grove Hill and the less steep road to the east, Peterborough Road. Headed 'Take Heed', the plaque was placed here in 1969 on the 70th anniversary of what is thought to have been Britain's first fatal car accident, or, at least, Britain's first car accident in which the driver died. Edwin Sewell was the poor man and the accident happened on 25 February 1899 when the brakes of his Daimler Wagonette failed as he was going down Grove Hill. He was killed instantly; his passenger died later. Peterborough Road had been constructed 20 years earlier to provide a less precipitous route up and down the hill – a pity he did not use it instead.

Passing the New Schools, the Vaughan Library and the Chapel on the left, you are now in the heart of the school. It is concentrated here at the north end of the High Street because this is where the school originally started in the early 17th century, but all the buildings are much later in date, reflecting the great era of expansion and reconstruction in the mid- to late-19th century when Harrow transformed itself into a progressive, modern public school and numbers rose from under 70 to over 500. As Church Hill joins from the right, you pass between two of the oldest boarding houses, Druries on the right, where poet Lord Byron and politician Lord Palmerston boarded as boys, and Headmaster's on the left. The headmaster used to live here as well, but now has his own house elsewhere.

Flambards
Now you are in the High Street proper, dipping and winding along the crest of the hill in a north–south direction. At certain times of day it will be packed with boys in their straw boaters and blue blazers going off to eat or hurrying between classes. Beyond Headmaster's are the school bursary and bookshop. Opposite, at the beginning of West Street, are the outfitters and school tuck shop. On the far side of the bookshop are three more boarding houses: Moretons, Flambards and The Park. Flambards and The Park are connected historically because they are both relics in

their way of a medieval estate in Harrow that existed side by side with the main one, which belonged to the Archbishops of Canterbury – the Archbishops of Canterbury were, until the reign of Henry VIII, Lords of the Manor of Harrow. Flambards is the successor to the original manor house of Harrow's other estate, named after the family that owned it in the Middle Ages. There are 14th- and 15th-century brasses to some of the Flambards in **St Mary's Church**, which you come to later in the walk. In 1797 James Rushout acquired the Flambards estate through marriage, but finding it too small for him, built The Park instead. The school acquired The Park as a boarding house in 1831.

The Cat Museum
In the little square ahead cat lovers should look out for an antiques shop called The Other Shop on the left-hand side of the road, for they will surely not want to miss the Cat Museum here. Actually, it is not really a museum as such, more a private collection of feline memorabilia put together by the owner of the shop, Kathleen Mann, over the past 20 years and now, in response to public demand, put on show by her in the converted Victorian scullery beneath the shop. Admission is free, but the premises are rather cramped, so only two people can visit at a time.

The other Harrow school
After slipping into the private road called Harrow Park to see the easterly views from the first corner, exit from the square via the road going downhill next to the King's Head Hotel. The next section of the walk is a circuit that takes in Byron Hill Road, Crown Street and West Street to see the other old streets that have always been part of Harrow village. There are some pretty houses of varying ages and descriptions and some good views off to the west.

At the bottom of Byron Hill Road turn right into Crown Street. To the left now is the John Lyon School, another school set up with funds left by the founder of Harrow School, but long after the original Harrow School. It was in 1572 that public-spirited local farmer John Lyon endowed the original Harrow School. The first school was intended mainly as a free school for local children, but fee-paying children from elsewhere were also allowed to attend. Over the centuries the fee-paying children gradually ousted the local children, even though the school tried to encourage local children to attend. In the end, following the passage of the Public Schools Act in 1868, Harrow School ceased to provide free places for local children and established the John Lyon School for them instead.

Workhouse and Old Schools
At the end of Crown Street turn right into West Street. The large white building on the left is the former parish workhouse, dating from the 18th century, where poor people who could not maintain themselves were given spartan accommodation in return for arduous labour. When you get back to the High Street at the top of the hill, turn left and walk along the left-hand side of the road past Druries and into Church Hill. Now you are really at the heart of historic Harrow School, for the building on the left with the clock on top is the original school building, called the Old Schools. Although John Lyon petitioned Elizabeth I for permission to endow his school in 1572, funds only became available in 1608 after both he and

his wife had died. Work on the new school then began and the building opened in 1615 with a single large classroom, masters' accommodation above and storerooms below. This Jacobean building is the left-hand section of the Old Schools and survives unchanged. Inside, every available surface in the classroom, known since the 19th century as the Fourth Form Room, is covered with the carved names of generations of pupils, including, close together, those of Byron and fellow writer Thomas Sheridan. In 1820 the original school building was extended in identical style to the right. This now houses the Old Speech Room Gallery with its collection of school treasures. From the yard outside, where the game of squash was invented, there are wonderful views west as far as the North Downs and the Chilterns.

Sacred Grove

From the Old Schools make your way up Church Hill and into the churchyard of St Mary's Church. (The big house up ahead is The Grove, another school boarding house, and there are good views east here, sometimes as far as **Westminster Abbey** and the British Telecom Tower.) The church is probably the reason why the village of Harrow is here in the first place, for the name 'Harrow' is thought to be an ancient word meaning temple or sacred grove. In pagan times the summit of a hill would have been a natural site for a shrine or some other place of religious significance.

The Archbishop of Canterbury consecrated the first church in Harrow in 1094. Nothing remains of the original building, but sections of the existing church date from only half a century later. The chancel was constructed out of local oak in 1242. The nave and roof and the 200-foot (60-m) spire – a northwest London landmark in every direction – were added in the 1400s. Somewhere in the churchyard, in an unidentified spot, Byron's daughter Allegra, who died when she was only five, is buried and there is a little plaque to her fixed to the south porch. Inside the church there are various memorials commemorating Harrow School founder John Lyon, and a large collection of brasses.

Peachey stone

The path takes you past the church to a famous viewpoint with a viewfinder to help you identify the various sights. This spot is also a place of pilgrimage for Byron lovers, for it is the site of the Peachey stone, the flat-topped tomb, now railed in, where as a boy the poet dreamed away hours gazing over the countryside and developing his poetic imagination.

If you go straight on here you will pass through the lower cemetery onto the western slope of Harrow Hill. But the route of the walk goes to the right to descend the northern slope. When you meet the road coming up the hill, take the sign-posted path to the right and follow it down to the main road. The station and the end of the walk is 100 yards (90m) or so to your left.

CHIPPING BARNET AND MONKEN HADLEY

Summary: This circular walk explores the two neighbouring villages of Chipping Barnet and Monken Hadley out on London's northern fringe. Features of the circular walk, which starts and finishes at High Barnet station, are Barnet and Hadley parish churches, no fewer than six sets of almshouses, many fine Georgian mansions, Barnet's Elizabethan grammar school, **Barnet Museum**, Monken Hadley Common, Hadley Green where the Battle of Barnet is supposed to have been fought during the 15th-century Wars of the Roses, and houses connected with three great figures of the Victorian era: explorer David Livingstone and novelists William Thackeray and Anthony Trollope. Four hundred feet (122m) above sea level, Barnet and Hadley also offer some fine views south and east across the valleys of two little rivers, the Dollis Brook and Pymmes Brook respectively.

Start and finish:	High Barnet station (Northern Underground Line).
Distance:	4 miles (6.4km).
Time:	3 hours.
Refreshments:	Variety of cafés, pubs, restaurants and fast-food outlets in Barnet High Street at the start and finish of the walk; the Windmill pub in Hadley Highstone at the rough halfway point; and the Black Horse pub towards the end of the walk.

Turn right out of High Barnet station and walk up the hill to the High Street. Turn right here and carry on up the hill. Crossing Meadway you can see down into the valley of the Pymmes Brook. East Barnet down in the valley was the original Barnet village and remained for centuries the centre of the parish. Chipping Barnet grew up to the west of the village at a point where the Great North Road breasted its first major hill on the way out of London to York. Being a natural place for travellers to stop and change horses, it developed in the 18th century as a great coaching centre, with fine large inns and fleets of horses standing ready for the harness. By the end of the century at least 150 mail- and stagecoaches were passing through the village daily, not to mention post-chaises, private carriages, carts and wagons. After the railway arrived at East Barnet in 1850, a footpath was made linking the new station with Chipping Barnet. This subsequently developed into Meadway. Chipping Barnet got its own station, High Barnet, 20 years later.

Further up the High Street on the left, the Felix and Firkin pub occupies part of the site of the 18th-century Red Lion, probably the biggest and grandest of the old coaching inns in Chipping Barnet. The fine inn sign protruding way out over the street is a relic of the original inn. A few doors up on the right you come to Ye Olde Mitre Inne, dating from the century before the Red Lion and obviously more typical of an earlier age. It is the oldest pub in Barnet and one of Barnet's few surviving 17th-century buildings.

Follow the High Street round to the right as it passes through The Squeeze between the shops and **St John's Church**, of which more later. Round the corner the street is much wider because the market that gave Chipping Barnet its name ('chipping' means market) was held here from the Middle Ages into modern times. Today, the market, held every Wednesday and Saturday, has its own site in St Albans Road behind The Spires shopping centre.

The Battle of Barnet

Walk all the way up the right-hand side of the street until you come to Hadley Green. This ancient tract of common is reputed to be the site of the Battle of Barnet, one of the most important engagements of the Wars of the Roses. After being deposed and forced into exile by Warwick the Kingmaker, Edward IV returned to England in March 1471, captured Henry VI and then, with only 2,000 men behind him, defeated and killed Warwick at Barnet one foggy day in April. This victory, plus another one at Tewkesbury shortly after, established him securely on his throne for the rest of his life.

Bear right now by the garage, cross East View and continue between Joslin's Pond and Ossulstone House in the direction of Monken Hadley, which the walk comes to shortly. From the late 17th century onwards villages around London boasting large heaths and commons were invaded by wealthy Londoners seeking healthy situations for country houses well away from the overcrowded and insanitary city. With its green on one side, common on the other and its elevated position, Monken Hadley was one of the most sought after resorts. By the time sugar refiner John Horton built Ossulstone House in the 1760s, a virtually complete row of gentlemen's residences connected Barnet with Hadley.

Thackeray's grandfather

Beyond Ossulstone House and The Cottage there is now a gap in this row. Here, formerly, stood an old house that once belonged to the grandfather of the novelist William Thackeray. After his grandfather's time Thackeray himself got to know Hadley quite well because his cousin was rector here. By that time the house had passed into other hands. Between 1829 and 1934 it was the home of Hadley's lords of the manor. The last lord of the manor, Miss Rhoda Wyburn, gave the fields behind the house to the public and after her death in 1935 the house was demolished to provide access to the new open space. The former fields are now crossed by a bridle path connecting Hadley Green with East Barnet.

Dr Livingstone

After World War II the gap in the row was a lot bigger because three of the houses on the far side (The Elms, The Mercers and Thackeray House) were destroyed by bombs. Since then they have been rebuilt exactly as they were before and now it is almost impossible to tell from looking at them that they are not genuine. Beyond the new-old houses you come to Hadley House, the grandest house in the row and the original manor house of Monken Hadley. Beyond the manor house are Fairholt and Monkenholt, both dating from the mid-18th century, and then Monken Cottage followed by Livingstone Cottage. In 1857–58 the latter was the residence of the famous explorer, Dr David Livingstone. He had just come back to England from Africa for the first time and it was here that he wrote *Missionary Travels and Researches in South Africa*. Although the time he spent here was very short, it was nevertheless one of the happiest periods of his life for he had his family with him all the time, a rare occurrence in the great traveller's life. The plaque was put up by his daughter in 1913 on the centenary of his birth.

Trollope's sister

After Livingstone Cottage, keep to the right. Beyond Hollybush House, Grandon has connections with another great novelist of the 19th century, Anthony Trollope. In January 1836 Trollope's consumptive sister, Emily, moved here hoping that Hadley's situation would lead to an improvement in her health. It didn't and the poor girl died just a few weeks later. Go past Sir Roger Wilbraham's almshouses, founded in 1612, and follow the road round to the right into the centre of Monken Hadley village. When you get to White Lodge, cross the road and enter **St Mary's**

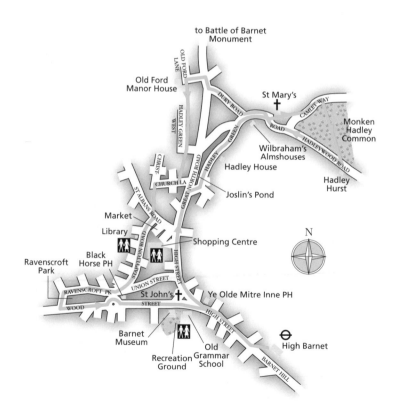

churchyard. Emily Trollope and Thackeray's grandparents, among many others, are buried here.

Above the west door of the the church the date 1494 denotes when the medieval church was substantially rebuilt. The coats of arms close by, put up when the west door was renovated in 1956, represent the Archbishop of Canterbury and the Bishop of London and their respective provinces at the time. In the church there are various brasses and old monuments, the most striking of which is the portrait of almshouse benefactor Sir Roger Wilbraham and his wife Mary, carved by well-known Jacobean sculptor Nicholas Stone.

Unlike Chipping Barnet, Monken Hadley has preserved its identity as a pretty country village with church, manor house, rectory and cottages. The village was originally a clearing in a vast tract of woodland, hence the name Hadley, which means 'high place cleared in a wood'. In the 1130s Geoffrey de Mandeville, Earl of Essex, founded a hermitage in the village and presented it to the Monastery of Walden in Essex. The monastery owned the village all through the Middle Ages and so it acquired its prefix of Monken, a corruption of 'monachorum' meaning 'of [i.e. belonging to] the monks'. After the dissolution of the monasteries, Monken Hadley passed into lay hands but, like Chipping Barnet, no one family owned it for long enough to establish a squirearchical dynasty. This is perhaps one reason why the village was so popular as a retreat for wealthy merchants and professional men from London.

Monken Hadley Common

Pass between the church and the flint-faced Pagitt's almshouses on the right. Justinian Pagitt founded this almshouse in 1678: the plaque was put up in 1978 to mark its tercentenary. The path through the churchyard brings you out on Monken Hadley Common with Hadley Wood ahead down in a dip. Monken Hadley grew up on the western edge of Enfield Chase, a medieval hunting park. When the Chase was divided up into enclosed fields for farming in 1779, the village received the land that is now called Monken Hadley Common as compensation for loss of grazing and other rights in the old Chase. Today the Common covers 190 acres (77 ha) and stretches east nearly 2 miles (3km) as far as Cockfosters.

Hadley Hurst

Turn left along the road. At the entrance to the Church of England primary school, the original village school founded in 1832, turn right across the road and head across the Common, bearing slightly left along a path leading towards a red-brick house on the extreme left with two superb cedars in front. This is just one of many fine houses on the south side of the common: approaching them from this direction is the best way of admiring them. When you reach the red-brick house – Hadley Hurst, built around 1705 – turn right along the path worn in the broad verge. The white house called Hurst Cottage is a slightly earlier and slightly less grand house than Hadley Hurst. Attached to it on the left is a small house rather more recogniz-able as a cottage. This one was built in the 16th century and is probably the oldest building in the village, apart from the church.

Further on along the row, Gladsmuir was the home of the Quilter family from 1736 until the early 20th century. More recently it belonged to the novelist Kingsley Amis; it was during his tenure that in 1972 the poet Cecil Day Lewis died in the house.

Carry on back towards the village, passing the rectory on the right and then going through the Common gates. Retrace your steps through the centre of the village, this time on the right-hand side of the road and passing the 17th-century Pagitt's almshouses. Beyond St Mary's Church you pass two large neo-Georgian houses set well back from the road in their own grounds. These were built in the early 1960s and replaced the so-called Hadley Priory, the largest house in the road leading from Hadley Green to the church. Although the house was built in the 16th century it was never a priory, but it was made to look like one around 1800 when the owner attached a sham Gothic front to it and gave it its religious-sounding name. The Priory was demolished in the 1950s.

When you reach the Green, again turn right along Dury Road, named after a family that lived in the vicinity in the 18th century. There are more Georgian houses here, but there are many more Victorian cottages, reflecting the expansion of the population at that time – and also the presence of Hadley Brewery. From at least 1770 this stood by the larger of the two ponds (the one with the wall along one side). Beer was brewed here until 1938. After World War II the old brewery became a distribution centre – latterly for Whitbread's Breweries – until it was demolished in 1978.

Hadley Highstone

At the end of Dury Road, turn right on the Great North Road and then, opposite the Old Windmill pub, cross the road into Old Fold Lane. As you do so, look right and you can just see a junction of roads and a patch of green. This is the site of the stone monument commemorating the Battle of Barnet, put up in the 18th century on the spot where the Kingmaker is supposed to have met his end. Because of the monument, this part of Hadley is known as Hadley Highstone.

When Old Fold Lane bends right by the golf club (the clubhouse is a Regency house extended, in the Barnet direction, in the 1920s), turn left past Old Fold Manor House. Old Fold Manor was part of South Mimms, a village about 2 miles (3km) northwest of here. The moat of the original medieval manor house survives on the 18th tee of the golf course. This later house was built sometime around the middle of the 18th century.

Follow the path beside the green all the way back to Chipping Barnet. When you reach the junction of Gladsmuir Road and Christ Church Lane, turn right into the latter, passing on the left one of the old pumping stations of the East Barnet Gas and Water Company. When the road bends right, turn left into Christ Church Passage. At the end cross St Albans Road diagonally left and enter Stapylton Road. Walk all the way down this road, passing the library and the shopping centre. At the bottom Stapylton Road joins Union Street, one of a number of new roads laid out in the 1830s as Chipping Barnet expanded beyond its historic confines of High Street and Wood Street. At the end of Union Street, turn right past the Victorian almshouses of the Leathersellers' Company, one of the City livery companies, and then go left into Ravenscroft Park. The little park here is the last remaining patch of Barnet Common, a large tract of open land which once stretched all the way from the Black Horse pub to the neighbouring village of Arkley. The developer of Ravenscroft Park, Thomas Smith, paid for the landscaping of the park in 1880. The park seems sunken now because it used to contain two large ponds that were only drained in 1992. The boundary stone at the end of the railings by the park marks the western limit of both Barnet parish (beyond is South Mimms) and the long-defunct Whetstone and Highgate Turn-pike Trust, which once levied tolls on the roads in the area to pay for their upkeep.

Mrs Palmer and the Barnet poor

At the end of Ravenscroft Park turn left into Blenheim Road. At the junction with Wood Street you see the old tollgate-keeper's cottage across the road, and on the right the almshouses founded by Mrs Eleanor Palmer, the daughter of Henry VII's treasurer. In 1558 Mrs Palmer left property in Kentish Town to provide an income for the relief of Barnet's poor, but it was not until 1823 that the first almshouses were built with her money. They were subsequently rebuilt in 1930 and then modernized in 1987. About 100 yards (90m) beyond the almshouses you can see the junction with Wellhouse Lane. This leads eventually to Well Approach where there is a little mock-Tudor well house in the midst of a 1930s housing estate. The well house covers the remains of a chalybeate spring (i.e. a spring containing dissolved iron salts) which was developed as a spa in the 1650s and in the the following decade twice visited by diarist Samuel Pepys.

Turn left along Wood Street. Bells Hill on the right shows you how steeply the ground falls away to the south into the valley of the Dollis Brook. The historic part of Wood Street really starts beyond the Black Horse pub and the roundabout. On the right the Elizabeth Allen free school functioned from 1824 until 1973. Local resident Mrs Allen actually left money for the school in 1727, but until the National School was set up in 1824 her bequest was used for the old grammar school seen later in the walk. The former Allen school building now provides sheltered accommodation for the elderly.

Barnet Museum

On the left is another almshouse, this one founded by John Garrett in 1728 for six elderly widows. A little further on from the Garrett almshouse and on the same side of the road is the fourth and last of Chipping Barnet's almshouses, the Jesus Hospital, founded by James Ravenscroft in 1679. Ravenscroft, of a prominent Barnet family, graduated from Jesus College, Cambridge, and went on to become a lawyer and a merchant. Just before the Registry Office, No. 31 Wood Street on the right is the Barnet Museum, run by the local history society. Ahead, Barnet church became a parish church in its own right in 1866. Since the Middle Ages until that time, it had officially been no more than subsidiary to the main parish church down in East Barnet. A wealthy brewer called John Beauchamp paid for the rebuilding of the original church in 1420. Then that 15th-century building was rebuilt and enlarged in the 1870s. Many of the old monuments were preserved, the best being that to James Ravenscroft's father, Thomas, who died in 1630.

Opposite the church and set back from the road is the last of Chipping Barnet's historic buildings to be seen on the walk. This is the Elizabethan grammar school, built in 1573 and the main school in the village until the 19th century. It was to this school that Elizabeth Allen's money was devoted for the century following her original bequest. The school moved to new premises in 1932. The old building, now part of Barnet College, is occasionally used for public concerts and other events.

Outside the old schoolhouse, cross back over the High Street to the north side and turn right. Make your way back down the hill past the Mitre and eventually to the station, where the walk ends.

ENFIELD

Summary: This is a circular walk round the former village of Enfield. Now a north London suburb, the village once lay between the Enfield Chace hunting park to the west and fields and market gardens stretching down to Ponders End and the River Lee in the east. It was on the Lee that in 1804 the government established the arms factory that later produced the famous Lee-Enfield rifle. Enfield has obviously been built up since those days, but it retains many attractive and historic features, all of which are included on the walk. The most notable are the old houses along Gentlemans Row, the New River and riverside walks, the Elizabethan grammar school, **St Andrew's Church** with its fine collection of memorials and handsome old vicarage, and houses associated with writer Charles Lamb. It's worth trying to combine the walk with a separate visit to 17th-century **Forty Hall**, a country house a mile or two north of Enfield which now houses the local history museum.

Start and finish:	Enfield Chase station (mainline trains from King's Cross and Moorgate via Finsbury Park); Enfield Town station (mainline trains from Liverpool Street).
Length:	3 miles (4.8km).
Time:	2½ hours.
Refreshments:	Fast-food outlets and Oliver's coffee house (in shopping centre) in Church Street in the walk's early stages; Crown and Horseshoes pub on the New River at the halfway point; café in Town Park in the final section.

Come out of Enfield Chase station and turn right under the railway bridge. The first railway came to Enfield in 1849; this line opened in 1871. Walk down the hill past the Wheatsheaf pub and Chase Green on the left. This area was once part of Enfield Chace, an 8,000-acre (3,250-ha) royal hunting park dating from medieval times. When Enfield Chase was divided up in 1779, a portion was allotted to the villagers of Enfield as compensation for the loss of common rights in the old Chase. When the common fields of Enfield were in turn enclosed in 1803, the allotment from the Chase, covering 12 acres (5 ha), was preserved in the form of Chase Green, Enfield's first public park. Cross Old Park Avenue and the bridge over the New River. The gate into the Chase from Enfield stood just about here, on the village side of the bridge and at the entrance to Church Street. The New River, an artificial canal constructed in the early 17th century to bring fresh water to the City of London from springs in Hertfordshire, effectively divided the village from Enfield Chase.

Royal palace

Cross Cecil Road and continue on into Church Street, the high street of the old village. Beyond Sarnesfield Road, Little Park Gardens on the left commemorates an old house called Little Park, demolished in 1888 and one of the first of Enfield's many mansions to fall victim to Victorian development. Burleigh Way further on was laid out over Burleigh House, knocked down in 1913. Opposite the market-place, Pearson's department store on the right was built in the 1920s on the site of Enfield's manor house, known as the Palace. The manor house acquired its grand title when Enfield became royal property in 1421. In the 16th century Henry VIII's daughter Elizabeth inherited Enfield and the neighbouring estate of Worcesters: she and her half brother, later Edward VI, spent a good deal of time at Worcesters as children. Later, as Queen, Elizabeth rebuilt Enfield's decaying manor house in the form of a two-storey gabled house with a central block and wings. Almost from the beginning the house was let out, usually to royal servants. About 1670 Dr Robert Uvedale, who had been master of Enfield grammar school, opened a successful private boarding school in the manor, which survived right down to 1896. Destruction of the old house was finally completed in 1928. Nothing remains of it now except one panelled room with a fine plaster ceiling and a carved stone fireplace, both of which have been re-erected in No. 5 Gentlemans Row.

Enfield market
When you reach Sydney Road, look across Church Street to the right-hand side of the bank and you will see the former parish beadle's house and lock-up, built in 1830. It later became the vestry house and is now a solicitor's office. Now cross Church Street to the market-place. Although Enfield was first granted the right to hold a market in 1303, the modern one (on Thursdays, Fridays and Saturdays) was not started until 1612. From the beginning the proceeds were dedicated to parish poor relief. The original site of the market was a small green. Then it was enlarged by the acquisition in 1632 of a house called The Vine, which for a time served as the market house. The present octagonal market building dates only from 1904.

Fine memorials
From the market-place go into the churchyard. Although Enfield was the second largest parish in Middlesex, St Andrew's was its only church until 1831. In the 1820s the church was extensively reconstructed, but it kept both its medieval appearance and many of its original memorials. The best are in the northeast corner. One is a brass, said to be the finest in Middlesex, commemorating a soldier's wife, Lady Joyce Tiptoft, who died in 1446; the other is a fine 17th-century sculpture of Sir Nicholas and Lady Rainton. City merchant and twice Lord Mayor of London, Sir Nicholas bought the old royal estate of Worcesters just north of Enfield and rebuilt the old manor house that Queen Elizabeth had used as a child. His new house, called Forty Hall, survives and is now Enfield's local-history museum.

Make your way round the east end of the church. Now you can see to your left, across the churchyard, the original Elizabethan schoolhouse of Enfield grammar school. To the right is the handsome vicarage of St Andrew's with its central Dutch-style gable. You can get a better view of it by standing on the plinth of the Mitton tomb next to the wall. Although the vicarage has all the appearance of a Georgian house, the oldest section of it, on the Silver Street side, is timber-framed inside and has been dated to the 13th century. Not many church houses of this antiquity survive in London, and certainly not still in church occupation.

Gentlemans Row

Walk on towards the churchyard gate. Just before you reach it, turn left along the footpath leading to the white house with black shutters. Continue past this house into Holly Walk. Follow this round by the car park on the left and the girls' school, founded in 1909, on the right. Keep right when the path forks. You now pass some cottages on your left, and on your right a sports ground bordered by the New River. Eventually you come out on Gentlemans Row (of which more in a moment). Turn right here, and at the end of the road, by Brecon House, turn left, cross the New River and carry straight on through the alley. You will emerge, eventually, on Chase Side next to Chase Green. Cross the road and turn right.

Development in this area started after the creation of Chase Green in 1803. After a while you come to an elegant terrace called Gloucester Place. The pretty little cottages here were built in 1823. At the end of the terrace look across the road to the white house (No. 87) and the brick house to the left of the white house (No. 89). Both these houses were successively home to the writer Charles Lamb and his mentally unstable sister Mary, and bear plaques to that effect. After retiring from the East India Company in 1825, Lamb occasionally took lodgings in Enfield. In 1827 he and his sister became tenants of The Poplars, the white house. After two years Mary's condition was so bad and she was away from home so much that Charles could not cope with the housekeeping and moved next door into Westwood Cottage to lodge with retired tradesman Mr Westwood and his wife. He stayed here for four years. In 1833 Charles and Mary left Enfield and moved to nearby Edmonton to live with Mary's guardian. Charles died there two years later.

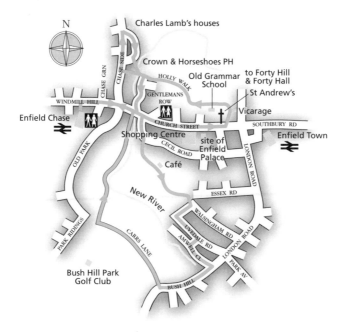

Beer garden

Cross the road to the Lamb houses, turn right and walk along Cricketers Arms Road. Keep left into Chase Side Place and pass the modern Cricketers pub. At the end of the Place turn left. Here you meet the New River again. Here also is the Crown and Horseshoes pub, with its large beer garden behind. Turn right along the riverside. Having passed the wooden bridge, turn left across the next iron bridge (the one you crossed earlier in the other direction). Now you are at the top of Gentlemans Row. From the 17th century onwards, people began building houses along the village side of the New River facing west across the the river to the Chase. Many of these houses were quite substantial and so in the 18th century they became known collectively as Gentlemans Row. After 1779, when the old Enfield Chase was split up and enclosed, more houses, not so grand as the original ones, were built on the other side of Gentlemans Row, making it, at least for half its length, more like a regular street.

The next section of the walk follows the Row all the way down to its beginning in the centre of the village. The Row is lined with 18th- and 19th-century houses of varying sizes and styles, some cottages and some larger residences, such as Brecon House and, a little further on, Archway, which arches over the entrance to Chapel Street. Beyond Archway go left of the garden in the middle of the road and continue along the Row. Most of the houses have a special plaque indicating that they have been 'listed' (i.e. protected) by the local council. White-painted Clarendon Cottage, No. 17, was another of Lamb's Enfield homes (this was the one he occasionally rented before moving to The Poplars). At the end of the Row the biggest house provides offices for council services. To the right the New River flows through a pretty public garden. In the earlier section near the pub the river was roughly at the same level as the houses beside it. But here, as you can clearly see, it is several feet higher. This is because it was originally constructed to follow the 100-foot (30-m) contour, a design constraint that produced some rather bizarre loops and diversions, including one all the way around Enfield village. In 1859 the Enfield section was straightened and then, in 1890, piped underneath the village. Bypassed, the Gentlemans Row stretch then became super-fluous and would have been filled in had there not been a public campaign to preserve it for its ornamental value. Today, therefore, the New River just here is not a river at all but a linear lake. The main channel still carries water to Stoke Newington, whence it is distributed via the mains.

Town Park

Gentlemans Row brings you out at the bus station. Turn right and then, in front of Trinity Church, go left across the road, using the zebra crossing. Walk on down Cecil Road and go straight on through the gates into the 27-acre (11-ha) Town Park, created in 1903 out of the grounds of Chaseside and other large houses that formerly stood on the south side of Church Street. When the path forks, bear left beside the tennis courts. To your right you can see the embankment of the old New River course as it skirts the foot of Bush Hill.

Follow the path round to the right past the pavilion/café and then to the left towards the main gate. Just before you reach the main gate, cut right and go through the little gate leading into Walsingham Road. Immediately turn right. Follow the road round to the left (Uvedale Road) and then right into Whitethorn Gardens and left into Amwell Close (Amwell was one of the Hertfordshire sources of the New River). Keep to the high path on the right and then, when you reach the main road (Bush Hill), turn right and walk up the hill.

Bush Hill Park
At the top turn right at the Bush Hill Park Golf Club sign and join the footpath just to the right of the club gateway. The clubhouse, which you can see to your left at the end of the long straight drive, is, in origin, 18th century, but the history of the park in which it stands goes right back to before the Domesday survey of 1086. It is therefore much older than Enfield Chase, which was not emparked until a century or more later. After the restoration of the monarchy in 1660, Old Park, which was royal property, was granted to one of the restoration's major architects, George Monck, Duke of Albemarle. Later, the 550-acre (225-ha) estate passed through many different hands before eventually coming into the possession of the Bush Hill Park Golf Club early in the 20th century.

The footpath goes straight through the middle of the golf course. When you reach the bollards at the end, turn right along the tarmac path leading down the hill back towards the New River. At the river go left (either side will do) and walk for some way beside the water. Eventually you come out back on Church Street. Turn left up Windmill Hill and make your way back to the station, where the walk ends.

❖❖

WALTHAMSTOW

❖❖

Summary: A circular walk round Walthamstow, a former village in northeast London on the Essex side of the River Lee opposite Tottenham on the London side. Walthamstow – meaning 'a place where travellers are welcome' – is a rare little oasis of history in the otherwise often ugly sprawl of contemporary east London. It owes its survival to the fact that the centre of Walthamstow has shifted twice away from its historic core as the once country village has grown into today's suburb. Walthamstow's medieval church, 15th-century Ancient House, 16th-century almshouses, 18th-century workhouse and **Vestry House** (now the local history museum) and 19th-century cottages and schools, are all seen on the walk. Also featured is the **William Morris Gallery** housed in the Georgian mansion where the great Arts and Crafts designer lived as a boy. The walk between the village and the house is not particularly attractive, but unfortunately cannot be avoided. The **Walthamstow Village Festival** takes place in July.

Start and finish:	Walthamstow Central station (Victoria Underground Line; mainline trains from Liverpool Street) (Walthamstow Queens Road station is served by mainline North London Line trains between Gospel Oak and Barking).
Length:	2¾ miles (4.4km).

Time: 2¼ hours.

Refreshments: Orford Road in Walthamstow village in the walk's early stages
                 has a bakery, café/take-away, Chinese take-away/fish and chip
                 shops, two pubs, two Italian restaurants and an Indian take-away.
                 At the end of the walk, the High Street, near the station, has
                 cafés, restaurants, sandwich bars and fast-food outlets.

Turn right out of the station and walk up Selborne Road to the traffic lights. Cross
the main road and go straight on into St Mary Road. At the end of the road continue on into Church Path. This takes you past some pretty Victorian cottages, and then
a row of rather older ones built in 1825, before bringing you out in the original
village centre of Walthamstow, called Church End to distinguish it from other settle-
ments in the parish such as Kings End in the south and Chapel End (where there was
a chapel-of-ease to the main parish church) in the north. On the right are the old
school and workhouse, of which more later. On the left are the Squires almshouses,
founded in 1795 by Mrs Squires for six tradesmen's widows. Mrs Squires lived at
Newington and died the year after the almshouses were founded.

Ancient house

Carry on past the almshouses into Church Lane. On the left now is **St Mary's
Church**, standing in its 3-acre (1.2-ha) churchyard. The many fine tombs reflect
Walthamstow's former status as an up-market residential area. From the late Middle
Ages rich City merchants such as Sir George Monoux, of whom more in a minute,
built country houses in the beautiful wooded countryside around the village. By
the middle of the 19th century, the still-rural parish was well sprinkled with fine
gentlemen's seats. Several are still standing today, including Walthamstow House in
Shernhall Street to the east of the village and The Chestnuts to the south in Hoe
Street. Neither of these feature on the walk, but the 18th-century Water House and
Brookscroft and the 19th-century Orford House do.

Opposite the church is the so-called Ancient House, a timber-framed structure
dating from the 15th century. Some sources say that a previous house on this site
was the manor house of the de Toni family, who were granted the manor of
Walthamstow after the Norman Conquest. In the 19th century Ancient House was
converted into four shops, hence the large windows on the ground floor. Now it is
a private home again. The bare plot on the other side of the entrance to Orford Road
was the site of the village inn, the Nag's Head, until it was rebuilt behind Ancient
House in Orford Road in 1859.

Walk on past Ancient House. The small but elegant house on the far side (No. 10
Church Lane) was built in 1830 for a family of local builders called Reed. A little
further on in Bishop's Close is the Chestnuts, built by the Rev. J. Roberts, headmaster of the Monoux School (which you come to shortly) from 1820 to 1836. It
was partly a residence for himself and partly a boarding house for the private pupils
he taught at the school. Bishop's Close was later built in the grounds of the house.

Vinegar Alley

Continue on down Church Lane for some way. Just beyond the pillar box near the
end, turn left into Vinegar Alley. This takes you back through the churchyard towards

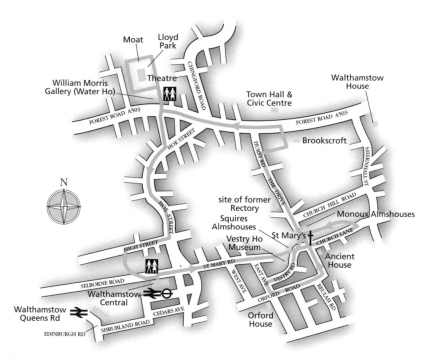

the east end of the church. To the right, opposite the church, are the Monoux Almshouses and Grammar School for boys, founded in 1527 by City merchant and former Lord Mayor of London Sir George Monoux. The school was in the brick part at the far end (rebuilt in 1955 following bomb damage during World War II) and, in the early days at least, the master lived in the protruding section in the middle. The much-expanded school moved to a new site in Chingford Road in the 19th century and is still there today.

Although Monoux was never lord of the manor of Walthamstow, he was one of the village's most generous benefactors. As well as funding the almshouse and school, he also paid for the rebuilding of the 13th-century parish church. After his death in 1544 he was buried in St Mary's and commemorated by a brass that can still be seen in the church. His house in northern Walthamstow near Chapel End survived until 1927 and is now covered by Monoux Grove.

At the west (tower) end of the church, turn left and bear right at the fork. On the right now, on the far side of the churchyard, is the old St Mary's infants school, founded in a barn on the vicar's glebe in 1824 and then provided with this handsome building four years later. The vicar at the time, the Rev. William Wilson, was a pioneer of infant education and St Mary's was the first school of its kind established by the Church of England. The building was last used as a school in 1978 and is now the church's Welcome Centre.

Parish workhouse

Back in Church End, cross the road, turn right and follow it round to the left as it becomes Vestry Road. The road takes its name from the building on the right, built by the parish in 1730 as a combined workhouse and vestry office (the vestry was the local authority in those days). The parish poor were moved to a new workhouse in Stratford in 1840 and the building subsequently became, among other things, a police station and a private house before being turned into the Vestry House local history museum in 1931. A plaque on the wall by the barrel marks the site of the old parish watchhouse and lockup. Nearby stands the top of a column from the old General Post Office in St Martin's-le-Grand in the City. A local resident brought it to Walthamstow after the post office was demolished in 1912. On the other side of the road is the National School. This was built in 1819 to take the overflow from the old Monoux School and was in use until 1906. Since 1924 the building has been used by the National Spiritualist Church.

Carry on along Vestry Road, crossing the deep railway cutting made in 1870, and following the road round to the right past the playground and the old (1903) postal sorting office on the left. As the plaque on the sorting office says, this area was once the Bury Field, or Church Common, one of three large areas of common land in the old rural Walthamstow. All the commons were enclosed in 1850 and subsequently built over with streets and houses.

New centre of Walthamstow

At the end of Vestry Road, turn left into East Avenue. The large house ahead is Orford House, built in the early 19th century on the edge of Church Common for Whitechapel merchant John Case. Now it is a social centre with a bowling green in the garden behind. Before you reach the house, turn left by the Queen's Arms pub into Orford Road and walk along past the shops. Orford Road was built from the 1860s onwards as the new centre of Walthamstow: further on you pass the new school (now the Asian centre) and the new town hall (now a nursery school), which were put up at that time. As Walthamstow continued to expand, the centre of the growing town moved to yet another new site, still further from the old village. Today, Orford Road serves the Walthamstow Village conservation area and surrounding streets.

Follow the road when it bends round to the left and crosses back over the railway line, passing the rebuilt Victorian Nag's Head pub on the far side. Cross straight over Church Lane and walk past the west end of the church once more, but this time in the opposite direction. Carry on past the almshouses into Church Hill. Beyond the almshouses on the right is the new rectory; on the left is the old vicarage, absorbed into Walthamstow High School in 1974. The old rectory, owned all through the Middle Ages by the Priory of Holy Trinity, Aldgate, in London, stood across the road, ahead and to the left, until its demolition at the end of the 19th century.

The Ching valley

Cross straight over the road ahead (Church Hill/Prospect Hill) and walk along The Drive. Although you cannot see it, the ground now drops away on all sides as you approach the top of the hill that once protected Walthamstow village from the worst of the north winds. At the end of The Drive the steepness of the descent into the Ching valley becomes apparent. Go straight over into Hurst Road, and, halfway down, turn right by the Hurst Road Health Centre sign into the path to the right of the railings. This brings you out in front of a block of flats. At the far end there is a car-turning area and next to it more railings. Turn left here and follow the path downhill again to the junction with Forest Road. On the right now is Brookscroft, another of old Walthamstow's surviving 18th-century mansions. Once it looked out over woods and fields. Now, converted into a YMCA hostel, it surveys the Borough of Waltham Forest's impressive civic centre, opened in 1941.

William Morris's home

Turn left along Forest Road. At the lights cross straight over and at the zebra crossing cross the road and go through the gates into Lloyd Park. Go through the gate to the right of the mansion, Water House, and walk around the moat in the park behind in either a clockwise or an anti-clockwise direction. The original house stood on the island in the centre of the moat. The present house was built in the mid-18th century and was later one of the boyhood homes of Arts and Crafts designer William Morris. Born nearby in Forest Road in 1834, Morris came here with his family in 1848. Eight years later the family had to leave because of financial problems brought on by a banking crash in the City. The house was later bought by newspaper publisher Edward Lloyd, hence the name of the park, and then in 1950 converted into a museum celebrating the life and work of the great designer, craftsman, poet and socialist.

Walthamstow Market

Exit Lloyd Park by the same gate and cross straight over the main road into Gaywood Road. At the top, turn right on Hoe Street. Follow this winding road for some distance until you pass the cinema and reach the lights. Here turn into the modern High Street, the post-Orford Road town centre and the site of Walthamstow's 1-mile (1.5-km) street market. Originally called Marsh Lane, High Street connected the village with the marshes down by the Lee. As Walthamstow expanded, costermongers started setting up the stalls here from the 1880s and so the market, now one of the longest in Europe, grew up. When you reach the town square, turn left along the tree-lined avenue and make your way back to the station, where the walk ends.

❖❖

WIMBLEDON

❖❖

Summary: A circular walk on high ground round the former south London village of Wimbledon, famous for its common and the international lawn tennis championships. The walk passes close to the spot where the Wimbledon tennis (originally croquet) club was founded in 1868 and explores the part of the common, ringed with fine Georgian mansions, that lies closest to the village. Other features are Wimbledon's High Street and local history museum, its historic parish church with 17th-century memorial to Lord Wimbledon and 19th-century grave of engineer

Sir Joseph Bazalgette, architect of London's amazing sewer system, 17th-century Eagle House and **Southside House**, and fine views of London. The map points the way to the **Wimbledon Windmill Museum** on the common and the **Wimbledon Lawn Tennis Museum** down near Wimbledon Park, both of which are slightly too far away to be included on the walk.

Start and finish:	Wimbledon station (District Underground Line; mainline trains from Waterloo and London Bridge stations).
Length:	3¾ miles (6km).
Time:	2½ hours.
Refreshments:	Plenty of places near the station and in the shopping centre at the start and finish of the walk, and also in the High Street in Wimbledon village proper. At the approximate halfway stage there are pubs in Crooked Billet and and also in Camp Road a little further on. From the Camp Road area it's only about 10 minutes walk to the Wimbledon Windmill museum in the middle of Wimbledon common where there is a café and toilets.

From the station forecourt turn right along the main road. Cross at the traffic lights and go straight on, passing the library on your right. At the end of the shops the main road starts to climb the hill towards the historic centre of Wimbledon, which has retained much of its village identity precisely because the railway had to be built half a mile away down here in the valley bottom. Just before the climb starts, turn right into Woodside. Walk along here and then take the first left into St Mary's Road. Follow this road as it winds its way uphill to the top of the plateau on which Wimbledon and its common sit, 150 feet (45m) above sea level. St Mary's Road was once called Hothouse Lane because it connected Lord Spencer's house at the top of the hill (of which more in a minute) with his kitchen garden at the bottom.

Eventually you reach the junction with Arthur Road in front of the church. Here you are well inside the boundaries of the old village. To your right, though you can't see it, is the edge of the Wimbledon plateau overlooking the broad valley of the River Wandle. On this magnificent site, taking full advantage of the views, stood the first, second and fourth of the four manor houses built in Wimbledon between the 16th and 18th centuries. The first, completed in 1588, belonged to the Cecils, a powerful courtier family, who had come to the village about half a century before. (Sir Edward Cecil, third son of the builder of the house and a professional soldier, inherited the estate and was created Viscount Wimbledon in 1625.) The third was built by the Duchess of Marlborough, who bought the estate from a failed Huguenot financier in 1724. When her house burned down later in the century, her descendant, Lord Spencer, replaced it with Wimbledon's fourth and last manor house, completed in 1799.

Only half a century later, in 1846, the Spencers left Wimbledon. Their Wimbledon Park estate, landscaped in the mid-18th century by Capability Brown and extending down the hill into the valley bottom, was mostly sold off for development. The local council later acquired one part, including the lake, and opened it to the public. Another part was bought by the All England Lawn Tennis Club and subsequently developed as the home of the Wimbledon tennis championships. Up on top of the plateau, property developer John Beaumont built Stag Lodge in front of you and in 1872 laid out Arthur Road over the gardens of Lord Spencer's house. The house itself was demolished in 1948 and replaced with a school in the 1970s. All that is left of it today is a well house across the road from the school entrance, built in 1798 to cover Lord Spencer's private artesian well and converted into a private house about the time the school was built. Nothing at all remains from the previous houses on the site.

Between the Cecils and the Duchess of Marlborough, the Wimbledon estate belonged to Huguenot merchant and financier Sir Theodore Janssen. Finding the Cecils' house, though only a century or so old, pretty much in ruins, Janssen knocked it down and used the bricks to build a brand new house on a new site to the left of where you are standing now, in the vicinity of Alan Road. Chronologically, Janssen's was Wimbledon's second manor house. Poor Janssen did not enjoy his new creation for long. Only four years after completing the house in 1720, he was ruined by the South Sea Bubble scandal in the City and forced to sell up to the Duchess of Marlborough. His house survived until 1900. The only relic of it now is a length of kitchen garden wall in one of the roads built over the site.

Memorials in the church

Beyond Stag Lodge, **St Mary's Church** has been an important religious centre for the best part of 1,000 years. In the Middle Ages it was the parish church not just for Wimbledon but for the whole of the Archbishop of Canterbury's manor of Mortlake, which, besides Mortlake (where the Archbishop had his manor house) and Wimbledon, also included Putney, Roehampton and East Sheen. Though relatively modern (the church was rebuilt in 1789 and 1841 to make more space), St Mary's

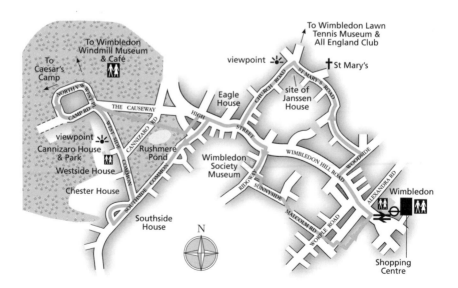

contains many old memorials, particularly the large black marble tomb of Lord Wimbledon in the 17th-century Cecil Chapel and the fine memorial to James Perry in the entrance lobby. Perry, a Wimbledon resident, owned and edited the *Morning Chronicle* newspaper in the early years of the 19th century and had a large flour mill down on the River Wandle. Round the back of the church you can see the tomb of Sir Joseph Bazalgette, one of the greatest British engineers of the 19th century and the builder of London's remarkable sewer system.

Looking over the churchyard wall, the upper parts of Wimbledon's historic former rectory are visible. Built beside the church around 1500, this substantial structure, reflecting the standing of the rector of the living, is, by a margin of a century or so, the oldest building in Wimbledon. After Henry VIII forced the Archbishop of Canterbury to surrender his Wimbledon property in 1536, the Cecil family leased the rectory from the crown as a country house before building themselves their great manor house on the other side of the church. The present rectory is a more modern, and more modest, house close by.

Fine view of London

Turn left at the junction with Arthur Road and continue along St Mary's Road. From the roundabout junction with Church Road there is a fine view to the north towards central London: if you cross over to the entrance to Burghley Road the British Telecom Tower in the West End stands out prominently. Turn left now into Church Road (turning right down the hill will bring you to the Wimbledon lawn tennis museum). Large houses line both sides of the road, those on the left being built on the site of Janssen's house. This was originally called Wimbledon House to distinguish it from the Spencers' Wimbledon Park. Later it was renamed Belvedere House, not because of its hilltop site but because that was the name of the road in Lambeth where the then owner of the house ran his prosperous timber business.

Beyond Belvedere Avenue you come to Old House Close, a modern development laid out on the site of a late 17th-century merchant's house pulled down in the 1960s. Beyond the close the little houses and shops of the village start. This next section of Church Road, together with the short High Street, was really – apart from the large mansions dotted about – all there was to Wimbledon for centuries until the railway brought commuters, particularly from the 1860s onwards. At the junction with the High Street, the nucleus of the village, turn right along the oldest section of the street and cross to the other side at the lights. Continue and then turn left when you get to Southside Common. This soon brings you to the beginning of Wimbledon's great tract of common land where the villagers once grazed their animals and gathered turf and firewood.

What you see here is only the southeastern tip of Wimbledon Common, perhaps one-twentieth of it at most. Attracted by the healthy situation and proximity to the City, wealthy Londoners started building houses here during the late 17th century after all the best plots in the village had been taken (by Eagle House, which you see later in the walk, for example). By the end of the 18th century the south, west and east sides of this little section of the Common – more a large village green really – had been almost completely built up. The old houses on the east side have all gone now. On the west side (opposite you) most of the mansions fortunately remain. Here on the south side there are just a handful of survivors. Claremont House on the left, built in 1650 by retired City merchant Thomas Hilliard, is one. Beyond Claremont House, the crescent at the entrance to Murray Road is the old entrance drive of Wimbledon Lodge, home of the Murray family from 1812 to 1905 when the house was pulled down. On the corner of Lauriston Road the former coach house of Lauriston House still stands, bearing a plaque to William Wilberforce. He inherited the house from his uncle in 1777 and lived here until he started his anti-slavery campaign nine years later.

King's College School
At the junction with West Side Common you come to King's College School, founded in 1829 under the auspices of King's College, part of London University. The school moved here from central London in 1897 – taking over an existing house and its 8-acre (3-ha) grounds – and is now a well-known and highly successful boys' public school with associated junior school. On the far side of the school you pass the entrance to Wright's Alley, an ancient right of way between the common and the village fields below the Ridgway. Next is the late 17th-century Southside House, one of Wimbledon's finest houses and the ancestral home of the Pennington-Mellor family who still occupy it.

The Crooked Billet
A little further down the hill, turn right by the Gothic House (1763) and cross over into Crooked Billet, a collection of workmen's houses carved out of the Common when the big houses were being built. A 'billet' is a piece of wood cut to the right length for fuel, but the curious name presumably comes from the eponymous pub. Go past the rebuilt Cinque Cottages (originally built in 1872 for poor men over the age of 55) and turn right, passing in front of the Crooked Billet pub and the Hand in Hand. At the end of Crooked Billet turn left along the west side of the Common.

The first mansion is Chester House, dating from the 1690s and a century later the home for 20 years of the radical John Horne Tooke, one-time rector of Brentford. Next, where the tarmac gives way to the unsurfaced path, is Westside House, built in the time of Queen Anne by London merchant William Bourne. Continuing on, the pink and white house set well back from the road is Cannizaro House, also built by Bourne and in the 19th century the home of an impoverished Sicilian nobleman called the Duke of Cannizaro. Though the house is now a hotel and restaurant, its magnificent grounds – reached by a gate just beyond the hotel entrance – are public property and are well worth a look, both for themselves and for the views to the west across the valley of the Beverley Brook.

Wimbledon Windmill Museum
At the end of West Side, cross straight over into West Place, like Crooked Billet another collection of mainly workmen's cottages built on a patch of common in the 18th century. When you reach the corner, paths lead on into the main part of Wimbledon Common. The one marked as a cycle track and going straight on from the road is the way to the Wimbledon Windmill Museum in the centre of the Common. It takes about 10 minutes to reach it, and it is well worth visiting as there is a café (and public toilet) there too.

Plate 43: Walthamstow

The Monoux almshouses in Walthamstow were founded in the 16th century by Sir George Monoux,
local resident and Lord Mayor of London in 1514 (see page 226).

Plate 44: Wimbledon
The old windmill on Wimbledon Common is well worth a short
detour from the main route of the Wimbledon walk (see page 232).

Plate 45: Mitcham
The green at Mitcham in south London has been used for cricket matches
ever since the game began roughly 300 years ago (see page 234).

Plate 46: Carshalton
Grove Park and one of the ponds forming the source of the
River Wandle at Carshalton in south London (see page 243).

Plate 47: Dulwich
This pretty Victorian park-keeper's cottage stands at the western end of
Dulwich Park, near the gateway into Dulwich village (see page 246).

Plate 48: Greenwich
*Greenwich's historic waterfront buildings – now occupied by a university and
a museum – were originally part of a 17th-century royal palace (see page 248).*

Plate 49: Blackheath
Sir John Morden founded Morden College in 1695 as an almshouse
for his fellow Turkey Company merchants (see page 256).

Plate 50: Bexley
Seventeenth-century Hall Place is the architectural highlight
of the Bexley walk in south-east London (see page 260).

Caesar's Camp

Meanwhile the walk turns left, following the road round the houses to the junction with Camp Road. About 10 minutes' walk down the road to the right, in the middle of a golf course, is an Iron Age hill fort misleadingly called Caesar's Camp – now little more than a circular space surrounded by a nearly levelled ditch and rampart. On the left just here is the old village school, established in 1758 and used as such up until after World War II. It is now a private girls' school, but the original school building with its central octagon is still standing. Turn left past the school and then past the village's modern almshouses, built on the site of the old parish workhouse. When you get to the Common again, take the path between the roads heading back across the Common towards the village and passing the Rushmere Pond on the way.

Instead of re-entering the village by means of Southside Common, take the unsurfaced road called The Green to the left of it. This brings you back to the High Street opposite the entrance to Marryat Road, the site of Wimbledon House Parkside, one-time home of the novelist Captain Frederick Marryat's parents. Turn right along the High Street, passing first the Rose and Crown pub and then Eagle House, Wimbledon's oldest house apart from the Old Rectory. Built in 1613 by one of the founders of the East India company, it became a school at the end of the 18th century and was extended forward to the High Street at that time in order to create extra space. When the school moved out at the end of the 19th century the house was fortunately saved from demolition. It is now used as an office by the Islamic Heritage Foundation.

Prehistoric track

Keep going along the High Street and carry on when you get to the Church Road junction. This next section of the High Street was only created from the mid-19th century onwards when the village started to expand – the shops on the left where the Belvedere House garden had been were not built until 1924. Just before the road sets off down the hill, turn right into Ridgway, thought to have originated as a prehistoric track running along the southern edge of the plateau to a ford over the Thames at Kingston. On the corner of Lingfield Road is the **Wimbledon Society Museum**, a local-history museum housed in the premises of the original village club and hall which were opened in 1859.

Cross over Ridgway here and turn left down Oldfield Road, a row of labourers' cottages dating from about 1820. Near the bottom go right into the passageway. This brings you out on Sunnyside Place. Here turn left and then, when the road comes to an end, carry on downhill via Sunnyside Passage. Both this and the previous passageway represent former footpaths leading from Wimbledon to the neighbouring village of Merton down in the valley. Sunnyside Passage brings you into Malcolm Road and Malcolm Road brings you to Worple Road. In a field a few hundred yards to the right of this point the Wimbledon croquet club was founded in 1868 and the first croquet championship held two years later. The new game of tennis was added in 1877, when the club was renamed the All England Croquet and Lawn Tennis Club. Later croquet was dropped and in 1920 the club bought its current site in the former Wimbledon Park. Cross straight over Worple Road and continue on into the next passage (lampstand at entrance). At the end, turn left, then right into Alt Grove. At the end of Alt Grove turn left along the path by the railway line and carry on until you reach the main road and station opposite, where the walk ends.

❖❖❖

MITCHAM

❖❖❖

Summary: This circular walk explores the former south London village of Mitcham, a place with an unusually varied history encompassing railways, cricket and industry on the River Wandle besides the more traditional churches, historic buildings and famous former residents. Featured on the walk are **Mitcham Cricket Club** and the green where the game has been played for over 300 years, The Canons, a 17th-century house now home to the **Merton Heritage Centre**, the parish church, the **Wandle Industrial Museum** and tranquil Ravensbury Park with the River Wandle flowing gently through it. Two Mitcham mills once powered by the Wandle are still in existence. One is glimpsed on the walk; the other can be seen by taking a short diversion. **Mitcham's annual fair** takes place every August on Mitcham Common.

Start and finish:	Mitcham station (mainline trains from Waterloo – change at Wimbledon, and from Victoria – change at Mitcham Junction). On Sundays there is no service at Mitcham, so travel from Victoria to Mitcham Junction and walk (approximately 1 mile/1.6km).
Length:	3 miles (4.8km)
Time:	2½ hours.
Refreshments:	Fish and chip shop, burger bar, café and Burn Bullock pub in London Road near the start and finish of the walk, and Enzo's café (mentioned in text) in Ravensbury Park towards the end. Otherwise wide choice of fast-food outlets in the Upper Green area of Mitcham off the walk route.

Come out of Mitcham station onto the London Road and turn right past the old station house with the arch in the middle. The railway arrived at Mitcham when the Wimbledon to Croydon line opened in 1855. The line made use of an earlier track that had been laid by the Surrey Iron Railway in 1803. Connecting Wandsworth with Croydon, this was the world's first public railway. Horses pulled wagons along the tracks and users paid fees at tollgates as on a turnpike road. The railway was intended mainly for commercial use and played a valuable part in promoting industrial development in the Wandle area south of Mitcham village in the early 19th century.

Cricket Green

Carry on up London Road towards the village centre. After a while you come to Cricket Green, formerly Lower Green East and the larger of the two open spaces that together make up the Lower Green and the historic heart of Mitcham. (The Upper Green a few hundred yards north of here is now the main shopping centre of the modern town of Mitcham.) All the historical landmarks in Mitcham are illustrated and described on the information panel across the road at the corner of the green.

The green itself, of course, is the Mitcham cricket pitch, one of the oldest such pitches in the country. For reasons that are not now clear, Mitcham emerged before 1700 as one of the great early centres of cricket. The game was played on the Cricket Green from at least 1685, and in 1707 the villagers challenged an All-London team to a match on Lamb's Conduit Fields in Holborn, which the rustics unfortunately lost. The first recorded match in Mitcham was played in 1711, and the game has thrived here ever since, making the village a shrine for devotees.

To both left and right are former coaching inns given handsome Georgian facelifts around 1750. The fact that both were modernized and enlarged about the same time is clear evidence of the growth of road traffic at this time. The one on the right was originally called the King's Head, but it was renamed in 1975 after Burn Bullock, the famous Mitcham cricketer who was a member of the local club from the age of 17 and landlord of the pub from 1941 until his death in 1954. Burn Bullock's wife Lil continued to run the pub until her retirement in 1975. Inside, the walls are covered with cricketing photographs.

Mitcham Cricket Club

Turn right by the pub. Behind the Georgian section you can clearly see the inn's original half-timbered part, certainly more than 300 and possibly as much as 400 years old. Beyond the pub is the pavilion of the Mitcham Cricket Club, with its verandah for watching play. Crossing the road to the pitch was a relatively easy matter when the pavilion was built in 1904. Now, with the great increase of traffic, it is infinitely more hazardous. Maybe it's just as well the clubhouse lease prevents the club from having its own bar!

Carry on along Cricket Green, passing Mary Tate's almshouses built in 1829 on the site of her family's Mitcham house. The Tates had several other houses elsewhere, including Burleigh Park in Northamptonshire where Miss Tate lived. She was the last of her line, hence this bequest. Just beyond the Queen's Head pub, cross the road to the obelisk on the north side. Mitcham went through several years of drought in the early 1820s. When an artesian spring suddenly appeared on this spot, locals took it for a miracle and the lord of the manor's son, the Reverend Richard Cranmer, commemorated the event with this monument, erected in September 1822.

The Cranmer family lived in The Cranmers, a large house to the right, off what is now Cranmer Road. Robert Cranmer, descendant of the 16th-century Archbishop Cranmer and a wealthy East India merchant, bought the Mitcham estate in 1656. It remained in his descendants' hands until shortly before World War II when the property was sold for development. The house was then demolished and replaced by a hospital.

Monastic estate

Continue past the obelisk into Madeira Road and then after a short time turn left through the gates of The Canons. In the Middle Ages four separate manors emerged in Mitcham, all belonging originally to the church. The most important, lying to the east of the village centre, was Mitcham Canons, a property of the Priory of St Mary Overie in Southwark. The monastic estate was administered from a manor house just to the east of Lower Green. In 1680 this ancient building was demolished and replaced by The Canons, now the Borough of Merton's Heritage Centre and local history museum. The Canons and Eagle House, a beautiful early 18th-century mansion just to the north of the Upper Green and unfortunately too far away to be included on the walk, are the only two of Mitcham's historic mansions to survive into modern times. Eagle House was built by court physician Fernando Mendez on land that once belonged to the great Sir Walter Raleigh.

Turn right down the side of the house to the back garden. Here you can see the carp pond and stone dovecote, dated 1511, belonging to the original medieval house. Turn left along the back of the house, and then right, along the garden wall. When you reach the car park you can see dead ahead of you a stone placed in the wall in 1816 by Mrs E. M. Cranmer to mark the eastern boundary of her property. Turn left along this wall and then right when you reach the playing fields.

The handsome Georgian mansion on the right now is Park House, built in 1780 for Francis Gregg, City lawyer and senior figure in the Skinners livery company. Gregg was also manager of the Earl of Carlisle's extensive estates in the north, and served as MP for one of the Earl's pocket boroughs in the 1790s. When you reach Mitcham Common, turn left along Commonside West and walk past the Windmill pub, which dates from about 1870 and recalls a former windmill. When you reach the lights, cross the road and walk along the path across the Common. Known as Three Kings Piece, this section of the common is the venue for Mitcham's annual August fair.

Five generations of Charts

At Commonside East, turn left past the row of cottages and the Three Kings pub. In front is a duck pond, at least 300 years old, fed by a covered-in stream running alongside Commonside. At the junction with the main road, the weatherboarded Clarendon House was at one time the home of the Chart family who were noted local builders and administrators. John Chart built the parish church in 1821. Five generations of Charts served in the local vestry and its successors. William Chart was appointed vestry clerk in 1761. His descendant, Colonel Stephen Chart, retired as town clerk in 1946.

At the traffic lights just beyond Clarendon House, cross the main road and turn left back along Commonside West. When you get to the lights where you turned onto the Common, turn right along Cold Blows, an aptly named footpath that once connected the village with the common fields on the far side of Commonside East. The path brings you back to Cricket Green and to some of the elegant houses overlooking it from the northeast side. Carry straight on across the Green towards the Victorian vestry hall, Mitcham's first town hall, designed by a Chart and built in 1887 on the site of the village lockup.

Cross London Road and pass between the vestry hall and the Wandle Industrial Museum on the right. In the 18th and 19th centuries Mitcham was well known for its Wandle-based industries and for its herbs. The Wandle mills turned out flour, paper, colourful calico cloth and tobacco products, particularly snuff and Mitcham 'shag'. The herb fields and distilleries produced lavender, camomile, wormwood, aniseed, liquorice and damask rose, and associated essential oils and waters. In 1805 the firm of Potter and Moore, which had pioneered industrial-scale lavender water distillation over half a century earlier, had at least 500 acres (200 ha) of medicinal and aromatic herbs under cultivation. No trace of the herb industry remains in Mitcham today, but the Ravensbury snuff mill and the Mitcham flour and paper mill (the latter glimpsed at the end of the walk) still stand on the Wandle.

Go straight across Lower Green West now, passing on your left the old village school topped with a cupola and clock tower. Built as a Sunday school for 150 children in 1788, it became a National day school in 1812 and then one of England's new elementary schools in 1870. From 1897 until 1987, when the church sold it, it served as the parish rooms. It has now been converted into flats and artists' studios.

14th-century chapel

As you continue into Church Road you pass a newer school on the left. At the entrance behind the fence you might just be able to make out a ruined arch. This is the only surviving portion of Hall Place, the manor house of Vauxhall, one of medieval Mitcham's three other manors besides Mitcham Canons. The now lonely arch was the entrance to the house's private chapel, constructed in 1349. Further along busy Church Road you come to the vicarage on the left and then the parish church of **St Peter and St Paul** on the right. Mitcham once had its traditional small medieval parish church, but it had to be replaced by this larger one in 1821 in order to accommodate the village's growing population.

Cross the road by the church into Church Path (to be on the safe side use the zebra crossing round the corner ahead). At the end of the row of cottages, continue on along the footpath, called Baron Path because it once led to Baron House, named after an 18th-century barrister occupant. Two centuries before Oliver Baron lived here, Queen Elizabeth I stayed in the house on two of the five visits she made to Mitcham in the 1590s. In those days Mitcham was highly regarded as a pleasant retreat from the teeming, insanitary streets of the capital. Elizabeth's favourite Sir Walter Raleigh owned property in Mitcham, and John Donne, the famous poet and dean of St Paul's, lived in the village from 1605 to 1611.

Ravensbury Park

Having crossed the railway line and reached the end of the path, turn right onto Morden Road and then, just beyond Morden Gardens, left into Ravensbury Park. Follow the path round to the right past Enzo's café and across one of the channels of the Wandle. At the toilets the path forks. The right one leads to the Ravensbury snuff mill, in production until 1925 but now converted into flats. The walk takes the left fork, passing on the right the site of the old manor house of Ravensbury Manor, one of medieval Mitcham's four separate manors. At the bridge an information panel recounts the history of the area and tells how the last owners of the estate before it was developed and part preserved as a public park were the Bidder family, descendants of an engineering associate of George Stephenson of Stephenson's *Rocket* fame.

Private bank

Carry on along the path beside the Wandle. Having crossed two small bridges you pass some houses on your left. Here, until 1846, stood Mitcham Grove, generally reckoned to have been the most beautiful of Mitcham's many secluded and gracious country houses. Between 1786 and his death in 1828, it was the home of Henry Hoare, senior partner of the private bank still flourishing in Fleet Street in the City and one of Mitcham's most public-spirited and generous residents. Hoare bought the house from Alexander Wedderburn, the lawyer and later Lord Chancellor, who in turn had been presented with it by Clive of India after successfully defending him against charges of corruption in the early 1770s.

The path brings you out on the London Road again. From the bridge on the right, the white Mitcham mill, where flour and paper were once produced, can be glimpsed a short distance upstream. The route of the walk, however, is to the left. Mitcham station, where the walk ends, is up ahead by the traffic lights.

❖❖

CARSHALTON

❖❖

Summary: This circular walk reveals the delights of Carshalton, a particularly attractive village on London's southern fringe. The village is centred on large ponds which form the more important of the two sources of the River Wandle. On the walk you see the ponds and the Wandle (which in the 18th century drove mills that made Carshalton a thriving industrial centre), the old parish church, the Borough of Sutton's heritage and ecology centres, the ecology centre's island nature reserve, two of the three large houses that dominated the village up to the 1890s and the third house's 18th-century park with grotto and cascade (the house itself no longer exists). It's worth trying to combine the walk with a separate visit to nearby **Little Holland House**, the arts and crafts house designed and furnished single-handed by Frank Dickinson, whose home it was until his death in 1961 (direction shown on map).

Start and finish: Carshalton station (mainline trains from Victoria).
Length: 2¾ miles (4.4km).
Time: 2¼ hours.
Refreshments: In the village centre there are pubs, sandwich bar and deli, bakery and coffee house, fish and chip shop, burger bar, Indian restaurant/take-away and wine bar. West of the church are the Greyhound Hotel and Heritage Centre tea room.

Come out of Carshalton station and turn right down the hill. At the bottom turn left into West Street and walk in the direction of the village. Traditional weatherboarded houses, painted white, are a feature of this part of Carshalton. Beyond the Racehorse pub (an allusion, perhaps, to the fact that the Derby is run on the Epsom Downs to the south of Carshalton), the park wall and the Water Tower of Carshalton House come into view. Just beyond the Water Tower a gate in the wall allows you a view of the house.

Carshalton House

When it was just a small country village, Carshalton was dominated by three large houses whose estates intruded right into the centre of the village. Here in the western part was **Carshalton House**, built around 1707 by Edward Carleton. After Carleton went bankrupt six years later, merchant Sir John Fellowes bought the house. But he encountered financial problems of his own when the South Sea Company, of which he was the head, collapsed after the bursting of the South Sea Bubble, one of the most notorious financial scandals in British history. Carshalton House was confiscated to compensate the victims of the scandal, but Fellowes' brother generously bought it back, paying twice the amount Sir John had given for it less than 10 years before. In possession once more, Sir John added the Water Tower to the mansion's amenities. Its prime purpose, achieved through a rooftop reservoir, was to supply water to the house – even to the upper floors – but it also contained an orangery, a changing room and a Delft-tiled plunge bath, one of the earliest in the country.

In 1850 the last of Carshalton House's private occupants was replaced by the Board of Ordnance, which used the mansion as a school for its military cadets. In 1892 the Daughters of the Cross arrived and opened St Philomena's girls' school. Over 100 years later the school is still here. Founded in Liège in 1833, the Daughters are a Roman Catholic organization and carry on the educational work of the convent of St Philomena.

Ecology Centre

Cross West Street at the gate into Carshalton House and walk along Festival Walk by the side of the dried-up watercourse. Long ago a stream from the chalk downs used to flow into a lake in the grounds of Carshalton House and thence down this

239

channel into the River Wandle. The Old Rectory on the left, built about the time of Queen Anne, like Carshalton House, and raised well up to protect it from flooding, was never the rectory as such, but the private home of a number of well-to-do rectors in the 18th century. The village's official rectory was in the High Street until it was pulled down to make way for a shopping precinct in the 1960s. The present rectory is a modern house up the hill behind the church. Since the 1930s the Old Rectory has been public property and is now used, along with the grounds of a large 19th-century house called The Lodge, as the **Sutton Ecology Centre**. The Centre's nature reserve is well worth a visit. Just outside the main entrance stands the tallest London plane tree in Britain (see the plaque at its base).

Festival Walk takes you past the Ecology Centre and brings you out at Carshalton's famous ponds, one of two major sources of the River Wandle. The other and less important source is at Waddon ponds, a few miles to the east near Croydon. The two streams originating from these sources come together at Hackbridge and then flow

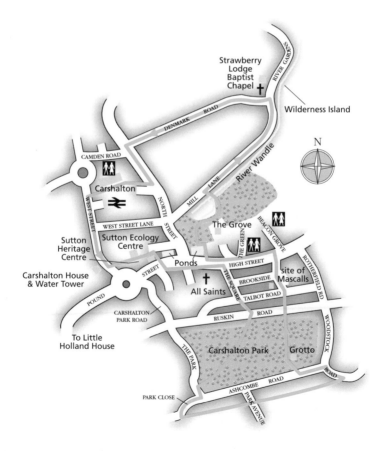

north towards the Thames at Wandsworth. Originally there was only one pond here, but the building of a causeway across the middle into North Street during the Middle Ages divided it into two. Since that time the near pond has been public property and the far one part of the Stone Court/Grove estate, of which more later. Natural springs gushing out of the chalk downs immediately behind the village used to fill the ponds, but now they have to be topped up from the mains because of a general lowering of the water table in the area. This geological change has also drained all Carshalton's other streams and ponds, streams and ponds that once made the village famous for its fresh trout and watercress.

Arts and crafts

The Lodge to your left was built in 1866 on what had been the orchard and kitchen garden of Stone Court. Ahead right is a fine view of the church and the High Street. Immediately to the right is Honeywood, a house dating from the 17th century and once the home of the 19th-century author and civil servant Mark Rutherford, real name William Hale White. White lived in several houses in the neighbourhood and, being a friend of William Morris and John Ruskin, eventually built himself an arts and crafts-inspired house in Park Hill. Honeywood was later bought by the council and in 1990 converted into the **Sutton Heritage Centre** and local history museum. (Coincidentally, a few doors up from White's Park Hill house there is another arts and crafts house – Little Holland House, the home of the 20th-century designer and craftsman Frank Dickinson – see map for directions.)

Anne Boleyn's Well

Turn right past the entrance to Honeywood (note the dry watercourse running under the house) and walk up to the main road. This is the east end of Pound Street: stray animals were kept in the village pound until collected by their owners. Ahead is the elegant Greyhound Hotel, Carshalton's oldest and principal inn. Cross the road to the hotel and turn left. Opposite the entrance to North Street is a disused well surrounded by railings at the foot of Church Hill, known locally as Anne Boleyn's Well. A modern statue of Queen Anne (she was Henry VIII's second wife) is set into the corner of the new house in Church Hill. Legend has it that Anne's horse kicked at a boulder here one day and in doing so brought forth a gushing spring. The rather less exciting truth is that in pre-Reformation days there was a little chapel here dedicated to Our Lady of Boulogne. Over time the name Boulogne simply became corrupted into Boleyn.

Monuments and stables

Pass to the right of the well and follow the raised path that leads past the entrance to the church. Medieval in origin, **All Saints** was enlarged to such an extent in the 1890s that the old nave was relegated to the status of a subsidiary chapel. Here is to be found the Purbeck marble tomb of Nicholas Gaynesford, sheriff of Surrey and the builder of the original Stone Court across the road by the easterly Carshalton pond. Many other old monuments, including those of Sir John Fellowes and Sir William Scawen, 17th-century lord of the manor of Carshalton, are also in the church.

Just beyond the church is one of the oldest buildings in Carshalton, an ancient butcher's shop, now a wine bar. Carry on past the shop, turn right into The Square and walk up past the library towards Carshalton Park, once the grounds of Mascalls, Carshalton's ancient manor house which was later renamed Carshalton Park. On the other side of the road is the remaining section of the Carshalton Park orangery, later used as stables. Before streets were built along the bottom side of Carshalton Park, The Square was a wide cul-de-sac, its top end closed off by the park wall and the stable entrance. Carry on up the road, cross Talbot Road into the path, cross Ruskin Road and enter Carshalton Park.

Squire of Carshalton

Having bought Carshalton Park in 1696, merchant Sir William Scawen planned to replace the ancient manor house of Mascalls with a brand new house. Unfortunately, he died before he was ready to start building. His nephew and heir managed to complete the 2-mile (3-km) park wall, the orangery and various other structures, but then the money ran out. So the great new house designed by Italian architect Giacomo Leonie was never built. The Scawens sold up in 1781 and were succeeded by the Taylors, a family of West Indian sugar planters and slave owners. The Taylors themselves sold up in 1895. Part of the park was then developed with housing and part – complete with some fine old trees – preserved as a public open space.

Ahead, the deep hole called the Hogpit started out before the Scawens' time as a chalk pit and was later excavated to form a deep pond, now dried up. Branch right up the hill, with the Hogpit on your left, and when the path stops continue straight on across the park. Exit opposite the hospital and turn left, occasionally glancing back for the views. At the top, before the road bends left, turn right into The Park cul-de-sac. Walk to the far end, continue on along the footpath and then turn left when you meet the track. This was formerly an old road that ran across the hill just outside the park wall. Large sections of the latter survive on the left-hand side. To the right, on top of the plateau, were the original common fields of Carshalton. Cross the first road you come to – Park Avenue – and continue on down into the low point. Then climb. At the end you will have to negotiate an overgrown section before finally emerging on Woodstock Road. Here turn left, and then left again, into Ashcombe Road and then right into the park once more.

The grotto

At this point you are right on top of the grotto, one of the park features built by Thomas Scawen in the 18th century. From the shell-covered grotto, which housed a source spring of the Wandle, water flowed down towards the High Street over a series of cascades, passing close by Mascalls near the bottom. Near where it joined the Wandle, the stream powered a mill forming part of the Carshalton Park estate. Nowadays the grotto is derelict and the canal dry, but the whole structure is still an impressive feature.

The Grove

Walk down the left-hand side of the canal under the avenue of trees. Exit the park crossing Ruskin Road and continue. Talbot Road crosses the canal by means of a handsome little balustraded bridge, possibly a feature of the gardens around Mascalls, for the old house stood just here on the left until 1927.

When you reach the High Street, turn left, cross at the traffic lights and continue. Opposite the Coach and Horses turn right through the gates into the grounds of The Grove. This is the third, and most central, of the three large houses that once dominated Carshalton village. Sheriff Nicholas Gaynesford built the first house on the site in the 15th century. Gaynesford's house was called Stone Court because it was built of stone and thus contrasted sharply with other houses in the village which were either chalk and flint, or brick. A later house was christened The Grove after a clump of trees in the grounds with a temple in the middle, cleared away during the 19th century. The present house, a Victorian–Edwardian hotchpotch, is largely the work of Sir Samuel Barrow, a wealthy tanner who owned the house between 1896 and 1923. The local authority bought it the following year and now uses it for offices.

Carshalton corn mill
Follow the path round to the left by the lake and then, before crossing the 18th-century bridge over the outflow, turn right, keeping the water on your left. Near the first bridge you come to once stood what was called the Upper Mill, the original Carshalton corn mill, which finally went out of service in the 1880s after at least 800 years of operation (there is a reference to it in the 11th-century Domesday Book). Barrow later used the mill's power source to drive electricity-generating turbines for his house.

At the second bridge, cross the Wandle and turn right into Mill Lane, the name reflecting the presence of many water mills in this industrial part of the village. From the late 17th century onwards, various entrepreneurs began to harness the Wandle's power to drive other kinds of mills in addition to the old village corn mill. Industrial milling reached its peak around 1800, when Carshalton's mills – producing flour, paper, leather, snuff, drugs, linseed oil, sheet copper and gunpowder – employed nearly 60 per cent of the local population. On the left Victorian mill workers' cottages still survive, but on the right the old mills, most of which ceased operation towards the end of the 19th century, have been cleared away and replaced by housing. Once heavily polluted, the Wandle now flows sweetly again.

Butter Hill
Continue along Mill Lane. Just before the railway bridge you pass one of the original bridges over the river leading into Butter Hill. The snuff mill driven by the grotto canal in Carshalton Park stood about halfway up the hill on the right. Carry on under the bridge to the entrance of Denmark Road. Ahead on the right you can see the signboard at the entrance to Wilderness Island, a 6-acre (2.5-ha) nature reserve bordered by the Wandle and run by the Ecology Centre. Long before the railway arrived in 1868, the land covered by the reserve formed part of the rather larger Shepley estate, an industrial area first developed by early industrialist and gunpowder-maker Josias Dewye in 1692. Dewye lived across the road in a large house rebuilt in the 18th century as Strawberry Lodge. This still stands opposite the reserve entrance and now, comprehensively restored, belongs to the Baptist Church.

Turn left now into Denmark Road. Follow this round to the end and then turn left into North Street. Go under the railway line and then right up the incline to the station entrance, where the walk ends.

◆◆

DULWICH

◆◆

Summary: Set in woods, parks and playing fields, semi-rural Dulwich in south London has been carefully preserved by the major landowner in the area, the Dulwich College Estate. On the walk you will see old Dulwich College (17th-century almshouses and chapel) and new Dulwich College (Victorian public school), the **Dulwich Picture Gallery** (England's oldest public art gallery), 18th-century cottages, shops and mansions, Dulwich tollgate, Dulwich Park and the Sydenham Hill Woods nature reserve, one of the closest wildlife reserves to central London.

Start:	West Dulwich station (mainline trains from Victoria).
Finish:	North Dulwich station (mainline trains from London Bridge).
Length:	3½ miles (5.6km).
Time:	2 hours.
Refreshments:	Nowhere to stop until you get to the Dulwich Wood House pub on Sydenham Hill, about halfway round and at the end of a fairly steep climb. Further on there is another pub at the bottom of the hill, cafés in Dulwich Park and at Dulwich Picture Gallery, and more pubs in Dulwich Village.

Come out of West Dulwich station onto Thurlow Park Road and turn right, away from the traffic lights. Walk past the entrances to Gallery Road on the left and Alleyn Park on the right into Dulwich Common. This road used to run across the common ground of Dulwich Manor until, in the 19th century, the common was enclosed and divided up. In 1870, 40 acres (16 ha) were used for the new buildings and playing fields of Dulwich College, which you can see on your right. Dulwich College was originally founded in 1619 as a school and almshouse by Dulwich's childless lord of the manor, a wealthy actor and friend of Shakespeare called Edward Alleyn (pronounced Allen). The initial educational provision was for 12 poor boys, but in the 19th century the school expanded into a leading public school. The original College buildings still stand in the centre of Dulwich and you see them later in the walk.

Bears, bulls and mastiff dogs

The left-hand side of Dulwich Common is lined with old houses. The fifth house along, Old Blew House, is supposed to be the oldest house in Dulwich, though it was obviously refaced in the 18th century. Alleyn, who owned most of the land in Dulwich having bought the estate in 1605 with the proceeds of his acting, his successful business ventures and the fees from his lucrative post of Master of the Royal Game of Bears, Bulls and Mastiff Dogs, owned the house and donated it to his native parish, St Botolph Bishopsgate in the City, for the benefit of its poor.

When you get to the crossroads turn right into College Road and cross over by the pond. Continue along College Road until you come to Pond Cottages, a row of 18th-century cottages once lived in by farmworkers and mill-hands. The central pair are covered in black weatherboard, once a common style of building in Dulwich. The school physical education centre is at the end of the lane.

Continue along College Road past the school buildings and more playing fields and tennis courts. After a while you come to the Dulwich tollgate: the money

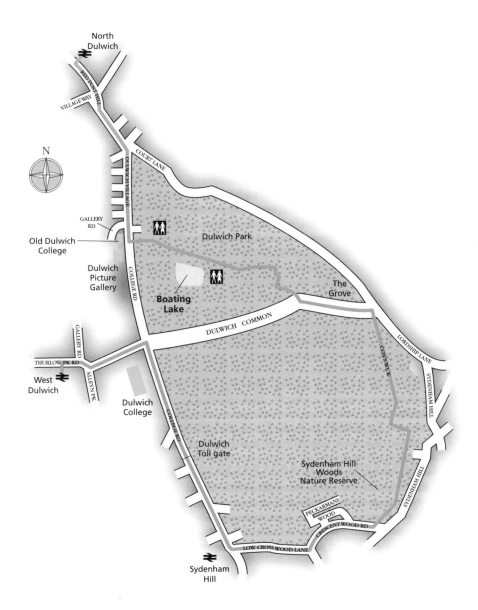

collected from motorists is used to pay for the upkeep of College Road, which is privately owned by the College Estate. Tollgates (or turnpikes, as they were called) were once a common sight in England, but most of them disappeared in the 1860s when local councils took over road maintenance from the turnpike owners. Dulwich tollgate is the only one left in London and raises some £17,000 a year.

Go past the gate and continue along College Road up the hill. After a while the white posts by the roadside start again and you come to Sydenham Hill station. Directly opposite, turn left through the wicket gate into Low Cross Wood Lane. A steep climb brings you to the summit of the hill and the Dulwich Wood House pub. Turn left here along Crescent Wood Road. When you get to the last of the modern houses on the left (No. 65), turn into Peckarmans Wood leading round behind them for a panorama over central London, 5 miles (8 km) away. In summer, much of it is obscured by trees, but on a clear day you can still make out **St Paul's Cathedral** and the International Financial Centre in the City, and Canary Wharf Tower in Docklands.

Ancient woodland

Retrace your steps back to the road. Turn left and then immediately left again and go through the gate into Sydenham Hill Woods nature reserve. Follow the path down the slope to the noticeboard. Managed by the London Wildlife Trust, the reserve is based on an ancient wood and incorporates a disused railway cutting, last used in 1954, and the ruins of several 19th-century houses, demolished in the 1960s. Take the right fork at the noticeboard (the walk is aiming for point 7 on the noticeboard map – the noticeboard is at point 1). Point 2 is in the middle of the site of an old tennis court. Point 3 is marked by a Lebanese cedar. The ruin at point 4 has been designed to look like the remains of a Gothic abbey. Turn right here and right again at the fork (go left if you want to go down to the pond – in which case go right round the pond and then rejoin the path). Pass point 8 and on the left now you can see the railway cutting. Walk straight ahead, go down the bank, cross the footbridge over the cutting where Impressionist Camille Pissarro once set up his easel, and turn right into Cox's Walk. Over to the left of you is Dulwich and Sydenham Hill golf course.

Cox's Walk brings you to the junction of Dulwich Common and Lordship Lane. The Grove pub is on the corner. There has been a pub here for nearly 300 years. In 1704 it was called the Green Man and the innkeeper was John Cox. Under his son's management, water from a well in the garden, which was found to have medicinal properties, was developed into a fashionable local spa called Dulwich Wells. Later the inn was converted by Dr Glennie into a school for young gentlemen. The doctor's most famous pupil was the poet Lord Byron, who spent two years here while a London specialist treated his club foot. Byron left the school in 1801 to go to Harrow.

Polish national gallery

Cross over to the other side of Dulwich Common and turn left. Walk along beside the modern flats and just beyond the end turn right through Rosebery Gate into Dulwich Park. Follow the road round to the left and then take the first path on the right into the inner ring. Turn left (there should be a small pavilion to the right) and then left again into the main path going through the middle of the park towards the children's playground and bowling green. In this part of the park there is also a café, an aviary and a boating lake.

Continue past the café along the right-hand side of the lake and then go straight on along the car road to Old College Gate with the old college ahead of you. To the left is the Dulwich Picture Gallery, set back from the road in its own grounds. When Alleyn died in 1626 he left the college some pictures, but not enough to warrant a purpose-built gallery. In 1811, at the suggestion of one of the college fellows, the landscape painter Sir Francis Bourgeois left the college another 370 pictures, including many first-class works collected for an unrealized national gallery in Poland. Architect Sir John Soane was commissioned to design a gallery for the pictures, which became the first public picture gallery in England.

Return to Old College Gate and walk to the right towards Dulwich Village along the right-hand side of the road. The old college on the left is grouped around three sides of a square, the fourth being open towards the fountain that marks the junction of three roads: College Road, Gallery Road, and ahead, Dulwich Village. If you look back into the courtyard of the college, the end wing is the chapel, the right-hand side the offices of the College Estate, and the left-hand side the present-day almshouse providing 16 homes, four more than Alleyn initially provided for. At the beginning of Gallery Road is the 19th-century schoolhouse designed by Charles Barry, architect of the Houses of Parliament.

Georgian suburb

Next to the fountain is a triangular milestone, dated 1772, giving distances to both the Treasury in Whitehall and to the Standard in Cornhill – 5 miles (8km) in each case. This was useful information for the kind of people (civil servants, lawyers, City merchants and bankers) who were the first occupants of the fine Georgian houses that continue in a virtually unbroken line along the right-hand side of the village street from this point. The other side of the street was (and still is) reserved for the village shopkeepers and tradesmen.

Walk straight along Dulwich Village as far as the old burial ground in the triangle that is formed by the junction of Court Lane and Dulwich Village. Alleyn gave it to the village in 1616, when the village had no church or graveyard of its own, and it was used until 1858. Dulwich's 35 victims of the 1665 Great Plague are buried here.

Continue along Dulwich Village past a row of modern shops and then the parish hall. At the junction with Village Way, with Lyndenhurst (1757) on the corner and Pond House (1739) to the left of it, cross over into Red Post Hill. The walk ends at North Dulwich station on the right.

❖❖❖

GREENWICH

❖❖❖

Summary: This is a circular walk around the Georgian riverside town of Greenwich in east London. Greenwich is famous for the old royal palace and park, the **Old Royal Observatory** and the Greenwich meridian, as well as the concentration of maritime history in the shape of the **National Maritime**

Museum and the **Cutty Sark** and *Gypsy Moth IV*. From a steep hill behind the town there are panoramic views of Greenwich, the Isle of Dogs, the River Thames, and the Millennium Dome. Greenwich is a World Heritage site.

Start and finish:	Island Gardens station (Docklands Light Rail). Greenwich Pier (riverboats from Westminster and other central London piers) and Greenwich station (mainline trains from Charing Cross) are possible alternative approaches.
Length:	3½ miles (5.6km).
Time:	2½ hours.
Refreshments:	Plenty of pubs and restaurants (especially fish restaurants) in Greenwich itself. Otherwise try the riverside pubs (particularly the Cutty Sark on Ballast Quay which you pass towards the end of the walk) or the café halfway round the walk in Greenwich Park. There is also a basic open-air café across the river from Greenwich in Island Gardens where the walk starts and finishes.

Turn right and left out of Island Gardens Station into Ferry Street, left again into Saunders Ness Road and then right into Island Gardens. From here there is a classic view of Greenwich on the opposite side of the river. From left to right the riverside features visible are: the four-chimneyed electricity generating station for London's Underground system; **Trinity Hospital** (all white); the Trafalgar Tavern (light brown); the Old Royal Naval College with the **Queen's House** in the middle and the park beyond; the masts and rigging of the *Cutty Sark*; the dome of the Greenwich foot tunnel (to match the one to your right); the diminutive form of the round-the-world-yacht *Gypsy Moth IV*; and, finally, the waterfront at Deptford, where Henry VIII established the first royal dockyard.

The Old Royal Naval College and the Queen's House were originally part of a huge new royal palace begun by the Stuarts in the 1600s to replace the rambling old Tudor palace dating from the 1400s. The Queen's House was built first, then came the riverside section, divided into blocks to preserve the view from the Queen's House. During building, which spanned a century, royal plans for Greenwich changed and the palace-to-be became a royal almshouse for aged or disabled seamen equivalent to the soldiers' hospital at Chelsea. The 19th century saw the hospital buildings taken over by the Old Royal Naval College and the Queen's House by a school for sailors' orphans. The Queen's House, with colonnades and wings added, now belongs to the National Maritime Museum, while the former college buildings are divided between Greenwich University and Trinity College of Music.

Maritime history
Enter the dome to your right and use the foot tunnel to cross the river to Greenwich. The tunnel was opened in 1902 for dockers employed in the West India Docks on the Isle of Dogs behind you. You emerge from the tunnel on a riverside plaza with the *Cutty Sark* straight ahead and *Gypsy Moth IV* to your right. The *Cutty Sark* was built in 1869 for the China tea-trade but really made her name freighting wool from Australia. She was the fastest clipper of them all and on a good day could

cover over 350 miles (563km). The *Gypsy Moth IV* was the yacht in which 65-year-old Sir Francis Chichester completed the then fastest solo circumnavigation of the world in 1966–67.

The old town centre of Greenwich and **St Alfege's Church** are straight ahead of the tunnel entrance. Aim for the church. When you get to the main road (Cutty Sark Station on the right) turn left and then cross over (using the traffic lights at the end of the road if necessary) to get into Greenwich market. As you go through the arch into the covered courtyard, built in 1831, look up and behind you to see the admonition to the market traders: 'A false balance is abomination to the Lord but a just weight is his delight.' The old food market no longer functions but there is an arts and crafts market here at weekends.

Leave the market through the corresponding arch at the far end and turn right on Nelson Road. Turn left in front of St Alfege's Church into Greenwich High Road. Alfege was an 11th-century Archbishop of Canterbury who was brought to Greenwich by Danish invaders and murdered on the site of the church in 1012. King Henry VIII was baptized in the old church. The present church was the first to be built under a new church building act of 1712.

Beyond the church, turn left into Stockwell Street. On the corner of Nevada Street opposite Ye Olde Rose and Crown pub there is a fine example of an old coaching inn in something like its original state. To the left of the yard, on the restaurant, there is a painted sign that gives you some information about the old inn, and also the Stock Well.

Civil rights for children
Continue on into Crooms Hill. On the left is the old Greenwich Theatre. Then follow a terrace of houses built in 1702 with a bequest from a local benefactor, John Roan, Yeoman of His Majesty's Harriers (died 1644). The idea was that the houses would generate an income to educate 'poor town-borne children of East Greenwich … until the age of fifteen years'. The owners of the houses, although freeholders, still pay their annual £1.34 (or thereabouts) to the John Roan Secondary School in Maze Hill. Opposite this terrace there is another one composed of rather grander Georgian houses. The two at the top house the **Fan Museum**.

Further along on the right, on the corner of the entrance to Gloucester Circus, there is a plaque to Benjamin Waugh, ex-congregationalist minister and founder, in 1888, of the National Society for the Prevention of Cruelty to Children. Almost singlehandedly, Waugh conceived the idea of civil rights for children and in 1889 got an act of Parliament passed that meant that children who were maltreated by their parents could be taken into protective custody.

From this point Crooms Hill runs up the steep hill alongside **Greenwich Park**. Elsewhere a high brick wall surrounds the park, but here the wall has been replaced by railings so that the houses have a view into the park. Sir William Hooker's gazebo on the right was obviously built while the wall was still *in situ* so that he could see over it into the park. Just inside the park here is an old conduit house, part of the original water supply for Greenwich Palace.

Beyond the Catholic church, branch right up the cobbled path on the other side of the green. St Ursula's Convent School is on the right now and the beginnings of Blackheath lie ahead. Turn left along the gravel road leading away from the school entrance. When you get to the tarmac road look back at the view across south London. In the centre, about 6 miles (9km) away, you can see disused Battersea Power Station, with its four distinctive chimneys. Cross over to the large house with the bricked-up windows and the postbox by the front door. This is Macartney House, where General Wolfe lived in the 18th century. Aged only 32, Wolfe captured Quebec by leading his army up steep cliffs above the St Lawrence River and then launching a surprise attack on the French garrison. He was killed in the attack and later buried in St Alfege's Church.

Turn right along the lime avenue planted to commemorate the Queen's Silver Jubilee in 1977. After a while you come to Ranger's House, formerly the official residence of the Ranger of Greenwich Park. In the distance, opposite the house, you can see the aerial of the Crystal Palace television transmitter, about 5 miles (8km) away. Further round to the right, the view is of the tower blocks of south London and the London Eye near Westminster Bridge.

London panorama

Continue along the avenue and turn left round the corner of the park wall. You can now see the full extent of Blackheath, a windy plateau crossed by the main road from London to Canterbury and Dover. Blackheath village is on the far side. Follow the park wall past the pond on the right (relic of gravel digging) to the gate in the middle and turn left into the central avenue. Turn right through the small gate in the railings and go into the park's flower garden. On the right is a huge sweet chestnut, planted as long ago as the 1660s. Follow the path round between the lake on the left and the deer enclosure on the right. Just before the path dips into a hollow, turn right and then left along the side of the main lawn area, which is dotted with flower beds and trees. Go through the gate at the end of the path and cross over to the bandstand. Turn left along the roadway and then at the crossroads turn right along the central avenue, past the Planetarium. Aim for the statue of General Wolfe silhouetted against the sky at the far end.

The view from the statue is stupendous. Away to the left are the tower blocks of the City. **St Paul's Cathedral** is plainly visible, but the tallest building is the International Financial Centre. The squat structure to the left of the tower is the new Lloyd's building. Ahead are the cranes and new buildings in the old docklands on the Isle of Dogs, dominated by Canary Wharf Tower, at 800 feet (244m) Britain's tallest building. Over 100 feet (30m) below is the Queen's House and the National Maritime Museum and, on the riverside, the Old Royal Naval College. To the right are Greenwich Power Station and the Millennium Dome.

On the left is the Old Royal Observatory. Charles II commissioned it in 1675 for 'the finding out of the longitude of places for perfecting navigation and astronomy'. The royal astronomers started by fixing the meridian here, where they were working. Denoted by a brass strip set in the ground, you can see it running through the cobbled courtyard and down the wall outside. Although the Royal Observatory did not succeed in its main longitude quest, over the next couple of centuries the majority of the world's navigation charts came to be based on the Greenwich Meridian, and Greenwich Mean Time was accepted as the international standard in 1884. The Royal Observatory's telescopes are now stationed in the Canaries.

Take the path behind you, leading away from the observatory and Wolfe's statue. After passing the 800-year-old Queen Elizabeth's Oak, a casualty to the gales of recent years, you eventually come to the gate on the east side of the park. Just outside the park on the edge of Maze Hill is Vanbrugh House, an extraordinary building complete with turrets and towers and castle-type battlements. The house was designed by and for Sir John Vanbrugh, around 1720 when he was appointed architect to Greenwich Hospital, and is now divided into flats.

Turn left past the house and go down to the bottom of Maze Hill, passing the entrance to Maze Hill station. Cross the main road (Trafalgar Road) into Hoskins Street. Walk straight down to Old Woolwich Road and turn right. Follow this for some way until you get to Hadrian Street and turn left. At the end turn left again into Pelton Road and walk down to the end to join the riverside walk extending left and right in both directions. To the right, the Thames Path leads along a still-working section of the river to the Thames Barrier.

Turn left past the old Harbour Master's office and walk along Ballast Quay. Round the corner is the Cutty Sark pub with fine views of the river, especially of Blackwall Reach and the Millennium Dome to the right. At the end of the quay continue straight on where the path narrows. Round the corner the path broadens out again on the quay in front of the electricity generating station. Once again you are standing on the meridian line.

Greenwich reclaimed

Beyond the power station is Trinity Hospital, an almshouse for retired Greenwich men, which was founded under the will of Henry Howard, Earl of Northampton, who died in 1614. Northampton was brought up at Greenwich and after Queen Elizabeth's death in 1603 bought the manor and Greenwich Castle. He was bitterly disappointed when James I reclaimed Greenwich as a royal possession, settling it on his queen, Anne of Denmark, for whom Inigo Jones then built the Queen's House. Compared with its giant power station neighbour Trinity Hospital is tiny, but it has an enormous garden which stretches right back to Old Woolwich Road. Stones in the wall opposite the entrance record exceptionally high tides on the Thames.

From the hospital, continue on into narrow Crane Street behind the Trafalgar Tavern, opened in 1837. Turn right, round the corner of the pub, and then left along the terrace in front of the Old Royal Naval College. Further along, the path rejoins the pier. If you want to see the college's famous Painted Hall and Chapel, the entrance is on the left through the visitor centre. To finish the walk, return to Island Gardens Station via the foot tunnel (or, to avoid the tunnel, cross the piazza to Cutty Sark Station).

❖❖

BLACKHEATH

❖❖

Summary: A circular walk round the south London village of Blackheath, on the south side of Blackheath itself, directly opposite Greenwich. The energetic could easily do the Greenwich and Blackheath walks in one day. Blackheath is one of those places – like Wimbledon and Monken Hadley – that was discovered at an early date by wealthy Londoners seeking healthy situations for country residences. As a result it boasts some of the finest Georgian architecture in London, particularly the Cator estate and the Paragon, both seen on the walk. Other sights, besides the 'black' heath itself, include **All Saints Church**, the 1695 Morden College almshouse, said to be the work of Sir Christopher Wren, Pagoda House where the notorious Queen Caroline is reputed to have conducted her affairs, and the grave where astronomer Edmond Halley of Comet fame is laid to rest.

Start and finish: Blackheath station (mainline trains from Charing Cross).
Length: 3 miles (4.8km).
Time: 2½ hours.

Refreshments: Plenty of pubs, bars, take-aways and restaurants (including Indian, Italian and French) in Tranquil Vale and Montpelier Vale in the village centre. Otherwise try the Hare and Billet and Princess of Wales pubs on the heath, the first just after the beginning of the walk and the second near the end.

Turn left out of the station and walk through the centre of Blackheath village. When the road divides in front of the triangle, bear left into Tranquil Vale and walk up the hill. Compared with most other London villages, Blackheath is a relatively modern phenomenon. It started out just here as a small hamlet consisting of a few cottages, a public well called Queen Elizabeth's Well (its site is in Tranquil Passage which runs through the middle of the triangle) and the Crown pub, which you soon come to on the corner of Camden Row. In the early days the hamlet was known as Blount's Hole after the owners of the neighbouring big house, Wricklemarsh. Sir John and Lady Morden bought Wricklemarsh from the Blounts in 1669. During Lady Morden's long widowhood in the early 18th century, Blount's Hole acquired the equally unflattering name of Dowager's Bottom! Blackheath village gradually expanded as more and more houses were built around the heath from the 1690s onwards. Development really took off in the 19th century when the Kid Brook was covered over and the railway laid on top. Blackheath station opened in 1849.

The little village grew up at the point where four roads crossed the Kid Brook, two heading south towards Lee and Lewisham, and two heading north to link up with the main road across the heath connecting London and Dover. Tranquil Vale was the road leading towards London; its sister, Montpelier Vale, headed off towards Dover. Continue along Tranquil Vale past the entrance to Camden Row and the well-known Mary Evans Picture Library and you come out on the southern edge of Blackheath. Some say the heath's name comes from its black, barren soil, but it is more probably a corruption of 'bleak'. Certainly the heath, a treeless plateau 125 feet (38m) above sea level, is empty and windswept enough today. In the days when it was covered with gorse and scrub and infested with highwaymen and footpads it must have been truly forbidding. The heath originated as waste or common land for the inhabitants of the four neighbouring manors of Lewisham, Greenwich, Charlton and Kidbrooke.

To the right now is the parish church of All Saints, built in the mid-19th century when the new village had grown to the point when it merited its own place of worship. Ahead is a cluster of buildings in the middle of the heath, hiding what is known as Blackheath Vale. The Vale is actually a huge pit dug in the days when Blackheath was an important source of sand and gravel. After World War II most of the pits were filled in with bomb rubble, but not the Vale, which had long since been colonized by cottages, a livery stable, a school and even a brewery. Today only the houses and the school survive.

City merchant
Walk on up the hill. At the top you come to a handsome semicircle of houses composed of Lloyd's Place, Grote's Buildings and Grote's Place. Lloyd's Place was built in the 1770s by John Lamb and takes its name from John Lloyd, a resident of No. 3 in the 1780s. Grote's Buildings and Place were a largely speculative development by

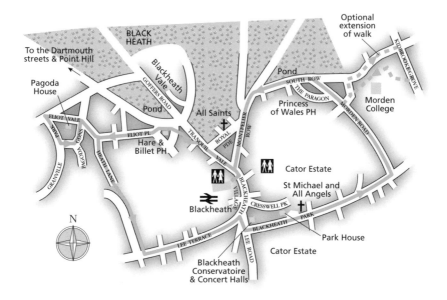

City merchant Andrew Grote in the 1760s. The land belonged to Morden College, which wanted to create a fund for paying its chaplain. Grote built Lindsey House – the red-brick detached house behind the trees at the left end – for himself and then sold the other, terraced, houses to recoup his investment. All these houses enjoy fine views across the heath to All Saints Church and South Row and, beyond, to the houses along Shooters Hill Road and the spire of St John's Church.

Walk straight on across the green towards the clump of trees surrounding the Hare and Billet pond, probably an old gravel pit. As you pass between the pond and the pub you see to the right the roofs of the houses in Blackheath Vale. Straight ahead in the distance are houses built on the west side of the heath in the second half of the 18th century. The most prominent one – white stucco with a pitched roof – is actually a pair and dates from 1776. Near these houses, close to Greeenwich and the London Road, are Dartmouth Row and neighbouring streets, laid out by Lord Dartmouth, lord of the manor of Lewisham, in the 1690s and the first streets to be developed in the Blackheath area.

Turn left at the pub and cut across past Eliot Cottages to Eliot Place. The houses here were built between 1795 and 1802 on land belonging to the Eliot family, Earls of St Germans (hence St Germans House at No. 11). The central house, No. 6, is perhaps the most handsome. Built in 1797, five years later it became the home and private observatory of merchant and amateur astronomer Stephen Groombridge. Now Morden College almshouse uses it for out-pensioners. The last house in the terrace, No. 2, was the home of naval officer and polar explorer Sir James Clark Ross, after whom Ross Island and Ross Sea off Antarctica are named. Next door is the grand Heathfield House, built for Rotherhithe shipowner John Brent. The earliest and grandest house in Eliot Place, it has now been given a modern extension and divided up into flats.

Pagoda House

Go straight on down the hill into Eliot Vale and then up the far side, following the road round to the right. As you cross the entrance to Pagoda Gardens look left and you will see the house with the curly roof that gives the road its name. Standing by the pillar box, you can see away to the right on the other side of the heath a red-brick house called **Ranger's House**. Next to it used to stand another mansion called Montagu House. Montagu House's grounds were mainly on this side of the heath, laid out on the south-facing slope of the hill, and the 18th-century Pagoda House was a kind of summer house. When the Prince Regent's notorious wife Caroline was living at Montagu House in the early 19th century she was a regular user of Pagoda House. It was here that she was rumoured to have conducted her affairs and housed her illegitimate children. In reality she probably got up to nothing more suspicious than overseeing her little nursery school and tending her garden. The Regent, later George IV, had Montagu House knocked down in 1815 and divorced Caroline five years later.

Follow the road round to the left past Aberdeen Terrace, which consists of large 19th-century houses built on land once belonging to the Pagoda. When the Terrace turns left, keep going and on the far side of the green, behind the bushes, turn left down Granville Park. When you get to Pagoda Gardens turn left and then at the T-junction turn left again. Now you have a close-up view of Pagoda House.

Quaggy valley

Back on Eliot Vale, turn right and then a little further on right again into Heath Lane. Passing Eliot Vale House on the left and turning into a footpath, this goes down the hill into the former valley of the Kid Brook, crosses the railway line and the old course of the river and then climbs up the far side to meet Lee Terrace, the road connecting Blackheath (to your left) with Lewisham (to your right). Some distance ahead, down in the valley of the Quaggy river, lies Lee. The church here, St Margaret's, is Lee's new parish church, built in 1841. The ruins of the original one stand in the closed graveyard 100 yards (90m) or so to the right. Astronomer Edmond Halley, of Halley's Comet fame, is buried here.

Turn left on Lee Terrace and head back towards Blackheath, passing some fine 19th-century houses and some less impressive 20th-century infilling. As you pass Dacre Park there is a good view to the right over the Quaggy valley.

The Cator Estate

You arrive back in the village at the point where Lee Terrace meets Lee Road coming in from the right. Cross over to the partly ivy-covered Blackheath Conservatoire (founded 1881) and turn right. Immediately beyond the Concert Halls turn left through the gates into Blackheath Park and the Cator Estate. With the exception of Kidbrooke Grove near Morden College and the fine houses round the heath, the Cator Estate was, and indeed still is, the most select part of Blackheath village.

The old name for the Cator Estate was Wricklemarsh and it was as such that the Blounts and then the Mordens owned it. After Lady Morden's death in 1721, Wricklemarsh was bought by Sir Gregory Page. One of the few people to escape from the 1720 South Sea Bubble scandal with his fortune intact, Page demolished the old Tudor house and built a vast new one on the heights overlooking the Kid valley. It was all in vain, however, for his nephew and heir, who found his uncle's house far too large, promptly sold it to Beckenham timber merchant John Cator. Cator auctioned off the fabric of the house and developed the northern fringe of the estate beside the heath into what is now Montpelier Row, South Row and The Paragon. Building on the interior of the estate started a little later and continued over a considerable period of time.

Laid out along the crest of the ridge dividing the valleys of the Kid and the Quaggy rivers, Blackheath Park is the main thoroughfare of the estate and the location of some of its earliest and finest houses. The row on the left starting at No. 7, for example, dates from about 1806 when street development started. Just beyond it is a wooden fence atop a low brick wall. Behind here, set well back in a large garden, is the earliest and finest house on the estate, a silvery stone mansion constructed in 1788 with materials salvaged from Sir Gregory Page's house. Since the end of the 19th century it has belonged to the Catholic Church.

Now comes a row of three pretty detached villas and then St Michael and All Angels Church, built in 1828. The junction of Blackheath Park with Pond Road next to the church marks the site of the great house built by Sir Gregory Page in the 1720s. From its hilltop site it had wonderful views north over the heath to Greenwich and south over the Quaggy valley.

Gounod's plaque
Carry on along Blackheath Park and then near the end, turn left into Morden Road. No. 17 just beyond The Plantation on the right has a blue plaque on it recording the stay of French composer Charles Gounod in October 1857. At the end of Morden Road you leave the Cator Estate by another set of gates and return to the heath. To the right is Morden College, the almshouse founded in 1695 by childless Sir John Morden of Wricklemarsh for fellow merchants of the Turkey Company. Said to have been designed by Sir Christopher Wren and built in spacious landscaped grounds on a knoll overlooking the Kid Brook, the College – much expanded – is still in operation today. It is not very easy to see the actual College building from this point, but a better view can be obtained from the footpath (see dotted line on map) which starts to your right at the end of the green railings and runs all the way through the College grounds.

The Paragon
Walk straight on up the hill onto the heath. To your right is St German's Place. Ahead you can see **Greenwich Park** and the Canary Wharf Tower beyond. To your left is The Paragon, the first section of the line of houses built along the northern perimeter of the Cator Estate from 1795 onwards. As its immodest name suggests, The Paragon is the finest Georgian set piece in Blackheath and one of the finest of its period anywhere in London. As you walk past you will see that it is composed of seven blocks linked by colonnades forming a crescent facing northeast across the heath towards St German's Place. The blocks were designed, as were South Row and Montpelier Row which follow, by surveyor Michael Searles. Each block contained two houses so there was a total of 14 residences in all. Unfortunately they were very badly damaged during World War II. However, afterwards they were acquired by a responsible developer who regarded their restoration as something of a personal crusade. The original 14 houses are now split up into 100 flats.

Colonnade House

South Row continues the Cator Estate perimeter development. Cator Manor, the first house, is not an old manor house but a neo-Georgian house built on the site of outbuildings blitzed during World War II. Pond Road, named after the remnant of an ornamental lake that existed up until 1955, is the old drive up to Sir Gregory Page's Wricklemarsh. Beyond Pond Road more modern housing replaces another section of South Row destroyed during World War II. Then comes Colonnade House, built in 1804 for William Randall, shipbuilding partner of John Brent whom we encountered earlier at Heathfield House. Brent, Randall and a third partner made a fortune building warships at the time of the Revolutionary Wars with France.

At the end of South Row you come to the Princess of Wales pub (named after George IV's wife Caroline, who was never actually crowned). A plaque on the front records the fact that it was here in 1871 that the English team for the first-ever rugby international was selected. The team included four players from Blackheath Rugby Club, one of the oldest in the country.

Blackheath has always been used for sport. Golf was played here from early times, the old sand and gravel pits making excellent bunkers. James I (James VI of Scotland, which is the 'home' of golf) is said to have introduced the sport to the area while staying at Greenwich Palace in the early 17th century. The local club, in existence by the 1780s, later developed into the Royal Blackheath Golf Club and is now generally regarded as the oldest in England. Since 1923 it has been based at Eltham.

Round the corner from the Princess of Wales pub, South Row turns into Montpelier Row. At the far end of the Row you return to the centre of the village. Follow Montpelier Vale down the hill to the junction with Tranquil Vale and make your way back to the station, where the walk ends.

❖❖

BEXLEY

❖❖

Summary: Bexley is a pretty little village literally on the edge of southeast London. One side is built up; the other is meadow and woodland. This circular walk begins in the village centre, with its historic cricket club, 18th-century almshouse and workhouse, handsome Georgian village houses and ancient church and manor house. It then moves on, via woodland and the River Cray, to **Hall Place**, a lovely old Tudor mansion set in immaculate grounds and home to the Bexley Local History Museum. From Hall Place, where there are toilets and a café, it's only a short walk back to the village via Bourne Road.

Start and finish: Bexley station (mainline trains from Charing Cross).
Length: 3¼ miles (5.2km).
Time: 2½ hours.

Refreshments: Hall Place at the furthest extremity of the walk has a café and pub-restaurant and is the obvious place to stop. Otherwise Bexley High Street at the start and finish of the walk has a 16th-century pub, various restaurants (Chinese, Italian, Greek, Indian), fish and chip shop, tearooms and sandwich bar, wine bar and brasserie, Bexley bakery and Old Mill pub-restaurant. Towards the end of the walk, Dennis the Butcher in Bourne Road makes award-winning pies.

Turn right out of the station and follow Station Approach down the hill to the junction with the High Street. Turn right and then immediately right again into Tanyard Lane. This takes you through the former tanning yard and under the railway line into the riverside meadowland. Across the meadows you can see the backs of some of the houses in North Cray Road. Follow the path until you reach **Bexley Cricket Club**. Founded by 1746, the club is one of the oldest in Kent and has been based at this pitch since about 1840. Match scores survive from 1802. The most celebrated match in club history took place in 1805, the year of the Battle of Trafalgar, when humble Bexley dismissed the great county of Kent for only six runs.

Turn right at the car park and go back under the railway line into Manor Way. When you reach Hurst Road cross slightly to the left and go into a footpath (the entrance is marked by a 'No Cycling' sign). This brings you out on Parkhill Road, the old main road from Eltham to Dartford. The houses on the other side of Parkhill Road, built from 1869 onwards for middle-class commuters attracted to Bexley by the recently-arrived railway, were the first signs that the old country village was changing into a London suburb. St John's Church was completed for the new inhabitants in 1881 and became a parish church in its own right in 1936.

Almshouses and workhouse
Turn right past the church and playground, and walk down the hill into the winding village High Street, which begins at the junction with Hurst Road. On the left, the long low building is Styleman's Almshouses. John Styleman made a fortune in India and lived in a large house in Danson, one of the outlying hamlets of Bexley parish. He died in 1734 and left money for the almshouses, but they were not built until several years after his widow's death in 1750. Ahead, the Georgian house with steeply pitched roof on the corner by the station entrance represents another 18th-century method of dealing with the poor: from the 1780s until 1834 this house served as the parish workhouse.

Beyond the old workhouse is the Railway Tavern, and then on the left, at No. 57 High Street, Jackson House. Built in 1676 with a double-height porch, Jackson House is one of Bexley's finest houses. In the 18th century it was home to the local builder. Still on the left, the building with the clock tower is the Freemantle Hall, built in 1894 as a public hall for the village. Just beyond is the 16th-century King's Head pub, probably the oldest building in the village centre apart from the church.

The mill
When you reach the little roundabout at the junction with Bourne Road, follow the High Street round to the right past the George pub (dating from at least 1717) and

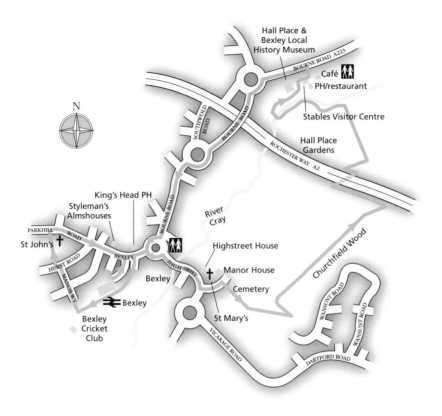

Hall Place &
Bexley Local
History Museum

BOURNE ROAD A223

Café

PH/restaurant

N

SOUTHWOLD ROAD

BOURNE ROAD

Stables Visitor Centre

ROCHESTER WAY A2

Hall Place
Gardens

King's Head PH

Styleman's
Almshouses

BOURNE ROAD

River
Cray

Churchfield Wood

PARKHILL ROAD

St John's

HURST ROAD

MANOR WAY

BEXLEY

HIGH STREET

Highstreet House

Manor House

Bexley

Cemetery

WANSUNT ROAD

WANSUNT ROAD

Bexley

Bexley
Cricket
Club

St Mary's

VICARAGE ROAD

DARTFORD ROAD

cross under the railway line once more. On the far side of the railway you come to
the river crossing. Bexley – meaning 'clearing among the box trees' – grew up at the
point where the Eltham-Dartford and Crayford-Orpington roads converged to cross
the River Cray. The Old Mill restaurant on the right is a modern replica of the 18th-
century corn mill, built in 1775 and burned down in 1966. Beyond is Cray House,
built at the same time as the mill, possibly for the mill owner. The cottages on
the opposite side of the road are mainly early 19th century with the exception of
No. 101 in the middle. This has a bit of style and probably dates from the mid-18th
century when Bexley was described as having many handsome, modern-built
houses, inhabited by genteel families of fortune.

Following the High Street round to the right you come to the wisteria-clad
Highstreet House, the finest house in the village with the exception of the Manor
House. Built in 1761 over the foundations of an earlier house, it was, as the plaque
on the front states, the home of the Kent historian and antiquary John Thorpe. Born
in 1715, the son of a Rochester surgeon, he lived here until 1789, when his wife
Catharina died. Thorpe died three years later. There is a plaque to his wife on the
churchyard side of the garden wall.

Brasses and monuments
Walk beside the churchyard wall and turn left into Manor Road. St Mary's, with its unique cone and pyramid spire, dates from the early Middle Ages. Inside, the oldest memorial is a 15th-century brass commemorating Henry Castilayn, park keeper to Bexley's then lord of the manor, the Archbishop of Canterbury. Slightly later monuments, dating from the 16th century, represent the leading local families of Champneis, Austen and Styleman. Outside, the oldest tomb – belonging to the Payne family – dates from 1603. On the right you pass the entrance to Manor Farm House and then the footpath leading up the hill to an area that used to be called, for obvious reasons, Coldblow. Beyond the footpath is the modern church hall, built on the site of the medieval tithe barn demolished about 1910, and the Victorian Manor Cottage.

Manor Road finishes at the entrance to the old manor farmyard, now the Bexley Sand and Ballast Company. The Manor House, rebuilt in the 18th century, is to the left, but is hardly visible unless you go into the churchyard and peer over the fence. Bexley was ruled from this manor house in the Middle Ages when the village formed part of the great estate of the Archbishops of Canterbury. After Bexley passed into lay hands in the mid-16th century, its new owner built a new manor house, seen later on the walk, a mile northeast of the village.

The walk now turns right into the lane leading to the churchyard extension, opened in 1857 and in 1990 turned into a protected ecological area. If you look back when you reach the corner of the wall, there is a good view of the upper part of the manor house across the old farm orchard. Carry straight on along the now narrow path heading uphill through the cemetery. At the end, go through the gate and continue up the hill on the tarmac path leading through meadow land towards Churchfield Wood on top of the hill. Just before the path forks, turn left into Churchfield Wood (there is a Cray Riverway waymark here) and follow the lower of the two paths (the one on the edge of the wood next to the fence). From the path you can clearly see the sand and gravel workings beside the Cray.

When you reach the far side of the wood by the main road, exit via the stile and turn left down the tarmac path towards the railway line. Follow the path underneath the road and then round to the right, keeping tight to the embankment. When you reach the path leading up to the road level, take it and cross the bridge over the railway line, walking into the face of the oncoming traffic. On the far side, turn right down the steps back onto ground level and go through the gate into the grassy area beside the railway line, following the Cray Riverway waymark. Walk straight along here with the railway on your right and the hedge boundary of Hall Place gardens on your left. At the corner of the hedge turn left and follow the hedge all the way up to the river. Here turn left again and go straight on through the gate into the Hall Place grounds and walk along beside the river.

Hall Place and gardens
After acquiring the Bexley estate from the Archbishop of Canterbury in the 1530s, the king almost immediately leased it to merchant and ex-Lord Mayor of London, Sir John Champneis. Using old stone salvaged from demolished monasteries, Champneis built himself a fine house about 1 mile (1.6km) northeast of the village, on the north bank of the Cray. In the early 1600s James I granted the manor and

Champneis' house to the antiquary and herald William Camden, author of Camden's *Britannia*. When Camden died in 1623 he left the estate to Oxford University to fund a history professorship. The university remained Lord of Bexley Manor into modern times. Meanwhile, the house – known as Hall Place – was acquired by Sir Robert Austen in 1649, the year of Charles I's execution. By adding a brick section on the south side that faces the river, he more than doubled the house in size. Today, half silvery Tudor stone and half weathered 17th-century brick, the building is more or less as Austen left it at his death in 1666.

Beyond the first bridge – leading into the maintenance yard and marking the approximate site of the old watermill demolished in 1926 – the house comes into view, presenting its 17th-century brick face. At the second bridge, cross the river and turn back towards the house, aiming for the gap in the hedge. You can now see the older stone part of the house and how the later section was simply added on to the south side. The Tudor part has two wings projecting to the north, but the 17th-century part is a quadrangle with a courtyard in the middle. Hall Place is now owned by the local council and houses offices and the Bexley Local History Museum.

Once through the hedge look left and you will see the topiary garden started by the last private occupant of the house, the Countess of Limerick. She died in 1943. The figures at the front – looking like large teddy bears, but in fact intended to be heraldic beasts – were added by Bexley Council a decade after the countess's demise, to mark the Queen's coronation. Follow the path round to the east side of the house where the public entrance is and then turn right past the granary (brought from Manor Farm in Bexley village in 1988) and the stables (now the Visitor Centre). Go out of the gate into the car park and turn left.

Development pressure

Turn left again out of the car park and walk along Bourne Road in front of the north front of the house, screened from the road by a fine pair of 18th-century gates. Continue on up to the roundabout. If you were to turn right here you would come to Bexleyheath. Built following the enclosure of Bexley's ancient common in 1819, Bexleyheath took development pressure off old Bexley and thus ensured the latter's survival as a more or less country village. The walk, however, goes left. Follow the pavement over the motorway and River Shuttle back towards Bexley, which you re-enter at the second roundabout. As you approach the village centre once more, you pass on the right various institutions that reflect the growth of the village in the Victorian era and later: the National Schools, opened in 1834 and converted to industrial use 140 years afterwards; the Victoria Homes almshouses, built to mark Queen Victoria's Diamond Jubilee in 1897; the local library, built at the junction of Albert Road in 1912; and the 1905 Baptist chapel across Albert Road from the library.

Across Bourne Road from the library is the old Refell's Brewery, in business from 1874 until 1956 and now converted into a business park. Further on, also on the left, you pass the entrance to a row of old workshops leading down to the railway viaduct, and then the original 1846 Baptist chapel with a louvre in the roof, converted into shops many years ago. At the roundabout you meet up with the High Street once more. Turn right here and make your way back to the station where the walk ends.

BIBLIOGRAPHY

This is an edited list of the sources used in research for this book. More complete lists will be found in the individual works from which the walks in this compilation have been selected. One title in particular should be singled out for special mention: the *London Encyclopedia*, edited by Ben Weinreb and Christopher Hibbert. It is an invaluable reference work and should be on the bookshelf of anyone interested in London's fascinating past.

Arthure, Humphrey, *Life and Work in Old Chiswick*, 1982
Ashton, John, *The Fleet*, 1888
Barker, Felix, *Greenwich and Blackheath Past*, 1993
Barker, Felix and Jackson, Peter, *London, 2000 Years of a City and its People*, 1983
Barker, Felix, and Silvester-Carr, Denise, *Crime and Scandal: The Black Plaque Guide to London*, 1995
Barton, N., *The Lost Rivers of London*, 1992
Batey, Mavis, *et al.*, *Arcadian Thames*, 1994
Begg, Paul, and Skinner, Keith, *The Scotland Yard Files*, 1992
Bell, Walter, *Fleet Street in Seven Centuries*, 1912
Berridge, Clive, *The Almshouses of London*, 1987
Blatch, Mervyn, *A Guide to London's Churches*, 1978
Blomfield, David, *The Story of Kew*, 1992
Blomfield, David, *Kew Past*, 1994
Boast, Mary, *The Story of Rotherhithe*, 1980
Boast, Mary, *The Story of Dulwich*, 1990
Boast, Mary, *A Trail Walk around Old Rotherhithe*, 1994
Brazil, David, *Naked City*, 1987
Butler, Ivan, *Murderers' London*, 1992
Byrne, Richard, *Prisons and Punishments of London*, 1989
Byrne, Richard, *The London Dungeon Book of Crime and Punishment*, 1993
Byron, Arthur, *London Statues*, 1981
Cameron, A., *Hounslow, Isleworth, Heston and Cranford. A Pictorial History*, 1995
Campbell, Duncan, *The Underworld*, 1996
Canham, Roy, *2000 Years of Brentford*, 1978
Clegg, Gillian, *Chiswick Past*, 1995
Cloake, John, *Richmond Past*, 1991
Cluett, Douglas, *Discovering Sutton's Heritage*, 1995
Courlander, Kathleen, *Richmond*, 1953
Crowe, Andrew, *The Parks and Woodlands of London*, 1987
Darby, Madge, *Waeppa's People*, 1988
Druett, Walter, *Pinner through the Ages*, 1965
Druett, Walter, *Harrow through the Ages*, 1971
Ebel, Suzanne, and Impey, Doreen, *A Guide to London's Riverside. Hampton Court to Greenwich*, 1985
Essex-Lopresti, Michael, *Exploring the Regent's Canal*, 1987
Fairfield, Sheila, *The Streets of London*, 1983
Forshaw, Alec, and Bergström, Theo, *The Open Spaces of London*, 1986
Gelder, W. H., *Monken Hadley Church and Village*, 1986
Gladstone, Florence, and Barker, Ashley, *Notting Hill in Bygone Days*, 1969
Gosling, John, and Warner, D., *The Shame of a City*, 1960
Green, Brian, *Dulwich Village*, 1983
Grimwade, Mary, and Hailstone, Charles, *Highways and Byways of Barnes*, 1992

Hawkins, Roy, *Green London*, 1987
Hibbert, Christopher, ed., *Royal London*, 1987
Higgs, Tom, *300 Years of Mitcham Cricket*, 1985
Jennett, Sean, *Official Guide to the Royal Parks of London*, 1979
Jones, A. E., *An Illustrated Directory of Old Carshalton*, 1973
Kelland, Gilbert, *Crime in London*, 1986
Law, A., *Walthamstow Village*, 1984
Lawson, Andrew, *Discover Unexpected London*, 1979
Lucas, Norman, *Britain's Gangland*, 1969
McAuley, Ian, *Guide to Ethnic London*, 1987
Meller, Hugh, *London Cemeteries*, 1985
Mercer, John, *Bexley, Bexleyheath and Welling. A Pictorial History*, 1995
Milward, Richard, *Wimbledon. A Pictorial History*, 1994
Montague, Eric, *Mitcham. A Pictorial History*, 1991
Murphy, Robert, *Smash and Grab*, 1993
Norrie, Ian, *Hampstead, Highgate Village and Kenwood*, 1983
Pearson, John, *The Profession of Violence*, 4th edn, no date
Perlmutter, Kevin, *London Street Markets*, 1983
Pevsner: various London volumes in *The Buildings of England* series
Prokter, Adrian, *A Guide to the River Thames from Battersea to Woolwich*, 1983
Rasmussen, Steen Eiler, *London the Unique City*, 1982
Rhind, Neil, *Blackheath Village and Environs, 1976–1983*
Richardson, John, *Highgate Past*, 1989
Rosen, Barbara, and Zuckerman, Wolfgang, *The Mews of London*, 1982
Rumbelow, Donald, *The Complete Jack the Ripper*, 1988
Saunders, Ann, *Regent's Park*, 1981
Saunders, Ann, *The Art and Architecture of London*, 1984
Spurgeon, Darrell, *Discover Greenwich and Charlton*, 1991
Spurgeon, Darrell, *Discover Bexley and Sidcup*, 1993
Sugden, Philip, *The Complete History of Jack the Ripper*, 1994
Survey of London: various volumes in this ongoing series begun in 1900
Tames, Richard, *Soho Past*, 1994
Taylor, Pamela, and Corden, Joanna, *Barnet, Edgware, Hadley and Totteridge. A Pictorial History*, 1994
Tester, P., *Bexley Village*, 1987
Thornbury, G. W., and Walford, Edward, *Old and New London, 1880–86*
Trench, Richard, and Hillman, Ellis, *London Under London*, 1985
Twickenham Local History Society, *Twickenham 1600–1900, People and Places*, 1981
Verden, Joanne, *Ten Walks around Pinner*, 1991
Victoria County History: volumes for Essex, Hertfordshire, Middlesex and Surrey, various dates
Wade, Christopher, *Hampstead Past*, 1989
Weinreb, Ben, and Hibbert, Christopher, eds, *The London Encyclopaedia*, 1993
Wheatley, H., and Cunningham, P., *London Past and Present*, 1891

OPENING TIMES

Alfred Dunhill Collection 48 Jermyn Street, London.
020 7290 8622. Monday–Wednesday, Friday
9.30am–6.30pm, Thursday 9.30am–7pm, Saturday
10am–6.30pm.

All Saints Church All Saints Drive, Blackheath. 020
8852 4280. Monday–Friday 10am–12 noon. Access
by arrangement.

All Saints Church Church Gate, Fulham, London. 020
7736 4457. Monday–Friday 10am–3pm.

All Saints Church Church Street, Isleworth,
Middlesex. 020 8568 4645. Ruins of old church
visible through door.

All Saints Church High Street, Carshalton. 020 8647
2366. May–September: daily 2pm–4pm.

Apothecaries' Hall See City Information Centre listing.

Bank of England Museum, Threadneedle Street,
London. 020 7601 5545 or
www.bankofengland.co.uk/Links/setframe.html.
Monday–Friday 10am–5pm.

Banqueting House Whitehall, London. 0870 751 5178
or www.hrp.org.uk. Monday–Saturday 10am–5pm.

Barnet Museum 31 Wood Street, Chipping Barnet.
020 8440 8066. Tuesday–Thursday 2.30pm–4.30pm,
Saturday 10am–12 noon, 2pm–4pm.

Bexley Cricket Club Manor Way, Bexley. 01322
524159 or www.bexleycc.co.uk for fixture list.

Boston Manor House Boston Manor Road,
Brentford. 020 8583 4535. April–October: Saturday
and Sunday 2.30pm–5pm.

British Museum Great Russell Street, London. 020
7323 8000 or www.thebritishmuseum.ac.uk.
Saturday–Wednesday 10am–5.30pm, Thursday–Friday
10am–8.30pm.

Brompton Oratory Brompton Road, London. 020
7808 0900. Daily 6.30am–8pm.

Brunel's Engine House Railway Avenue, Rotherhithe.
020 7231 3840 or www.brunelenginehouse.org.uk.
Tuesday–Sunday 1pm–5pm.

Buckingham Palace Buckingham Palace Road,
London. 020 7766 7300 or
www.royalresidences.com. *Royal Mews* Monday–
Thursday 12 noon–6pm (August–September
10.30am–4.30pm). Ring for *Queen's Gallery/State
Rooms* opening times.

Burgh House New End Square, Hampstead. 020 7431
0144. Wednesday–Sunday 12 noon–5pm.

Bushy Park Park Office, The Stockyard, Hampton
Court Road, Hampton, Middlesex. 020 8979 1586
or www.royalparks.co.uk/bushy/infmain.html.

Cabinet War Rooms Clive Steps, King Charles Street,
London. 020 7930 6961 or www.iwm.org.uk. Daily
9.30am–6pm.

Carshalton House and Water Tower St Philomena's
School, Pound Street, Carshalton. 020 8773 4555.
House access by arrangement. *Water Tower*
April–September: Sunday 2.30pm–5pm. *Hermitage*
May–September: first Sunday of month.

Carlyle's House 24 Cheyne Row, London. 020 7352
7087. April–October: Wednesday–Friday 2pm–5pm,
Saturday and Sunday 11am–5pm.

Cat Museum The Other Shop, 49 High Street, Harrow-
on-the-Hill. Thursday–Saturday 10.30am–5pm.

Catamaran Cruisers 020 7987 1185 or
www.catamarancruisers.co.uk.

Central Criminal Court Old Bailey, London. 020
7248 3277. Monday–Friday 10.30am–1pm,
2pm–4pm.

Chapel Royal St James's Palace, London. 020 7930
4832 or www.royal.gov.uk/palaces/chapel.htm.
Sunday services 8.30am and 11.15am. For up-to-date
times check in preceding Saturday's *Times*,
Independent or *Daily Telegraph*.

Charterhouse Sutton's Hospital Charterhouse
Square, London. 020 7251 5002 or www.charter-
house.org.uk. April–August: guided tours Wednesday
2.15pm.

Chelsea Old Church 4 Old Church Street, London.
020 7795 1019 or www.domini.org/chelsea-old-
church. Days vary, 10am–1pm, 2pm–4pm.

Chelsea Physic Garden 66 Royal Hospital Road,
London. 020 7352 5646 or
www.chelseaphysicgarden.co.uk. April–October:
Wednesday 12 noon–5pm, Sunday 2pm–6pm.

Chiswick House Burlington Lane. 020 8995 0508.
April–September: Monday–Friday 10am–5pm.
Saturday 10am–2pm. October–March: closed except
for groups.

Christie's Fine Art Auctioneers 8 King Street,
London. 020 7839 9060. Viewing galleries: Monday,
Wednesday, Thursday and Friday 9am–4.30pm.
Tuesday 9am–8pm, Sunday 2pm–5pm.

City Information Centre St Paul's Churchyard,
London. 020 7332 1456 or
www.corpoflondon.gov.uk. October–March:
Monday–Friday 9.30am–5pm, Saturday 9.30am–
12.30pm. April–September: Monday–Saturday
9.30am–5pm, Sunday 9.30am–5pm.

Clink Museum 1 Clink Street, London. 020 7403 6515
or www.clink.co.uk. Daily 10am–9pm.

College of Arms Queen Victoria Street, London. 020
7248 2762 or www.college-of-arms.gov.uk. *Earl
Marshal's Court* Monday–Friday 10am–4pm.

Courtauld Gallery Somerset House, Strand, London.
020 7848 2526 or www.courtauld.ac.uk. Daily
10am–6pm.

Cutty Sark King William Walk, Greenwich. 020 8858
3445 or www.cuttysark.org.uk. Daily 10am–5pm.

Dickens House Museum 48 Doughty Street, London.
020 7405 2127 or www.dickensmuseum.com.
Monday–Saturday 10am–5pm, Sunday 11am–5pm.

Dr Johnson's House 17 Gough Square, London. 020
7353 3745 or www.drjh.dircon.co.uk.
May–September: Monday–Saturday 11am–5.30pm.
October–April: Monday–Saturday 11am–5pm.

Dulwich Picture Gallery Gallery Road, Dulwich Village, London. 020 8299 8700 or www.dulwichpicturegallery.org.uk. Tuesday–Friday 10am–5pm, Saturday and Sunday 11am–5pm.

Fan Museum 12 Crooms Hill, Greenwich. 020 8305 1441 or www.fan-museum.org. Tuesday–Saturday 11am–5pm, Sunday 12 noon–5pm.

Faraday Museum Royal Institution of Great Britain, 21 Albemarle Street, London. 020 7409 2992 or www.ri.ac.uk. Monday–Friday 9am–6pm.

Farm Street Church 114 Mount Street, London. 020 7493 7811. Monday–Sunday 7am–7pm.

Fenton House Windmill Hill, Hampstead. 020 7435 3471. Wednesday–Friday 2pm–5pm, Saturday and Sunday 11am–5pm.

Florence Nightingale Museum 2 Lambeth Palace Road, London. 020 7620 0374 or www.florence-nightingale.co.uk. Monday–Friday 10am–5pm, Saturday and Sunday 10am–4.30pm.

Forty Hall Forty Hill, Enfield. 020 8363 8196. Wednesday–Sunday 11am–4pm.

Foundling Museum 40 Brunswick Square, London. 020 7841 3600 or www.foundlingmuseum.org.uk. Tuesday–Saturday 10am–6pm, Sunday 12 noon–6pm.

Fulham Palace Bishops Avenue, Fulham, London. 020 7736 3233. March–October: Wednesday–Sunday 2pm–5pm. November–February: Thursday–Sunday 1pm–4pm (please note that at the time of writing, the palace is only open Saturday and Sunday, 2pm–4pm until further notice, because of restoration work). *Grounds* Daily.

Golden Hinde St Mary Overie Dock, Cathedral Street, London. 0870 011 8700 or www.goldenhinde.co.uk. Daily, ring for opening times.

Greenwich Park Park Office, Blackheath Gate, London. 020 8858 2608 or www.royalparks.gov.uk/parks/greenwich_park.

Greenwich Tourist Information Centre Pepys House, 2 Cutty Sark Gardens, Greenwich. 0870 608 2000. Daily 10am–5pm.

Gresham College Barnard's Inn Hall, Holdbom, London. 020 7831 0575 or www.gresham.ac.uk. Ring for details of free public lectures.

Grosvenor Chapel South Audley Street, London. 020 7499 1684 or www.grosvenorchapel.org.uk. Monday–Friday 9.30am–1pm.

Guards Chapel Wellington Barracks, Birdcage Walk, London. 020 7414 3228. Monday–Friday 10am–12.30pm, 1.45pm–4pm.

Guards Museum Wellington Barracks, Birdcage Walk, London. 020 7930 4466. February–December: daily 10am–4pm.

Guildhall Guildhall Yard, London. 020 7606 3030 or www.cityoflondon.gov.uk. *Guildhall* open when not being used for events, phone for details. *Guildhall Clock Museum* 020 7332 1868. Monday–Saturday 9.30am–4.45pm. *Guildhall Art Gallery* 020 7332 3700. Monday–Saturday 10am–5pm, Sunday 12 noon–4pm.

Hall Place and Bexley Heritage Trust Bourne Road, Bexley. 01322 526574. April–October: Monday–Saturday 10am–5pm, Sunday 11am–5pm. November–March: Monday–Saturday 10am–4pm. *Grounds* daily.

Ham House Ham Street, Richmond, Surrey. 020 8940 1950 or www.nationaltrust.org.uk.

End March–end October: Daily except Thursday and Friday 1pm–5pm. *Garden* daily except Thursday and Friday 11am–6pm.

Hampton Court Palace East Molesley, Surrey. 0870 752 7777 or www.hrp.org.uk. April–October: Monday–Sunday 10.am–6pm. November–March: Monday–Sunday 10am–4.30pm.

Harrow Museum and Heritage Centre Headstone Manor, Pinner View, Harrow. 020 8863 6720. Thursday and Friday 12.30pm–5pm (dusk in winter), Saturday and Sunday 10.30pm–5pm (dusk in winter).

Harrow Old Speech Room Gallery Old Schools, Church Hill, Harrow-on-the-Hill. 020 8872 8205. Daily except Wednesday 2.30pm–5pm.

Harrow School Guided Tours 020 8423 1524 or email tours@harrowschool.org.uk or write to Mrs Perena Shrayne, Harrow School, 57 High Street, Harrow-on-the-Hill, Middlesex HA1 3HT.

Hayward Gallery Belvedere Road, London. 020 7921 0813 or www.hayward.org.uk. Daily 10am–6pm (Friday closes 9pm).

Highgate Cemetery Swains Lane, Highgate, London. 020 8340 1834 or www.highgate-cemetery.org. Ring for opening times.

HMS Belfast Morgan's Lane, Tooley Street, London. 020 7940 6300 or www.hmsbelfast.iwm.org.uk. Summer: daily 10am–6pm. Winter: daily 10am–5pm.

Hogarth's House Hogarth's Lane, Great West Road, London. 020 8994 6757 or www.cip.org.uk/heritage/hogarth.htm. April–October: Tuesday–Friday 1–5, Saturday and Sunday 1pm–6pm. November–March (except January): Tuesday–Friday 1pm–4pm, Saturday and Sunday 1pm–5pm.

Horse Guards Parade Whitehall, London. Monday–Saturday 11am, Sunday 10am.

Houses of Parliament London. 020 7219 2033 or www.parliament.uk. Ring for details of debates and select committees. Visits may be booked through MPs.

Hyde Park The Park Manager, The Ranger's Lodge, Hyde Park, London. 020 7298 2100 or www.royalparks.gov.uk/parks/hyde_park.

Jewel Tower Old Palace Yard, Abingdon Street, London. 020 7222 2219. April–October: daily 10am–5pm. November–March: daily 10am–4pm.

Keats House Keats Grove, Hampstead, London. 020 7435 2062 or www.keatshouse.org.uk. Daily except Monday 1pm–5pm.

Kensington Gardens Park Office, Magazine Storeyard, Magazine Gate, Kensington Gardens, London. 020 7298 2100 or www.royalparks.gov.uk/parks/kensington_gardens.

Kensington Palace (State Apartments and Royal Ceremonial Dress Collection), Kensington Gardens, London. 0870 751 5170 or www.hrp.org.uk. March–October: daily 10am–6pm. November–February: daily 10am–5pm.

Kenwood House and Iveagh Bequest Hampstead Lane, Hampstead. 020 8348 1286 or www.english-heritage.org.uk. Summer: daily 11am–5pm. Winter: daily 10am–4pm.

Kew Bridge Steam Museum Green Dragon Lane, Brentford, Middlesex. 020 8568 4757 or www.kbsm.org. Daily 11am–5pm.

Leighton House Museum and Art Gallery 12 Holland Park Road, London. 020 7602 3316 or

www.rbkc.gov.uk/leightonhousemuseum. Daily
except Tuesday 11am–5.30pm.

Lincoln's Inn Chapel Lincoln's Inn, London.
Monday–Friday 12 noon–2.30pm.

Little Holland House 40 Beeches Avenue, Carshalton.
020 8770 4781. First Sunday of every month
1.30pm–5.30pm. Closed January.

London Aquarium County Hall, Westminster Bridge
Road, London. 020 7967 8000 or
www.londonaquarium.co.uk. Daily 10am–6pm.

London Canal Museum 12–13 New Wharf Road,
King's Cross, London. 020 7713 0836 or www.
canalmuseum.org.uk. Tuesday–Sunday 10am–4.30pm.

London Dungeon 28 Tooley Street, London. 020 7403
7221 or www.thedungeons.co.uk. April–mid July: daily
10am–6pm. Mid July–September: daily 10am–8pm.

London Planetarium Marylebone Road, London.
0870 400 3000 or www.madame-tussauds.co.uk.
Monday–Friday 9.30am–5.30pm. Saturday and
Sunday 9am–6pm.

London Silver Vaults Chancery House, Chancery
Lane, London. 020 7242 3844 or
www.thesilvervaults.com. Monday–Friday
9am–5.30pm, Saturday 9am–1pm.

London Transport Museum Covent Garden Piazza,
London. 020 7565 7299 or www.ltmuseum.co.uk.
At the time of writing, the museum is closed for
refurbishment, call for further details.

London Zoo Regent's Park, London. 020 7722 3333
or www.londonzoo.co.uk. March–September: daily
10am–5.30pm. October–February 10am–4pm.

Madame Tussaud's Waxworks Marylebone Road,
London. 0870 400 3000 or www.madame-
tussauds.co.uk. Monday–Friday 9.30am–5.30pm,
Saturday and Sunday 9am–6pm.

Mansion House Walbrook, London, EC4. 020 7626
2500. Only groups of 15 or more admitted. Appoint-
ments by written request; two-month waiting list.

Marble Hill House Richmond Road, Twickenham,
Middlesex. 020 8892 5115. April–October: Saturday
10am–2pm. Sunday 10am–5pm. Group visits available
on weekdays, call for details.

Merton Heritage Centre The Canons, Madeira Road,
Mitcham. 020 8640 9387. Tuesday, Wednesday, Friday
and Saturday 10am–4pm.

Mitcham Cricket Club Cricket Green. April–
September: matches most Saturdays and Sundays.

Mitcham Fair Three Kings Piece. 12–14 August.

Monument Monument Street, London. 020 7626 2717.
Daily 9am–5pm.

Mount Pleasant Sorting Office Farringdon Road,
London. 020 7239 2311. Tours by appointment
Monday–Friday; two weeks notice required.
No under-12s.

Museum of Garden History Lambeth Palace Road,
London. 020 7401 8865 or www.cix.co.uk/~muse-
umgh. Daily 10.30am–5pm.

Museum of London London Wall, London. 020
7600 0807 or www.museum-london.org.uk.
Monday–Saturday 10am–5.50pm, Sunday 12
noon–5.50pm.

Museum of Richmond Old Town hall, Whittaker
Avenue, Richmond, Surrey. 020 8332 1141 or
www.museumofrichmond.com. Tuesday–Saturday
11am–5pm.

Museum of St Bartholomew's Hospital West
Smithfield, London. 020 7601 8152/8150.
Tuesday–Friday 10am–4pm.

National Army Museum Royal Hospital Road,
London. 020 7730 0717 or www.national-army-
museum.ac.uk. Daily 10am–5.30pm.

National Gallery Trafalgar Square, London. 020 7747
2885 or www.nationalgallery.org.uk. Daily
10am–6pm (Wednesday closes 9pm).

National Theatre South Bank, London. 020 7452 3400
or www.nationaltheatre.org.uk. Guided tours
Monday–Saturday 10am–10.45pm.

Natural History Museum Cromwell Road, London.
020 7942 5000 or www.nhm.ac.uk. Monday–
Saturday 10am–5.50pm, Sunday 11am–5.50pm.

New Caledonian Antiques Market Bermondsey
Square. Friday morning.

Old Operating Theatre 9A St Thomas Street, London.
020 7188 2679 or www.thegarret.org.uk. Daily
10.30am–5pm.

**Old Royal Observatory, Planetarium, National
Maritime Museum, Queen's House** Greenwich
Park. 020 8858 4422 or www.nmm.ac.uk. Daily
10am–5pm (in summer, museum and observatory
close at 6pm).

Orleans House Gallery, Riverside, Twickenham,
Middlesex. 020 8831 6000 or
www.richmond.gov.uk/orleans_house_gallery.
Tuesday–Saturday 1pm–5.30pm, Sunday
2pm–5.30pm (October–March closes 4.30pm).
Gardens 9am–dusk.

Pinner Fair Wednesday after Spring Bank Holiday.

Pollock's Toy Museum 1 Scala Street, London. 020
7636 3452 or www.pollockstoymuseum.co.uk.
Monday–Saturday 10am–5pm.

Queen's Chapel of the Savoy Savoy Hill, Strand,
London. 020 7836 7221. Tuesday–Friday
11.30am–3.30pm.

Ranger's House Chesterfield Walk, Blackheath. 020
8853 0035. Ring for opening times.

Regent's Park Park Office Storeyard (Inner Circle),
The Regent's Park, London. 020 7486 7905 or
www.royalparks.gov.uk/parks/regents_park.

Richmond Park Park Office, Richmond Park, Surrey.
020 8948 3209 or
www.royalparks.gov.uk/parks/richmond_park.

'Roman' Bath 5 Strand Lane, London. 020 7641 5264.
Visible through window at all times; access by
arrangement.

Royal Academy of Arts Burlington House, Piccadilly,
London. 020 7300 8000 or www.royalacademy.org.uk.
Saturday–Thursday 10am–6pm (Friday closes 10pm).

Royal Botanic Gardens Kew Gardens, Surrey. 020
8332 5655 or www.rbgkew.org.uk.
March–September: Monday–Friday 9.30am–6.30pm,
Saturday and Sunday 9.30am–7.30pm.
September–October: daily 9.30am–6pm.
November–February: daily 9.30am–4.15pm.

Royal Courts of Justice Strand, London. 020 7947
6000. Monday–Friday 9.30am–4.30pm. *Courts*
10.30am–4pm with lunch adjournment 1pm–2pm.
Closed August–September.

Royal Hospital Chelsea Royal Hospital Road,
London. 020 7881 5204 or www.chelsea-
pensioners.co.uk. *Museum* Monday–Saturday

10am–12 noon and 2pm–4pm, Sunday 2pm–4pm (closed Sunday October–March). *Gardens* daily (except week of Chelsea Flower Show, late May).

St Alfege's Church Greenwich High Road, Greenwich. 020 8293 5595 or www.st-alfege.org. Check website or call for opening times.

St Andrew-by-the-Wardrobe Church Queen Victoria Street, London. 020 7248 7546. Monday–Friday 10am–4pm.

St Andrew's Church Church Street, Enfield. 020 8363 8676. Monday–Friday 9am–3pm, Saturday 9am–1pm.

St Anne's Church Kew Green, Kew, Surrey. 020 8940 4616. Saturday 10am–12 noon and most weekend afternoons in summer.

St Anne's Church Newell Street, London. 020 7987 1502. Monday–Friday 2.30pm–4.30pm, Saturday 2pm–5pm, Sunday 10.30am–1pm.

St Bartholomew-the-Great Church West Smithfield, London. 020 7606 5171. Tuesday–Friday 8.30am–5pm (November–February closes 4pm), Saturday 10.30am–1.30pm, Sunday 2.30pm–6pm.

St Bartholomew-the-Less Church Smithfield Gate, West Smithfield, London. 020 7601 8066. Daily 8am–8pm.

St Bride's Church Fleet Street, London. 020 7427 0133 or www.stbrides.com. Monday–Friday 8am–6pm, Saturday 11am–3pm, Sunday 10am–1pm and 5pm–7.30pm.

St Bride Printing Library Bride Lane, Fleet Street, London. 020 7353 4660 or www.stbride.org. Tuesday 12 noon–5.30pm, Wednesday 12 noon–9pm, Thursday 12 noon–5pm.

St Clement Danes Church Strand, London. 020 7242 8282. Monday–Saturday 9am–4pm, Sunday 9am–3pm.

St George's Church Hanover Square, St George Street, London. 020 7629 0874. Monday–Friday 9am–3.30pm.

St James's Church 197 Piccadilly, London. 020 7734 4511. Daily 8am–6.30pm.

St James's Church St James's Walk, London. 020 7251 1190. Monday–Friday 9am–5pm.

St James's Park and Green Park, Park Office The Storeyard, Horse Guards Approach, St James's Park, London. 020 7930 1793 or www.royalparks.gov.uk/parks/st_james_park.

St John's Church Church Row, Hampstead, London. 020 7794 5808. Monday–Saturday, most Sundays 9am–5pm.

St John's Church High Street, Chipping Barnet. 020 8449 3894. Saturday morning.

St John's Church High Street, Pinner. 020 8886 3869. Daily.

St Lawrence Jewry Church Guildhall Yard, London. 020 7600 9478. Monday–Friday 7.30am–2pm.

St Luke's Church Sydney Street, London. 020 7351 7365. Monday–Friday 9.30am–12.30pm.

St Margaret's Church Parliament Square, London. 020 7654 4847. Monday–Friday 9.30am–3.45pm, Saturday 9.30am–1.45pm, Sunday 2pm–5pm.

St Martin-in-the-Fields Church Trafalgar Square, London. 020 7766 1100 or www.stmartin-in-the-fields.org. Daily 8am–6pm.

St Martin-within-Ludgate Church Ludgate Hill, London. 020 7248 6054. Monday–Friday 10am–4pm.

St Mary Abbots Church Kensington High Street,

London. 020 7937 2419. Daily 9am–6pm.

St Mary Magdalen Church Bermondsey. 020 7357 0984 or www.stmarysbermondsey.org.uk. Access by arrangement.

St Mary-at-Hill Church Lovat Lane, London. 020 7626 4184. Monday–Friday 11am–4pm.

St Mary-le-Bow Church Cheapside, London. 020 7248 5139 or www.stmarylebow.co.uk. Monday–Friday 7.30am–6pm (Friday closes 4pm).

St Mary-le-Strand Church Strand, London. 020 7836 3126 or www.stmarylestrand.org. Monday–Friday 11am–4pm, Sunday 10am–3pm.

St Mary's Church Church End, Walthamstow. 020 8520 1430. Access by arrangement.

St Mary's Church Church Hill, Harrow-on-the-Hill. 020 8422 2652 or www.harrowhill.org. Monday–Friday 9am–11am.

St Mary's Church Church Road, Barnes. 020 8741 5422 or www.stmarybarnes.org. Monday–Saturday 10.30am–12.30pm.

St Mary's Church Hadley Green Road, Monken Hadley. 020 8449 2414. Second Sunday every month 2pm–4pm.

St Mary's Church High Street, Putney, London. 020 8788 4414. Access by arrangement.

St Mary's Church Riverside, Twickenham, Middlesex. 020 8744 2693. Weekday mornings.

St Mary's Church St Marychurch Street, Rotherhithe. 020 7231 2465. Daily.

St Mary's Church St Mary's Road, Wimbledon. 020 8946 2605 or www.stmaryswimbledon.fsnet.co.uk. Daily. If church is closed, enquire at adjacent Fellowship House Monday–Friday 9am–1pm and 2.30pm–4pm (except Wednesday 2.30pm–6pm).

St Michael Paternoster Royal College Hill, London. 020 7248 5202. Monday–Friday 9am–5pm.

St Michael's Church South Grove, Highgate. 020 8340 7279 or www.stmichaelshighate.org.uk. Saturday 10am–12 noon and occasional afternoons.

St Michael's Church St Michael's Alley, Cornhill, London. 020 7248 3826 or www.st-michaels.org.uk. Daily except Saturday 8.30am–5.30pm.

St Nicholas's Church Church Street. 020 8995 4717. Sunday 2.30pm–5pm.

St Olave's Church 8 Hart Street, London. (020 7488 4318. Monday–Friday 9am–5pm.

St Paul's Cathedral St Paul's Churchyard, London. 020) 7236 4128 or www.stpauls.co.uk. Monday–Saturday 8.30am–4pm.

St Paul's Church Bedford Street, London. 020 7836 5221 or www.actorschurch.org.uk. Monday–Friday 8.30am–5.30pm, Sunday 9am–1pm.

St Paul's Church 302 The Highway, London. 020 7680 2772 or www.stpaulshadwell.org. Access arranged through the Parish Office, opposite the church.

St Paul's Church St Paul's Road, Brentford. 020 8568 7442 or www.parishofbrentford.org.uk. Daily.

St Peter and St Paul's Church Church Road, Mitcham. 020 8648 1566. Access by arrangement.

St Peter's Church Vere Street, London. 020 7399 9555. Monday–Friday 9am–5pm.

St Sepulchre's Church Holborn Viaduct, London. 020 7248 3826. Tuesday 5.30pm–7pm, Wednesday 11am–3pm, Thursday 12 noon–2pm.

Science Museum Exhibition Road, London. 0870 870

4868 or www.sciencemuseum.org.uk. Daily
10am–6pm.

Serpentine Gallery Kensington Gardens, London. 020
7402 6075 or www.serpentinegallery.org. Daily
10am–6pm.

Shakespeare's Globe Exhibition New Globe Walk,
Bankside, London. 020 7902 1400 or
www.shakespeares-globe.org. October–May: daily
10am–5pm. May–October (performance season):
daily 9am–12 noon.

Shakespeare Temple Hampton Court Road,
Hampton, Middlesex. 020 8831 6000 or
www.garrickstemple.org.uk. Access by arrangement.
Temple April–September: Sunday 2pm–5pm. *Lawn*
daily dawn–dusk.

Sir John Soane's Museum 13 Lincoln's Inn Fields,
London. 020 7405 2107 or www.soanes.org.
Tuesday–Saturday 10am–5pm. First Tuesday of every
month 6pm–9pm. Tour Saturday at 2.30pm.

Skinners' Hall 81/2 Dowgate Hill, London.
www.skinnershall.co.uk. A selection of City livery
halls are open for guided tours a few days each year.
Tickets must be obtained in advance through the
City Information Office (see listing).

Southside House 3 Woodhayes Road, Wimbledon. 020
8946 7643 or www.southsidehouse.com. Guided
tours March–October: Saturday, Sunday, Wednesday
2pm, 3pm, 4pm.

Southwark Cathedral Montague Close, London. 020
7367 6700 or www.southwark.anglican.org/
cathedral. Daily 8am–6pm.

Spanish and Portuguese Synagogue Off Bevis
Marks, London. 020 7626 1274. Daily 11.30am–1pm.
Guided tours usually at 11.30am Sunday and Tuesday
and at 12 noon Monday, Wednesday and Friday, but
ring in advance to check.

Spencer House 27 St James's Place, London. 020 7499
8620 or www.spencerhouse.co.uk. Guided tours
Sunday 10.30am–5.30pm (except January and August).

Strawberry Hill St Mary's University College,
Waldegrave Road, Strawberry Hill, Twickenham,
Middlesex. 020 8240 4114. April–October:
pre-booked tours Sunday 2pm–3.30pm.

Sutton Ecology Centre The Old Rectory, Festival
Walk, Carshalton. 020 8770 5820 or
www.sutton.gov.uk/environment/ecologycentre.
Nature reserve 10am–dusk. *Information sessions*
Saturday 10.30am–1pm, 2pm–4.30pm.

Sutton Heritage Centre Honeywood, Honeywood
Walk, Carshalton. 020 8770 4297 or
www.sutton.gov.uk/leisure/heritage/honeywood.
Wednesday–Friday 11–5, Saturday and Sunday
10am–5pm. *Tearoom* Wednesday–Sunday 10am–5pm.

Syon House Syon Park, Brentford Gardens, Middlesex.
020 8560 0881 or www.syonpark.co.uk. End
March–October: Wednesday, Thursday, Sunday
11am–5pm. *Gardens* Daily 10.30am–5pm or dusk.

Tate Modern Bankside, London. 020 7887 8000 or
www.tate.org.uk/modern. Sunday–Thursday
10am–6pm, Friday–Saturday 10am–10pm.

Thames Passenger Boat Services Westminster Pier,
Victoria Embankment, London. 020 7930 4097 or
www.westminsterpier.co.uk.

Theatre Museum Russell Street, London. 020 7943
4700 or www.theatremuseum.org. Tuesday–Sunday

10am–6pm.

Tower Bridge Experience Tower Bridge, London. 020
7403 3761 or www.towerbridge.org.uk.
April–September: daily 10am–6.30pm.
October–March: daily 9.30am–6pm.

Tower of London Tower Hill, London. 0870 756 6060
or www.hrp.org.uk. March–October:
Tuesday–Saturday 9am–6pm, Sunday and Monday
10am–6pm. November–February: Tuesday–
Saturday 9am–5pm, Sunday and Monday 10am–5pm.

Travellers Club 106 Pall Mall, London. 020 7930
8688. Large group tours only, by arrangement
four–five weeks in advance.

Trinity Hospital High Bridge, Greenwich. 020 8858
1310. Access by arrangement with Warden or through
Greenwich Tourist Information Centre (see listing).

Vestry House Museum Vestry Road, Walthamstow.
020 8509 1917. Monday–Friday 10am–1pm,
2pm–5.30pm, Saturday 10am–1pm, 2pm–5pm.

Victoria and Albert Museum Cromwell Road,
London. 020 7942 2000 or www.vam.ac.uk. Daily
10am–5.45pm. Wednesday and every last Friday of
the month 10am–10pm.

Wallace Collection Hertford House, Manchester
Square, London 020 7563 9500 or
www.wallacecollection.org. Daily 10am–5pm.

Walthamstow Village Festival. July. Ring 020 8496
3000 for exact date and details.

Wandle Industrial Museum Vestry Hall Annexe,
London Road, Mitcham. 020 8648 0127 or
www.wandle.org. Wednesday 1pm–4pm, first Sunday
of every month 2pm–5pm.

Wellington Museum, Apsley House, Hyde Park
Corner, London. 020 7499 5676 or www.english-
heritage.org.uk. April–October Tuesday–Sunday
10am–5pm. November–March 10am–4pm.

Westminster Abbey Broad Sanctuary, London. 020
7654 4900 or www.westminster-abbey.org.
Monday–Friday 9.30am–3.45pm (Wednesday closes
at 6pm), Saturday 9.30am–1.45pm.

Wetlands Centre Queen Elizabeth Walk, Barnes. 020
8409 4400 or www.wwt.org.uk. Daily 9.30am–5pm.

Whitefriars' Crypt Freshfields Bruckhaus Deringer, 65
Fleet Street, London. 020 7936 4000. Crypt visible
from outside at all times. Access by arrangement with
Premises Manager, Freshfields Bruckhaus Deringer.

William Morris Gallery Lloyd Park, Forest Road,
Walthamstow. 020 8527 3782 or
www.lbwf.gov.uk/wmg. Tuesday–Saturday
10am–1pm, 2pm–5pm. First Sunday of every month
10am–1pm, 2pm–5pm.

Wimbledon Lawn Tennis Museum All England
Club, Church Road. 020 8946 6131 or www.wim-
bledon.org. Daily 10.30am–5pm (Times may change
during championships).

Wimbledon Society Museum Ridgway. 020 8296
9914. Saturday and Sunday 2.30pm–5pm.

Wimbledon Windmill Museum Windmill Road,
Wimbledon Common. 020 8947 2825. April–
October: Saturday 2pm–5pm, Sunday 11am–5pm.

Winston Churchill's Britain at War Experience
64–66 Tooley Street, London Bridge, London. 020
7403 3171 or www.britainatwar.co.uk.
October–March: daily 10am–5pm.
April–September: daily 10am–6pm.

267

INDEX